T0257611

Human-Computer Interaction: Design, Developments and Applications

Human-Computer Interaction: Design, Developments and Applications

Edited by **Stanley Harmon**

WILLFORD PRESS
New York

Published by Willford Press,
118-35 Queens Blvd., Suite 400,
Forest Hills, NY 11375, USA
www.willfordpress.com

Human-Computer Interaction: Design, Developments and Applications
Edited by Stanley Harmon

International Standard Book Number: 978-1-68285-255-2 (Hardback)

Printed in the United States of America.

Contents

Preface

Human-computer interaction is an applied field of research and study that aims to analyze the user interface and evaluate the interaction between humans and computers. The topics included herein on semantic systems, privacy, security and trust management, social computing and social intelligence are of utmost significance and bound to provide incredible insights to readers. It strives to provide a fair idea about this discipline and to help the readers develop a better understanding of the latest advances within this field.

The researches compiled throughout the book are authentic and of high quality, combining several disciplines and from very diverse regions from around the world. Drawing on the contributions of many researchers from diverse countries, the book's objective is to provide the readers with the latest achievements in the area of research. This book will surely be a source of knowledge to all interested and researching the field.

In the end, I would like to express my deep sense of gratitude to all the authors for meeting the set deadlines in completing and submitting their research chapters. I would also like to thank the publisher for the support offered to us throughout the course of the book. Finally, I extend my sincere thanks to my family for being a constant source of inspiration and encouragement.

Editor

Artificial neuro fuzzy logic system for detecting human emotions

Mohammad Malkawi[1,2*] and Omayya Murad[3]

* Correspondence: mmalkawi@
aimws.com
[1]Jadara University, Irbid, Jordan
[2]Cambium Networks, USA
Full list of author information is
available at the end of the article

Abstract

This paper presents an adaptive neuro/fuzzy system which can be trained to detect the current human emotions from a set of measured responses. Six models are built using different types of input/output membership functions and trained by different kinds of input arrays. The models are compared based on their ability to train with lowest error values. Many factors impact the error values such as input/output membership functions, the training data arrays, and the number of epochs required to train the model. ANFIS editor in MATLAB is used to build the models.

Keywords: Fuzzy logic, Neural networks, Hybrid ANFIS, Human emotion detection, MATLAB

Introduction

The problem of emotion detection based on the measured physiological changes in the human body had received a significant attention lately (Nie et. al. 2011) [1]. However, the instant detection of each human's emotions had not been thoroughly studied. The problem is that each person manifests emotions in a manner different from others. In social networks, for example, a person sending a message across the net may experience certain emotional status which need to be transmitted to the other party in the same manner voice or image are transmitted.

The human emotional status is rather intangible [2], and therefore cannot be directly measured. However, these emotions can be correlated to external and/or internal factors, which are rather tangible things, and hence they can be measured and analyzed. The internal factors come from different parts of the body in several forms such as electroencephalography (EEG), heart rate (HR), heart rate variability (HRV), pre-ejection period (PEP), stroke volume (SV), systolic blood pressure (SBP), diastolic blood pressure (DBP), skin conductance response (SCR), tidal volume (Vt), oscillatory resistance (Ros), respiration rate (RR), nonspecific skin conductance response rate (nSRR), skin conductance level (SCL), finger temperature (FT), and others (Kreibig 2010) [3].

These factors' measurements are provided in wide ranges and often their impacts vary from a person to a person and for different postures for the same person. For example, a given measurement of some factors may relate to a person being happy, while the same measurements may reveal a rather "sad" status for another person. This kind of behavior lends itself naturally to fuzzy sets and fuzzy logic (zero and one, true and false or black and white cannot present this kind of data) [4].

In this paper, we will use fuzzy operations [5] to represent the knowledge about each factor. This will enable us to detect the emotion of a person using fuzzy inputs of the various factors. For example, we can use a fuzzy rule such as "IF (Temperature is High) AND (Heart Rate is High) THEN (Person is Excited)." Although fuzzy sets and operations are useful for representing the knowledge base, they fail to model the individual behavior of each and every person. Obviously, a model that is able to adapt to various categories of human responses would be preferred. Consequently, an adaptive learning mechanism is required to adjust the model if we were to cater for the differences in emotions between various humans. This requirement calls for the use of an adaptive learning system such as artificial neural networks (ANN) (Abraham 2005) [6]. However, the ANN model does not allow the use of fuzzy sets or rules, which is the more natural way of representing the relation between human emotions and human physical and physiological parameters. ANN uses exact and crisp values for representing the model's input.

In order to utilize the benefits of both fuzzy logic and artificial neural networks, we will use the hybrid approach, which combines fuzzy logic and artificial neural networks in a single model.

The analysis and detection of human emotions using an expert system has a direct impact on several fields of the human life such as health, security, social networks, gaming, entertainment, commercials and others [3,7]. The system will enable social networks (SN) participants to exchange emotions in addition to text, images, and videos.

In health related applications, for example, the interaction between a patient and doctor (in some critical cases) may become difficult or impossible [3], where the patient cannot explain his/her feelings to the doctor (e.g. coma infants, autism). The proposed system would enable the doctor to analyze and detect the patient's emotions, even when the patient is unable to correctly define his emotional status.

In social networks people exchange all types of information such as text, video, images, and audios. The proposed model would enable communicating parties to detect the emotional status of their partners in a seamless automatic manner. In essence, a person chatting with a friend on the social network would be able to tell whether the other partner is sad, angry, embarrassed, afraid or happy without the need for the partner to explicitly state the emotional status.

Security is another area where the proposed model can be of significant impact. The model can be used to predict a crime before it occurs by detecting a criminal behavior based on the emotional status of the person attempting to commit a crime or breach the security at given facilities. This is based on the psychological status of the criminal before committing a crime. At an airport facility, for example, the system can identify individuals with certain emotional postures based on perceived measures of the individual's heart rate, EEG frequencies, body temperatures and other measurable factors.

Gaming and entertainment is yet another area where the prediction of a person's current emotion status is very useful. The system can detect the modes of customers based on the various factors studied and analyzed in this paper.

The rest of this paper is organized as follows. Related work is presented in Section 2. Section 3 provides an overview of the various factors which impact the human emotions. Section 4 presents the ANFIS model, used to build the neuro/fuzzy model. Section 5 presents and analyzes the model results. Conclusions are presented in Section 6.

Related work

Human emotion detection and analysis is an important field of study. Some scientists have focused on external effects on human emotions for commercial objectives, such as the use of Electroencephalogram (EEG) measurements for determining the level of attention of a subject to a visual stimulus such as a television commercial displayed on a screen [7].

Timmons at al. [8] introduced a medical instrument that allows doctors to monitor their patients using sensors like insulin and blood pressure sensors. Ohtaki et al. [9] developed wearable instruments capable of indoor movements tracking and monitoring of concurrent psycho–physiologically indicated mental activity. The instrument used electro dermal activity (EDA), heart rate, and vascular change sensors for emotion detection. EDA can be used to detect the human emotional response by measuring the skin humidity, which reflects the activity of the Eccrine sweat glands [9].

In another related study, Petrushin & Grove [10] provided a method for detecting emotional state using statistical analysis of perceived measurements. In their study, they use parameters extracted from a voice speech as an input to an artificial neural network (ANN) to get the related emotion; ANN was used as an adaptive classifier which is taught to recognize one emotional state from a finite number of states [10]. Affectivea [11] introduced a wearable sensor which is capable of quantifying human emotions such as fear, excitement, stress, boredom etc. The devise can be used by doctors to analyze the emotions of autism patients by monitoring their motion and temperature.

Santosh and Scott [12] proposed the use of wearable wireless sensor system for continuous assessment of personal exposures to addictive substances and psychosocial stress as experienced by human participants in their natural environments. It was observed that physiological stress and response vary from person to person, and for the same person with respect to postures and physical activity; it has also been observed that human emotions can be correlated to behavioral patterns such as smoking and speech [12,13].

Nie et al. [1] evaluated the relationship between the Electroencephalography (EEG) and the human emotions and concluded that EEG can be used to classify two kinds of emotions: negative and positive. Yuen et al. [13] believe that the states of the brain change as feelings change, therefore, EEG is suitable for the task of recording the changes in brain waves, which vary according to feelings or emotions; a neural network was used to train the model. Leupoldt A et al. [14] observed the emotion influence on respiration sensation, skin conductance response and EEG. Kreibig [3] conducted a survey of several research studies to find the relationship between autonomic nervous system (ANS) and the human emotions. ANS includes the cardiovascular, the electrodermal, and the respiratory responses. The survey shows that the ANS response appears in negative emotions clearer than in positive emotions. Kreibig summarized the results of the survey in one table which shows the impact of several measurable factors on both negative and positive emotions. We will rely on this data for the construction of our model and we will choose fourteen factors out of the factors listed by Kriberg. The factors are selected on the basis of their measurability and the availability of sensors for these factors. The model will include all 22 different emotions (11 positive and 11 negative emotions).

Human emotions analysis and detection

Human emotions are intangible things; however there are several factors which can be used to detect them [3]. The factors impact the human emotions and the emotions of different people in different ways. The amount of information presented by the various factors is enormous, thus drastically increasing the complexity of any model used to correlate the factors to the emotions. In order to simplify the model by reducing the amount of data required to evaluate the model, we make use of fuzzy logic, where the input parameters are quantified with linguistic variables such as low, normal, and high which represent a wide range of input values. Following is a brief description of the factors used in our model and their impact on human emotions [15-17].

1. Electroencephalography(EEG):EEG measurements [18,19] are given in frequency ranges, and can be represented with four linguistic variables, namely alpha, beta, theta and delta with ranges 13–15, 7.5-13, 2.5-8, and <4 Hz respectively, (Figure 1).
2. Heart Rate (HR): Three heart rate ranges are identified, and categorized with fuzzy linguistic variable low (LHR) from 20 to 70 bpm, normal (NHR) from 45 to 100 bpm and high (HHR) from 84 to 120 bpm as shown in Figure 2

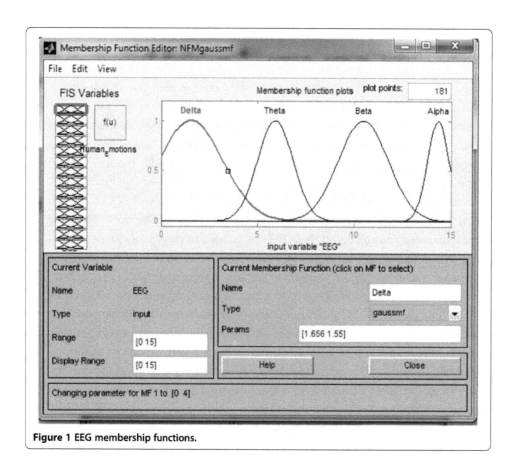

Figure 1 EEG membership functions.

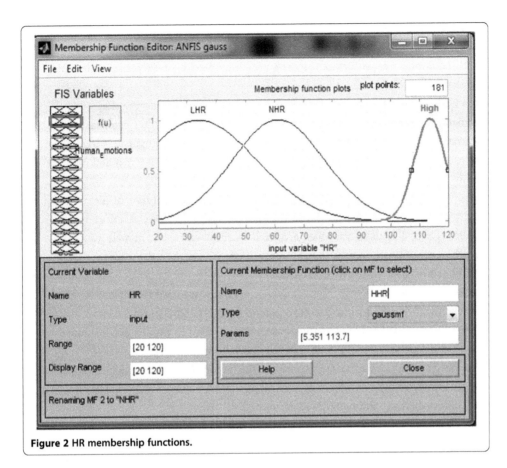

Figure 2 HR membership functions.

3. There are several frequency-domain measures which pertain to HR variability at certain frequency ranges; and these measures are associated with specific physiological processes. HRV has three ranges of frequencies, high, low and very low with ranges 0.15-0.4, 0.04-0.15 and 0.003-0.04 Hz respectively. HRV is known to decrease with anxiety and increase with amusement. Three linguistic variables (very low, low and high) with Gaussian functions are used to represent HRV.

4. Pre-Ejection Period (PEP). The PEP is defined as the period between when the ventricular contraction occurs and the semi lunar valves open and blood ejection into the aorta commences Three linguistic variables are used to implement PEP, namely low (LP) from 0 to 800 ms, normal (NP) from 0 to 1000 ms, and high (HP) from 500 to 1100 ms. PEP is known to increase with acute sadness, while it experiences an increase or decrease with joy

5. Stroke Volume (SV): Stroke volume is defined as the amount of blood pumped by the left ventricle of the heart in one contraction, and its normal range is from 0 ml to 250 ml. SV remains almost invariant for the positive emotions, while it responds actively to negative emotions e.g. it decreased with disgust, fear, and sadness [3]. Three linguistic variables are used to implement SV, namely low (LSV) from 10 to 144 ml, normal (NSV) from 10 to 250 ml, and high (HSV) from 240 400 ml.

6. Systolic Blood Pressure (SBP): Three linguistic variables are used to implement SBP, low (100–121), normal (110–134), and high (120–147). SBP is known to increase with fear and anxiety

7. Diastolic Blood Pressure (DBP): Three variables are used to implement DBP namely low (LDBP) from 77 to 87, normal (NDBP) from 81 to 91and high (HDBP) from 81 to 91. DBP increases with anger, anxiety, and disgust, while it decreases with acute sadness [3].

8. Skin Conductance Response (SCR): SCR is the phenomenon that the skin momentarily becomes a better conductor of electricity when either external or internal stimuli occur that are physiologically arousing. Three linguistic variables are used to implement SCR namely low (0–0.2 ms), normal (0.1-1 ms) and high (0.85-1.5 ms) [20,21].

9. Tidal Volume (Vt): Tidal volume represents the normal volume of air displaced between normal inspiration and expiration when extra effort is not applied Three linguistic variables are used to implement Vt, namely rapid breath (100–150 ml/breath), quiet breath (200–750 ml/breath) and deep breath (600–1200 ml/breath) [15,20].

10. Oscillatory Resistance (Ros): Three linguistic variables are used to implement Ros, namely low (0–0.49), normal (0.4-0.88) and high (0.5-1) [20].

11. Respiration Rate (RR): Three linguistic variables are used to implement RR namely, low (5–10), normal (7 to 23) and high (15–24) breath/min [20].

12. Nonspecific Skin Conductance Response (nSRR): nSRR is used to measure the moisture level of the skin and is implemented with three linguistic variables, low (0–2), normal (1–3) and high (2–5) per min [20].

13. Skin Conductance Level (SCL). SCL measures the electrical conductance of the skin and is used as an indication of psychological or physiological arousal. Three linguistic variables are used to implement SCL namely low (0–2), normal (2–25) and high (20–25) ms.

14. Finger Temperature (FT): Three linguistic variables are used to implement FT namely low (65-75°F), normal (75- 85°F) and high (80-90-°F) [20].

Output membership functions

There are twenty-two different emotions impacted by the factors described above. In the artificial neural fuzzy system the output can be based on the Mamdani or the Sugeno models [5]. We will use the Sugeno model in this study, without loss of accuracy or generality of the overall results of the model, since both models equally represent the real system, differing only in the performance of the models, where the Sugeno model exhibits better performance than the Mamdani model [5]. For Sugeno model, we use both a single point constant and linear outputs functions to represent each of the emotions.

Using the Sugeno model, each output is represented by exactly one fuzzy rule and one constant value. The initial distribution can be uniform across all output emotions, since the final values will be adjusted after training. In our model, we use constant representation ranging from 1 to 22 as shown in Figure 3

The initial choice of the output values does not have an impact on the accuracy of the model, because the training part of the model adjusts the final output values based on the training data. For example, the initial value for the anger emotion is 1, for anxiety is 2. After training with the ANFIS model, the output values will be adjusted based on a set of training data.

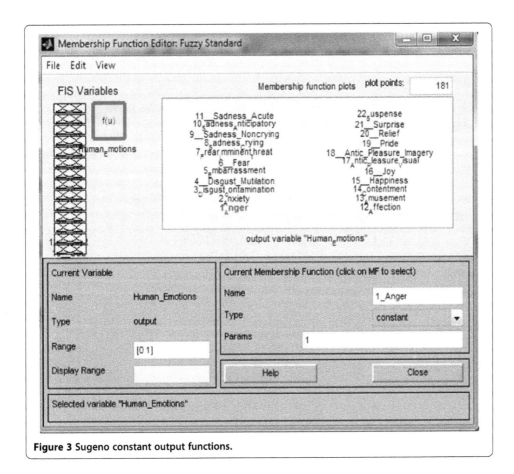

Figure 3 Sugeno constant output functions.

The Sugeno linear output model has the general form:

$$a_0X_0 \ + \ a_1X_1 \ + \dots \ + \ a_iX_i \ + \ z$$

Where a_i is a constant parameter and X_i is input variables. For constant functions, the values of a_i is equal to zero and, hence $Y = z$ (constant value). For the linear function model, the a_i values are entered through the ANFIS editor, while X_i are the values of the input factors

The correlation between the input and the output variables is done through a set of fuzzy rules. Each rule uses AND/OR connectors to connect various input factors with a particular output emotion. For example, rule 1 shows all the input factors which produce the anger emotion; the initial weight of the rules is set to 1 and will be adjusted after training the system.

Rules

The correlation between the input and the output variables is done through a set of fuzzy rules. Each rule uses AND/OR connectors to connect various input factors with a particular output emotion. Five of the 22 different rules used in our model are listed below for illustration. Each rule corresponds to one and only one output emotion. For example, rule 1 shows all the input factors which produce the anger emotion; the initial value of the anger emotion is set to 1. In the ANFIS model, rules are also assigned weights. The initial weights for all rules are set to 1.

1. If (EEG is Beta) and (HR is HHR) and (HRV is LF) and (PEP is LP) and (SV is LSV) and (SBP is HSBP) and (DBP is HBP) and (SCR is HSCR) and (Vt is RapidL) and (Ros is HRos) and (RR is HRR) and (nSRR is HnSRR) and (SCL is HSCL) and (FT is LFT) THEN (Emotion is Anger - 1) (1)

2. If (EEG is not Alpha) and (HR is HHR) and (HRV is VLF) and (SV is NSV) and (SBP is HSBP) and (DBP is HBP) and (SCR is HSCR) and (Vt is RapidL) and (Ros is HRos) and (RR is HRR) and (nSRR is HnSRR) and (SCL is HSCL) and (FT is LFT) THEN (Emotion is Anxiety - 2) (1)

3. If (EEG is not Alpha) and (HR is HHR) and (HRV is HF) and (PEP is LP) and (SV is LSV) and (SBP is HSBP) and (DBP is HBP) and (SCR is HSCR) and (Vt is RapidL) and (Ros is HRos) and (RR is HRR) and (nSRR is HnSRR) and (SCL is HSCL) and (FT is LFT) THEN (Emotion is Disgust_contamination –3) (1)

4. If (EEG is not Alpha) and (HR is LHR) and (PEP is LP) and (SV is NSV) and (SBP is HSBP) and (DBP is HBP) and (SCR is HSCR) and (Vt is RapidL) and (Ros is NRos) and (RR is HRR) and (nSRR is HnSRR) and (SCL is HSCL) and (FT is HFT) THEN (Emotion is Disgust_Mutilation –4) (1)

5. If (EEG is not Alpha) and (HR is HHR) and (HRV is VLF) and (PEP is LP) and (SBP is HSBP) and (DBP is HBP) and (SCL is HSCL) THEN (Emotion is Embarrassment –5) (1)

Experimental results and discussions

In this study, using NFIS editor in MATLAB which supports building a hybrid neuro-fuzzy systems, six models are built with three input membership functions, namely the Gaussian membership function (gaussmf), a combination of two Gaussian functions (gauss2mf), and a product of two sigmoid shaped member functions (psigmodmf). We use the Sugeno constant and linear output functions. The rule in Sugeno fuzzy model has the form

If (input 1 = x) and (input 2 = y)

THEN output z = ax + by + c.

For the constant Sugeno model, the output level z is constant c, where a = b = 0. The output level z_i of each rule is weighted by firing strength w_i of the rule.

The performance metrics of the models include the trainability, the training time, and the training error. The characteristics of the six models are given in Table 1: Model Characteristics

For each of the models shown in Table 1: Model Characteristics, we build a neuro/fuzzy structure with 5 layers as shown in Figure 4. The general structure of the ANFIS

Table 1 Model characteristics

Model Name	Input Memberships	Output memberships
Gauss/Const	Gaussmf	Const
Gauss/Linear	Gaussmf	Linear
Gauss2/Const	Gauss2mf	Const
Gauss2/Linear	Gauss2mf	Linear
Psigmf/Const	Psigmf	Const
Psigmf/Linear	Psigmf	Linear

model is the same for all models. The models differ in the specifications of the membership functions and the output specifications. However, the general structure remains the same for all.

Training

Training is used to adjust the model parameters, particularly the input membership function parameters, and the corresponding output values. For example, after training, the width (c) and the height (σ) of Gaussian function curve are adjusted to produce the desired output. The adjustment and tuning depend on the accuracy of the training data.

Training requires two kinds of data arrays, training array and testing array. A training array is a two dimensional array [m × n], where m is the number of rows containing input values, and n = a + 1, where a is the number of input factors; in our model, n = 15. Each row contains values for each of the 14 input factors; the last column holds the value for the corresponding emotion output. The testing array holds the data in the same way as the training array, but the data in this array is more accurate and smaller than the data of the training array. We use three sets of training arrays. The correct values training Array (CTA) has 815 records; each is selected based on the rules given in Table 1. The noisy training array (NTA) with 815 records; the noise is introduced by violating the rules of Table 1. The small training array (STA) has 465 records.

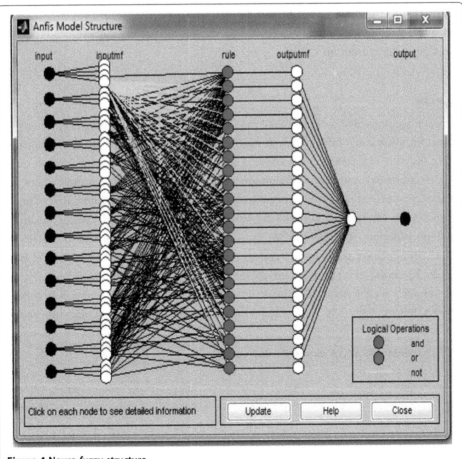

Figure 4 Neuro fuzzy structure.

Results

Table 2 shows the parameters for the SCR factor before (σ BT, c BT) and after (σ AT, c AT) training with NTA array.

We noticed similar behavior for all factors using the three different functions and the different arrays; although the magnitude of change is different for each experiment. We also noticed that the output values of the emotions had changed from the initial values. Figures 5 and 6 show the Gaussian membership function before and after training respectively.

Training under CTA data arrays produced smaller error values than those for NTA. The STA training data produced the lowest error values. The choice of training data set has an impact on the outcome of the emotions. Using different training data sets may very well produce different emotions output. This is consistent, however, with the fact that different categories of people may respond differently to emotions stimuli. Table 3 and Figure 7 show the human emotions response to 10 different trials with different input values for each trial under a model that had been trained for 10,000 epochs with CTA, STA, and NTA using psigmf/Linear functions. The table demonstrates how the models behave under different training sets.

The first experiment (column 2 HE-BT) indicates that the human emotion was 22 (suspense) before training and after training it became 15.4 (happiness), 6.48 (fear) and 8.3 (sadness crying) for NTA, CTA and STA respectively. Note that different training sets produce different models. In reality, there could be different training sets representing different human behavior and different human responses. So it is essential to know which category (or training set) an individual belongs to before attempting to define his/her current emotion.

Conclusions

In this paper, we presented a neuro/fuzzy model for the detection of human emotions using fourteen measurable human factors which are known to impact human emotions in varying degrees. The factors are converted into fuzzy variables and used in a set of rules to detect one of twenty two different emotions. The model is trained and the output parameters representing emotions can are adjusted using a set of training data. The developed models can be used in social networks such as Facebook and Twitter, health organizations especially for coma, infant or autism patients, security systems like airports and critical places, and gaming industry. The experiments show that the model is sensitive to the choice of input membership functions as well as the output function.

In this research, we developed a neuro-fuzzy system that deals with 14 human factors that impact human emotions. These human factors are used as input data for the

Table 2 SCR training with NTA date set – 800 epochs

SCR Factor	σ			c		
	BT	AT		BT	AT	
		Const	Linear		Const	Linear
LSCR	0.08	0.09	0.08	0.06	0.06	0.05
NSCR	0.12	0.16	0.12	0.73	0.73	0.73
HSCR	0.22	0.1	1.21	1.24	1.28	1.24

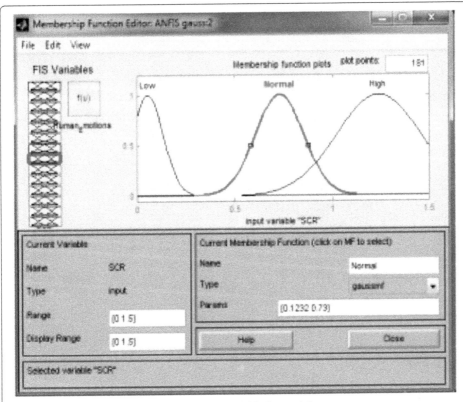

Figure 5 Charactersistic for Gaussian/Constant model before training.

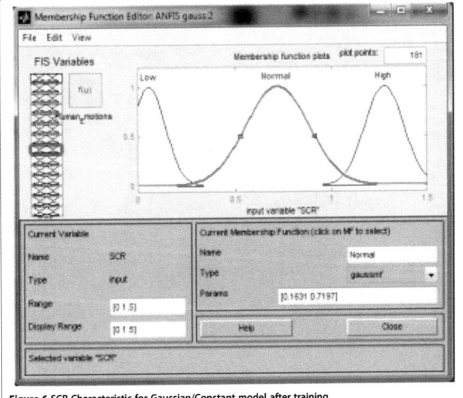

Figure 6 SCR Characteristic for Gaussian/Constant model after training.

Table 3 Human emotions response after training for 10,000 epochs with NTA, CTA, and STA (Psigmf/Linear)

HE-STA	HE-NTA	HE-CTA	HE-BT	Output
8.3	15.4	6.48	22	1
Sadness	Happiness	Fear	Suspense	
Crying		Imminent threat		
11.1	16.1	11.3	20	2
Sadness	Joy	Sadness	Relief	
Acute		Acute		
13.8	16.1	15.4	16	3
	Joy	Happiness	Joy	
10.7	16	11.8	17	4
Sadness	Joy	Affection	Antic Pleasure	
Acute			visual	
10	16	4.52	21.1	5
Sadness anticipat	Joy	Embarrass.	Surprise	
15.9	16.1	15.7	16.3	6
Joy	Joy	Joy	Joy	
12.7	16	15.2	15.8	7
Amusem.	Joy	Happiness	Joy	
10.9	10.6	3.91	13.7	8
Sadness	Sadness	Disgust	Contentment	
acute	Acute	mutilation		
8.29	9.54	7.13	12.8	9
Sadness	Sadness	Fear	Amusement	
crying	anticipat	imminent		
21	16.1	20.7	9.01	10
Surprise	Joy	Surprise	Sadness Non-cry	

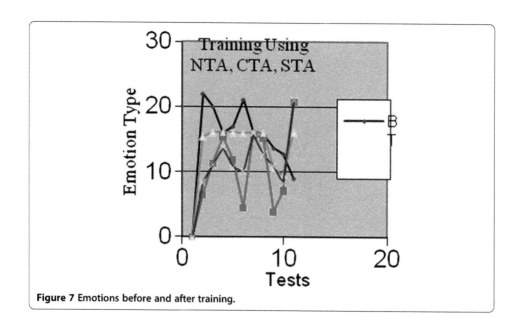

Figure 7 Emotions before and after training.

system. These input factors are entered into some specific rules which correlate human emotions to one or more of these factors. A training mechanism is developed, which allows the neuro-fuzzy system to be trained in a manner to detect current human emotions. The developed system benefits the advancement of social networks, security systems, gaming industry and others.

Competing interests

The authors declare that they have no competing interest.

Authors' contributions

MM and OM carried a neuro-fuzzy system for detecting human emotions, participated in the sequence alignment and drafted the manuscript. MM and OM read and approved the final manuscript.

Author details

[1]Jadara University, Irbid, Jordan. [2]Cambium Networks, USA. [3]Department of Computer Science, Jadara University, Irbid, Jordan.

References

1. Nie D, Wang X, Shi L, Lu B (2011) "EEG-based emotion recognition during watching movies". International IEEE EMBS Conference on Neural Engineering Cancun, Mexico, pp 667–670
2. Owaied H, Abu-Arr'a M (2007) 'Functional model of human system an knowledge base System', the international conference on information & knowledge engineering, pp 158–161
3. Kreibig S (2010) 'Autonomic nervous system activity in emotion: a review', biological psychology. 84:394–421. doi:10.1016/j.biopsycho.2010.03.010. Listed among Biological Psychology's Most Cited Articles and Most Downloaded Articles
4. Zadah L (1965) Fuzzy sets. Ntional Science Foundation under Grant, U.S
5. Negnevitsky M, et al. (2005) Fuzzy expert system. In: (ed) Artificial intelligent a guide to intelligent systems, 2nd edition. Pearson Education, England
6. Abraham A (2005) 'Artificial neural networks', handbook of measuring system design. USA, John Wiley & Sons, Ltd, pp 901–908
7. Silberstein R (1990) Electroncephalographic attention monitor. US patent 4:955,388
8. Timmons N, Scanlon W (2004) 'Analysis of the performance of IEEE 802.15.4 for medical sensor body area networking', sensor and Ad Hoc communications and networks, 2004. IEEE SECON. First Annual IEEE Communications Society Conference, Ireland, pp 1–4
9. Ohtaki Y, Suzuki A, Papatetanou (2009) 'Integration of psycho – physiological and behavioral indicators with ambulatory tracking of momentary indoor activity assessment'. ICROS – SIC, International Joint conference 2009, Japan, pp 499–502. 2009
10. Petrushin V, Gove B (2002) 'Detecting emotions using voice signal analysis'. US patent 7:222. 075,B2
11. Affectiva (2011) Affectiva. http://www.affectiva.com/q-sensor, viewed by 11 June 2011
12. Santoch K, Scott M "Auto sense: a wireless sensor system to quantify personal exposure to Psycological stress and addictive substances in natural environment". viewed by 13 June 2011 http://sites.google.com/site/autosenseproject/research
13. Yuen C, San W, Rizon M, Seong C (2009) "Classification of human emotions from EEG signals using statistical features and neural network". International Journal of Integrated Engineering:71–79. In International Journal of Integrated Engineering
14. Leupoldt A, Vovl A, Bradley M, Keil A, Lang P, Davenport P (2010) 'The impact of emotion on respiratory-related evoked potentials'. Society for Psychophysiological Research, USA, pp 579–586
15. Cacioppo J, Tassinary L, Berntsong G (1999) 'The hand book of psychophysiology, 3rd edition
16. Sherwood L (2010) Human physiology from cells to systems, 7th edition
17. Osumi T, Ohira H (2010) The positive side of psychopathy: emotional detachment in psychopathy and rational decision-making in the ultimatum game. Personality an Individual Differences 49:451–456
18. Niedermeyer E, da Silva FL (2004) Electroencephalography: basic principles, clinical applications, and related fields. Lippincot Williams & Wilkins. ISBN 0781751268
19. Bos D (2006) 'EEG-based emotion recognition'. The influence of visual and auditory stimuli University, pp 734–743. Online ISBN 978-3-642-24955-6
20. Kaluer K, Voss A, Stahl C (ed) (2011) Cognitive method in social psychology
21. Seo S, Lee J (2010) 'Stress and EEG'. Convergence and Hybrid Information Technologies Marius Crisan, In Tech, pp 413–426

2

Panoramic human structure maintenance based on invariant features of video frames

Shih-Ming Chang[1*], Hon-Hang Chang[2], Shwu-Huey Yen[1] and Timothy K Shih[2]

---

* Correspondence:
rest306@hotmail.com
[1]Department of CSIE, Tamkang
University, Taipei, Taiwan
Full list of author information is
available at the end of the article

Abstract

Panoramic photography is becoming a very popular and commonly available feature in the mobile handheld devices nowadays. In traditional panoramic photography, the human structure often becomes messy if the human changes position in the scene or during the combination step of the human structure and natural background. In this paper, we present an effective method in panorama creation to maintain the main structure of human in the panorama. In the proposed method, we use an automatic method of feature matching, and the energy map of seam carving is used to avoid the overlapping of human with the natural background. The contributions of this proposal include automated panoramic creation method and it solves the human ghost generation problem in panorama by maintaining the structure of human by energy map. Experimental results prove that the proposed system can be effectively used to compose panoramic photographs and maintain human structure in panorama.

Keywords: ASIFT algorithm; Human structure maintenanc; Panoramic creation

Introduction

Generation of panorama from a set of individual photos has been a useful and attractive research topic within the researches in the domain for several years so far. Even though the researchers focused more into personal computer based solutions at the beginning nowadays much focus is being diverted to mobile platform based solutions making it a very convenient and attractive application for the users. As an example many recent smart mobiles are equipped with applications that are capable of generating even a 360° panorama in a scene. The panorama generation solution presented in Yingen Xiong's method [1] consumes less processing time as the processing is done in memory. Wang Meng [2] presented an approach to create a single view point full view panorama photograph from a set of image sequence. Individually ordered frames which are extracted from a panning video sequence have been used as the input making it simple for both shooting and stitching. Going forward another step of panorama generation Wagner Daniel et al. [3] presented a method for the real-time creation and tracking of panoramic maps on mobile phones. Specially, the maps generated are accurate and allow drift-free rotation tracking. But, most of the current technologies used for panorama generation are targeted for natural landscape capturing. Hence, in the situations where human objects appear in the background, the result of panorama may contain blurred human objects, as the structure of human object cannot be detected very precisely via feature extraction, which in turn results in low quality panorama. In regular feature extraction method, defining feature points in human object is very difficult unless there are obvious feature points available on the clothes. Therefore in this paper, we present our efforts in generating a panorama which show the landscape and human objects in the background without any blurred effects.

On the other hand more information of the natural scenery and buildings that we want to capture can be obtained via panoramic photography. Hence, ppanoramic photography can be considered best suited where the user needs more natural scenery in one picture. Even though panoramic photos can be created using commercially available image processing tools in several steps by appropriately segmenting available human objects and combining relevant background features together from the source frame sets, it is very time consuming manual work and the results are not satisfactory. There, in the combining step, most of the images cannot be combined via simple manual methods even in the same scene, b due to the problem of always existing cylindrical distortion exists in camera lenses which is difficult to recognize by the user in the source images. Therefore, we also propose an automated calibration mechanism in the proposed method which in turn reduces steps and time consuming in manual methods.

In summary the main goal of our work is to develop a system to take panoramic photographs, eliminating blurred effects created due to the human objects in frames with the background. Presented solution also reduce the steps comparing to the manual methods, allowing the user to obtain a panoramic photograph via our panning shooting method in video.

The schematic steps of proposed method is shown in Figure 1. User first captures a short video focusing main human character following a designed circle path like in the left part of Figure 1. Then the frames are extracted from the short video via proposed system and selects 6 source image out of that frame set and produce panorama after proposed method. Composition of the paper is organized as follows. Section III and IV discusses the human structure maintenance and panorama creation phases consecutively. Experimental results and analysis are presented in Section V. We conclude our contributions and future works in Section VI.

Related works

Feature extraction

Feature extraction can be done by matching the similar objects between difference images. We can regulate and track objects via the information obtained from feature extraction.

Figure 1 The schematic steps of the proposed approach.

Even though human eye can detect the features in different images it is not an easy task to be done in computers. One famous method which is used to detect features is the Scale-Invariant Feature Transform (SIFT) algorithm by Matthew Brown [4] and Saeid Fazli [5]. SIFT algorithm is a very robust method that can detect and describe local features in the image and it can find some features in different images as well. It uses Difference of Gaussian (DOG) function and image pyramid technology to find extreme values in different scale-space. Then a linear least square solution and threshold value is used to decide height-contrast feature points or to excise low-contrast feature points and use each feature points' gradient direction and feature points, strength to allocate the feature points. Therefore, the information of feature is very credible and can be used in calibration images using calibration matrix.

Though SIFT algorithm can describe local features very robustly, the cost of process time is very large, and some features are not very import and apparent in image. In order to solve the problem of cost, Yingen Xiong [1] and Zhengyou Zhang [6] presented the Speeded Up Robust Features (SURF) algorithm that can be used which is faster than SIFT algorithm. But the number of features that can be extracted is less than SIFT algorithm.

Panorama creation

In recent years, panorama creation has been attracted by many researchers in the world developing very robust solutions. Matthew Brown et al. [4] used SIFT algorithm for feature matching in source images where their source images were not in order as per their research. Hemant B. Kekre et al. [7] presented a panorama generation approach to nullify effect of rotation of partial images on process of vista creation. Their method is capable of resolving the missing region in the vista caused due to the rotation of partial image parts used during the vista creation. Helmut Dersch [8] presented the open source of panorama creation that can be create panorama via parameters of open source functions. Image inpainting has been used during the process to fill the missing region. That missing view regeneration method was also able to overcome the problem of missing view in vista due to cropping, irregular boundaries of partial image parts and errors in digitization. Wang Meng [2] presented an approach to create a single view point full view panorama photograph. Song Baosen et al. [9] then presented another panorama generation based research to enlarge the horizontal and vertical angles of view for an image.

To fulfill the fast developing mobile devices market panorama creation solutions for mobile devices has been presented in recent years. Yingen Xiong et al. [1] proposed a fast method of panorama creation for mobile devices. In order to reduce the process time they used the default direction of photography instead of the method of calibration. A smoothly varying affine stitching field which is flexible enough to handle parallax while retaining the good extrapolation and occlusion handling properties of parametric transforms was presented by Wen-Yan Lin et al. in [10]. Their algorithm which jointly estimates both the stitching field and correspondence permits the stitching of general motion source images, provided the scenes do not contain abrupt protrusions.

Human structure maintenance

The panoramic photograph creation process of the proposed method have two main phases as human structure maintenance and panorama creation, respectively as shown in the flow chart of Figure 2. The proposed system is semi-automatic allowing users to adjust the output based on their preferences. We discuss the human structure maintenance in Section III and the panorama creation method in Section IV.

Preserving the full human

Most of the technologies for panoramic creation nowadays often used for natural landscapes or interior landscapes and the panorama can be constructed in a very good quality. That is because such landscape backgrounds are static during the small time of capturing. But when the panorama is being captured with human objects in the foreground, the result of panorama may be resulted a poor quality human object as shown in the example in Figure 3. The reason for such bad quality human object is the deformation of the feature structure of human due to the calibration of the structure of images. It is required to retain the main human and more scenery in the resultant panorama. The background structure can be maintained using feature matching and camera calibration but the structure of main human may look distorted after camera calibration. In order to solve this problem, some of panoramic creation technologies also use the image editing method. Using editing method is a good idea to solve the problem of deformed human object in

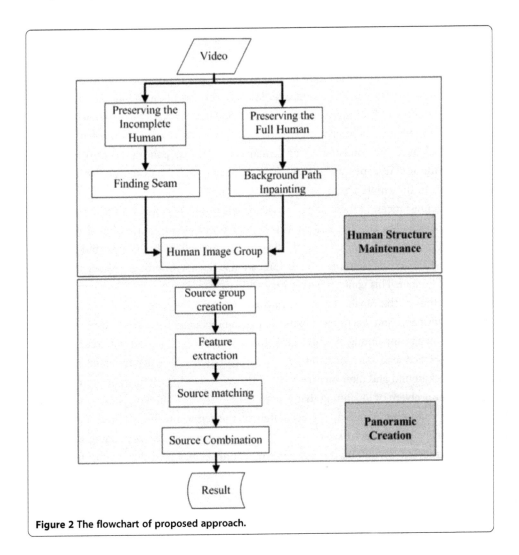

Figure 2 The flowchart of proposed approach.

Figure 3 The poor result of human in panoramic creation.

image, but editing method have to spend most time to adjustment the object and land-scapes with artificial.

In order to solve the problem of human panoramic creation, we use the inpainting technology. Because general panoramic creation may produce a panorama with blurred human object or human object with a wrong structure details. Therefore, we obtain the position of human from source images, then find the largest region position of human and recover it into panorama. The panoramic image often maintain the largest dimensions (the height and width of image) and information. The complete human object will be available in the panorama after merging the relevant parts from the source images. Finally, since we have the information of human, we can use panoramic creation to produce the natural landscapes without the human object, and then recover the largest human object into the empty region in the panoramic image.

In normal circumstances, in the pictures or videos taken for the generation of the panorama, human objects do not move in a short time, and background information also have similar regions in difference source images. But, we cannot obtain the background information that is shielded due to human. Therefore, we use the surrounding region patch to fill structure of human. This concept is very easy and fast. But, this concept does not guarantee the structure in the repaired regions. In this way, the structure cannot be retained and the resultant panorama becomes unnatural. In maintenance of structure in repair regions, we use image inpainting method [11]. Image inpainting method can retain the structure in specified area via user definition. The repair patch consider the similarity of structure in background and filter incorrect structure via inpainting method.

An important problem of inpainting that is used in the proposed method is the structure of background cannot be repaired very accurately in the regions to be repaired. Because image inpainting method has to select the sequence of repair regions depending on the similarity of structure. Therefore, the structure of boundary has a distinguishing feature that captures the complete human from source images and recover into panoramic image.

In order to solve the problem of the structure in repaired region, we have to add the original background information around the boundary of human object. The sequence selection of repair region of image inpainting finds the structure that can be obtained from background information and human boundary. Two of the methods in image processing, dilation and expansion, can control the size of the object boundary, effectively. We use dilation method to obtain the large area of object region than original object boundary and the expansion region has the background information. An example of dilation method is shown in Figure 4. Note that, to avoid the wrong structure to be found in image inpainting method, the expansion region of human boundary is not allowed to expand too much in the proposed method. If the expansion region of human boundary in source images are too large, the image inpainting method may find different structure and introduces bad quality into panoramic.

After this step, the repair structure of human boundary becomes similar and prevent the clutter of structure in repaired regions. The panoramic image becomes a disarray and unnatural in repaired regions via image inpainting method as shown in the example in Figure 5. Steps of the proposed method are presented in the following algorithm and a sample result is shown in Figure 6.

Algorithm: Human panoramic creation- Preserving the Full Human

Data: Human source images

   Result: Human inpainting image

   begin

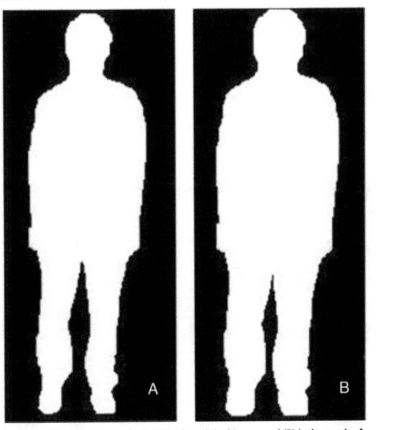

Figure 4 The example of dilation method, (A) is the original image and (B) is the result of dilation method.

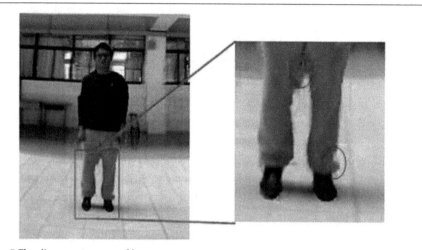

Figure 5 The disarray structure of human.

I. Select source image and find the largest human region in each source image.
II. Using panoramic creation method produce the panorama with a hole region of human.
III.Using dilation and expansion method for largest human region obtain human boundary correspondence information.
IV.Differentiate the foreground and background region of human boundary.
V. Using image inpainting method repair human boundary.
VI. Recover human region into panoramic image.

Preserving the incomplete human

In most cases, user cannot control the distance between camera and human. When the human is close to camera and it is required to obtain more background in panorama, the human structure becomes incomplete in some frames. We cannot use the method

Figure 6 The integrity structure of human.

described in part A, because the incomplete human may be in the same height as in frames. In order to solve the problem in incomplete human, we use energy map and find the seam in proposed method.

Some of panoramic creation methods often use the average value of RGB (or other color space value) on the overlapping region in the combination of source images. The average value is a fair-minded method, but, use of average value method may produce the ghost effect in panoramic image. The average value needs to rely on robust panoramic position method and accurate camera parameters, and there should not any moving or apparent object in source images. Therefore the average value method is not very reliable for our method of this step. Hence we use image stitching method in the proposed method as steps given below.

The concept in proposed method of image stitching is to find the optimal seam in the overlapping region between two images and to remove the ghost problem in the matching structure in panoramic image. Main steps of image stitching can be divided into three parts as registration, calibration and blending [4,12], and using dynamic programming method to find optimal seam. We can find the best seam (the shortest path) via dynamic programming method, this problem can be common in graphs. For each pixel in the source image can be converted into nodes and the relationship of neighboring pixels can be regarded as path between two nodes. Therefore the source image can be converted into a multi-stage graph. We use the concept of seam craving to find optimal seam in overlap region between two images and the schematic diagram is shown in Figure 7. The red line is the optimal seam between image A and image B.

The concept of seam craving [13] is used energy map to find the optimal seam and avoid the important area in image. The important area in the current part is definition area of human. We hope to avoid the human area in combination step of panoramic creation. And the energy map with seam carving can avoid the important area reducing the ghost effect problem as well. The energy map M_E can be generated by summing all values with smaller energy coefficients of the following direction up to down or left to right. All energy coefficients will increase downward or rightward. Figure 8 is the example of energy map constructed and the energy map M_E that can be defined as in Equation (1) where (x, y) represent the current position, the M_S is the image after sobel

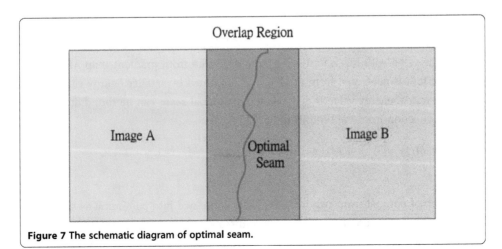

Figure 7 The schematic diagram of optimal seam.

32	33	24	12	43
32	33	24	12	43
32	25	24	24	26
64	49	36	36	38
15	35	34	19	26
64	71	70	55	62
45	47	58	67	20
79	111	113	122	75

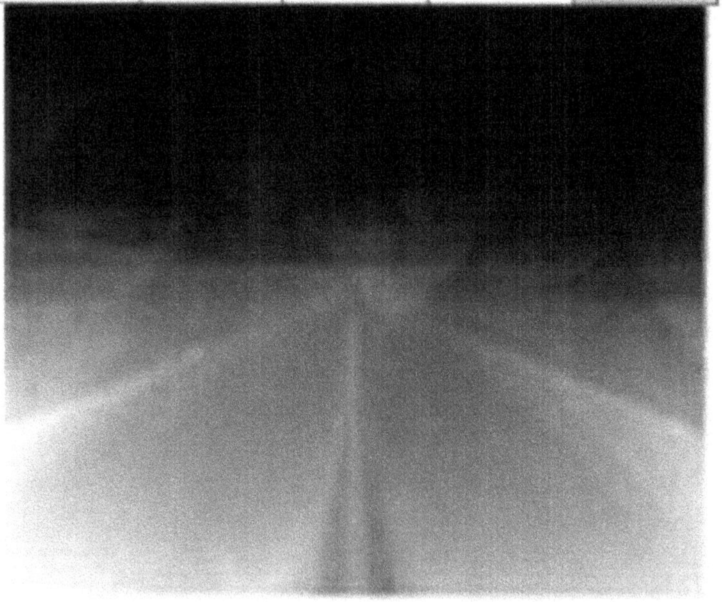

Figure 8 The example of Energy map generating phase and energy map.

processing. The value with black font represents the value from gradient map M_s; the value with red font is generated from energy value summed by smaller energy value in last row. Afterwards, energy value is generated; the optimal seam can be found and removed in the direction from the bottom to up.

$$M_E(x,y) = M_S(x,y) + min(M_E(x-1,y-1), M_E(x-1,y), M_E(x-1,y+1)) \tag{1}$$

After the step of optimal seam two images can be combined into panorama as shown in Figure 9. Red lines on top of Figure 9 are found seams on the overlapping region via energy map value. We found 30 seams on the overlapping region, respectively. After

Figure 9 Seam in overlapped region of images (top: original images of seams, bottom: combined photo with overlapped region is marked in red).

matching the most similar patch on the overlapping region and define the current seam as the optimal seam. Note that, because human area often presents in the center of panoramic image. Therefore, the overlapping region and to find optimal seam will be used on the surrounding of source images. The optimal seam for the overlapping region after combination step is showing in the down of Figure 9, and green area is the overlapping region of current source images.

Panoramic creation
Matching position of images
In order to establish a complete panorama, one important factor is to find the correct structure in source images. Most of the current methods use artificially marking of the structure points in the images. This is very time-consuming when there are large number of images. One shortcoming of artificially marking is the accuracy of the matching construction. Because the position of marks in images becomes different when we have visual differences or when there are artificial errors of marking the structure points. But, identification correct structure or graphics is also difficult target in automatic processing of computer. Therefore, many useful methods have been proposed based on feature matching and structure identification.

As described in Section 2, SIFT algorithm [5,12], can be used to detect and describe the local features on source images which even captured in difference view angles. A sample of SIFT algorithm is shown in Figure 10A. As previously mentioned, SIFT

Figure 10 The human result of SIFT and ASIFT algorithm, (A) is the result of SIFT algorithm and (B) is the result of ASIFT algorithm.

algorithm very time consuming during the processing and not effective for the images which captured in large shooting angles. Another worth noting drawback is the inefficiency in detecting features if the structure is too smooth or if there are many same feature. In order to improve above shortcomings, Morel proposed Affine-SIFT (ASIFT) [14] that can be used to find more features even in the images captured in large shooting angles between images. A sample result is shown in Figure 10B. ASIFT algorithm use six parameters to compute and record the zoom, rotation and translation of images. Morel proposed two important concepts that are against any prognosis and simulating all views depending that can be find more feature in large angle of shooting images. Because ASIFT algorithm increase some concepts that will become robust than the SIFT algorithm. But in processing time, ASIFT algorithm will spend more processing time than SIFT algorithm. According to our experiment the difference is very small.

In some cases, where there are many similar many similar features in one image, ASIFT algorithm may still have the wrong feature matching. Hence, we use a simple concept to filter the wrong feature matching via slope. For example, assume that we find the A frame and B frame have the same feature in Y axis and distance is 10 pixels. In subsequent frames, we find the C frame also have the same feature with A frame and B frame, but the feature point is in Y axis, distance is 5 pixels and 5 pixels in X axis. In this way, the concept of fixed displacement cannot use to filter wrong feature matching. Therefore, we use the slope S in all coordinates of feature matching, because we obtained video in same scene and same moving direction of photography, so most of the same feature matching will be same corresponding between two frames and have most same slope in feature matching. Through the slope concept, we can filter wrong feature matching between two frames, and to reserve the true feature matching information. At the same time, we can reduce the processing time in compute calibration parameters matrix. Steps of slope concept are in the following algorithm.

Algorithm: Matching Position of Images

Data: Source frames

Result: Feature Coordinate information

begin

I. Use ASIFT algorithm to find matching information with two images. Definitions (X_A, Y_A) and (X_B, Y_B) present the matching coordinates of source A and B and compute the slope S:

$$S = {}^{Y_B - Y_A} \big/ {}_{X_B - X_A} = \frac{\Delta Y}{\Delta X} \qquad (2)$$

II. If $S \neq 0$, using SAD method in a small range bounded by a 3×3 pixels block compute the number of matching information.

III. Using coordinates of matching information compute calibration matrix via the maximum number of S, then repeat for all source frames.

Image calibration

Image calibration is very important in image processing, image combination and stereo vision. The combined image becomes poor in quality on the boundary of source images even though source images were taken in same time and same scene during a short time. The reason is the cylindrical distortion available on camera lenses which cannot be avoided during the time of capturing of videos and images with camera. Figure 11 shows an example of a simple merging of a source image set without using any calibration methods.

In order to guarantee the structure and to avoid distortion in panorama, we have to determine the photography of panorama. In the proposed method we set the direction of capturing the scene as a circular path to obtain a source video of a small time. Then a set of frames are separated from the short video to be used as the source frame set. After that ASIFT algorithm is used to obtain the coordinate information of matching features based on the source images. After this step, we need to compute the camera parameter matrix [6,15] and transformation matrix in order to compensate the distortions in adjacent frames, although we obtained the source videos as smooth as possible.

We use the homography matrix [15] to ensure that all source images can be projected into the same plane maintaining the correct structure and information in panoramic

Figure 11 The result of easy combination.

image and defined as in Equation (1). Therefore it is required to calculate the homography matrix via matching information that can be extracted by ASIFT algorithm.

$$sm' = Hm \tag{3}$$

where, s is the scale matrix, H is the homography matrix, $m = (x, y, 1)$ and $m'=(x', y', 1)$ is a pair of corresponding points matrix in the original image and in panorama plane. The m and m' are the corresponding feature point in difference frame. The scale martix s will not affect the result of homography matrix, so we set the smallest constant into s. Then the homography matrix H, corresponding feature point m and m' can be expanded by,

$$S \begin{bmatrix} x' \\ y' \\ 1 \end{bmatrix} = \begin{bmatrix} H_{11} & H_{12} & H_{13} \\ H_{21} & H_{22} & H_{23} \\ H_{31} & H_{32} & H_{33} \end{bmatrix} \begin{bmatrix} x \\ y \\ 1 \end{bmatrix} \tag{4}$$

where, H_{ij} represents each element of the homography matrix. Equation 4 can be further simplified as follows,

$$\begin{aligned} x'(H_{31}x + H_{32}y + H_{33}) &= H_{11}x + H_{12}y + H_{13} \\ y'(H_{31}x + H_{32}y + H_{33}) &= H_{21}x + H_{22}y + H_{23} \end{aligned} \tag{5}$$

Since Equation 4 have eight parameters (i.e., the scale of H is variable and h_{33} is usually normalized to 1 [15]) at least four pairs of corresponding points are required to solve eight parameters and the expanded equation is given below.

$$0\begin{bmatrix} x_1 & y_1 & 1 & 0 & 0 & 0 & -x_1'x_1 & -x_1'y_1 \\ 0 & 0 & 0 & x_1 & y_1 & 1 & -y_1'x_1 & -y_1'y_1 \\ x_2 & y_2 & 1 & 0 & 0 & 0 & -x_2'x_2 & -x_2'y_2 \\ 0 & 0 & 0 & x_2 & y_2 & 1 & -y_2'x_2 & -y_2'y_2 \\ x_3 & y_3 & 1 & 0 & 0 & 0 & -x_3'x_3 & -x_3'y_3 \\ 0 & 0 & 0 & x_3 & y_3 & 1 & -y_3'x_3 & -y_3'y_3 \\ x_4 & y_4 & 1 & 0 & 0 & 0 & -x_4'x_4 & -x_4'y_4 \\ 0 & 0 & 0 & x_4 & y_4 & 1 & -y_4'x_4 & -y_4'y_4 \end{bmatrix} \begin{bmatrix} H_{11} \\ H_{12} \\ H_{13} \\ H_{21} \\ H_{22} \\ H_{23} \\ H_{31} \\ H_{32} \end{bmatrix} = \begin{bmatrix} x_1' \\ y_1' \\ x_2' \\ y_2' \\ x_3' \\ y_3' \\ x_4' \\ y_4' \end{bmatrix} \tag{6}$$

Moreover according to the characteristic of homography matrix these points in the three-dimensional space must be on the same plane. Thus the following algorithm clusters all feature points and calculate the best homography matrix.

Algorithm : Finding Optimal Homography Matrix

Data: Coordinates of matching information

   Result: Homography matrix

   begin

I. Cluster feature points according to color features via mean-shift algorithm.
   i. Transform the color space into *CIELuv*.
   ii. Create a 2D array *arrayLU* and give the L and U dimension parameters of *CIELuv*.
   iii. According to the *arrayLU* perform the clustering process and eliminate small regions by merging with neighbor regions.

II. For each group calculate the homography matrix by using the feature points within the group. Solve at least four pair of corresponding points. If there is no sufficient number of points the group is neglected.

III. The homography matrix of each group is fed into Equation (3) to calculate the value of H^*m and compare the deviation dev between the actual m' and the calculated H^*m, where num is the number of matching feature pairs.

$$dev = \sum_{i=0}^{num} \left(m_i' - Hm_i \right) / num \qquad (7)$$

IV. Define the optimal homography matrix is the one with the minimum deviation that is the one with the smallest dev.

After above steps, we can obtain the calibration parameters matrix. In the proposed method, we use calibration parameters matrix to transform source images into panoramic images as a example result shown in Figure 12. Note that we also have used the color adjustment method of poisson [16,17] during the combination of the source images. This color adjustment was not applied in Figure 11. Therefore, we can clearly detect that even the source images are taken in same time same scene, the light is different when we take images or video. Hence, we have to add color adjustment method when images are combined that can be obtained the conformity panoramic images.

Experiment results

In this section, the results of the experiment are discussed. Without using any supporting device for the camera (like tripod) input videos were captured to simulate a regular user who uses a regular camera. The main human did not move in a short time as previously mentioned. For each video, we take the time about 12~16 second that we have been try to keep for one cycle of circle in our photography. We only take video in outdoor, because user often want to retain the natural landscape and human in one image. Although the proposed method also can be used in interior scenes.

The specification of PC with 1.8 GHz CPU and 2 GB RAM is used for our experiment. All of source video, 6 frames were obtained automatically to compose the panorama.

Figure 12 The result of image combination.

Time taken in each phase of the process for the eight videos was measured and displayed in Figures 13 and 14. However time taken in the generation of panorama phase for eight source videos is largely different. The reason for this probably is the color complexity and structural complexity of the input frame set like S04 and S06 in Figure 14. The Panorama Creation ensures that main human subject appears clearly in panorama as discussed in Section 3 and 4.

In the photography environment, we do not restrict much in distance and brightness. Because we transform video to panorama assuming the rate of the camera moving is not fast. When the rate of the camera moving is too fast, we obtain largely blurred frames. In this way, we obtain low quality results of panorama. Several selected experimental results are shown in Figure 14.(A) to 14.(P). S1~S4 videos were captured in outdoor and the resultant panorama clearly shows that the main person in the panorama. S5 and S7 were captured in outdoor and the resultant panorama clearly shows that main of two persons in the panorama. S6 and S8 videos were captured again in outdoor and the resultant panorama clearly shows that main of three persons in the panorama,

Conclusion

This paper proposes a novel method for generation of panorama image from a video captured from a simple digital camera by a novice user. It further provides details of composing a human panoramic image which provides more scenery information in one image. Main concepts of the proposed method are use of inpainting method and energy map method in human maintenance for panoramic creation. User does not need to tag or give a label of source images. We also combined the advantage of traditional panoramic creation and image stitching in proposed method and proved that proposed method is effective in use as per the shown results in experiment results section.

In panoramic creation, the processing is required to pay more attention to reduce the time taken for the processing. And often it is required to concentrate in feature matching

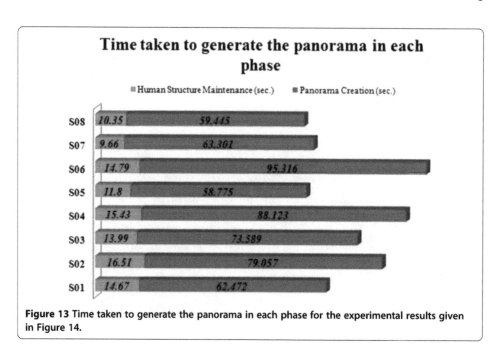

Figure 13 Time taken to generate the panorama in each phase for the experimental results given in Figure 14.

Figure 14 Experimental results (left: one frame from source video, right: resultant panorama).
(A) S1: original video. (B) S1: panorama result. (C) S2: original video. (D) S2: panorama result. (E) S3: original video. (F) S3: panorama result. (G) S4: original video. (H) S4: panorama result. (I) S5: original video. (J) S5: panorama result. (K) S6: original video. (L) S6: panorama result. (M) S7: original video. (N) S7: panorama result. (O) S8: original video. (P) S8: panorama result.

step, because of the feature information are important in image position matching and in computing the homography matrix. Therefore, all source images need to be coordinated in same step of feature matching which results an increase in time complexity when the amount of source images is large in input processing. Authors are working on a proper solution to remove the empty black color regions around the boundary of the panorama and to develop that proposed solution for the mobile devices as well.

Competing interests
The authors declare that they have no competing interest.

Authors' contributions
All authors contributed to the content of all sections, read and approved the final manuscript.

Authors' information
Shih-Ming Chang is a PhD student at Department of Computer Science and Information Engineering of Tamkang University, Taiwan. He acquired the Master degree in Department of Computer Science and Information Engineering of Tamkang University of Taiwan in 2009. His research interests are in the area of Computer Vision, Interactive Multimedia and multimedia processing.
Hon-Hang Chang is a PhD and student and currently reading at the Department of Computer Science and Information Engineering, National Central University (NCU), Taiwan (R.O.C.). He acquired his Master's degree in Department of Photonics and Communication Engineering of Asia University of Taiwan in 2011. His research fields are image processing, information hiding and water marking.
Shwu-Huey Yen is currently an associate professor in Computer Science and Information Engineering (CSIE) department of Tamkang University, New Taipei City, Taiwan. She is also an author of over 50 journal papers and conference papers. Her academic interests are signal processing, multimedia processing and medical imaging.
Timothy K. Shih is a Professor of the Department of Computer Science and Information Engineering, National Central University, Taiwan. He was a Department Chair of the CSIE Department at Tamkang University, Taiwan. Dr. Shih is a Fellow of the Institution of Engineering and Technology (IET). In addition, he is a senior member of ACM and a senior member of IEEE. Dr. Shih also joined the Educational Activities Board of the Computer Society. His current research interests include Multimedia Computing and Distance Learning. Dr. Shih has edited many books and published over 440 papers and book chapters, as well as participated in many international academic activities, including the organization of more than 60 international conferences. He was the founder and co-editor-in-chief of the International Journal of Distance Education Technologies, published by the Idea Group Publishing, USA. Dr. Shih is an associate editor of the ACM Transactions on Internet Technology and an associate editor of the IEEE Transactions on Learning Technologies. He was also an associate editor of the IEEE Transactions on Multimedia. Dr. Shih has received many research awards, including research awards from National Science Council of Taiwan, IIAS research award from Germany, HSSS award from Greece, Brandon Hall award from USA, and several best paper awards from international conferences. Dr. Shih has been invited to give more than 30 keynote speeches and plenary talks in international conferences, as well as tutorials in IEEE ICME 2001 and 2006, and ACM Multimedia 2002 and 2007.

Author details
[1]Department of CSIE, Tamkang University, Taipei, Taiwan. [2]Department of CSIE, National Central University, Taoyuan, Taiwan.

References
1. Xiong Y, Pulli K (2010) Fast image stitching and editing for panorama painting on mobile phones. In: IEEE Comput Soc Conf Comput Vis Pattern Recogn Workshops (CVPRW). San Francisco, CA
2. Wang M (2009) Panorama Painting: With a Bare Digital Camera. In: Image and Graphics, 2009. ICIG'09. Fifth International Conference. Xi'an, Shanxi
3. Wagner D, Mulloni A, Langlotz T, Schmalstieg D (2010) Real-time panoramic mapping and tracking on mobile phones. Virtual Reality Conference (VR), Waltham, MA
4. Brown M, Lowe DG (2007) Automatic panoramic image stitching using invariant features. Int J Comput Vis 74(1):59–73
5. Fazli S, Pour HM, Bouzari H (2009) Particle filter based object tracking with sift and color feature. International Conference on Machine Vision, Dubai
6. Zhang Z (2000) A flexible new technique for camera calibration. IEEE Trans Pattern Anal Mach Intell 22(11):1330–1334
7. Kekre HB, Thepade SD (2008) Rotation invariant fusion of partial image parts in vista creation using missing view regeneration. WASET Int J Electr Comput Eng Syst (IJECSE) 47:660
8. Helmut D (2007) Panorama Tools. Open source software for immersive imaging international VR photography conference, 2007. http://webuser.fhfurtwangen.de/~dersch/IVRPA.pdf, Accessed June 15-20 2007
9. Song B, Yongqing F, Wang J (2011) Automatic panorama creation using multi-row images. Inf Technol J 10:1977–1982
10. Wen-Yan L, Siying L, Yasuyuki M, Tian-Tsong N, Loong-Fah C (2011) Smoothly varying affine stitching. Computer vision and pattern recognition (CVPR). IEEE Conference, Providence, RI

11. Criminisi A, Perez P, Toyama K (2004) Object removal by exemplar-based inpainting. IEEE Comput Soc Conf Comput Vis Pattern Recogn 2:721–728, 2003

12. Matthew B, Lowe DG (2003) Recognising Panoramas. In: Proceedings of the 9th International Conference on Computer Vision (ICCV2003). Nice, France, pp 1218–1225

13. Avidan S, Shamir A (2007) Seam carving for content-aware image resizing. ACM Transactions on Graphics (TOG) 26(3):10

14. Morel J-M, Guoshen Y (2009) ASIFT: A new framework for fully affine invariant image comparison. SIAM J Imag Sci 2(2):438–469

15. Criminisi A, Reid I, Zisserman A (1999) A plane measuring device. Image Vis Comput 17(8):625–634

16. Sun J, Jia J, Tang C-K, Shum H-Y (2004) Poisson matting. ACM Trans Graph 23(3):315–321

17. Pérez P, Gangnet M, Blake A (2003) Poisson image editing. ACM Trans Graph 22(3):313–318

3

Automatic evaluation technique for certain types of open questions in semantic learning systems

Eman Elsayed[*], Kamal Eldahshan and Shaimaa Tawfeek

* Correspondence:
emankaram10@hotmail.com
Department of Math and Computer
science, Faculty of Science (girls),
Al-Azhar University, Cairo, Egypt

Abstract

In this paper, we propose a methodology to enhance the evaluation tools in semantic learning systems. Our proposal's aim is to evaluate two types of open questions in hybrid exams. The proposed technique in the first type MOQ (Multi Operations Question) uses the matrix concept for fuzzy score. But POQ (Proof Open Question) is more complicated so we use direct connect to learning objects which saved as ontology based. Also take into consideration the dependence among learning objects so we merge the universal ontology with weight matrix.

The proposed methodology has been applied to the case study of the mathematical multi operations question and the proof question on a logic course in a hybrid exam.

Keywords: Ontology based; E-learning; Evaluation tools; Hybrid exam; HCC; MOQ; POQ

Introduction

Recently, using computers and information technology are making revolution in education systems. They have many advantages as low costs and internationality. Until now, the new generation of e-learning systems is applicable in many fields and hybrid fields as in reference [1]. Consequently, online exams are widely used. Online exams are more convenient and flexible relative to traditional exams. They also reduce the overall expenses of processing exams especially in saving papers, storage, and materials' costs. The easiest type of questions is closed questions as multiple-choice questions. It is straightforward and does not require any text mining, Artificial Intelligence (AI), Natural Language Processing (NLP) techniques or algorithms [2].

However, multiple-choice questions can't determine the skills of students in writing and expressing. In some fields, educators prefer to have essay questions to grade more realistically students' skills.

Open questions are considered to be the most appropriate, because they are the most natural and they produce a better degree of thought. They help to evaluate the understanding of ideas, the students' ability to organize material and develop reasoning, and to evaluate the originality of the proper thoughts. We can say that using open questions evaluation tools is good for understanding the different human skills. That's human-centered computing (HCC) feature. We can classify this work as a version in preprocess of analysis the human skills. Where there are three large areas of HCC activities (production, analysis and interaction). We work deeply in this area in reference [3]. Also we used weight matrix with ontology to evaluate proof questions to ameliorate the evaluation. Where, we can evaluate the student's ability to relate the knowledge among each other. In this work, we generate a new scoring function by using weight matrix to measure the student's ability to connect knowledge in her/his mined.

However, they are much more difficult to evaluate than more restricted tests such as multiple choice tests. When student calculates some mathematical formula; not only the final result is interesting for us but also the deduction process is important too. We can evaluate the deduction path. We can check if the student understands this problematic or not by evaluating the steps.

The features of open questions in reference [4] are: No fixed method, No fixed answer or many possible answers, Solved in different ways and on different levels (accessible to mixed abilities), take a permission to a natural mathematical way of thinking, Develop reasoning & communication skills and open' creativity and imagination when relates to real-life context.

There are many types of open questions as a problem to solve with missing data/hidden assumptions, Proof questions, multi steps problem, Problem to explain a concept/procedure/error, Problem Posing, Real-life/Practical problems, Oral questions, investigative problems [compare, contrast, classify, test hypothesis and generalize] and so on.

In this paper, we focus on the POQ and MOQ.

There are different kinds of communication infrastructures between e-learning content objects and e-learning platforms. For successful application of any IES (Intelligent Educational System), it is necessary to get information about a learner's knowledge [5,6]. So we propose to direct connection of the learning materials to an evaluation tool.

The knowledge is represented through ontology as an artificial intelligent knowledge representation method [7]. This technology is currently being used for representing human knowledge and as critical components in knowledge management, semantic web, business to business applications, bioinformatics, e-learning, etc. In particular, using ontologies in E-learning for different purposes is commonly accepted in the community [6]. Ontologies allow representing, in a shareable and reusable manner, the knowledge involved in the evaluation processes. The learning objects in the same level of Ontology based are related if they are in the same ontology class. So in proof questions, we can generate weight matrix as in FCM [8]. In correct solution only the weight function calculates weight for rules was used. But we used only 1 if there is a relation (dependent) and 0 if there is no relation (independent). Then we can use the sum of this matrix as another variable to evaluate the student.

The paper is organized as follows. Section two presents the literature review, section three for proposal methodology, then section four implements the proposed method in the case study and finally the conclusion and further work.

Literature review

Several methodologies have been proposed to solve the problems in automatic evaluation of open questions. Some of them are summarized below:

Chang et al. [9] made a comparative study between the different scoring methods. They also studied the different types of exams and their effect on reducing the possibility of guessing in multiple choice questions.

And Rein [10] proposed an intelligent system to help in mathematical problems. The system is similar in concept to the programming languages' technology that is called Intelligence technology where software developers will be assisted through programming by showing them possible actions and mistakes while typing.

Also Mu et al. [11] discussed an approach for the automatic grading of code assignments. The developed tool assesses some of the issues with the code such as evaluating the performance and logical errors.

SMT (Satisfiablility Module Theory) solver is one of the methods for a certain type of proof. It isn't applied on exam until now. It is formal method example. There are many SMT solvers as in references [12-14]. SMT solver makes an automatic theorem prove. The SMT solver job is a decision problem to determine if a given logic formula is satisfiable with respect to a combination of theories expressed in first-order logic. There is yearly competition SMT-COMP [15].

In MOQ type, the evaluation by using the set of correct answers is the traditional method. But this method wasn't respect answer's order steps [16]. There is also the evaluation by using vector concept. It is more complicated but respect the order of the answer. So the solution must be exactly similar the template of the model answer.

Reference [8] proposed a FCM to determine the concepts dependences. That is by using the network graphic representation. Fuzzy concepts used to represent learning material domain concepts' knowledge dependencies, adaptive learning system knowledge representation [17]. It also represents the concept's impact strength over the other related concepts.

Proposed method

In this section, we present our proposal to handle the evaluation tool to evaluate the hybrid exam. Exactly the exam has the three types of questions, which presented into three subsections. MOQ section has a variable number of operations or steps, POQ section and the old type which is the closed question.

Proof open questions (POQ)

The proof questions are mathematical type of open questions. This type may be based on inference and reasoning through the constructed solutions. Also this type has dependence among concepts. When we solve problems there are some rules that may/may not depend on each other ex. Calculate average depend on the summation and the division over the summation.

In this part, we propose to connect the answers directly with the learning content's objects not with the model answer. So this part of the proposal tool built on the semantic knowledge representation" *universal ontology model*" where the extent domain ontology may require updates to solve domain problems. This helps to prevent the restriction over specific and determined answers. In contrast to such a thing, we have a variety and flexibility to handle different meanings and provide the flexibility to process over any constructed model.

The connected process in each step of the evaluation tool depends on the keys from solution. The keys in the POQ are the rules and theorems which are used. The student implements rules in such a way to solve problems. This satisfies the aim of the course.

The semantic e-learning system contains ontology modeling that has a design feature for further using in Content Management System (CMS).

We use CMS to implement our technique through interact admin with the knowledge represented by ontology in an appropriate way supported by their e-learning web application system. We make a bridge between a semantic system built using a semantic web language and the online e-learning web applications, using our system in e-learning tests capacitate our users to interact and access their open questions included in online exams.

We could load the developed course content model over CMS. In case a change occurs in a syllabus' learning contents (ex. updating, modifying) i.e. insert new learning objects or introduce new items or even deleting from our learning syllabus contents. We associate the required model answers in the generated model with their corresponding constructed questions. The developed system considers only the required concepts and answers that belong to their questions. The constructed answers are checked over the generated model.

Each correct equation gains its percentage score value that is stored into the student Database. After submitting these values, the teacher may preview the student's answers and their scores evaluations, hence scoring and feedback for each student performance and cognitive abilities measurements can be obtained.

Multi operations question (MOQ)

For the second questions part that if we have the open question type has a variable numbers of steps, where the solution steps aren't unique. In this type of questions used the matrices concept to merge vector evaluation technique and set evaluation technique i.e.

Set evaluation technique $+_h$ vector evaluation technique = matrix evaluation technique

Where $+_h$ means hybrid technique. This update is the main idea in the algorithm of the evaluation tool can automate the human rate in scoring. Also using the matrices concept makes the proposed method adequate for any answer that has ordered steps.

In general, we find that some final solution values are dependent on the previous existing values, i.e. we can't reach the final correct answer value if the previous one related to it is wrong. So while writing created solution values, the steps should be set in a correct order with correct values. In most cases the order for each solution is important. The vector evaluation restricts the position for each value in the answer template, with the sets evaluation concern with the number of all possible values without restricting its position in the solution. So we propose the evaluation matrix technique which has a set of array values, generates the set of all possible correct values that have a probability to exist in the solution, related to the position importance of each item in the created solution, and evaluates answers relatively and absolutely. So we could measure the similarity between student answers and a certain row in the generated solutions' matrix.

To prevent plagiarism sometimes teachers require descriptive details for each answers' question so decrease the number of steps and decrease scores as well. Each item in the evacuation matrix is assigned a specific score. If a correspondence exists between student and teacher items then score is gained, otherwise it isn't. The sum of all these scores represents the student's total score. The general form of the evaluation matrix that contains the set of all possible is:

$$
I_T = \begin{bmatrix}
A & B & C & D & E \\
\{A,B\} & C & D & E & O \\
\{A,B,C\} & D & E & O & O \\
\{A,B,C,D\} & E & O & O & O \\
E & O & O & O & O
\end{bmatrix}
\begin{matrix}
100\% \\
80\% \\
60\% \\
40\% \\
20\%
\end{matrix}
$$

The general form for student solution that has the set of all possibly created values is:

$$
I_{ST} = \begin{bmatrix} x_{z1} & x_{z2} & \cdots & x_{zm} \end{bmatrix}
$$

z = reference the row number in the evaluation matrix, m= number of student solution values.

Algorithm steps

I-*Input:* Teacher's question, teacher's model answers and student's solutions.

II-The processes:

Count mathematical operations (n-elements) in a teacher's question.

Assign each item in a teacher row answer solution a specific score.

Create a matrix.

Insert teacher's answers/items within this matrix as a first row.

Generate next row, the 1st item is 2nd item in the previous row then proceed in this way until reach last item.

Put the student's solution values into an array.

Compare between the student solution array and each row in the created matrix.

If there is a similarity between the array and a certain row, then calculate the percentage which depends upon several variables as the row number and the teacher request. Otherwise the score is zero.

Total score= question mark * percentage.

III- *The output* is the total score.

Through this algorithm we can generate the set of all possible values within our matrix make the system more accurate and support descriptive details. Question is evaluated absolutely, relatively, or absolutely and relatively whether a correspondence exists between item-item or item-set of items. The characteristics of vectors and sets are combined together to form matrix structure model.

Now, we explain the main relations between the proposed evaluation tools and the e-learning system. We must talk about these relations because the proposed evaluation tools especially POQ tool can't work dependently. It used learning objects from e-learning system. But our proposal depend on new generation of e-learning which build the learning object by using Ontology based. In this case the e-learning system called semantic e-learning.

The Figure 1 shows the infrastructure of the evaluation part in the proposed semantic e-learning. The CMS is a control management system or the control panel of the e-learning system. The teacher can control the icons from this side. He/She- if has experience in using ontology- can change or insert the learning objects by using the update learning contents icon. It is gate to connect to the universal ontology of many related courses in certain field. This ontology instead of learning objects database. The other

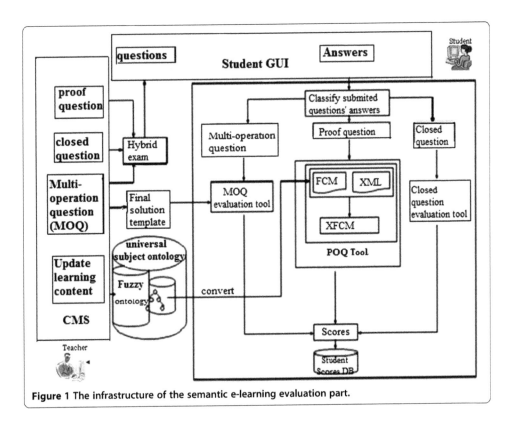

Figure 1 The infrastructure of the semantic e-learning evaluation part.

icons in CMS side are gates to send the hybrid exam to the students or to send the model answers (final solution template) to MOQ tool. The student has the exam and can send the answers from student GUI. The student's answers are classified in this first version in three parts. The first part is the original closed questions which use original tools in the e-learning system. The second type of questions sends to MOQ tool which explained in more details in Section Multi Operations Question (MOQ) and applied in Section Handle MOQ. The third part of questions is POQ which handling in POQ tool. The POQ tool needs certain information from learning objects ontology. The connection between Ontology and POQ tool is by XML to OWL converter in protégé platform or by semantic web rule language (SWRL) tool also from protégé platform. Section Proof Open Questions (POQ) and section Handle POQ explain more details about POQ type of questions and application in certain example. Then the proposed POQ and MOQ tools calculate the score and save the result in the student's database.

Implementation

In this section, we apply the proposal on certain course by Protégé platform and its plugin library in subsection Create Learning Object Materials Ontology to handle OWL ontology. Also we use SCORMCLOUD for Drupel which needn't to separate LMS. The algorisms were presented in subsections Handle POQ and Handle MOQ were uploaded as icons as evaluation tools. The proposed algorithms were written by PHP web scripting language and WampServer connecting scripts codes. So we use XML language to connect OWL to PHP.

To present our proposal, we needed real example. So we created simple part of Ontology based for Boolean algebra course by protégé platform which displayed in subsection Create Learning Object Materials Ontology. Then in subsection Handle POQ we presented different solutions for example of proof question and displayed part of the PHP code to handle the scoring function and how connected to ontology and also the weight function. That is for matching the solutions with rules. Finally, in subsection Handle MOQ we presented example for multi operations question and how matrix was generated and part of score function for this type.

Create learning object materials ontology

The first step is building the ontology of the course domain. This is done by defining ontology classes and arranging them in a hierarchy super class and subclass using top-down approach [18,19]. In this approach, we define the concepts and the rules. Common concepts are followed by more specific ones and the properties in the slots. Then we fill the instance's slot value. Constructing the classes hierarchy high levels and their sub-classes, make a relation between each main class and its sub classes. Identify the main and sub-concepts, relations, slots values, and instances. One of the fundamental using of the Boolean operations "OR, AND" and "NOT" are axiomatic and Algebraic proofs. A Boolean algebraic function that is put in algebraic form can be simplified using Boolean algebraic axioms, laws and theorems. Simply we insert the following part of Boolean algebra in Ontology based. Table 1 is a summary of some Boolean algebra functions from [20].

According to our implemented case, the developed technique POQ evaluation tool focused on Boolean algebra rules' axioms, laws and functions ontology modeling. The Ontology model represents Boolean algebra logic concepts, information and learning objects, which satisfy our system's educational knowledge needs, arrange main concepts (axioms, laws, theorems) and their hierarchical concepts into classes and subclasses respectively i.e. Starts with defining the classes of Boolean algebra rules' axioms, laws, theorems. Each class of these classes has a number of classes related to it represented as sub-classes (ex. axiom 1, axiom 2, ..., theorem 1, theorem 2, ...). A relation is defined between the main class and its sub classes. Each axiom, law and theorem contains two operations; one in OR Form and the other in AND Form. We make the values of these operations as an instance for a class that is related to, specifying the domain and the cardinality for each slot. We define the slots/properties values and fill the instance's slot value for those classes. Protégé platform was used to introduce our ontology model,

Table 1 Part of Boolean algebra functions

Description	OR form	AND form
Axiom 1	$x + 0 = x$	$x \cdot 1 = x$
Axiom 2	$x + y = y + x$	$x \cdot y = y \cdot x$
Axiom 3	$x \cdot (y + z) = (x \cdot y) + (x \cdot z)$	$x + y \cdot z = (x + y) \cdot (x + z)$
Axiom 4	$x + x' = 1$	$x \cdot x' = 0$
Theorem 1	$x + x = x$	$x \cdot x = x$
Theorem 2	$x + 1 = 1$	$x \cdot 0 = 0$
Theorem 3	$(x') = x$	
Associativity	$x + (y + z) = (x + y) + z$	$x \cdot (y \cdot z) = (x \cdot y) \cdot z$
Absorption	$x + x \cdot y = x$	$x \cdot (x + y) = x$
DeMorgan's Law	$(x + y)' = x' \cdot y'$	$(x \cdot y)' = x' + y'$

tools and semantic data. That because Protégé language is OWL (Ontology Web Language).

The OWL is suitable for web applications. We used protégé and its XML plug-in to save Axiom's rules model as xml file format for import and export XML files to PHP code. The connection between Ontology based and POQ tool executes by using "simplexml_load_file" PHP function.

The visualization plug-in tool has been used to visualize our ontology modeling ex. jambalaya tool plug in. Figure 2 shows the Boolean algebra Rules' Ontology visualization by Jambalaya tool.

Handle POQ

The main contributions of the mathematical Proof Open Questions (POQ) evaluation part is to develop an intelligent semantic method to automate the POQs evaluation, and design a technique that contains ontology modeling in which users can interact with the knowledge represented by ontology in an appropriate way supported by their Drupal e-learning which is a CMS freely available under the GPL [21].

In this research, the POQ evaluation tool has a consistently universal mathematical syllabus ontology model for a number of mathematical courses each course has its independent ontology model (ex. Abstract algebra, geometric algebra, Boolean algebra, ...) those different ontologies hypothetically represent independent learning courses' contents, aligned and merged them together with a matching and adequate concepts. Each course contains its belonging chapters, and each chapter contains a number of concepts available for different lessons, merging those ontologies together into a unified universal ontology model.

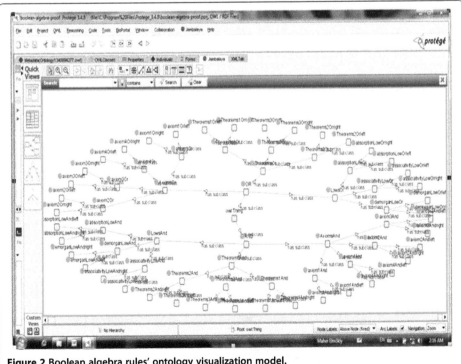

Figure 2 Boolean algebra rules' ontology visualization model.

Now to present how the system evaluates the POQ, we present the following scenario:

The teacher is asked to set the POQ as" **X+X'+Y=X+Y"** in the input box in order to be sent to the students. Then the tool connects to Boolean algebra ontology base. The proposed "simplexml_load_file" PHP function code converts the XML ontology to the PHP variables as in Figure 3.

Once the tutor sends the question, the student can receive it. Then student is asked to solve it and put constructed answers in input boxes as in Figure 4.

When the student submits these values into the system, the POQ's answers are connected directly to the POQ evaluation tool. The tool converts the classes or sub-classes of the axioms or theorem in the key column to xml file to connect with the PHP tool code. But if the student doesn't insert any axioms in the key column the whole Boolean algebra ontology is converted.

As we mentioned earlier, our system contains the part of Axiom1 rule's OWL/RDF ontology model which is further converted into the corresponding xml file.

When the student submit the first constructed solution item, the system checks both the rule and its value that exists in the right and left hand sides over the scripting file hierarchical tags. A score is gained for each correct solution item array, otherwise no scores are evaluated. Calculate the percentage scores' values to be stored into the student's DB.

These solutions' items and scores could be previewed, thus the teacher receives the student's answers and the evaluations for each correct solution.

The score function in our proposal tool sets value for each correct solution step, student gain a specific score value for each correct solution part. That value is increased as a student proceed in a correct steps, until student reach the final correct result, even if he/she doesn't set all steps in details' solutions, i.e. in case a student reaches the final solution result after any number of steps, then he could gain the score set for the problem. Figure 5 shows part of how score code checks solution arrays with rules arrays in each step. Although, the students can submit different solutions as in Figure 4 the POQ tool can evaluate it. In case of the correct answers, the POQ tool transfers to other scoring level. It is weight function as shown in Figure 6. By weight function we

```
//Initialize the XML parser                      //Specify element handler
$parser=xml_parser_create();                     xml_set_element_handler($parser,"start","stop");
//Function to use at the start of an element     //Specify data handler
function start($parser,$element_name,$element_attrs)  xml_set_character_data_handler($parser,"char");
{                                                //Open XML file
  switch($element_name)                          $fp=fopen("orAnd.xml","r");
  {                                              //Read data
    case "SLOT-VALUES":                          while ($data=fread($fp,4096))
    echo "--slotValue --<br />";                 {
    break;                                         xml_parse($parser,$data,feof($fp)) or
    case "SLOTS":                                  die (sprintf("XML Error: %s at line %d",
    echo "Slot: ";                                 xml_error_string(xml_get_error_code($parser)),
  }                                                xml_get_current_line_number($parser)));
//Function to use at the end of an element       }
function stop($parser,$element_name)             //Free the XML parser
{                                                xml_parser_free($parser);
  echo "<br />";
}
//Function to use when finding character data
function char($parser,$data)
{
  echo $data;
}
```

Figure 3 A part of converter code XML to PHP.

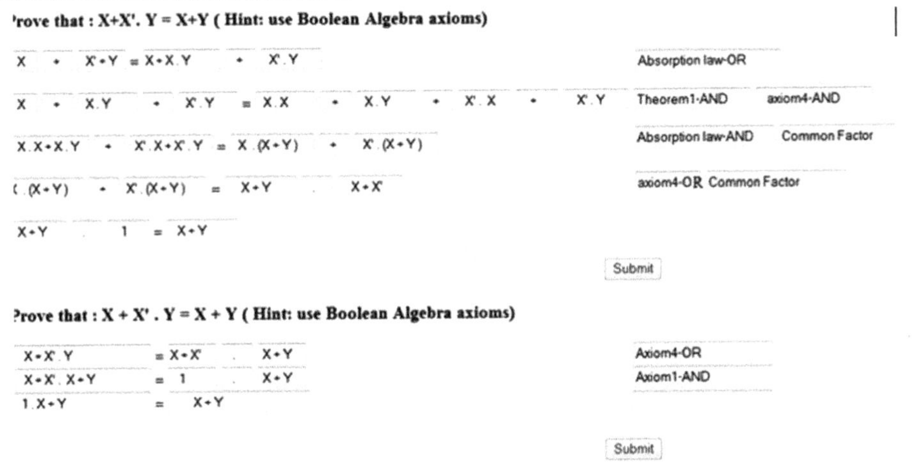

Figure 4 Two students' answers for the same question.

can measure the student's ability of connected knowledge to receive to the correct answers. The function steps are as the following:

First step is generation the square matrix for used rules. Where, the matrix values are 0 if the two rules are independent else one i.e. the two rules in the same ontology class or not.

Second step is summation the weight matrix values.

Then the third step is comparison between the used rules number (n matrix dimension) and summation of weight matrix values.

The output is as in Figure 7 for solutions in Figure 4. Where, the score for each student is 100% but the first one uses rules- theorems, Axioms or Lemmas- independent but the second student uses the dependent rules.

But if the student's answer is incomplete, then the score will be as shown in Figure 8. Also the developed system helps admin to easily delete, modify or update the courses' contents by modifying/deleting learning objects or even introducing new concepts. This is to gain access and preview the learning objects.

Handle MOQ

We implemented the proposed algorithm in section Multi Operations Question (MOQ) by PHP web scripting language and WampServer connecting scripts codes. PHP programming

```
$score = 0;
$k = $x+$x'; //value1 in axiom1-OR
$m = 1;          //value2 in axiom1-OR
$axm1-OR  = array($k,$m);
$l_fi_stp = array($w,$y); //values in 1st L.H.S
$r_fi_stp = array($p,$q); //values in 1st R.H.S
$fi_stp   = array($l_fi_stp,$r_fi_stp); // values for both sides in 1st step
    ...
$stps = array($fi_stp,$sc_stp,$thr_stp,$fr_stp);
foreach($axm1-OR as $value)
    {
        foreach($fi_stp as $value1)
        if($value == $value1)
        $score =+ .20;
    }
```

Figure 5 The student's score code.

```
$a=array();
$d= array( $_POST['inputxf'] ,$_POST['inputyf'],$_POST['inputxf'], $_POST['inputxf']); // Student submits Rules, variable number.
$n=count($d);
for ( $i = 0; $i<$n; $i++ )
for ( $j = 0; $i<$n; $j++ )
{ a[$i][$j]=0; //generate weight matrix, and intialize its values.
}
$Rules= array(array ( array($axiom1), array($axiom2), array($axiom3), array($axiom4)),
        array ( array($theorem1),array($theorem2),array($theorem3)),
        array ( array($Associativitylaw),array($AbsorptionLaw),array($DeMorganLaw) ) );

$axiom1=array($axiom1_AND,$axiom1_OR);
                                ...
$sum=0;
foreach($d as $value)
while( $element = each($axiom1))
    for ( $i = 0; $i<$n; $i++ )
    for ( $j = 0; $i<$n; $j++ )
{ if( $value==$element["value"])
}    {
    $a[$i][$j]=1; }
}else {
    a[$i][$j]=0;    }

    $sum+=a[$i][$j]                  ...

if($sum >=$n)
echo "";
else if($sum < $n)
echo "Ability to use new concepts";
```

Figure 6 Part of weight function.

language enables us to build the evaluation matrix with multiple dimensional arrays which contains vectors and sets. There are varieties in the student solution vector length so using PHP language is moderate. We aren't restricted to build n x n-matrix with n^2-elements where each vector created contains its own set. Once we had mathematical question and their corresponding solution values, the matrix rows elements could be generated. The following example will show the implementation of the algorithm. The system student's interface of online MOQ type is shown in Figure 9.

Suppose that the open mathematical question is I=2/2*4+1-2 and the final solution of I is equal to 3. The steps from the model answer are

i) $2/2 = 1$,   ii) $1 * 4 = 4$,   iii) $4 + 1 = 5$,   iv) 5-2 = 3.

We know that there are some arithmetic operations that have higher parentheses (executed *, / before +,-) more than the other operations. We has 4-operations/steps for 4-equation all should solve in correct order. The student answer (1,4,5,3) is correct 100%. But to be more specific, some students reach the final correct solution by summarize the number of steps/operations required. We take in consideration this point, so the first row in the evaluation matrix contains the detailed (standard) correct values (1,4,5,3) as a vector of array values, in other problems we may have two or more

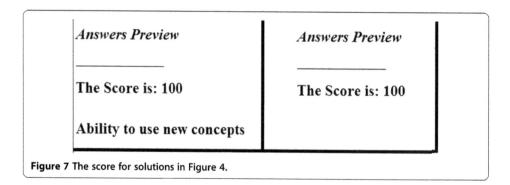

Figure 7 The score for solutions in Figure 4.

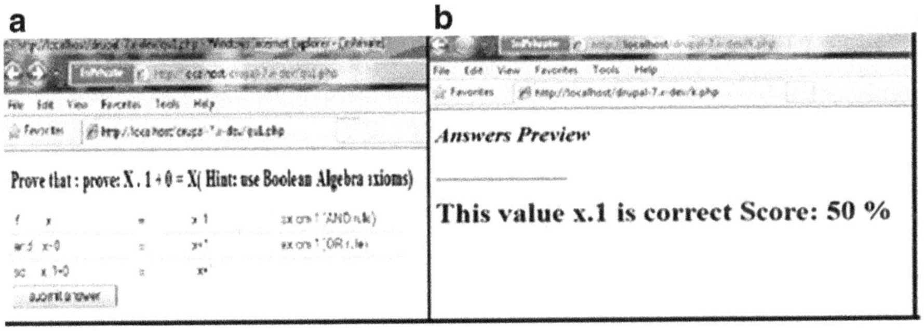

Figure 8 The student's incomplete answer in part a and the student's score in part b.

operations/steps that should be solved with the same parentheses. So we represent all the possible sets of solution for each step in its corresponding order. The 2nd row contains a number of correct elements less than the 1st one i.e. student's solution values are (4,5,3) or (1,5,3) represent a vector of array values. On the other hand we represent these possible items in the evaluation matrix as ({1,4},5,3). Both arrays are combined together. So as we move down along the evaluation matrix the number of generated correct values expected to be in each row is less than the number of values that exist in the previous one. The last row has the final correct solution.

To compare the solution matrix to the student's solution, If Z=3 i.e. the student array like the 3^{ed} row in the evaluation matrix, for each similar values we give a score as a correct answer otherwise the score is zero. The total score is the sum of all scores.

We need to notice that each item/element in the teacher template (model answer) has one/set of values. The MOQ tool generates the matrix of all correct answers.

$$\begin{bmatrix} 1 & 4 & 5 & 3 \\ \{1,4\} & 5 & 3 & 0 \\ \{1,4,5\} & 3 & 0 & 0 \\ 3 & 0 & 0 & 0 \end{bmatrix}$$

If the student's answer array is one row in the generated matrix, then the following score function to calculate the percentage will run else the student's answer is wrong and the percentage is zero (Figure 10). The score code in this type of question gives the same percentage for each step and the percentage depends on number of the complete answer's steps. But it's easy to make the percentage inserted from teacher's side.

Figure 9 An example of MOQ.

```
...
$d = array($z, $s, $b, $a);
        $n=count($d)
        $n=100/$n;
        reset($col);
        list($key, $value) = each ($col);
        reset($d)
        list($key, $value) = each ($d);
        if(count($col)!=count($d))
        $score=0;
        { foreach($col as $key=>$value)
if(each($col)==each($d)){
//echo "$key is $value<BR>\n";
        $score=$score+($n);
        echo "The Score is: $score %score % <BR>\n";
        ...
```

Figure 10 MOQ score function code.

The score result is as in Figure 11 if the student wrote the final correct answer directly. Then the student missed the score for details step.

Conclusion and further works

This paper proposed an evaluation tool for hybrid exams which have POQ and MOQ types of open questions. The methodology is based on semantic e-learning. Using direct connection between the learning objects universal ontology based and the evaluation tool have many advantage as we don't need model answers in POQ type and the student can use any correct theorem in her/his answer. Also using weight matrix solves the problem of dependence among learning concepts. Finally, using a fuzzy score matrix has benefits in case of MOQ which have order steps and could be answered by different ways.

In the future, In case of POQ the completed fuzzy weights matrix needs group of experts in the given field as mathematics therefore we recommend the authentication organization in education support a project to determine the weight of dependent among material concepts. Then when we want to create any open questions exam in

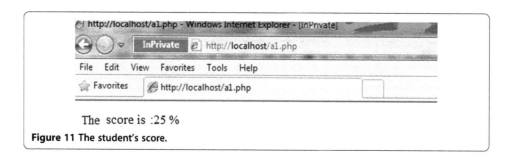

Figure 11 The student's score.

the proof type, we connect directly with the Universal Ontology of learning materials and it's Fuzzy Ontology which generates the fuzzy weight matrix automatically. Also we recommend the improvement of MOQ tool by creating AI questions bank. It will be Ontology based and connected it to the Universal Ontology for learning materials.

Competing interests
The authors declare that they have no competing interests.

Authors' contributions
All authors EE,KE and ST work together in conception, design, write and apply the proposed methods in this paper then they read and approved the final manuscript.

Authors' information
Eman Elsayed was born in Athens, Greece. She received a B.Sc. degree in Mathematics and Computer science from the Cairo University, Egypt in 1994, a M.Sc. degree in computer science from the Cairo University, Egypt in 1999, and a Ph.D. degree in computer science from Alazher University, Cairo, Egypt in 2005. She works as a Lecture of computer science in Mathematics and computer science Department, Faculty of science, Alazhar University. She is also member of Egyptian Mathematical Society EMS and Intelligent Computer and Information systems Society ICIS. She has graduated nine Ph.D. and M.Sc. students. She has been the Chair of over ten international conferences. She has authored two books in computer science, and over twenty published papers in data mining, ontology engineering, e-learning, operating system and software engineering.

References
1. Elsayed E (2011) Supporting convergent technologies by ontology-based for BNIC e-science. AIML conference, UAE. 2011
2. Ikdam A, Izzat A (2011) Automatic code homework grading based on concept extraction. International journal of software engineering and its applications, vol 5, No. 4. Yarmouk University, Irbid, Jordan
3. Elsayed E (2010) Graphology expert system, VAK-test, and graphics for E-course development. Egyptian Computer Science Journal ECS 34(4):11–20
4. Foong P (2002) Using short open-ended mathematics questions to promote thinking and understanding. National Institute of Education, Singapore. 2002
5. Larisa S, Riichiro M (2001) Ontology of test. Osaka University, Japan. http://www.ei.sanken.osaka-u.ac.jp/pub/larisa/402-115.pdf. Accessed 25 Oct 2012
6. Jesualdo T, Fernández B, Damián C-C (2006) OeLE: applying ontologies to support the evaluation of open questions-based tests. http://academic.research.microsoft.com/Publication/5639019/. Accessed 12 Nov 2012
7. Farida B-D, Malik S-M, Catherine C (2009) ODALA an ontological model for an automated evaluation of the Learner's state of knowledge: application to a Web-based algorithmic teaching. In: Bouarab D (ed) vol 4. No 1., Algeria. http://www.knowledgetaiwan.org/ojs/index.php/ijbi/article/viewPDFInterstitial/202/54. Accessed 13 Feb 2013
8. Konstantina C, Maria V (2013) A knowledge representation approach using fuzzy cognitive maps for better navigation support in an adaptive learning system. Chrysafiadi and Virvou SpringerPlus 2:81. doi:10.1186/2193-1801-2-81. http://www.springerplus.com/content/2/1/81
9. Chang S-H, Lin P-C, Lin Z-C (2007) Measures of partial knowledge and unexpected responses in multiple-choice tests. International forum of educational technology & society (IFETS), pp 95–109. http://ifets.info/journals/10_4/10.pdf
10. Rein P (2009) Prospects of automatic assessment of step-by-step solutions in algebra. Proceedings of the ninth IEEE international conference on advanced learning technologies. IEEE Computer Society, Washington, DC, USA, pp 535–537. 10.1109/ICALT.2009.123
11. Mu L, Qian X, Zhang Z, Zhao G, Xu Y (2008) An assessment tool for assembly language programming. International conference on computer science and software engineering, vol 5. IEEE Xplore Digital Library, Wuhan, Hubei, pp 882–884. doi:10.1109/CSSE.2008.111. ISBN 978-0-7695-3336-0
12. Miquel B, Robert N, Albert O, Enric R, Albert R (2008) The barcelogic SMT solver. In: Gupta A, Malik S (ed) Proceedings of the 20th international conference on computer aided verification. Lecture notes in computer science, vol 5123. Springer, Berlin, Heidelberg, pp 294–298. http://www.springerlink.com/index/10.1007/978-3-540-70545-1
13. Thomas B, Diego C, David D, Pascal F (2009) VeriT: an open, trustable and efficient SMT-solver. Automated deduction CADE-22, lecture notes in computer science, vol 5663. Springer, Verlag, pp 151–156. http://www.springerlink.com/content/f33m4615152325x3
14. Dutertre B, De Moura L (2006) The yices SMT solver. http://yices.csl.sri.com/tool-paper.pdf. Accessed 1 Dec 2012
15. David D (2011) Integration of SMT-solvers in B and event-B development environments. Universidade Federal do Rio Grande do Norte, Departamento de Informática e Matemática Aplicada, Natal, RN, Brazil
16. Radoslav F, Michal R (2010) Networked digital technologies, communications in computer and information science, Cairo, vol 88. Springer, pp 883–888. doi:10.1109/ISDA.2010.5687151. ISBN 978-1-4244-8134-7
17. Réka V (2007) Educational ontology and knowledge testing. Electronic Journal of Knowledge Management, EJKM 5(1):123–130

18. Emanuel R, Christian G, Heinz D (2010) Deriving ontologies and assessment rubrics for electronic documents with human support for automatic assessment purposes. Institute for information systems and computer media (IICM). Graz University of Technology A-8010, Graz, Austria. 2010

19. Lucía R, Milagros G, María L (2012) Conceptualizing the e-learning assessment domain using an ontology network. International Journal of Artificial Intelligence and Interactive Multimedia 1(6):20–28

20. Mukesh B BOOLEAN ALGEBRA. http://wikieducator.org/images/5/5e/CS_Revision_KIT_(CBSE-XII).pdf. Accessed at Jen. 2013

21. Bill F (2008) Drupal for education and E-learning. In: Akshara A (ed). Packt Publishing Ltd., Birmingham, Mumbai. First published: November 2008

4

Intention awareness: improving upon situation awareness in human-centric environments

Newton Howard[*] and Erik Cambria

* Correspondence: nhmit@mit.edu
Massachusetts Institute of
Technology, Cambridge, MA 02139,
USA

Abstract

As the gap between human and machine shrinks, it becomes increasingly important to develop computer systems that incorporate or enhance existing Situation Awareness. However, these tend to focus on raw quantitative parameters, such as position and speed of objects. When these situations are governed by human actors, such parameters leave significant margins of uncertainty. In this paper, we discuss the potential of applying the characteristics intrinsic to the human actors that comprise a given situation to Situation Awareness, and the capacity that these concepts have to improve situation-aware systems. We argue that intention-aware based systems offer an advantage over situation-aware based systems in that they reduce the informational burden on humans without limiting effectiveness. We argue that computational analysis and tracking of semantic and affective information associated with human actors' intentions are an effective way to minimize miscommunication and uncertainty, particularly in time-sensitive and information-saturated situations.

Keywords: Intention awareness, Situation awareness, Sentic computing

Introduction

As computer systems continue to improve in their information processing capability and become more integrated into the everyday lives of end-users, the potential scope of their roles increases as well. For instance, recent attempts to augment the human decision-making process, especially in dynamic and time-sensitive scenarios such as military command and control, game theory, home automation, and swarm robotics, have focused primarily on environmental details such as positions, orientations, and other characteristics of objects and actors of an operating environment. However, a significant factor in such environments is the intentions of the actors involved. While creating systems that can shoulder a greater portion of this decision-making burden is a computationally intensive task, performance advances in modern computer hardware bring us closer to this goal.

This paper discusses Intention Awareness (IA) as the process of integrating actors' intentions into a unified view of the surrounding environment. IA includes many of the basic principles of Situation Awareness (SA), such as consistent tracking and extrapolation of objects in the user's environment, but also exploits circumstantial semantics and sentics [1], that is, the conceptual and affective information associated with objects and actors of the operating environment. Consider the everyday example discussed below.

Everyday tasks, from handling fragile objects to navigating a highway to parking one's car at work, require a high degree of SA and spatial aptitude. Such tasks require the human actor to quickly adapt to new stationary and moving objects, as well as unpredictable moves that these may make, such as a pedestrian suddenly crossing the road. In the case of parking a car, the driver must account for the overall distribution of objects in the space of the parking lot at the time he/she plans to park, as well as the actions those objects may take based on the intentions of other human actors, hence the Parking Dilemma [2]. In order to properly understand and predict the actions of others in this space, the driver must predict what others will do, or their actions will otherwise appear random. For instance, a car may suddenly change course to move to a parking spot, which a driver considering the intentions of other drivers is more likely to detect and account for in his subsequent driving maneuvers.

While cars and other motor vehicles possess functions, such as turn signals, to assist in the conveyance of the driver's intention to other drivers, there still remains a significant gap between a driver's intentions and other drivers' awareness of them. Due to finite time and resources, routine activities such as this require integrating not only SA, but IA as well, in order to optimize the exchange of those resources for some other reward (in the above example, a parking space).

In this paper, we discuss and deconstruct the SA paradigm from four distinct perspectives. First, we review relevant theoretical work in SA and organizational theory fields in order to assess their strengths, weaknesses, and their alternatives. We apply the results of this assessment in the second section, where we provide a working definition of SA, and in the third section, we demonstrate the additional utility that IA offers in enhancing the predictive analytical capabilities of SA. In the fourth and final section we summarize these findings and point to specific areas that would benefit from future development and integration of IA.

SA has grown to include a large scope of environmental and informational attributes, which depend primarily on the nature of the situation. In a maritime navigational scenario, for example, the situational picture would include other ships, weather, wind, depth, buoy locations and heading. On the other hand, the parking scenario, which generally entails more direct association with other actors over limited resources, would include a greater emphasis on other driver's intentions. Thus, employing SA properly requires a significant devotion of cognitive (and, more recently, computational) resources as well as recognition of the appropriate level of focus for new input and ongoing analysis. That is, staying in the bounds of a sea channel takes on a lower priority in an emergency collision avoidance maneuver at sea.

In order to achieve this level of focus effectively, both human actors and their computer system counterparts need to be able to analyze the situation both with existing data and knowledge about other actors' goals. Data-driven analysis is based on tracking the status of existing goals as new data about the situation become available, and goal-driven analysis is the basis for the formation of new goals (if necessary) based on the results of data-driven analysis. Because each mode of analysis depends on the other, the situation-aware entity, human, or computer, must be able to switch dynamically between them.

Because warfare condenses and renders more urgency to the requirements of SA, many of its original concepts can be traced to scholarship on military operations, such as Clausewitz's writings on the "frictions" of war, one of the most important being uncertainty, or the "fog of war [3]." Apart from warfare, SA's innovations have proven useful in all scenarios, including any in which high-stakes, short-term variations are present.

As a result, study of aviation and air traffic control has also yielded significant insight into augmenting human SA [4]. This has resulted in a proliferation of definitions for SA, some more domain-specific than others. However, the most cited definition is that provided by Mica Endsley in 1988:

The perception of the elements in the environment within a volume of space and time, the comprehension of their meaning, the projection of their status into the near future, and the prediction of how various actions will affect the fulfillment of one's goals [5].

In this passage, Endsley is describing the critical process of *situation assessment*. Situation assessment is a combination of information acquisition and interpretation, which consists of four distinct but integrated stages:

1. *Perception:* acquiring the available facts.
2. *Comprehension:* understanding the facts in relation to our own knowledge of such situations.
3. *Projection:* envisioning how the situation is likely to develop in the future, provided it is not acted upon by any outside force.
4. *Prediction:* evaluating how outside forces may act upon the situation to affect our projections [Ibid].

Vidulich et al. [6] provide some elaboration on Endsley's previous definition describing SA as "the continuous extraction of environmental information, the integration of this information with previous knowledge to form a coherent mental picture, and the use of that picture in directing further perception and anticipating future events". Both Endsley and Viludich appear to agree that SA, which occurs in the *present*, has the primary goal of forming a coherent narrative between past, ongoing events, and likely future outcomes. While each of their definitions is technically compatible with the IA concept, the lack of implementation of IA at the time they published their theories on SA, and in the present to some degree, has been the primary cause of the conceptual gap between IA and SA.

As an outcome of situation assessment, SA can be viewed as a quadripartite end product of an actor's existence in a given scenario. Since SA occurs in four critical stages (per Endsley's definition), they can each be mapped to their own "level" in the SA hierarchy. *Perception* corresponds to level 1 SA, *comprehension* to level 2, and *projection* to level 3, respectively. Demonstrating the utility of this perspective, Jones and Endsley [5] were able to isolate 76% of SA failure in pilots could as problems in level 1 SA (perception of needed information) due to failures and/or shortcomings in the system or in cognitive processes themselves. The study also found that 20% of SA failures were attributable to level 2 SA (projection), and the remaining 4% involve problems with level 3 (projection).

While this study demonstrates a rough analytical approach to intentions and perceptions, it also shows the necessity of a more precise understanding of the interaction between intentions of human actors and the situations in which they find themselves. Endsley and Jones demonstrated significant correlation between these phenomena in their study, suggesting a need for further study. Of particular importance is the question of whether the limits of the human brain's capabilities impose a limit on computationally augmented SA. If so, a more cognitive-based approach to the SA problem is warranted.

Situation assessment is an intensive cognitive process that serves as a junction between the physical properties of objects (position, heading, etc.) and the human mind's portrayal of such objects. In order to successfully complete this process, the actor conducting situational assessment must be able to properly account for the intentions of the other actors that share the same situation. This is a shortcoming in many contemporary SA models, which give less priority to intentionality as a driver of human-dominant situations [2,5,7]. Due to the inherent structural differences in situational data and intentional information, not all systems that address the latter can also address the former, which produces a significant implementation gap despite the conceptual and potential application overlap between SA and IA.

It is also known that attention plays a significant part in successful SA [8-10]. Up to 35% of all SA failures in Endsley's study were traceable to attention; "all needed information was present, but not attended by the operator" [5]. Although it may appear to be explicitly tied to perception, attention is also affected by intentions and goals. "[A] gents deployed their attention in ways that are consistent with [their] operational goals" [4].

Goals are important in cognitive models in various other ways as well:

a) "*active goals direct the selection of the mental model,*"
b) "*goal and its associated mental model are used to direct attention in selecting information from the environment,*"
c) "*goals and their associated mental models are used to interpret and integrate the information*" [11].

Each of these precepts is representative of a classical interpretation of intentions in which cognitive states constantly "evolve" into hierarchical forms based on the demands of the environment.

Bruner and several other scholars of cognition and SA suggested that goal-driven planning is a subconscious cognitive process. Thus, the action resulting from this process can be viewed as hierarchical in nature [ibid]. Similarly, intention itself is comprised of several discrete layers, each having a unique relationship to consciousness; there are high-, medium-, and low-level intentions: "A hierarchy is formed by these three levels of intention that give us a relation between the means and ends" [12].

High-level intentions are the behaviors, as well as the beliefs and emotions that drive them, that one actor will use to influence another actor. Mid-level intentions are related to high-level intentions in that they are used to achieve the goals defined by high-level intentions, and low-level intentions provide a means to achieve goals defined by intentions at either of the higher levels. This hierarchy serves to simplify spatio-temporal reality by reducing it to states and actions.

In very general terms, we can describe all human activities as a series of proactive and reactive states and behaviors that cause transitions between states. Actors themselves have internal states, i.e., "states of mind," and they use these mind states to perceive the interactive environment they inhabit. Because human beings are themselves cognitive systems, and operate in a greater environment that contains other humans, any given situation can be described as a *system of systems*. Humans in this system are inherently intentional, exhibiting certain consistently rational behavior based on their intentions [13].

When we refer to rationality within this paper, we are specifically discussing "acting as best to satisfy [one's] goals overall, given what [one's] know and can tell about [one's] situation" [14]. In this sense "rationality is the mother of intention" [ibid]. According to this definition, intention can be described as a relationship between some object (primarily physical such as an artifact) and an actor's internal mind state - desire, belief, goal, purpose, etc. Intentionality[a] is thus "the character of one thing being "of" or "about" something else, for instance by representing it, describing it, refereeing to it, aiming at it, and so on" [ibid].

At the lowest level, we can view intention as the relationship between an environmental state and the objects with which it interacts and which act upon it. *Intentional stance* is an abstract tool that enables the predictive analysis of complex systems such as human actors, but does not account for the cognitive nature of those processes and the way that they operate [15].

If an intentional stance exists in a system by virtue of human presence, this takes us to the next phase in the process – identifying the system state and its components. Such a system can be characterized by myriad factors, including but not limited to beliefs, goals, wants, previous commitments, fears, and hopes. States within the system can be viewed as "attitudes" and grouped as such. Below is an example of one such grouping:

1. *Information attitudes*: preconceived notions that an actor has towards information about the surrounding environment.
2. *Proactive attitudes*: attitudes that direct a mind state to favor action.
3. *Normative attitudes*: obligations and permissions [ibid].

Prior research has, for the most part, followed a work template that concentrates primarily on one of these attitudes and/or notions and investigates others in relation to it. Research investigating the relationships among beliefs, desires, and intentions (BDI) assumes that these systems project inherently desired states (and that the nature of these desired states does not change with the environment) [16].

While BDI and classification systems for attitudes present researchers with a straightforward abstraction of environmental systems, there are a number of alternative, abstract views for the analysis of interacting systems such as human actors situated in a given environment. These types of systems can be regarded as exceptional cases, or intentional systems, because they involve the interaction of human actors and thus depend heavily on modeling intentionality. If the human actor must choose how to act in both a spatial and temporal frame, then we can model the system and its inputs by addressing the factors that contribute to those choices. In these systems, observers often note a consistent, rational behavior pattern that can be mapped to intuitive intentions on the part of the human actors in the system [14].

Intentional systems differ from conventional ones in that they possess several additional explanatory characteristics and capacities. First, they tend to view infrequent conditions as similar to more frequent ones because classification depends more on relevance to intentions than empirical frequency. This gives intentional systems the ability to create and analyze "multidimensional" states. This allows a simple, straightforward means to solve the problem of scaling and context.

We can thus construct a useful abstraction for giving a general description of systems that will extend past specificity of individual attitudes to include their interaction with other systems, even those that do not specifically include human actors, such as organizations and computer systems. To do so, we must consider multiple levels of abstraction based on the following criteria:

1. *Intentional states.* These must be defined in accordance with the relationship between states and relevant objects, if the system in question is intentional. The analysis must also distinguish between desires, beliefs, and intentions because these are fundamentally distinct intentional states.

2. *Types of choices.* Choices are defined based on the characteristics of interpretation, justification, and functionality of specific behavioral decisions. For instance, justifiable choices by some set of observers, primary or secondary, qualify for classifying choices – these qualifications are often made based on the mechanism by which those choices are made.

We can also specify two schemes, or classes, to simplify the definition of choice types in system characterization. The first defines the various types of intentional states, and the second defines types of choices to be made that will ultimately affect those states. Similarly, intention schemes (I-schemes) and choice, or rationality, schemes (R-schemes) can be used to map intentions to their logical behavioral conclusion.

All systems that include some degree of intentionality can thus be analyzed as instances of intentional systems with different levels of I-schemes and R-schemes. Systems composed of animal actors are equipped with this intentionality and rationality, but in a way that is distinct from their expression in human agents. In addition to humans, information systems such as computers and computer networks possess a similar rationality/intentionality scheme. Specifically, their behavior is guided by transitions from initial states to non-initial states by way of intrinsically motivated behavior, or intervention from without.

Distributing SA among human actors

Artman et al. [17] argue that systems driven by teams of actors need an additional dimension of analysis: "it is necessary to shift the unit of analysis from the individual to the whole cognitive system comprising a team of people as well as the artefacts which they use." This is due to the fact that, while examples of SA are often single-user centric, team-driven action multiplies the complexity of the SA picture by the number of actors involved, because the difference between each of their perceptions will create distinct outcomes. Thus, Artman et al. touch on a SA concept that is not entirely unrelated to IA, which is the multiplicity of actors. The primary distinction is that in IA, we address all actors that impact the environment, not just those that form a loose unit that functions as a larger actor (Figure 1).

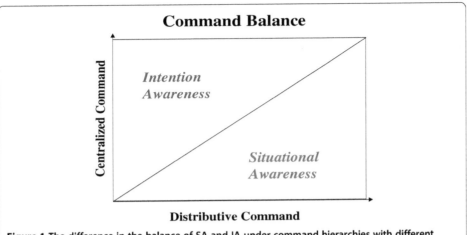

Figure 1 The difference in the balance of SA and IA under command hierarchies with different schemes of authority.

Intention awareness

IA is the process of integrating actors' intentions into a unified view of the surrounding environment. IA includes many of the basic principles of SA, such as consistent tracking and extrapolation of objects in the user's environment, but also exploits circumstantial semantics and sentics associated with objects and actors of the operating environment. Semantics and sentics, in fact, are key for sensemaking, in which they extend the meaningfulness that the system attributes to every single object/actor of the environment by considering it as an entity carrying specific conceptual and affective information, rather than simply a point in a space or time window. In the context of home automation, for example, a greater deal of intentions can be inferred, if the semantics and sentics associated with the object 'coffee machine' are known. Such semantics and sentics can be retrieved from external resources, e.g., affective common-sense knowledge bases for concept-level sentiment analysis [18]. For example, if the system has access to pieces of information such as 'a coffee machine is used for making coffee' and 'people generally like coffee', the repeated proximity of a human actor to the object 'coffee machine' can be exploited to infer the intention of the human actor to make coffee.

Intention in computation

The BDI model functions by establishing a decision tree whose nodes represent possible future outcomes, and assigning probabilities to each of these based on calculations of intent. Computational models of intention, such as the BDI software model, attempt to optimize the time spent allocating computational power for given tasks and actually executing them. While the BDI model is fairly rudimentary in its analysis of intent (essentially parsing past requests and actions to find trends), it epitomizes the increasing feasibility of implementing IA in computational systems. Four basic components of BDI allow speedy processing of intentional information:

- Beliefs
- Desires
- Intentions
- Events

BDI formal architecture consists of "beliefs," or the set of inference rules that an agent uses to derive basic intentional information. "Desires" represent the distinction between goal end-states and the current state. That is, desires are tasks actively pursued by the agent, such as performing a mathematical operation on a set of numbers. Intentions in BDI represent what has already been decided upon by the agent, but is not necessarily being achieved yet. For instance, the primary distinction between intentions and desires is the level of commitment. Intention, both in human and computational systems, requires some sort of signaling to transform from desire.

What is particularly significant about BDI modeling in software is its use of the intent/action chronological dichotomy to construct information-rich event narratives. While more mature implementations of intention in computational systems will be inherently intention-aware than BDI, this model illustrates the importance of actor-driven decision making.

Formal models of intention

In the Control Theory approach to system behavior analysis, *states*, or the distinction between intentions and whether they have been executed and *goals*, or short-term components of intention, are central. For instance, feedback control mechanisms are components of systems constructed for the purpose of reducing the difference between an actor's goal and their current state, and these systems tend to exhibit some form of efficiency or consistency, such as the consistent rational behavior we attribute to intentionality in humans [19-21]. The important distinction between goal and present systemic state is traceable to the type of applied *rationality*, i.e., in selecting strategies. "Feedback control reacts to sensory observations with actions designed to correct errors between observed and desired states," while "feed-forward uses a model of the world to predict what actions are required to achieve the goal" [22].

The distinguishing characteristic of feedback control is that is data-driven, and often results in reactive behavior. Observers can obtain information about past events, but such definitive information is largely unavailable when future events, beliefs, and perceptions are under analysis and, hence, projection plays a significant role in perception. Thus, feed-forward control results in proactive anticipatory behavior.

Control over a system is, simply put, a means of reducing the variety that the operating environment imposes. In a military environment, superior intelligence offers battlefield commanders greater control because this necessarily reduces variety (i.e., uncertainty). Ashby's Law of Requisite Variety tells us that "only variety in [response] can force down the variety due to [disturbance]; variety can destroy variety" [23]. Simply put, a system reacting to variety in the environment must have more inherent variety in order to seek its goals.

Reactive response in terms of possibly unlimited variety creates a unique problem. Specifically, the system's internal intrinsic variety must be maximized so that unexpected developments can be dealt without losing control. The best way to solve a problem, in fact, is to already know a solution for it. But, if we have to face a problem we have never met before, we need to use our intuition. Intuition can be explained as the process of making analogies between the current situation and the ones solved in the past to make a suitable decision at the present time. Such reasoning by analogy can be emulated, by means of sentic computing [1], through the ensemble application of semantic multi-dimensional scaling [24] and neural-network-based clustering [25].

Feed-forward controls assume that systems are reflective of the environment in which they are situated and that they can also predict states and actions by analysis of that system. As Ashby predicts, "Any regulator able to confine the fluctuations in the system to be regulated must not only have adequate amounts of variety available to control that system but also be or have a homomorphic representation of that system" [26]. In the early 1970s, Maturana and Varela developed the theory of Autopoiesis, which tends to support this perspective [27,28]. Autopoiesis is closely related to self-referentiality, or self-awareness attributes that we associate with human actors, and sees living systems as dualistic. That is, Autopoiesis covers both the internal organization of these systems, such as structure and metabolic functions, as well as their external component, or agency. The theory does this by presenting three key notions: operational closure, component production networks (which is an abstraction of the concept of metabolism), and spatio-topological unity between the individual and any physical borders he/she may encounter. Proponents of Autopoiesis claim that recursivity, or an organization's resemblance to a closed loop, is generated by the components and production processes inherent to the system that develops a complementary relationship between the network and border [2,28]. This system begins to develop a unique identity based on the set of couplings and shared components and processes within it, and thus a holistic character of its component processes [27,29]. Such a system must also be able to regulate the flow and consumption of matter and energy in order to facilitate self-constructive processes, as well as exchanges of material and information with the surrounding environment. The system must therefore be able to generate its defining factors, such as boundary conditions, that define it as such.

Based on this discussion, we propose a list of necessary attributes for systems incorporating intentionality in any way:

1. Self-existence is necessary because this will allow the system to increase its internal variety consistently.
2. The *Rule of Requisite Variety* must be satisfied in s series of transitory states at least once, which leads to the formation of intention.
3. We can also deduce that since intentions are hierarchical, they are so organized according to their inherent rationality. Thus, a system will exhibit more unconventional behavioral solutions to problems presented by the environment by forming intentions of its own volition, and then acting upon them. This is also observed in studies of AI and intentionality, such as in [15] citing [30] "that Sandy [,] of the Coffee shop Conversation [,] claims that the really interesting things in AI will only begin to happen when the program itself adopts the intentional stance towards itself."
4. Intentional systems with higher internal variety tend to reach their goals more frequently in constantly changing environments.
5. The internal state of a system tends to be richer in terms of intentionality and rationality than its external state.
6. Competing instances of rationality and intentionality contribute to an operating environment's current state, and state transitions can be attributed to the result of these phenomena. This type of competition helps to explain why the potential

internal variety of an individual system is greater than the actual scope of states that an operating system can exhibit.

7. Individual system intentionality can be independent, shared, complementary, and conflicting.

8. Because intentionality is hierarchical, there are equivalent mappings between actions and intentions.

9. Intentionality is shaped not only by semantics associated with the operating environment, but also by sentics each individual system associates with specific objects and events of that environment.

A number of scholars argue that goal-directed planning happens below the threshold of consciousness and that as a result, components of action are organized in a more hierarchical fashion [12,31]. Affective information processing, in fact, mainly takes place at unconscious level [32]. Reasoning, at this level, relies on experience and intuition, which allow considering issues intuitively and effortlessly through reasoning by analogy in a multi-dimensional space where the exact relationships between specific concepts are lost, but in which it is easier to infer how such concepts are semantically and affectively related [33]. Hence, rather than reflecting upon various considerations in sequence, the unconscious level forms a global impression of the different issues. In addition, rather than applying logical rules or symbolic codes (e.g., words or numbers), the unconscious level considers vivid representations of objects or events. Such representations are laden with the emotions, details, features, and sensations that correspond to objects and events of the operating environment.

Forming a hierarchy of high-, medium-, and low-level intentions presupposes that the intentional system in question possesses a highly nuanced comprehension of the operating environment in which other individuals' intentions are formed, as well as relevant details about the other individuals themselves.

We employ Lattice Theory to bring some insight to this complex problem of intentions, actions, and attributes. The Law of Modularity is of particular use here, since it tells us that for any three components of a lattice a, b an c, $x \leq b \rightarrow\rightarrow x \vee (a \wedge b) = (x \vee a) \wedge b$, using an AND operation to represent the joining operation, and the OR operation to portray the meet operations. What this tells us is that for a modular lattice, the highest lower bound on a partial order within the lattice is inversely isomorphic with the lowest upper bound.

We can then apply the Law of Modularity to our intentional hierarchy because in order to construct intentions, they must first be isomorphic because they influence each other in some way, no matter how trivial. For instance, we already know that the development of higher-level intentions gives rise to low- and middle-level intentions, and that high-level intentions can only be expressed through some combination of these. Interactions between any of these types of intentions are necessarily isomorphic, similar to those between high-level intentions, because they all exist within the same set of physical parameters. As a result, some interaction between subsets of intentions and actor systems will lead to unexpected results at lower levels. Representing intentions as lattice elements allows a better understanding of the intentional environment's inherent structure, as well as a better understanding of the interactions among them.

Using the lattice structures, we can represent these interactions between sets of intentions as follows:

1. Let the set of all of an individual's intentions be S, where $\{S: (l \cup m), h\}$.
   a. l is the set of low-level intentions;
   b. m is the set of mid-level intentions;
   c. h is the set of high-level intentions.
2. If $\{l, m, h\} \subseteq S$, $\forall\, i\in(l \cup m)$, $\exists\, j \in h$ such that we can define a mutually isomorphic relationship between i and j.

Assigning new information the proper value and priority in a rapidly changing environment remains a challenge to engineers and scholars of SA, since it is not simply the ability to acquire new information, but to interpret it in a way that is beneficial to the actor's intentions [34]. Here quality trumps quantity; that is, information must be useful more than it must be plentiful. As a simple example, imagine three email servers: one that filters no junk email, one that occasionally marks an important message as junk, and one that occasionally lets junk mail into the inbox. The third server is clearly the superior application of SA, since it prevents inundation (albeit imperfectly) without sacrificing the ultimate mission of the email server, which is to convey important information.

Applying psychological models of intent

In her research into human intentions, Zeigarnik argued that the "effect of intention is equivalent to the creation of an inner personal tension," meaning that one system is in disequilibrium of relative to surrounding systems. This relative equilibrium is a manifestation of the fundamental forces that cause equalization of other systems. This conclusion suggests that the human mind is itself a system with its own dynamic forces and subsystems. Zeigarnik made four basic assumptions in his theory [31]:

Assumption 1: The intention to reach a certain goal G (to carry out an action leading to G) corresponds to a tension (t) in a certain system S(G) within the person so that t(S(G))>0. This assumption coordinates a dynamic model (system in tension) with "intention."

Assumption 2: The tension system t(S(G)) is released if the goal G is reached. T(S(G))=if P accomplishes G. Zeigarnik uses the tendency to recall activities as a symptom for the existence of tension The expectation of the existence of such a system is based on the following:

Assumption 3: To a need for G corresponds a force f(P,G) action upon the person and causing a tendency of locomotion toward G. If t(S(G))>0 then f(P,G)>0. This assumption determines the relation between need and locomotion - motion from one place to another place. In other words it means a construct of tension in the person and the construct of force for locomotion in the environment.

Assumption 3a: A need leads not only to a tendency of actual locomotion towards the goal region but also to thinking about this type of activity; in other words, the force f

(P,G) exits not only on the level of doing (reality) but also on the level of thinking (reality); if t(S(G))>0 f(P,R)>0 where R means recall.

From these assumptions we can theorize that intentional systems such as humans have a stronger tendency to recall interrupted activities than finished ones. We can make the corresponding derivation as follows, where C is the completed task, U is the unfinished task, and the corresponding systems are represented by S(C) and S(U), respectively [2]:

1. $t(S(U))>0$ according to Assumption 1
2. $t(S(C))=0$ according to Assumption 2
3. $f(P,U)>f(P,C)$ according to Assumption 3a

Note: Zeigarnik computed the ratio as RU/RC=1.9, where RU is unfinished tasks, an RC represents completed tasks.

This model has several prerequisites regarding the dynamic character of this field, specifically with respect to the maintenance of tension and internal variety during a specific period of time. Since we expect this to be a very fluid field, any differences between the tension levels of the various systems will tend to disappear quickly as they tend toward equilibrium.

A human actor thus must have some degree of variance, or fluidity, in regard to the communication of his/her systems that cause tension. Thus type of fluidity must clearly vary between people and situations, but if we assume the constancy of structural relations between them, we can express them in the following way [2]:

Corollary: Let us indicate the absolute difference between the tension t(S1) and the tension t(S2) of two neighboring systems S1 and S2 at the time the tensions are being built up by the time since then elapsed by Ti, the tension difference at this time by , and the fluidity by . Then we can state, where symbolizes a monotonously increasing function. This means: the change in the tension difference of neighboring systems depends upon the time interval and the fluidity. Of course, this holds true only if the tensions of these systems are not changed by other factors such as, e.g., release of tension by reaching the goal?

Applying field theory to this new observation, we can make the following propositions:

a) Behavior is derived from the universe of coexisting facts;
b) These coexisting facts are similar in behavior to a dynamic field. That is, the state of any subfield depends on the rest of the field as a whole.

Proposition (a) presupposes we are dealing with a manifold, the internal relationships of which must use the concept of space for representation.

Spatial relationships between different psychological data cannot be represented in physical space, and instead must be treated as existing in mental space. It is everywhere accepted that the "life space" includes the person and his mental environment or world.

Locating and applying an appropriate geometry that can represent the spatiotemporal relationships of psychological facts is one of the first requirements of representing the mental space. With modern computational hardware, this is more possible today than ever before, especially in Zeigarnik's era. Today, one can find many geometries that permit mathematical understanding of the hodological space.

This is a finitely structured space, meaning that its subspaces and components are not infinitely divisible, but they are composed of certain units. Direction and distance are quantities that can be represented by "distinguished paths," which are easily correlated to psychological locomotion.

The geometry of hodological space is sufficiently well-defined that it can adequately represent most psychological processes, and it also permits an answer to the puzzling necessity to ascribe different psychological intentions and actions to locomotions in the same physical direction and dimension. This feature is particularly critical for the roundabout route problem: hodological space permits the description of structural relations inherent to the actor as well as in psychological operating environment.

Hodological space is equally useful for describing the structure and functions of groups of people. It is even more useful, however, when describing dynamic systems. Field theory tells us that behavior depends on the present field, not either the past or future fields. However, this stands in contrast to the theory of teleology, which opines that the future is the cause of behavior, and associationism, which opines that the past is the cause of behavior.

In addition, one must not make the mistake of assuming that directed factors are in themselves characteristic of teleology. These causal assumptions are even visible in physics, since physical force is a directed entity consisting of magnitude and the directional quality that allows its representation as a vector. The same goes for metapsychology, which resorts to constructs of similar vector-like character, such as psychological forces.

By defining directed forces in hodological space, we can adequately represent other teleological claims. The strange relationship between knowledge and dynamics that teleology has attempted to represent intuitively is made more comprehensible in one fundamental way: it becomes clear why ignorance serves as a barrier.

Zeigarnik's model provides a useful basis for modeling IA. The A-type model is the present model of the world. The type B model is a hypothetical future model of the world based on intentions and their ability to be achieved. A system of intentions can be used to define a map from a type-A-model to type-B-model, and finally, there is SA of the type-A-model. The fact that each agent at a given point in time has two models (SA and IA) creates many challenges to highlight, including the proliferation of multiple perceptions, expectations and awareness models that sometimes come into conflict with one another.

Thus emerges the four-part hypothesis [2]:

1. *Model A(X) − Model A'(X) 0.*
   - *Agent X type-A model at time t1 cannot be equal to Agent X type-A model at time t2.*
2. *Model B(X) − Model B'(X) 0.*
   - *Agent X type-B model at time t1 cannot be equal to Agent X type-B model at time.*

3. *Model A(X) – Model A(Y) 0.*
   - *Agent X type-A model at time t1 cannot be equal to Agent Y type-A model at time t2.*
4. *Model B(X) – Model B(Y) 0.*
   - *Agent X type-B model at time t1 cannot be equal to Agent Y type-B model at time t2.*

Intention awareness: a new role for intent in computation

Linking intent to SA-driven pictures of the environment requires more than simply creating an "intent" category in data analysis. From a computational perspective, intentions are causal inferences made from a series of events and a series of prior, linked intentions. Thus, in order for a system to possess IA, it must not simply infer based on available (i.e., situational) data, but must incorporate prior intentional analysis as one of its information sources. Thus, one of the fundamental distinctions between SA as we now know it and IA is that, while the former concerns *data analysis* that humans probably cannot process in the amount of time required, the latter concerns *information analysis*, a task that humans perform on a regular basis, but that can be enhanced by artificial systems (Figure 2).

One promising example of the extension of intention into SA is computational "sensemaking," or the process by which humans (or other reasoners) attach semantics and sentics to their observations of the operating environment in a parallel and dynamic way [35]. IA, in fact, is a viable means of improving synchronization in sensemaking between the human reasoner and associate system interfaces. This is due to two primary factors. The first is that IA is becoming increasingly viable thanks to advances in computer hardware performance. Second, since IA simultaneously frees some of the analytical

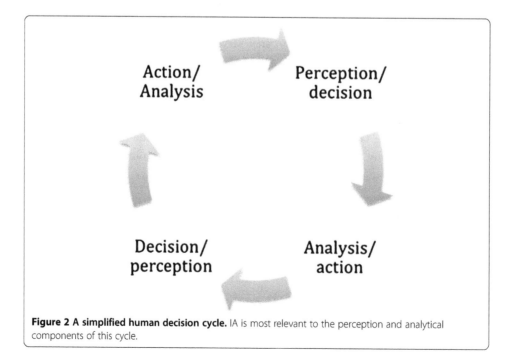

Figure 2 A simplified human decision cycle. IA is most relevant to the perception and analytical components of this cycle.

burden from human operators and uses similar structures as are found in human cognition, interface-based latency is minimized.

Conclusion

In popular applications, SA is seen as a proactive, purposeful behavior that is directed towards achieving a goal in a specific task environment. This view has been readily adopted in many different fields and contexts, where situations are by nature dynamic and subject to rapid, unexpected variation. Because commander's intent drives the mission, regardless of operational size or scope, it is tempting to cite military science as the primary beneficiary of advances in SA and IA systems. However, expansion upon some of the notions that drive the process of military organization and action reveals that we can apply the same concepts to any system requiring SA, e.g., game theory, home automation, cyber-security, and swarm robotics. This paper has argued that the next logical extension of SA is IA, or the independent analysis and awareness of intentions by computational systems that augment the human actor.

This is for two primary reasons. First, our understanding of cognitive processes has allowed a more computationally feasible problem of intent to be defined as the basis for IA models. Second, computational resources have made significant progress since the notion of SA was first proposed, so we currently experience an implementation gap where we have the resources but not the immediate capability to execute IA in field applications.

Endnote

[a]For the purposes of this paper, the concept of intentionality is the quality of having intentions, not to be confused with a quality of actions, as sometimes mentioned in the literature.

Competing interests
The authors declare that they have no competing interests.

Authors' information
Newton Howard (nhmit@mit.edu) is the director of the Synthetic Intelligence Lab at MIT and former Director of the Mind Machine Project. He received his Doctoral degree in Cognitive Informatics and Mathematics from La Sorbonne, France where he was also awarded the Habilitation a Diriger des Recherches for his leading work on the Physics of Cognition (PoC) and its applications to complex medical, economical, and security equilibriums. While a graduate member of the Faculty of Mathematical Sciences at the University of Oxford, England, he proposed the Theory of IA, which made a significant impact on the design of command and control systems and information exchange systems at tactical operational and strategic levels. He has served as the Chairman of the Center for Advanced Defense Studies (CADS), the leading Washington, D.C, National Security Group and is currently its board director. He is a national security advisor to several U.S. Government organizations. He recently published The Mood State Indicators (MSI) algorithm, which modeled and explained the mental processes involved in human speech and writing, to predict emotional states. Dr. Howard works with multi-disciplinary teams of physicists, chemists, biologists, brain scientists, computer scientists, and engineers to reach a deeper understanding of the brain. Dr. Howard's most recent work focuses on the development of functional brain and neuron interfacing abilities. To better understand the structure and character of this information transfer, he concentrated on theoretical mathematical models to represent the exchange of information inside the human brain. This work has proven applicable in the diagnosis and study of brain disorders and has aided in developing and implementing necessary pharmacological and therapeutic tools for physicians. He has also developed individualized strategies to incorporate solutions for psychiatric and brain prosthetics.

Erik Cambria (cambria@media.mit.edu) received his BEng and MEng with honors in Electronic Engineering from the University of Genoa, in 2005 and 2008 respectively. In 2011, he has been awarded his PhD in Computing Science and Mathematics, following the completion of an industrial Cooperative Awards in Science and Engineering (CASE) research project, which was born from the collaboration between the University of Stirling, Sitekit Solutions Ltd., and the MIT Media Laboratory, where he currently works as associate researcher (Synthetic Intelligence Project). His interests include AI, Semantic Web, KR, NLP, big social data analysis, affective and cognitive modeling, intention awareness, HCI, and e-health. Dr. Cambria is invited speaker/tutor in many international venues, e.g., IEEE SSCI, MICAI, and

WWW, associate editor of Springer Cognitive Computation, and guest editor of leading AI journals, e.g., IEEE Computational Intelligence Magazine, Elsevier Neural Networks, and IEEE Intelligent Systems. He is also chair of several international conferences, e.g., Brain Inspired Cognitive Systems (BICS) and Extreme Learning Machines (ELM), and workshop series, e.g., ICDM SENTIRE, KDD WISDOM, and WWW MABSDA.

Authors' contributions

NH developed the Intention Awareness in human centric environments concepts, and analyses. EC applied IA theory in Sentic environments. Both authors wrote, read and approved the final manuscript.

Acknowledgments

The authors would like to thank Ian Andrews, Rebecca Fahlstrom Sergey Kanareykin, David Johnson, Ammar Qusaibaty, and Adam Howard for their contribution to the ideas discussed in this paper and their assistance in reviewing and refining this article.

References

1. Cambria E, Hussain A (2012) Sentic Computing: Techniques, Tools, and Applications. ISBN: 978-94-007-5069-2. Springer, Dordrecht, Netherlands
2. Howard N (2002) Theory of Intention Awareness in Tactical Military Intelligence: Reducing Uncertainty by Understanding the Cognitive Architecture of Intentions. Author House First Books Library, Bloomington, Indiana
3. Spick M (1998) The ace factor: Air combat and the role of situation awareness. Naval Institute Press, Annapolis, MD
4. Endsley MR (2000) Theoretical underpinnings of situation awareness: A critical review. In: Endsley MR, Garland DJ (eds) Situation Awareness Analysis and Measurement. Lawrence Erlbaum Associates, Inc Publishers, Mahwah, NJ, pp 3–32
5. Jones DG, Endsley MR (1996) Sources of situation awareness errors in aviation. Aviat Space Environ Med 67(6):507–512
6. Vidulich M, Dominguez C, Vogel E, McMillan G (1994) Situation awareness: Papers and annotated bibliography, Armstrong Laboratory, Crew Systems Directorate, Human Engineering Division, Wright-Patterson, Interim Report for Period 15 January 1992 to 6 June 1994. AFB OH, AL/CF-TR-1994-0085
7. Lewin K, Cartwright D (eds) (1951) Field Theory in Social Science: Selected Theoretical Papers. Harpers, Oxford, England
8. Endsley MR, Smith RP (1996) Attention distribution and decision making in tactical air combat. Hum Factors 38(2):232–249
9. Endsley MR, Rodgers MD (1998) Distribution of attention, situation awareness, and workload in a passive air traffic control task: Implications for operational errors and automation. Air Traffic Control Quarterly 6(1):21–44
10. Gugerty L (1998) Evidence from a partial report task for forgetting in dynamic spatial memory. Hum Factors 40(3):498–508
11. Endsley MR (1995) Toward a theory of situation awareness in dynamic systems. Hum Factors 37(1):32–64
12. Gibbs RW (2001) Intentions as emergent products of social interactions. In: Malle BF, Moses LJ, Bladwin DA (eds) Intentions and Intentionality. MIT Press, Cambridge, MA
13. Dennett DC (1987) The Intentional Stance. MIT Press: A Bradford Book, Cambridge, MA
14. Haugeland J (1997) What is Mind Design, Mind Design II. MIT Press, Cambridge, MA
15. Van der Hoek W, Wooldridge M (2003) Towards a logic of rational agency. Log J IGPL 11(2):133–157
16. Bratman ME (1987) Intention, Plans, and Practical Reason. Harvard University Press, Cambridge, MA
17. Garbis C, Artman H (1998) Coordination and Communication as Distributed Cognition. In: Darses F, Zarate P (eds) Proceedings of Conference on the Design of Cooperative Systems (COOP'98). Cannes, France, pp 1–12
18. Cambria E, Schuller B, Xia YQ, Havasi C (2013) New avenues in opinion mining and sentiment analysis. IEEE Intell Syst 28(2):15–21
19. Ashby WR (1960) Design for a brain: The origin of adaptive behavior, Second Editionth edn. John Wiley & Sons Inc, New York
20. Ashby WR (1958) Requisite variety and implications for control of complex systems. Cybernetica 1(2):83–99
21. Wiener N (1948) Cybernetics or Control and Communication in the Animal and Machine. MIT Press, Cambridge, MA
22. Albus J, Meystel A (2001) Engineering of Mind: An introduction to the science of intelligent systems. John Wiley Inc., New York, NY
23. Ashby WR (1956) An Introduction to Cybernetics. Chapman and Hall, London
24. Cambria E, Song Y, Wang H, Howard N (2013) Semantic multi-dimensional scaling for open-domain sentiment analysis. IEEE Intell Syst. doi:10.1109/MIS.2012.118
25. Cambria E, Mazzocco T, Hussain A (2013) Application of multi-dimensional scaling and artificial neural networks for biologically inspired opinion mining. Biologically Inspired Cognitive Architectures 4:41–53
26. Krippendorff K (1986) A Dictionary of Cybernetics. The American Society for Cybernetics, Norfolk VA
27. Maturana H, Varela FJ (1980) Autopoiesis and Cognition: The realization of the living, Volume 42nd edn. D. Riedel Publishing Company, Dordrecht, Holland
28. Varela FJ, Maturana H, Uribe R (1974) Autopoiesis: The organization of living systems, its characterization and a model. Biosystems 5(4):187–196
29. Ruiz-Mirazo K, Moreno A (2004) Basic autonomy as a fundamental step in the synthesis of life. Artif Life 10(3):235–259
30. Wooldridge M (2000) Reasoning about Rational Agents. The MIT Press, Cambridge, MA
31. Bruner JS (1981) Intention in the structure of action and interaction. In: Lewis L (ed) Advances in Infancy Research. Ablex, New Jersey
32. Epstein S (2003) Cognitive-experiential self-theory of personality. In: Millon T, Lerner M (eds) Comprehensive Handbook of Psychology, vol 5. Wiley & Sons, Hoboken, NJ, pp 159–184

33. Cambria E, Olsher D, Kwok K (2012) Sentic Activation: A Two-Level Affective Common Sense Reasoning Framework, Proceedings of Twenty-Sixth Conference on Artificial Intelligence. AAAI, Toronto, Ontario, Canada, pp 186–192
34. Iyengar SS, Kamenica E (2007) Choice Overload and Simplicity Seeking. Center for Behavioral and Decision Research, Seminar Paper, Waterloo, Canada
35. Cambria E, Olsher D, Kwok K (2012) Sentic Panalogy: Swapping Affective Common Sense Reasoning Strategies and Foci. Proceedings of CogSci 2012 Conference, Sapporo, Japan, pp 174–179

An effective implementation of security based algorithmic approach in mobile adhoc networks

Rajinder Singh[1*], Parvinder Singh[2] and Manoj Duhan[3]

* Correspondence:
rajpanihar@rediffmail.com
[1]Deenbandhu Chhotu Ram
University of Science & Technology,
Murthal, Haryana, India
Full list of author information is
available at the end of the article

Abstract

Mobile Ad-hoc Network one of the prominent area for the researchers and practitioners in assorted domains including security, routing, addressing and many others. A Mobile Ad-hoc Network (MANET) refers to an autonomous group or cluster of mobile users that communicate over relatively bandwidth constrained wireless links. Mobile ad hoc network refers to the moving node rather than any fixed infrastructure, act as a mobile router. These mobile routers are responsible for the network mobility. The history of mobile network begin after the invention of 802.11 or WiFi they are mostly used for connecting among themselves and for connecting to the internet via any fixed infrastructure. Vehicles like car, buses and trains equipped with router acts as nested Mobile Ad-hoc Network. Vehicles today consists many embedded devices like build in routers, electronic devices like Sensors PDAs build in GPS, providing internet connection to it gives, information and infotainment to the users. These advances in MANET helps the vehicle to communicate with each other, at the time of emergency like accident, or during climatic changes like snow fall, and at the time of road block, this information will be informed to the nearby vehicles. Now days technologies rising to provide efficiency to MANET users like providing enough storage space, as we all know the cloud computing is the next generation computing paradigm many researches are conducting experiments on Mobile Ad-hoc Network to provide the cloud service securely. This paper attempts to propose and implement the security based algorithmic approach in the mobile adhoc networks.

Keywords: MANET; Network security; Wormhole attack; Secured algorithm

Introduction

Now days, lots of research is going on in the domain of mobile ad hoc networks. One of the major issues in the mobile ad hoc networks is the performance - in a dynamically varying topology; the nodes are expected to be power-aware because of the bandwidth constrained network. Another matter in such networks is security - as each node participates in the operation of the network equally, malicious nodes are intricate to identify. There are several applications of mobile ad hoc networks such as disaster management, ware field communications, etc. To analyze and detailed investigation of these issues, the scenario based simulation of secure protocol is done and compared with classical approaches. The scenarios used for the simulation and predictions depict critical real-world applications including battlefield and rescue operations but these can be used in many other applications also.

In ad hoc networks all nodes are responsible of running the network services meaning that every node also works as a router to forward the networks packets to their destination. It is very challenging for researchers to provide comprehensive security for ad hoc networks with the desired quality of service from all possible threats. Providing security becomes even more challenging when the participating nodes are mostly less powerful mobile devices.

Wireless Ad Hoc networks have been an interesting area of research for more than a decade now. What makes ad hoc networks interesting and challenging is its potential use in situations where the infrastructure support to run a normal network does not exist. Some applications include a war zone, an isolated remote area, a disaster zone like earthquake affected area and virtual class room etc.

In ad hoc networks all nodes are responsible of running the network services meaning that every node also works as a router to forward the networks packets to their destination. It is very challenging for researchers to provide comprehensive security for ad hoc networks with the desired quality of service from all possible threats. Providing security becomes even more challenging when the participating nodes are mostly less powerful mobile devices. In this paper an effort has been made to evaluate various security designs proposed.

Security aspects in mobile ad hoc networks

In any classical fixed or wireless network, the security is implemented at three stages: prevention, detection and cure. The key parts of prevention stage include authentication and authorization. The authentication is concerned with authenticating the participating node, message and any other meta-data like topology state, hop counts etc. Authorization is associated with recognition. The point where detection is the ability to notice misbehavior carried out by a node in the network, the ability to take a corrective action after noticing misbehavior by a node is termed as cure.

Assorted possible attacks that are implemented on ad hoc networks are eavesdropping, compromising node, distorting message, replaying message, failing to forward message, jamming signals etc. The central issues behind many of the possible attacks at any level of security stage are authentication, confidentiality, integrity, non repudiation, trustworthiness and availability.

Assumption and dependencies

- Basically Ad-hoc Networks depends upon any fixed infrastructure or any other mobile node to communicate, through forwarding and receiving packets.
- Comparing the security issues of wireless ad-hoc network with wired ad-hoc network, wired network has the proper infrastructure for forward and receiving packets, whereas in wireless network there is no proper infrastructure and it is accessible by both authorized users and hackers.
- In this wireless ad-hoc network there is no particular design to monitor the traffic and accessibility, these leads to third party intervention like malicious users.

In this manuscript, various issues are focused that affect the ad-hoc networks security mechanism and also to concentrate on pros and cons of Mobile networks protocols.

The focus on enhancing security and reliability to Mobile Ad-hoc Network (MANET) [1] is also addressed.

Many researches were done before to provide security to MANET [1] but none of the protocol shines in providing security and performance. There are many defects in the Mobile framework; this may cause unknown nodes to connect frequently without any proper routing. In order to prevent other nodes from trespassing we are going to concentrate on providing more security to Mobile Ad-hoc network.

There were so many research areas in MANET [1] in that security is the major concern among others.

The scope of securing MANET [1] is mentioned here

- Securing MANETs [1] is great challenge for many years due to the absence of proper infrastructure and its open type of network.
- Previous security measures in MANETs [1] are not effective in the challenging world with advancement in technology.
- Many layers often prone to attacks man in middle attack or multilayer attack, so proposal should concentrate on this layers.
- The proper intelligent approach [2] of securing MANETs [1] has not yet discovered.
- In this project we are going to concentrate on applying bio inspired intelligence [2] techniques for securing MANETs.

Problem identification

- The main objective of the manuscript is providing security to the existing systems mainly on the network layer to prevent the attacks like wormhole attacks [3] etc.
- To analyze the scope of multi layer attacks [4].
- To evaluate the techniques like Genetic Algorithms [5], Swarm Intelligence [6], Memetic Algorithms [7] etc.
- To analyze the needs of above mentioned techniques in different network layers especially in the multi link layer.
- To propose a unique technique for above mentioned attacks.
- Intelligent MANET [6] proposal to deal with all kinds of attacks.
- To validate the above techniques by implementing and analyzing its results with the existing systems.

Applications

- It provides a relative study of the systems under the parameters packet loss, packet delivery rate and network connectivity.
- A better understanding of the Quality of Service (QoS) parameters can be obtained and they can be used for solving various networking complexities.

Hardware requirements

The minimum requirements needed to perform operations are

- Intel Pentium Processor at 2 GHz or Higher

- RAM 256 MB or more
- Hard disk capacity 10 GB or more

Software requirements

The software required to perform the implementation are

- Linux Operating System (Ubuntu, Fedora)
- NS2, NAM tools
- GNU Plot

Manet security attacks

Malicious node [8] is one which causes attacks on various layers on MANET like application layer, data link layer, physical and network layer.

There were two types of attacks on MANET, they are

- Active attacks
- Passive attacks

Active attacks

In this attack, some harmful information is injected into the network, which causes malfunctioning of the other nodes or network operation. For performing this harmful information it consumes some sort of energy from other nodes, those nodes are called as malicious node.

Passive attacks

In this passive attack, the malicious nodes disobey to perform its task for some sort reasons like saving energy for its own use of moving randomly, by diminishing the performance of the network.

Network layer attack

Let us concentrate on various attacks on the network layer.

Wormhole attack

Wormhole attack [3] is also known as tunnelling attack, in this tunnelling attack the colluding attackers build tunnel between the two nodes for forwarding packets claiming that providing shortest path between the nodes and taking the full control of the nodes, which is invisible at the higher layers.

Figure 1 represents the wormhole attack, where S and D nodes are the source and destination, A B and C are the connecting nodes providing path between source and destination. M and N are the malicious nodes, tunnelled by colluding attackers.

Existing technique for preventing wormhole attack

In the previous techniques wormhole attack is prevented using the Location based Geo and Forwarding (LGF) Routing Protocol.

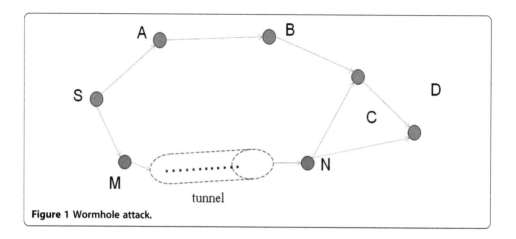

Figure 1 Wormhole attack.

Implementation of lgf routing protocol

There are several steps in implementing LGF routing protocol, consider source node S wants to communicate with destination node D (Figure 2).

- The Source node multicast the RREQ message to all the intermediate which contains the IP address of the destination node based on distance of the destination node.
- This protocol is tested with source node 100 M away from the destination node and the intermediate nodes as

DIST (S, 1) = 40 M

DIST (S, 2) = 53 M

DIST (S, 5) = 48 M

DIST (1, 3) = 60 M

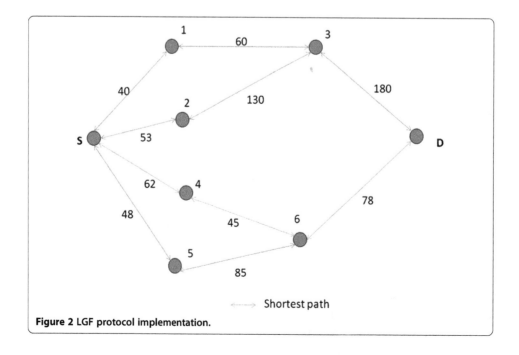

Figure 2 LGF protocol implementation.

DIST (2, 3) = 130 M
DIST (3, D) = 180 M
DIST (4, 6) = 45 M
DIST (S, 4) = 62 M
DIST (5, 6) = 85 M
DIST (6, D) = 78 M

- Compare distance between source and destination using the following code

  If (intermediate nodes < source node S to destination node D distance)

  {

  These are the nodes in between S to D, can conditionally transfer the RREQ packet to D.

  }

  Else

  {

  The intermediate node is out of transmission area, so send RREQ error message to S node

  }

- RREQ has been received in destination node, start D node sending RREP packet towards the intermediate node to reach the source node.
- S node received RREP packet from different intermediate nodes, compare the distance from different intermediate nodes.
- Select the shortest path between the source and destination node with respect to the received RREP packet and then send the original packets between S and D node this was the technique used in LGF protocol.

However the preventive measures of wormhole attack with this LGF protocol was not solved clearly.

Black hole attack

Black hole attack [8] is the serious problem for the MANETs, in this problem a routing protocol has been used by malicious node reports itself stating that it will provides shortest path.

In flooding based protocol, a fake route is created by the malicious node rather than the actual node, which results in loss of packets as well as denial of service (DoS).

In the Figure 3, S and D nodes are the source and destination nodes, A B C are the intermediate nodes and M is the malicious node. RREQ and RREP are the key terms for route request and route reply respectively. MREP is abbreviation for malicious reply.

Existing technique

Two tier secure AODV (TTSAODV)

TTSAODV protocol is proposed earlier to prevent the black hole attack. In these protocol two levels of security is provided

1. During route discovery mechanism and
2. During data transfer mechanism

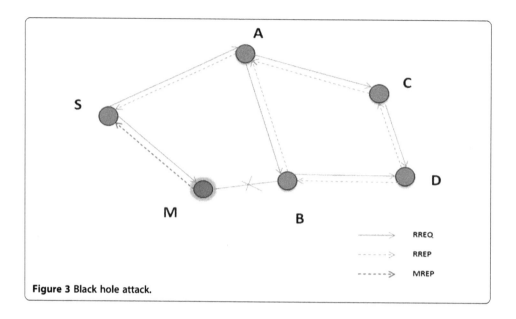

Figure 3 Black hole attack.

In this technique, black hole attack is easily identified either of these two techniques, even it fails in any of the mechanism. The major drawback in this technique causes enormous packet loss and delay in transferring packet.

Resource consumption attack

In the resource consumption attack, a malicious node can try to consume more battery life demanding too much of route discovery, or by passing unwanted packets to the source node.

Location disclosure attack

In the location disclosure based attack, the malicious node collects the information of routes map and then focus on further attacks. This is one of the unsolved security attacks against MANETs.

Multi layer attacks in manet

There are different types of multilayer attacks in MANET, they are as follows

- Denial of Service (DoS)
- Jamming
- SYN flooding
- Man In Middle attacks
- Impersonation attacks

Alpha numeric based secure reflex routing

In this, proposed algorithm prevents the worm-hole attacks by routing the data through the authorized nodes like LN, and AN nodes through this way the communication takes place.

In the proposed algorithm the worm-hole tunnel is prevented through the following steps (Figure 4).

Step 1

Since every connection through nodes is possible only through Leader Node and Access node so there is impossible for a malicious node to make tunnel from the source node.

Step 2

The Leader Node manages the routing table and also the details of all the nodes in its group, it also contains the details of whether the particular node is Access Node or normal node. The Leader node also maintains details about other groups Leader Node and its address with the help of its Access Nodes.

Step 3

The normal node in a group maintains a table that contains information of its Leader Node address and the common identifier generated by the Leader Node. The Access nodes have a table that maintains the other Leader Nodes common identifiers.

Step 4

The address of the Leader Node that has already involved in routing has stored in every packet, it is used for verification by other Leader Nodes.

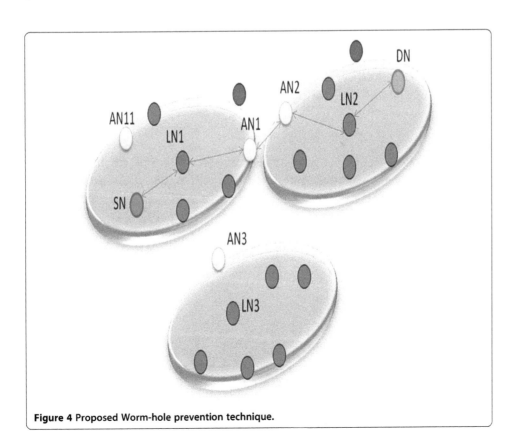

Figure 4 Proposed Worm-hole prevention technique.

Step 5

When a source node in a need of route to deliver packets to the destination node, it sends Route Request message to the Leader node, the Leader Node uses its common identifier to verify the packet with alpha numeric values.

Step 6

The leader Node checks whether the destination node is in house, if the destination node is present under the leader node, then it sends the packet directly. If the destination node is not in house then it sends Route Request message to all its Access nodes, The Access nodes using their common identifier verifies the alpha numeric values from Leader node then transfers that packet to the neighbours Access Node.

Step 7

The neighbour Access node checks whether the packet came from its neighbour Leaders node or from any malicious node by common identifier that has previously exchanged, then it sends the Route Request message to its Leader Node, this Leader Node verifies the Leader node details and include its details in that packet and forwards the original packet until it reaches the destination.

Step 8

Finally the destination node checks whether the packet came from its Leader node or from any malicious node using the identifier, after verification process is over it accepts the packet.

Step 9

Destination node sends the Reply Request message (RREP) to source node through the same route already followed for transferring packet.

Step 10

In case the any node involved in the routing moves away from one group into the another group, the previous process is not needed as it is already registered in that network, some other node in that group replace the previous node.

Step 11

Suppose if the source node or destination node moves away from its group, the foreign Access Node acts as a relay node for forwarding packets this process minimizes the time for authenticating in newer group.

Proposed architecture

Worm-hole attack prevention using alpha numeric reflex routing algorithm

In this technique, there won't be any possibilities for a malicious node to make tunnelling between the source and the destination nodes, as it is not included in the either of any groups. The packets are safe to reach the destination node efficiently.

Pseudocode for alpha numeric reflex routing algorithm

```
BEGIN
        Initialize nodes
        Initialize source and destination nodes
        FOR i = 0 to n DO
                LNᵢ ← Nodes with higher battery power, ability to manage other nodes
                IF (nodes in range of LN) THEN
                        Transmit common identifier
                ELSE
                        The node is under other LN
                END IF
        END FOR
        FOR i = 0 to n DO
                FOR j = j + 1 to n DO
                ANᵢⱼ ← Nodes receive common identifier from other LN
                IF (node accepts the common identifier and replies its details to LN) THEN
                        Node = trusted
                ELSE
                        Node = malicious
                END IF
                Source node → Forward RREQ
                IF (source node and destination node is under same LN) THEN
                        Forward RREQ → destination node
                ELSE
                        Forward RREQ → ANᵢⱼ
                        ANᵢⱼ → LNᵢ
                        LNᵢ → destination node
                END IF
                END FOR
        END FOR
END
```

Proposed algorithm to prevent black hole attack

In this proposed algorithm, the Expected broadcast count algorithm is introduced. With the help of this algorithm highest throughput is possible between the nodes but however the actual algorithm does not prevent the black hole attack.

Throughput refers to the average number of message transmitted in a given time, it is usually measured in bps or bits per second, and it is also mentioned as packet delivery ratio. Malicious node plays a major role in affecting throughput in black hole attacks.

Secure mesh network measurement technique is proposed in this project to prevent the black hole attacks during route discovery process between the source and destination node with the help of the throughput measurement values, this makes the routing process more consistent and efficient communication between the nodes.

Expected broadcast count algorithm

This *EBX* algorithm is used to increase throughput in MANETs, it is referred as the expected number of packets transmission and retransmission required to successfully deliver a packet in the network.

It is calculated using the delivery ratio of packets in destination node d_d and delivery ratio of packets in the source node d_s, d_d is the prospect of forward packet transmission and d_s is the reverse packet transmission.

These d_s and d_d values are calculated from the acknowledgement packets known as query, nodes commonly exchanges their query message with their neighbours after delivering each packet.

Suppose consider a link from $A \rightarrow B$ where A and B are the nodes, these two nodes determined themselves to send query message for particular time gap period g/τ, where as τ = jitter (packet delay variations).

A and B counts the number of query they received from each other during gap period *count* $(t - g, t)$ then A calculates the d_d from the equation.

$$d_d = count(t{-}g, t) / \left(\frac{g}{t}\right) \tag{1}$$

Where *count* $(t - g, t)$ is the number of query commenced by node B and received by node A.

The node B calculates the d_s in similar way to d_d.

$$d_s = count(t{-}g, t) / \left(\frac{g}{t}\right) \tag{2}$$

A and B swaps the d_s and d_d values to calculate the EBX.

$$EBX_{A \rightarrow B} = \frac{1}{d_s * d_d} \tag{3}$$

This equation is used to find *EBX* value for more routes, *EBX* value has more hops, and the routes with more number of hops may have lesser throughput due to the intrusion among hops in the same path.

Source and Destination nodes *EBX* value can be calculated through the following formula.

$$EBX_{S \rightarrow D} = EBX_{A \rightarrow B} \tag{4}$$

Less *EBX* value in the routes have fewer possibility of packet loss, and that route is more preferable than others routes (Figure 5, Table 1).

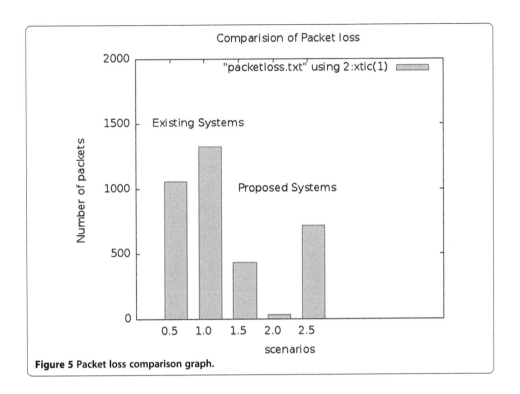

Figure 5 Packet loss comparison graph.

Intelligent manet algorithm

In this intelligent approach, nodes connected to this network is monitored by server agent, the server agent manages the details of the mobile nodes in a network like

- Behaviour of the node
- Speed of the node
- Direction of the node
- Position of the node

This technique prevents the malicious node from attacking other nodes (Figure 6).

Step 1

The nodes participating in the networks to access service like internet registers its identity with the server agent, the server agent replies with unique ID to the requesting node.

Step 2

The source node request route with the current access point to the destination node the current access point forwards the route request to the server agent.

Table 1 Packet loss comparisons

Scenarios	Time (in seconds)	Packet drop (in bits)
Existing system 1	6.5	10581
Existing system 2	6.5	13221
Proposed system 1	6.5	4372
Proposed system 2	6.5	322
Proposed system 3	6.5	715

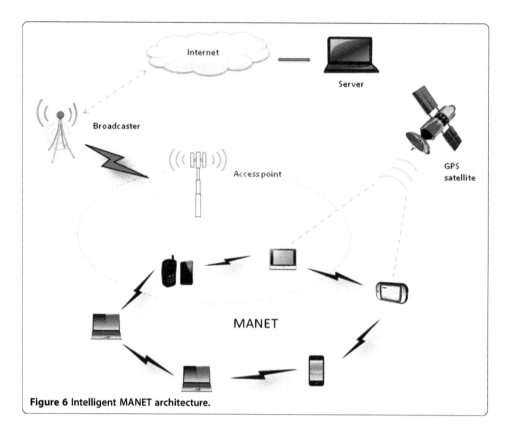

Figure 6 Intelligent MANET architecture.

Step 3

The server agent verifies the source ID, then it accepts the route request from sender then it gathers the information of receiver using destination ID from the list.

Step 4

The server agent then broadcasts the route request message using destination ID, the registered adjacent nodes that are nearer to the destination node which are ready to provide the service replies with the acknowledgement message to the server agent.

Step 5

The server agent chooses the adjacent node with the longest life time (the ability of the nodes to stay connected with the destination node) using the details collected from the ID, Such as nodes position, direction of motion and speed of the node.

Step 6

Then the server agent provides route reply message for the source node, after this authentication process, source node starts sending data packets in a secure way.

Step 7

In case any node moves away from the network, immediately the server agent replaces it with some other nodes to maintain the continuity of connection.

Step 8

In this technique, the malicious node or selfish nodes are completely eliminated from the network, as the server agent takes full control of the ad-hoc network.

Conclusion

Mobile adhoc networks are facing vulnerability and security issues from a long time. Assorted protocols and algorithmic approaches has been developed and implemented so far to avoid and remove the issues associated. In this manuscript, we have implemented an empirical and effective approach to optimize the packet loss frequency. The algorithmic approach is implemented in the network simulator ns2 to execute the scenarios and results.

Competing interests
The authors declare that they have no competing interests.

Authors' contributions
RS carried out the development of algorithmic approach, actual logic and implementation. PS and MD finally analyzed the results. All authors read and approved the final manuscript.

Author details
[1]Deenbandhu Chhotu Ram University of Science & Technology, Murthal, Haryana, India. [2]Department of Computer Science and Engineering, Deenbandhu Chhotu Ram University of Science & Technology, Murthal, Haryana, India. [3]Department of Electronics and Communications, Deenbandhu Chhotu Ram University of Science & Technology, Murthal, Haryana, India.

References
1. Clausen TH (2007) Introduction to mobile ad-hoc networks, Internet Draft
2. Yu C-F (1989) Security safeguards for intelligent networks. In: IEEE International Conference on World Prosperity Through Communications. ICC '89, BOSTONICC/89. Conference record, vol 3. GTE Lab. Inc, Waltham, MA, USA, pp 1154–1159
3. Choi S, Kim DY, Lee DH, Jung J-i (2008) WAP: wormhole attack prevention algorithm in mobile ad hoc networks, SUTC '08. IEEE International Conference on Sensor Networks, Ubiquitous and Trustworthy Computing pp 343–348
4. Li JH, Das S, McAuley A, Lee J, Stuhrmann T, Gerla M (2010) A multi-layer approach for seamless soft handoff in mobile ad hoc networks. Hui Zeng Intell. Autom., Inc. (IAI), Rockville, MD, USA, pp 21–26, GLOBECOM Workshops (GC Wkshps), IEEE
5. Leonard J (1997) Interactive Game Scheduling with Genetic Algorithms, Minor Thesis, RMIT (Royal Melbourne Institute of Technology University). Department of Computer Science
6. Prasad S, Singh YP, Rai CS (2009) Swarm based intelligent routing for MANETs. Int J Recent Trends Eng 1(1)
7. Garg P (2009) "A comparison between memetic algorithm and genetic algorithm for the cryptanalysis of simplified data encryption standard algorithm". Int J Netw Secur Appl (IJNSA) 1(1)
8. Sanjay R, Huirong F, Manohar S, John D, Kendall N (2003) Prevention of Cooperative Black Hole Attack in Wireless Ad Hoc Networks". International Conference on Wireless Networks (ICWN'03), Las Vegas, Nevada, USA

6

Adaptive polar transform and fusion for human face image processing and evaluation

Debotosh Bhattacharjee

Correspondence: debotosh@ieee.org
Department of Computer Science
and Engineering, Jadavpur
University, Kolkata 700032, India

Abstract

Human face processing and evaluation is a problem due to variations in orientation, size, illumination, expression, and disguise. The goal of this work is threefold. First, we aim to show that the variant of polar transformation can be used to register face images against changes in pose and size. Second, implementation of fusion of thermal and visual face images in the wavelet domain to handle illumination and disguise and third, principal component analysis is applied in order to tackle changes due to expressions up to a particular extent of degrees. Finally, a multilayer perceptron has been used to classify the face image. Several techniques have been implemented here to depict an idea about improvement of results. Methods started from the simplest design, without registration; only combination of PCA and MLP as a method for dimensionality reduction and classification respectively to the range of adaptive polar registration, fusion in wavelet transform domain and final classification using MLP. A consistent increase in recognition performance has been observed. Experiments were conducted on two separate databases and results yielded are very much satisfactory for adaptive polar registration along with fusion of thermal and visual images in the wavelet domain.

Introduction

Due to enhancement in accuracy, face recognition has gradually increased its recognition as a biometric trait for identification and authentication. Biometric security system is in active research areas for more than last four decades but till date a tractable, robust, and low cost solution is yet to be produced. Complications and difficulties arise in designing such a system lie heavily due to the requirement of unconstrained face recognition. Some constrained face recognition systems may be created specific to applications like monitoring daily attendance, recording frequency of visits for known personalities, or identity checking at non-critical official dealings, with ease, but to maintain security and surveillance e.g. to counter terrorism if some suspect is to be restricted to the protected area like an airport, unconstrained face recognition becomes a necessity. Many techniques have already been developed to tackle sources of different complications like, changes in illumination level and direction [1,2], variation in pose [3,4], changes in expression [5]; changes in skin colour [6], disguises due to cosmetics [7], glasses [8,9], skin colour [6], beard, moustaches [7] etc. These complications are multifaceted and it becomes deterrent to achieve better recognition performance when two or more complicacies are bundled together, some of them are given below:

i. Different illumination levels
ii. Direction of illumination may vary
iii. Distance of camera from the face may vary and, as a result, effective facial area is bound to be different. In this case if it is possible to crop the facial area still scaling of cropped images is necessary
iv. Rotation of head about one or more axes in 3-D space leads to significant differences in face images
v. Presence or absence of beard and/or moustache
vi. Presence or absence of spectacles and/or coloured-glasses, adornments
vii. Deliberate change in colour of skin and/or hair to appear before the designed system in disguise.
viii. Change in expressions and
ix. Others

In order to tackle all these detrimental factors let us take them into account one by one.

To handle different pose and sizes all the images of each and every person are to be registered against a frontal and neutral face design of that person. Illumination and disguise related problems are dealt with fusion of visual and its corresponding infrared or thermal face images. Finally, Principal Component Analysis (PCA) is used to manage the results of beard, moustache, glasses, and expressions. However, with all these tools in action, classification job is not necessarily a trivial one because all those tools are capable of handling these ill effects to some extent whereas they are not safe enough to abolish those unwanted circumstances. Therefore, like other complex pattern classification tasks, here also, an efficient classifier is needed for final acceptance. Here, one multilayer perceptron (MLP) has been chosen because of its simplicity.

Face recognition is an active research area and researchers are still trying different modalities to increase accuracy for recognition in an unconstrained environment. In this category one, inclusion is thermal infrared imagery [9], and another very recent addition is a using of fusion procedure [9] over different types of images.

Infrared (IR) or thermal images are considered a viable alternative to manage changes in illumination level and in detecting disguised faces [10-12]. Thermal or IR cameras capture images based on the heat patterns emitted from an object. Heat patterns emitted by an object depend on the body temperature and characteristics of the constituent material of the object. Since the blood vessel pattern, muscle, tissue etc. are different for each person, the radiated pattern of heat should be unique for each and every individual. The use of thermal face images has great advantages over visual images. Face recognition systems based on visual images results very poor under different illumination conditions, colours, disguises, and typical conditions like identical twins. However, these situations can be handled by IR images very easily but it has many drawbacks. Firstly, IR imagery depends on the temperature, and if there is a large difference in body temperature then the heat patterns generated by human body would certainly differ. Heat pattern produced by a person sitting in an air-conditioned room and the same person when sitting under strong sunlight must be different. As a matter of fact, IR images should be captured in a controlled environment i.e. with minimum variation in external temperature. Second, IR images are also sensitive to variations in the internal temperature of the face. Factors that could contribute to these variations include diseases (e.g. cold, fever etc.), facial expressions (e.g. open mouth, closed eyes), physical conditions (e.g. lack of sleeps), and psychological conditions (e.g. fear, stress, excitement). Finally, IR is opaque to spectacles and coloured glasses. This may introduce partial occlusion to the face images.

It is apparent from the above discussion; neither thermal images nor visual images are capable of tackling complications of face recognition, and therefore a combination of both the imaging modalities namely fusion of images have come up. Fusion is actually a natural mechanism built in man and other mammals. It serves as perceiving the real world by the simultaneous use of various sensing modalities [13]. The principal motivation for the fusion approach is to exploit the benefits of two or more modalities in one hand and simultaneously suppressing disadvantages of those on the other.

According to the method and data sources, image fusion techniques can be grouped into [14] following categories:

(i) Multiview fusion: images from the same source and taken at the same time but from different viewpoints.
(ii) Multimodal fusion: images coming from various sources like visual, thermal, X-ray etc.
(iii) Multitemporal fusion: images taken at different times
(iv) Multifocus fusion: images taken with different focal lengths.

For all these different categories, the fusion comprises of two primary steps: (i) image registration, which is nothing but spatial alignment of input images, and (ii) combining those aligned images.

Due to the rotation, tilting, and panning of head, it is difficult to match face images efficiently and the situation worsens when images are taken at different time intervals. Also, due to differences in distance from the camera to the source face, there may be a difference in dimension which is not so easy to ignore. Any unknown image should be registered against the probe images (neutral and frontal face image) stored in the images database. Many works have been made in this area in the past twenty years [15]. Recently Zokai and Wolberg [16] proposed an innovative design by using Log-Polar transform (LPT). LPT [16,17], is well known tool for image processing for its rotation and scale invariant properties. Scale and rotation in Cartesian coordinate appears as a translation in the log-polar domain. These invariant properties provide a significant benefit in registering images. Log-polar transformation utilizes the feature of applying greater weights to pixels at the centre of the interpolation region and logarithmically decreasing weights to pixels away from the centre.

In this paper, two different face recognition procedures have been performed, and their respective results are compared with each other. The general steps for each process are image registration, fusion of images in the wavelet domain, dimensionality reduction using PCA, and finally, classification of projected images using a multilayer perceptron neural network (MLPNN).

This paper deals with recognition of human face images in semi-uncontrolled environment. Here, semi-uncontrolled term has been used because uncontrolled environment may be any environment like wild where pose variation may be around 90 degrees, almost invisible face under overexposed or underexposed condition, very low resolution etc. Main contribution of this paper is to handle face recognition problem in moderate conditions of pose, illumination, disguise, and occlusions termed as semi-uncontrolled environment. Some techniques in literature exists where authors targeted one or two sources of complicacies but in the system, developed here, a comprehensive technique was developed, which is capable to handle combination of different ailments generally present in most of the face recognition systems.

The organization of the rest of this paper is as follows. In Overview of the present system section, the overview of the system is discussed. In Image registration section, details of image registration have been discussed. Fusion of visual and thermal images section describes the fusion of visual and thermal face images in detail. Principal component analysis section and Multilayer perceptron neural network section describe PCA and MLP respectively in brief. In Experimental results and discussions section, experimental results and discussions are given. Finally, Conclusion section concludes this work.

Overview of the present system

In the following sections, we present the techniques which form the elements of our system, shown in Figure 1 and which also describe our motivation for using them. Briefly, we explore the use of polar transform to register images against rotation and scale invariant face images, fusion of face images is made to achieve illumination invariance, principal component analysis to incorporate expression changes to some degree and ultimately, a multilayer perceptron is used for classification of images.

Image registration

Image registration is a means of finding correspondence between two images depicting common visual information, like, images of the same object taken at different conditions like changes in illumination levels and illumination direction, changes in the environment; many geometrical position e.g. orientations about X-, Y-, and Z-axes; with a difference in a time interval; and considered by several sensors, by which there may be a difference in resolution, intensity etc. In general, image registration works in four steps.

(i) Feature detection: Salient and distinctive features like corners, intersection and end points of lines, regions, edges, closed contours etc. are automatically detected. These features are described by critical data structures and termed as control points to establish a correspondence between images brought under registration.

(ii) Feature matching: Once control points are computed; correspondences between them are found through finding similarity between particular features computed.

(iii) Transform model estimation: Depending on corresponding control points, estimation of transformation is done. This estimation has to find the possible transformation functions and their respective parameters, so that once applied to transformed image; it becomes closest to the original one.

(iv) Image transformation: Final job is to transform the image as per transformation model discussed above. Once transformation is completed it may require resampling of images with appropriate brightness interpolation for pixels represented by non-integer coordinates.

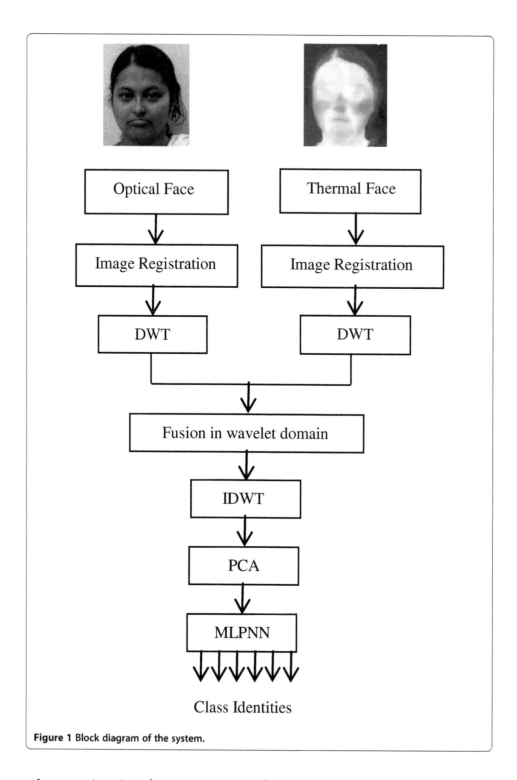

Figure 1 Block diagram of the system.

Image registration plays an important role in the fusion of images captured with different cameras with different features like viewing angle, resolution and focus.

Log polar transform

Log-Polar transform (LPT) is a process that converts an image described in Cartesian coordinate f(x, y) into the log-polar coordinate system s(r,θ). Image represented in log-polar coordinates are known for rotation and scale invariant properties. The transformation can be given as

$$r = \log_{10} \sqrt{(x-x_c)^2 + (y-y_c)^2}$$

$$\theta = \tan^{-1} \frac{y-y_c}{x-x_c}$$

where, (x_c, y_c) is the centre pixel of the transformation in the Cartesian coordinates.

Figure 2 shows an image in 2(a) and its corresponding log-polar transformed image in 2(d). Moreover, 2(b) and 2(c) are rotated images of the image in 2(a) and 2(e), 2(f) are log-polar transformed images of 2(b) and 2(c) respectively.

It is evident from Figure 2 is that the rotation in Cartesian coordinate system is mere shifting in log-polar coordinate system. Since, in case of shifting, detection is easier, and retranslation to its earlier state back can be done afterwards, log-polar transformation has been used in image registration very efficiently. The benefit of log-polar coordinate system over the Cartesian coordinate representation is that any rotation and (or) scale in the Cartesian coordinates are (is) represented as shifts in the angular and log-radius directions, respectively. Since log-polar transform uses non-uniform sampling, it becomes very efficient in object recognition. If the central message content becomes the centre of the transform then for that part more samples are taken, whereas for background etc., which are in the distant locations from the centre could influence very limited due to consideration of the lesser number of samples for those.

Adaptive polar transform

In some cases, the benefit of non-uniform sampling becomes disadvantageous. For example, in case of human face recognition, generally cropped images are considered and therefore the importance of all the parts should be given uniformly. In log polar transformation, the

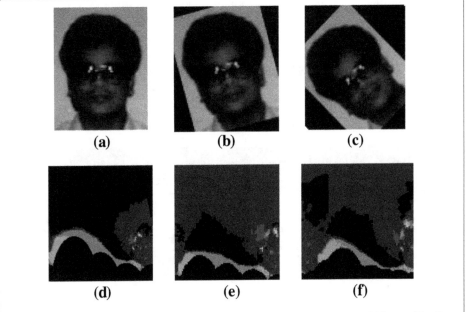

Figure 2 Log-Polar Transformation. (a) Original image, **(b)** rotated in 15 degrees and **(c)** rotated in 45 degrees; **(d)** – **(f)** are corresponding log polar transformed images of **(a)**-**(c)** respectively.

pixels which were away from centre point may be missed, and as a result, the part of pixels in the periphery in recognition becomes negligible and therefore the accuracy should degrade. To get rid of this disadvantage Matungka et al. [18] proposed a method called adaptive polar transformation. In adaptive polar transformation number of samples near centre and those at the periphery differ. It increases directly proportionally to the increase in radius.

In order to achieve consistent sampling over the circumference (C_i) at every sample of radius (r_i), the ith circular sample from centre through radius, number of samples in an angular direction (θ_i) should be adaptive i.e. θ_i should increase along with the increase in C_i. The circumference C_i at radius r_i is known to be $C_i = 2 \times \pi \times r_i$. For an adaptive polar transform of an image, $f(x, y)$, of size $2R_{max} \times 2R_{max}$ in Cartesian coordinate system into polar domain (with uniform samples over the circumference), $f_{apt}(x, y)$, is given as

for $i = 1$ **to** R_{max}

begin

$\theta = 2 \times \pi \times i$

for $j = 1$ **to** θ

begin

$f_{apt} (x, y) = (f(R_{max} + i \times \cos(2\pi j/\theta i), \ R_{max} + i \times \sin(2\pi j/\theta i))$

end for
end for

Adaptive polar transforms of Figure 2(a)-(c) are given in Figure 3(a)-(c) respectively. Registration of these images is made in the adaptive polar transformed domain using phase correlation because it is very easy to find the number of change by phase correlation and registration can be made by realignment opposite to shifting in transformed domain.

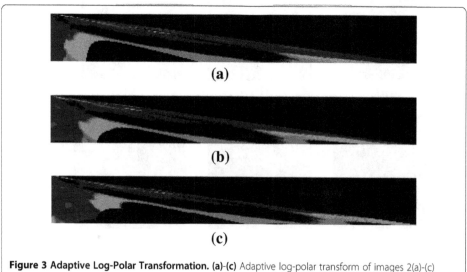

(a)

(b)

(c)

Figure 3 Adaptive Log-Polar Transformation. (a)-(c) Adaptive log-polar transform of images 2(a)-(c) respectively.

Phase correlation

Shifting theorem states that Fourier Transform of a function f(x+α) i.e. shifting of f(x) by an amount ∝ can be obtained by multiplying Fourier Transform of f(x) by $e^{-j\alpha x}$. This may be extended to 2-D (two-dimension) i.e. if f(x, y) is to be shifted by (α, β) then the shifted function would be

$$f_1(x, y) = f(x + \alpha, y + \beta)$$

and its corresponding Fourier Transform is

$$F_1(u, v) = e^{-j(\alpha u + \beta v)} F(u, v)$$

where F(u, v) is the Fourier transformed image of f(x, y). That means translation between two images in the spatial domain can be described as a phase difference in the frequency domain.

Cross correlation can be computed by the normalized multiplication in the frequency domain between the first image and the complex conjugate of the second image. To represent this phase difference as translation in the spatial domain, we apply the 2D inverse Fourier transform to it. The peak value of this inverse Fourier transform indicates the translation between the two images.

Figure 4 shows the use of cross-correlation in finding shifting of images. Figure 4(a), (b), and (c) show original image, change in the horizontal direction, and change in both horizontal and vertical direction respectively. Phase correlations of the original image given in Figure 4(a) with all these three images are shown in Figure 4(d)-(f) respectively. Figure 4(d) shows complete black representing no translation. Figure 4(e) shows translation in the horizontal direction and the number of translation is pointed by black arrow. Figure 4(f) shows shifting in both vertical and horizontal direction, and the number

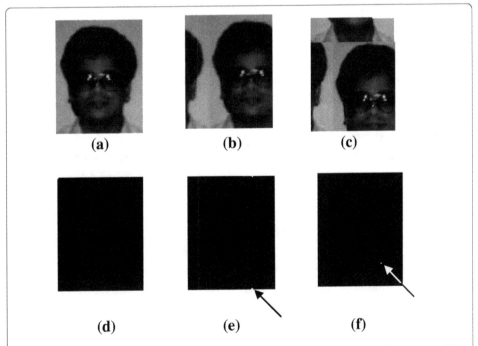

Figure 4 Cross-Correlation of Face Images. (a) Original image, **(b)** Shift in one spatial dimension, and **(c)** Shift in both the spatial dimensions; **(d)**, **(e)**, and **(f)** are images of phase correlations of **(a)** with **(a)**, **(b)**, and **(c)** respectively.

of translation is pointed by white arrow. Once the number of shifting is known then the images can be translated back to its original state. Since a rotation and scaling in Cartesian coordinate is represented in Polar coordinate a shifting in horizontal and vertical directions then retranslation of images in polar coordinate would produce scale and rotation invariant images.

Fusion of visual and thermal images

The fusion of images can be described as a means by which different images acquired through different sensors or modalities are combined to produce a new image with necessary and complementary information from the input images and capable of resolving inconsistencies or ambiguities encountered by classifiers used for classification of face images.

Human face recognition based on visual images has shown poor performance under uncontrolled working conditions. Among others, handling of larger variations in illumination level and disguises are very cumbersome. Whereas thermal face images are invariant towards variations in illumination levels as because those images are representations of the map for blood vessels. Other kind of visual impairments like disguise etc. can also be managed by thermal imaging. But in thermal images apart from blood vessels all other parts in the image are alike. As a matter of fact, two images of different persons may appear to be same by considering this similarity. Therefore to take the advantages of both the visual and thermal images combination of both the image types have been performed and the name of this blend comes under the field of image fusion.

Image fusion techniques

In image fusion, two or more images are combined, and a finally a single fused image is obtained which retains the necessary features from each of the original images. This image fusion is a lossy process because none of the original image can be reconstructed from a fused image. As discussed in Introduction, there could be many fusion situations. This existing design is a multimodal fusion, where images from two different sources namely visual and thermal are fused. In [19] pixel level fusion method has been applied. In that work, it has been assumed that each face is represented by a pair of images, one in the IR spectrum, and another is in the visible spectrum. For a particular imaging condition, both the thermal and visual images have been combined a priori to get corresponding fused images. During combining, 70% of a pixel in the visual image is added to 30% of the corresponding pixel in thermal images subject to a maximum. The best result reported is 95.71% of recognition accuracy on IRIS face database [20], but that idea didn't consider the entire IRIS face database. When it comes to the full database the performance degrades drastically, and the present method is an extension to that effort to acquire better recognition result for the whole face database. The purpose of such drastic reduction is quite logical from the fusion point of view. Since, in [19] pixel level fusion was considered, that should not work for the images with a subtle change in position of pixels due to expression, shift, tilt, or even noise. To overcome this category of problems, fusion of the wavelet coefficients is considered.

Wavelet-based fusion

Wavelet transform is a tool for time-frequency localization. It performs such localization by separating given signal into different frequency components and then each section is analysed with a resolution matched to its scale. Since face images are two dimensional discrete signals, 2-D discrete wavelet transforms are used in this situation. Several researchers have already applied wavelet transforms for fusing images in time-frequency domain [21-23]. Results of most of those investigations reveal that wavelet-based fusion algorithms outperform other image fusion algorithms.

In general, discrete wavelet transform decomposes a discrete signal into two subsignals of half of its length with the first one as a running average and another one as a difference or fluctuation. Considering all the discrete wavelet transforms Haar wavelet is the simplest transform. It has benefits like fast, requires less memory space, reversible etc., but it lacks capturing of all the high frequency components. This is because Haar wavelet captures through a window of size two starting from odd index and if there is a huge difference in components with even index in comparison with that of odd index then that the large difference is not taken into account during computation of high frequency components. To get rid of such demerit, in this work, Dubechies wavelet transform have been used. Keeping all other calculation same as Haar wavelet transform Daubechies wavelet uses overlapping windows and therefore all the changes are reflected in the high frequency coefficients. In this work, Daubechies 4-tap wavelet has been considered with the filter coefficients shown in Table 1. Here; H0 and H1 are input decomposition filters and G0 and G1 are output decomposition filters.

The fusion of images using wavelets [24,25] follows a standard procedure and is performed at the decomposition level. The input images are decomposed by a discrete wavelet transform and the wavelet coefficients are selected using a set of fusion rules and an inverse discrete wavelet transform is performed to reconstruct the fused image. Wavelet fusion methods differ mostly in the fusion rule used for selection of wavelet coefficients. Numerous fusion rules for combining the wavelet coefficients can be explored: (i) simple average, (ii) weighted average, (iii) Maximum, (iv) Maximum for high frequency components and minimum for low frequency components, (v) Maximum for high frequency components and average for low frequency components, and (vi) Maximum for high frequency components and the weighted average for low frequency components. It has been recognized that these combination schemes are having little effect on the overall performance of the fusion process. In this work, fusion rule "Maximum for high frequency components and the weighted average for low frequency components" has been chosen. The main reason for this choice is that the highest values capture the salient information (e.g. edges) in the images and a weighted average of low frequency coefficients to avoid the effects of noises.

Principal component analysis

Principal Component Analysis (PCA) is a well established tool for dimensionality reduction. A human face with thousands of pixels, if represented immediately, needs a

Table 1 Daubechies 4-tap wavelet coefficients

H0	H1	G0	G1
0.4830	0.1294	−0.1294	0.4830
0.8365	0.2241	0.2241	−0.8365
0.2241	−0.8365	0.8365	0.2241
−0.1294	0.4830	0.4830	0.1294

huge dimensional space for statistical analysis and subsequent classification. This will require extremely large memory space and processing capabilities for a large database which is common in real life applications. This problem is not as significant as storage space and processing requirement may be manageable, but the concept of "curse of dimensionality" may apply here. For a trainable classifier, it confirms that the required number of training samples grows exponentially with the increase in dimensionality. The fundamental objective of this step is dimensionality reduction by representing face space in lower dimensional space by generating features that are optimally uncorrelated. In the year 1987, Sirovich and Kirby used PCA to reduce dimensions for features vector of faces [26]. In the year 1991, Turk and Pentland used the same PCA again for dimensionality reduction in solving complex pattern recognition problem like problem of face recognition [27]. As reported in [28-30], PCA not only reduces the size of face images but also handles variations in face images due to changes in facial expressions.

Multilayer perceptron neural network

Artificial neural network (ANN) has already established its capability for classification of models due to its adaptivity, generalization strength, robustness, and fault tolerance. A Multilayer Perceptron (MLP) is a supervised neural network that has been used as a classifier in different pattern classification tasks successfully. This learning algorithm applied to multilayer feed forward networks here is consisting of processing elements with continuous differentiable activation functions. Such networks associated with the back propagation learning algorithm are also called backpropagation networks [31-35]. In this work, a multilayer neural network which incorporates backpropagation learning with momentum is used. This is a homogeneous system with tansigmoid transfer function in all the processing elements or neurons. The system consists of three layers. In the first layer, the number of neurons is equal to the size of the feature vectors achieved after dimensionality reduction and in output layer number of neurons is only one; a binary classifier. To be more specific for each course, there is a system to classify members of this class from others. Weights for the system are initialised with pseudorandom numbers. Weights associated with all the interconnections incident on node k are initialized with the pseudorandom numbers generated in the range $[-3/\sqrt{n_k}, 3/\sqrt{n_k}]$, where n_k is the number of interconnections to the kth node. Different parameters used to train the system are goal, learning rate (lr) and momentum constant (mc), epochs with values 10^{-6}, 0.06, 0.8, and 6,00,000 respectively.

Experimental results and discussions

For the performance analysis, several experiments were conducted. For this investigation, two face image databases were used. The first one is the IRIS database [20], and the second one is a face database created at our own laboratory and its proposed name is UGC-JU face database [36]. In all the experiments, images are normalized and cropped into corresponding images of size with width × Height as 40 × 50. Original images are normalized after registration of images with respect to frontal and neutral face images of each person. In order to obtain higher recognition accuracy, all the images are registered using variant of polar transforms and phase correlation. Corresponding registered visual and thermal face images are fused in the wavelet domain and then fused images are transformed back into the spatial domain. In this work, a multilayer perceptron neural network has been applied for classification of fused images. To evaluate the performance of the classification, the classifier used here is considered as binary classifier i.e. for each class, there is one classifier with elements of that class as positive exemplars and elements from other classes taken as negative exemplars. During the testing, four different results are possible: True Positives (TP), True Negatives (TN), False Positives (FP), and False Negatives (FN). False positive is considered when the outcome is incorrectly classified and marked as "yes" (or "positive"), when actually it is "no" (or "negative"). A false negative is marked when the outcome is incorrectly classified as negative but in real it is positive. Therefore, true positives and true negatives are correct classifications. Based on those four results other two statistical measures have been derived: Sensitivity and Specificity. Sensitivity is the measure that finds how good the test is in detecting real positives. It measures the proportion of actual positives, which are correctly identified and it is given as

$$\text{Sensitivity} = \text{TP}/(\text{TP} + \text{FN})$$

Whereas, specificity, is the measure that finds how well the test is at detecting real negatives. It measures the proportion of actual negatives, which are correctly identified and described as

$$\text{Specificity} = \text{TN}/(\text{FP} + \text{TN})$$

Another measure called accuracy is also calculated, which describes a ratio between number of samples correctly classified and total number of samples used in classification, given as

$$\text{Accuracy} = (\text{TP} + \text{TN})/(\text{TP} + \text{TN} + \text{FP} + \text{FN})$$

There are other measures exist, which can be computed from Specificity or Sensitivity and for that reason those are not computed here; those include:

$$\text{False positive rate} = \text{FP}/(\text{FP} + \text{TN}) = 1-\text{Specificity}$$

$$\text{False negative rate} = \text{FN}/(\text{TP} + \text{FN}) = 1-\text{Sensitivity}$$

Sensitivity, Specificity, and Accuracy measures computed for both the databases using different techniques implemented here are discussed in following sections.

IRIS thermal/visible database

This database [20] was initially formed in response to the IEEE Int'l Workshop on "Object Tracking and Classification in and Beyond the Visible Spectrum". The benchmark is used for educational and research purposes only and is available for all researchers in the international computer vision communities. The description relating to the database is given below:

Sensor Details: Thermal - Raytheon Palm-IR-Pro

Visible - Panasonic WV-CP234

Data Details: Total size of 1.83 GB

Image size: 320 × 240 pixels (visible and thermal), Total 4228 pairs of thermal and visible images with 176–250 images/person, 11 images per rotation (poses for each expression and each illumination) 30 persons - Expression, pose, and illumination.

Expression: ex1, ex2, ex3 - surprised, laughing, angry (varying poses)

Illumination: Lon (left light on), Ron (right light on), 2on (both lights on), dark (dark room), off (left and right lights off), varying poses.

Some visual and corresponding thermal images of a person are shown in Figure 5.

To measure the sensitivity, specificity, and accuracy, the IRIS database for visual and thermal face images were considered. There are several methods implemented for this experiment. Without fusion, visual and thermal face images are considered separately, and six different methods were investigated. They are based on dimensionality reduction using PCA and classification using Multilayer Perceptrons (MLP). Only difference is in registration; first process is without any registration at all; second one is registration with polar transform, and the third one is with adaptive polar transform for both thermal and visual counts to six different designs. When fusion is taken into consideration, unregistered, registered with polar transform, and registered with adaptive polar transform along with pixel fusion and wavelet fusion we got total six different designs. For the calculation of results, 3-fold cross-validation [37] was considered, and the results are shown in Table 2. All the images are partitioned into three subsets. Out of those three groups one is used for training and rest two are used for testing. From the results, in obtaining better recognition performance we can infer the followings:

i) Registration of face images produces better in comparison to an unregistered one.
ii) Adaptive Polar Registration produces better results that polar one.
iii) Fusion of visual and thermal face images outperforms the techniques which consider those individually.
iv) Wavelet based fusion produces better results that pixel fusion.

UGC-JU face database

This face database has been created at Department of Computer Science and Engineering, Jadavpur University, India under a project with a grant from University Grants Commission (UGC), India. Infrared images are captured using an FLIR 7 camera, and visual images are captured using Sony DSC-W350 digital camera at our own laboratory. Images are captured in pairs, one thermal and one visual, under different constraints. Every person sitting on a chair at a distance of about 2 feet from both the cameras. Each person has 34 different templates: different expressions with eye movements and emotions without changing head orientation, different views about x-axis, y-axis, and z-axis etc. for 20 persons.

All the experiments conducted on IRIS face database have also been conducted on UGC-JU face database [36], results obtained is shown in Table 3. Trend of results for

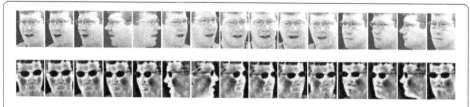

Figure 5 Some visual images (first line) of a person with corresponding thermal images (second line) from IRIS face database. (All are in grayscale).

Table 2 Experimental results on IRIS face database

Sl. no.	Method		Sensitivity	Specificity	Accuracy
1	Unregistered + No Fusion + PCA + MLP	Visual images	90.42	81.60	88.73
		Thermal images	87.04	84.62	85.38
2	Unregistered + Pixel Fusion + PCA + MLP		91.93	86.32	90.86
3	Unregistered + Wavelet Fusion + PCA + MLP		94.21	85.30	92.50
4	Log Polar Registered + No fusion + PCA + MLP	Visual images	90.18	80.80	88.39
		Thermal images	89.24	78.70	87.22
5	Adaptive Log Polar Registered + No fusion + PCA + MLP	Visual images	91.84	84.70	90.47
		Thermal images	90.99	82.80	89.42
6	Log Polar Registered + Pixel Fusion + PCA + MLP		92.53	86.70	91.41
7	Adaptive Log Polar Registered + Pixel Fusion + PCA + MLP		94.77	88.10	93.50
8	Log Polar Registered + Wavelet Fusion + PCA + MLP		95.84	92.80	95.26
9	Adaptive Log Polar Registered + Wavelet Fusion + PCA + MLP		98.46	97.90	98.36

different techniques obtained in this database is also similar as in the case of IRIS face database and therefore the inferences made in IRIS thermal/visible database section. Some visual and corresponding thermal images of a person of UGC-JU database are shown in Figure 6.

Comparative study

Discussion won't be complete without comparison of results of the present process is not made with other existing recent designs. Comparison is given in Table 4, where all the methods are not using the same database. Here, we have tried to compare our method with other through the same database and also result due to our database UGC-JU has also been depicted.

In Table 4, a complete overview with regard to acceptance rate of different fusion techniques has been presented. The IRIS thermal visible face dataset (which is one of the OTCBVS benchmark dataset) has been used for all the experiments conducted

Table 3 Experimental results on UGC-JU face database

Sl. no.	Method		Sensitivity	Specificity	Accuracy
1	Unregistered + No Fusion + PCA + MLP	Visual images	81.91	60.00	77.53
		Thermal images	76.32	54.87	72.06
2	Unregistered + Pixel Fusion + PCA + MLP		86.32	73.53	83.76
3	Unregistered + Wavelet Fusion + PCA + MLP		87.21	77.06	85.18
4	Log Polar Registered + No fusion + PCA + MLP	Visual images	85.44	72.35	82.82
		Thermal images	82.79	64.12	79.06
5	Adaptive Log Polar Registered + No fusion + PCA + MLP	Visual images	86.62	75.88	84.47
		Thermal images	84.26	68.82	81.18
6	Log Polar Registered + Pixel Fusion + PCA + MLP		88.38	80.00	86.71
7	Adaptive Log Polar Registered + Pixel Fusion + PCA + MLP		92.06	82.94	90.24
8	Log Polar Registered + Wavelet Fusion + PCA + MLP		92.94	87.65	91.88
9	Adaptive Log Polar Registered + Wavelet Fusion + PCA + MLP		96.77	91.77	95.77

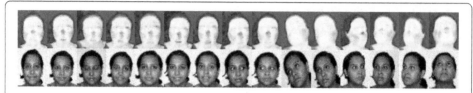

Figure 6 Some thermal images (first line) of a person with corresponding visual images (second line) from UGC-JU face database.

by M. K. Bhowmik et al. [19,39-45]. In [40], a pixel level fusion of visual and thermal image has been used, and 97.05% acceptance rate is achieved. In [45], fused images have been classified using radial basis function and multilayer perceptron and the listed images using RBF shown better accuracy than MLP, which is 96.0%. In [19], log polar transform of fused images has been analysed over MLP, and the acceptance rate is 93.81% which is much lesser than other techniques [40,42,45]. In [41], an optimum level fusion of visual and thermal images has been introduced, and 93% acceptance rate is achieved. In [42], a new dimension reduction technique, candid covariance-free

Table 4 A comparative study between different fusion methodologies

Sl. no.	Author	Techniques	Database used	Reported performance
1.	M. K. Bhowmik et al. [19]	log-polar transformed + PCA	OTCBVS (IRIS)	93.81%
2.	Mohammad Hanif et al. [38]	Gabor Filter Technique	Equinox	DWT - 90.31%
				OIF - 95.84%
3.	M. K. Bhowmik et al. [39]	Daubechies wavelet transform + PCA + ICA	OTCBVS (IRIS)	PCA - 91.13%
				ICA I - 94.44%
				ICA II - 89.72%
4.	M. K. Bhowmik et al. [40]	Pixel fusion + RBF	OTCBVS (IRIS)	97.05%
5.	M. K. Bhowmik et al. [41]	Optimum + Eigenspace projection + Multilayer Perceptron	OTCBVS (IRIS)	93%
6.	D. Bhattacharjee et al. [35]	Eigenspace projection + Multilayer Perceptron + Backpropagation learning	OTCBVS (IRIS)	95.07%
7.	M. K. Bhowmik et al. [42]	Pixel fusion + CCIPCA + SVM	OTCBVS (IRIS)	97.28%
8.	M. K. Bhowmik et al. [43]	Wavelet transformation + multiresolution analysis + MLP + RBF	OTCBVS (IRIS)	Feature level - 87.28%
				Decision level - 94.95%
9.	M. K. Bhowmik et al. [44]	Daubechies wavelet co-efficient + ICA + MLP	OTCBVS (IRIS)	91.5%
10.	M. K. Bhowmik et al. [45]	Eigenspace projection + MLP + RBF	OTCBVS (IRIS)	RBF - 96%
				MLP - 95.07%
11.	D. R. Kisku et al. [46]	Dempster-Shafer decision theory + SIFT features	ORL, IITK	ORL - 98.93%
				IITK - 96.29%
12.	R. Singh et al. [47]	Match score fusion + 2ν GSVM + Dezert Smarandache theory + SVM	Equinox	DSm match score fusion - 98.08%
				SVM - 95.05%
				DST - 96.51%
				2ν GSVM - 94.98%
13	Present method	Adaptive Log Polar Registered + Wavelet Fusion + PCA + MLP	OTCBVS(IRIS)	98.36%
			UGC-JU	95.77%

incremental principal component analysis (CCIPCA) is applied over the fused images, and finally those lower spaced fused images has been classified using different SVM kernel and 97.28% acceptance rate is achieved, which is the maximum of all fusion methodologies, those performed by M. K. Bhowmik et al. Since, Equinox database is not available so no comparison could have been completed. Results are compared for IRIS database only. All other methods, mentioned here, worked with IRIS database did not consider complete database for the evaluation of results, whereas the present method considered the entire database and has shown a very convincing result for acceptance of this method for development of the face identification system.

Conclusion

We present a fully automatic human face recognition system which efficiently registers face images using adaptive polar transformation. This technique also uses a wavelet based fusion method that combines visual and thermal faces images in a robust manner. Alternative methods were also implemented with lower computational cost, but recognition performance achieved is much lower than this. Different sources of complicacies when present in face images it becomes difficult to solve this recognition problem in efficient manner. This method has shown a very good performance in recognising almost all the possible complicacies to a large extent.

There are possibilities for further improvements of the existing design. Registration may be done based on some particular landmarks and considering symmetry of the face image to handle images captured across poses. Support vector machine (SVM) may improve classification result instead of a simple MLP. There may be fusion of different region classifiers used at various distinct region of the face images.

Competing interests

Author acknowledges the incessant and encouraging support of his wife Ms. Rituparna Bhattacharjee, which helped him in pursuing this research.

References

1. Liu Z, Liu C (2008) A hybrid color and frequency features method for face recognition. IEEE Trans Image Process 17(10):1975–1980. doi:10.1109/TIP.2008.2002837
2. Basri R, Jacobs DW (2003) Lambertian reflectance and linear subspaces. IEEE Trans Pattern Anal Machine Intel 25(2):218–233. doi:10.1109/TPAMI.2003.1177153
3. Hsieh CK, Chen YC (2007) Kernel-based pose invariant face recognition. In: Proc. IEEE Int. Conf. Multimedia and Expo., pp 987–990. doi:10.1109/ICME.2007.4284818
4. Ashraf AB, Lucey S, Chen T (2008) Learning patch correspondences for improved viewpoint invariant face recognition. In: Proc. IEEE Conf. Computer Vision and Pattern Recognition (CVPR '08), pp 1–8. doi:10.1109/CVPR.2008.4587754
5. Gizatdinova Y, Surakka V (2006) Feature-based detection of facial landmarks from neutral and expressive facial images. IEEE Trans Pattern Anal Machine Intel 28(1):135–139. doi:10.1109/TPAMI.2006.10
6. Kawato S, Ohya J (2000) Two-step approach for real-time eye tracking with a new filtering technique. In: Proc. IEEE Int. Conf. Systems, Man, and Cybernetics, pp 1366–1371
7. Pavlidis I, Symosek P (2000) The imaging issue in an automatic face/disguise detection system. In: Proc. IEEE Workshop on Computer Vision beyond the Visible Spectrum: Methods and Applications (CVBVS 2000)., p 15. doi:10.1109/CVBVS.2000.855246
8. Park JS, Oh YH, Ahn SC, Lee SW (2005) Glasses removal from facial image using recursive error compensation. IEEE Trans Pattern Anal Machine Intel 27(5):805–811. doi:10.1109/TPAMI.2005.103
9. Heo J, Kong SG, Abidi BR, Abidi MA (2004) Fusion of visual and thermal signatures with eyeglass removal for robust face recognition. In: Proc. IEEE Computer Society Conference on Computer Vision and Pattern Recognition Workshops (CVPRW'04)., p 122. doi:10.1109/CVPR.2004.35
10. Buddharaju P, Pavlidis I, Kakadiaris I (2004) Face recognition in the thermal infrared spectrum. In: Proceedings of the IEEE Workshop on Computer Vision and Pattern Recognition Workshop (CVPRW '04)
11. Pavlidis I, Buddharaju P, Manohar C, Tsiamyrtzis P (2006) Biometrics: face recognition in thermal infrared. In: Biomedical Engineering Handbook, 3rd Edition, CRC Press, pp 1–15
12. Dowdall JB, Pavlidis I, Bebis G (2003) Face detection in the near-IR spectrum. Image Vis Comput 21(7):565–578

13. Yin Z, Malcolm AA (2000) Thermal and visual image processing and fusion. In: SIMTech Technical Report (AT/00/016/MVS). Machine Vision & Sensors Group, Automation Technology Division, Singapore

14. Flusser J, Sroubek F, Zitova B (2007) Image Fusion: Principles, Methods, and Applications. In: Tutorial EUSIPCO

15. Zitova B, Flusser J (2003) Image registration methods: a survey. Image Vis Comput 21(11):977–1000. doi:10.1016/S0262-8856(03)00137-9

16. Zokai S, Wolberg G (2005) Image registration using log-polar mappings for recovery of large-scale similarity and projective transformations. IEEE Trans Image Process 14(10):1422–1434

17. Matungka R, Zheng YF, Ewing RL (2008) 2D invariant object recognition using log-polar transform. In: Proc. World Congress on Intelligent Control and Automation (WCICA '08)., pp 223–228

18. Matungka R, Zheng YF, Ewing RL (2009) Image registration using adaptive polar transform. IEEE Trans Image Process 18(10):2340–2354

19. Bhowmik MK, Bhattacharjee D, Basu DK, Nasipuri M (2011) Polar fusion technique analysis for evaluating the performances of image fusion of thermal and visual images for human face recognition. In: IEEE Workshop on Computational Intelligence in Biometrics and Identity Management (CIBIM), 11–15 April 2011, Paris., pp 62–69

20. OTCBVS (2013) OTCBVS Benchmark Dataset Collection., http://www.cse.ohio-state.edu/otcbvs-bench/. Accessed 20 November 2013

21. Nikolov SG, Canga EF, Lewis JJ, Loza A, Canagarajah CN, Bull DR (2004) Fusion of Visible and Infrared Image Sequences Using Wavelets. In: Technical report. The University of Bristol, Bristol, UK, p 202

22. Lewis JJ, O_Callaghan RJ, Nikolov SG, Bull DR, Canagarajah N (2007) Pixel- and region-based image fusion with complex wavelets. Informa Fusion 8:119–130

23. Zaveri T, Zaveri M (2011) A novel region based multimodality image fusion method. J Pattern Recogn Res 2(2011):140–153

24. Nunez J, Otazu X, Fors O, Prades A, Pala V, Arniol R (1999) Multiresolution-based image fusion with additive wavelet decomposition. IEEE Trans Geosci Remote Sensing 37(3):1205–1211

25. Singh S, Gyaourva A, Bebis G, Pavlidis I (2006) Face recognition by fusing thermal infrared and visible imagery. Image Vis Comput 24:727–742

26. Kirby M, Sirovich L (1990) Application of the Karhunen-Loeve procedure for the characterization of human faces. IEEE Trans Pattern Anal Machine Intel 12(1):103–108

27. Turk M, Pentland A (1991) Eigenfaces for recognition. J Cogn Neurosci 3(1):71–86

28. Lekshmi VP, Sasikumar M, Naveen S (2008) Analysis of Facial Expressions from Video Images using PCA. In: Proceedings of the World Congress on Engineering 2008 Vol I. WCE 2008, London, UK

29. Sun W, Ruan Q (2006) Two-Dimension PCA for Facial Expression Recognition. In: ICSP2006

30. Lin D (2006) Facial expression classification using PCA and hierarchical radial basis function network. J Inf Sci Eng 22:1033–1046, 1033

31. Bhowmik MK, Bhattacharjee D, Nasipuri M, Basu DK, Kundu M (2008) Classification of polar-thermal eigenfaces using multilayer perceptron for human face recognition. In: Proc. 3rd IEEE Conf. Industrial and Information Systems (ICIIS '08)., p 118

32. Bhowmik MK, Bhattacharjee D, Nasipuri M, Basu DK, Kundu M (2009) Human face recognition using line features. In: Proc. National Seminar on Recent Advances on Information Technology (RAIT '09)., p 385

33. Bhowmik MK, Bhattacharjee D, Nasipuri M, Basu DK, Kundu M (2008) Classification of log-polar-visual eigenfaces using multilayer perceptron. In: Proc. 2nd Int. Conf. on Soft computing (ICSC '08)., pp 107–123

34. Bhattacharjee D, Basu DK, Nasipuri M, Kundu M (2010) Human face recognition using fuzzy multilayer perceptron. Soft Comput 14:559–570

35. Bhattacharjee D, Bhowmik MK, Nasipuri M, Basu DK, Kundu M (2009) Classification of fused face images using multilayer perceptron neural network. In: Proc. Int. Conf. on Rough sets, Fuzzy sets and Soft Computing., pp 289–300

36. Seal A, Bhattacharjee D, Nasipuri M, Basu DK (2013) UGC-JU face database and its benchmarking using linear regression classifier. In: Multimedia Tools and Applications Journal of Springer., doi:10.1007/s11042-013-1754-8

37. Kohavi R (1995) A study of cross-validation and bootstrap for accuracy estimation and model selection. Proc 14th Int Joint Conf Artif Intel 2:1137–1143

38. Hanif M, Ali U (2006) Optimized visual and thermal image fusion for efficient face recognition. In: 9th International Conference on Information Fusion, Florence., pp 1–6

39. Bhowmik MK, Bhattacharjee D, Basu DK, Nasipuri M (2011) Independent Component Analysis (ICA) of fused Wavelet Coefficients of thermal and visual images for human face recognition. In: SPIE Defense, Security, and Sensing 2011 (track of Independent Component Analysis, Wavelets, Neural Networks, Biosystems and Nanoengineering, Conference 8058). Published by SPIE and SPIE Digital Library, in Orlando World Center Marriott Resort & Convention Center, Orlando, Florida, USA

40. Bhowmik MK, Bhattacharjee D, Nasipuri M, Basu DK, Kundu M (2009) Classification of fused images using Radial basis function Neural Network for Human Face Recognition. In: Proc. of The World congress on Nature and Biologically Inspired Computing. NaBIC-09, Coimbatore, India

41. Bhowmik MK, Bhattacharjee D, Nasipuri M, Basu DK, Kundu M (2010) Optimum Fusion of Visual and Thermal Face Images for Recognition. Proc of 6th Int. Conf on Information Assurance and Security (IAS 2010), Atlanta, USA, pp 311–316

42. Bhowmik MK, Bhattacharjee D, Basu DK, Nasipuri M (2012) Multisensor Fusion of Visual and Thermal Images for Human Face Identification using Different SVM Kernels. In: IEEE Conference on Long Island Systems, Applications and Technology (LISAT 2012). Farmingdale, New York

43. Bhowmik MK, Bhattacharjee D, Basu DK, Nasipuri M (2012) Human face Recognition Using Multisource Fusion. In: Track of Multi Sensor, Multisource Information Fusion: Architecture Algorithms, and Applications 2012 (DS223) SPIE Defense, Security and Sensing 2012, Baltimore Convention Center. Published by SPIE and SPIE Digital Library, Baltimore, Maryland, USA

44. Bhowmik MK, Bhattacharjee D, Nasipuri M, Basu DK, Kundu M (2012) Eye region based fusion technique of thermal and optical images for human face recognition in dark. Optical Eng J SPIE 51(7):2012

45. Bhowmik MK, Bhattacharjee D, Nasipuri M, Basu DK, Kundu M (2009) Image Pixel Fusion for Human Face Recognition. In: Published in International Journal of Recent Trends in Engineering [ISSN 1797-9617]. Academy Publishers, Finland, pp 258–262, Vol. 2, No. 2

46. Kisku DR, Tistarelli M, Sing JK, Gupta P (2010) Face Recognition by Fusion of Local and Global Matching Scores using DS Theory: An Evaluation with Uni-classifier and Multi-classifier Paradigm. In: IEEE Computer Vision and Pattern Recognition Workshop on Biometrics

47. Singh R, Vatsa M, Noore A (2008) Integrated Multilevel Image Fusion and Match Score Fusion of Visible and Infrared Face Images for Robust Face Recognition. Pattern Recognition Journal of Elsevier Science Inc, New York, USA, Vol. 41 Issue 3

7

Flexible context aware interface for ambient assisted living

James McNaull[2]*, Juan Carlos Augusto[1], Maurice Mulvenna[2] and Paul McCullagh[2]

* Correspondence:
McNaull-J1@email.Ulster.ac.uk
[2]School of Computing and
Mathematics, University of Ulster
Jordanstown, Shore Road,
Newtownabbey, Belfast
Full list of author information is
available at the end of the article

Abstract

A Multi Agent System that provides a (cared for) person, the subject, with assistance and support through an Ambient Assisted Living Flexible Interface (AALFI) during the day while complementing the night time assistance offered by NOCTURNAL with feedback assistance, is presented. It has been tailored to the subject's requirements profile and takes into account factors associated with the time of day; hence it attempts to overcome shortcomings of current Ambient Assisted Living Systems. The subject is provided with feedback that highlights important criteria such as quality of sleep during the night and possible breeches of safety during the day. This may help the subject carry out corrective measures and/or seek further assistance. AALFI provides tailored interaction that is either visual or auditory so that the subject is able to understand the interactions and this process is driven by a Multi-Agent System. User feedback gathered from a relevant user group through a workshop validated the ideas underpinning the research, the Multi-agent system and the adaptable interface.

Keywords: Ambient assisted living; Multi-agent systems; Interface adaption; Human computer interaction; Context aware computing; Multimodal interfaces

Introduction

The increasing older population [1] and current economic climate is resulting in health and social care provisions being stretched and this has provoked recent research into the development of assisted living systems that aim to provide efficient and effective assistance and support to older people in their own home. An Ambient Assisted Living (AAL) solution provides a subject with assistance during the day and feedback assistance based on day and night time activities and events through an **Ambient Assisted Living Flexible Interface (AALFI)**. It provides interventions adapted based on the current time of day, activity, detected events and changes of context in the environment. Feedback derived from past interventions may be beneficial in solving current issues. A Multi-Agent system (MAS) controls AALFI and the interaction method for interventions and feedback is adapted based on the subject's requirements profile. Current solutions known as Ambient Assisted Living Systems (AAL) have three identified shortcomings; **(i)** they normally concentrate on providing day based assistance and support and are not aware of activities and events that occur during the night, examples include a multimodal pervasive framework for ambient assisted living [2] where older people are supported through a multimodal interface and an intelligent home middleware system [3] that assists older people by acquiring, detecting and reasoning changes of context. These and other related projects outlined in Section "Related Research Areas and Projects" provide assistance during the day or in the case of NOCTURNAL [4] during the night. The research being carried out aims to provide a (cared for) person, the subject, with assistance during the day and adapt assistance based on the time of day, contextual changes and event that has occurred. In the future assistance may be adapted according to the older person's behaviour or mood. AALFI is aware of activities and events that occur during the night and is able to provide feedback type assistance the following day. AALFI complements the night time intervention assistance offered by NOCTURNAL with day based interventions, several new night time interventions relating to older person behaviour and feedback assistance based on day and night time events and activities. AALFI and the NOCTURNAL projects were developed in parallel, by related developing teams, and are mutually complementary. **(ii)** The interaction method may be inappropriate for the capability of the user which leads to further confusion and frustration, e.g. the systems may carry out actions that a person may not understand due to illegible text size and inappropriate colours. The wrong assistance may be offered to the older person causing confusion. Related research has investigated GUI layout [5], element placement [6] and font size and style used to convey information can have an effect on a subject's ability to interact with an interface; a study with 50 partially sighted and 100 sighted children found that larger fonts and clearer text are of benefit to partially sighted people [7]. To help alleviate any possible confusion AALFI can be adapted so that text, font or colour can be changed according to a subject's requirements and if a person's sight degrades over time, the interface can be further adapted through a care provider/person interface. Research into GUI content, placement, interface navigation and methods of conveying information have been used during the design of AALFI and planning for future work were further interface adaption may be implemented to include changing the layout of the interface and adapting other attributes. AALFI is currently installed on a 10 inch Windows Tablet PC and can function in a particular location or be moved to a different location by the older person. The approach which the NOCTURNAL project follows is to provide interactions through a static bed side interface. In the futures many Tablet PCs may be installed in key locations and the AALFI interface may be displayed on the interface where the older person is currently located. Auditory interactions may also implemented to allow an older person to interact with an interface through speech and sound [8]. The type of assistance that is offered to the older person is tailored to the limitations imposed by the subject's daily routine, activities and actions are often ignored and suitable feedback strategies have not been properly evaluated. **(iii)** Current state of the art AAL may often only provide intervention type assistance that corresponds to day based activities and not be aware of activities and events that occur during the night; when a subject may exhibit bad behaviours, or carry out activities that they do not remember the following day. AALFI provides intervention type assistance during the day in addition to feedback assistance for recognised events that occur during the day and night so that potential issues with the older persons behaviour may be drawn to their attention.

This article outlines the research ideas (Section "Research Aims"), supporting a subject by means of an adaptive multimodal interface, providing a subject with day and night time assistance, and facilitating interaction through visual and auditory modalities. Section "Related Research Areas and Projects" details the related research topics; Section "The Multi-Agent

System, Interventions and Feedback" highlights related research projects and the perceived limitations with current AAL systems. Section "Adaptable Multimodal Interaction" outlines the MAS architecture, intervention and feedback processes and discusses interventions and feedback strategies. Section "Evaluation and Results" details the multimodal interaction methods while Section "Conclusions" presents the findings from a validation exercise that was completed at Age NI headquarters [1] where participants helped to validate the research ideas, the MAS and associated adaptable multimodal interface. Conclusions regarding the research direction, further development and feedback from the workshop are provided in Acknowledgments.

Research aims

The aim of this work is the development and assessment of AALFI and this section details the three main research ideas, 'Supporting the subject through an adaptive multimodal interface that is driven and updated by a MAS', 'complementing the current support offered by the NOCTURNAL project' and 'providing interaction through visual and auditory modalities'.

Supporting the subject through an adaptive multimodal interface that is driven and updated by a MAS

AALFI provides several forms of assistance and support interactions based on the subject's requirements, detected context, event or action that has occurred. The interface is controlled and updated by a MAS that determines the correct intervention to make or feedback message to issue, the correct method to deploy the intervention or feedback message as either text messages or auditory interactions. A number of agent platforms were considered including JASON [9], JADE [10] and JADEX [11]. JADE offered the best means to develop the MAS; it is a mature technology that has been successfully tested in other AAL systems, including [12,13] and [14]. The JADE agents control the interface, choosing the appropriate content and interaction method for the interventions and feedback. A profile agent was implemented to adapt the interaction method so that either visual or auditory interactions are available to the subject depending on their current requirements profile.

Complement the intervention type night time assistance offered by NOCTURNAL with day time assistance and feedback type assistance

Providing assistance during the night has been successfully demonstrated by the NOCTURNAL project [3]. AALFI complements this night time assistance with intervention assistance during the day, offering several additional interventions during the night and providing feedback assistance to the older person that is based on activities that the older person carried out during the night. The assistance approach offered by AALFI differs from that of NOCTURNALs as AALFI provides assistance through a Tablet device that can be moved from room to room (NOCTURNAL offers assistance through a bed side device), provide feedback assistance in addition to intervention assistance (NOCTURNAL offers intervention type assistance) and supports the older person during the day (NOCTURNAL supports the person during the night). The research presented in this paper mainly concentrates on the day intervention assistance that AALFI offers in relation to common activities and events that may occur in an AAL scenario and on the feedback assistance that is offered in relation to historical interventions, activities and events that have occurred during the day and night.

Interaction through visual and auditory modalities

In order for successful and effective human computer interaction to occur, it is important to consider the user's requirements. Deficits may include sight issues and these can have an effect on how the person views and interacts with the interface. A person may be partially sighted or blind and not able to interact with a visual interface. In this case some form of speech and auditory interaction should be provided to the person so that they are able to carry out simple interactions.

The visual modality provides interactions through button, text and picture based interface. The text on navigation buttons may be altered so that the user can easily navigate and interact with the interface and understand the messages being displayed. The auditory modality includes text to speech interaction and the person is able to interact with a simple VoiceXML[a] speech menu; their speech is recognized by the Sphinx speech recognizer[b] and messages are spoken through the Java based free text to speech synthesizer[c]. With the auditory profile selected, the system listens for a key word before starting the interaction process; upon this trigger the main interaction menu is articulated and the subject is then able to carry out interactions with the interface.

Flexible assistance through a contact aware interface in an AAL environment

ALLFI offers flexible assistance strategies through a context aware interface in an AAL environment. The flexibility is made possible through the use different interaction technologies including touch screen, speech recognition and synthesised speech. The older person is able to choose the interaction technology by setting their individual interaction requirements and therefore personalise their interaction experience and how they receive assistance. These requirements may be updated at any time by the older person or their care provider so that future changing interaction requirements may be accounted for. To achieve interaction flexibility, AALFI is controlled and updated by a MAS that displays context aware attributes; sensor event data from sensors placed in the AAL environment is consumed to determine what has occurred and to choose the appropriate assistance. It is this consumption of sensor data that is key to the correct assistance being offered to the older person. Context awareness is an important and essential characteristic of the MAS. Context awareness in relation to a MAS is illustrated by [15] and MAS systems are shown to exhibit context aware attributes by [16] as they are able to decipher contextual changes that occur in an AAL environment. Without these context aware attributes and characteristics, the correct assistance would not be offered and AALFI would not be able to provide flexible assistance in relation to different situations that occur in the environment ranging from safety issues such as leaving cupboard, fridge, or back doors open to health issues such as not getting enough sleep, reminding a person to consume regular meals and offering advice based assistance at key times during the day.

Related research areas and projects

This section highlights several related research areas: Human Computer Interaction (a Multimodal interface has been implemented to allow a person to interact with AALFI), Context Aware Computing (the agents make use of contextual changes to identify what is occurring in the environment and what activity the person has carried out), Ambient Assisted Living (the research falls under the area of systems to assist people in their daily lives) and Multi-Agent Systems (AALFI is controlled by a Multi-Agent System).

Overview of human computer interaction, context aware computing, ambient assisted living and multi-agent systems

Examples of Human computer interaction (HCI) may include displays that are either mobile or stationary, interactive displays and tangible physical interfaces surfaces, touch screens and auditory interfaces [17]. As well as 'simple human computer interfaces', there may be multimodal interfaces that have several forms of input and interaction [18]. Many, sometimes competing, technical challenges may be faced by the developer and the person that makes use of the interface including ensuring that the interface is always available, extensible, efficient, secure and respects the users privacy [19]. HCI may be supported by visual or auditory interaction modalities. Auditory interactions may be of benefit to blind or partially sighted people that are not able to interact with a visual interface. A survey [8] has been completed by 50 blind and 100 sighted people, to investigate what interactions would be of benefit to a blind person. The survey found that font size, style and text size can have an effect on how a subject interacts with an interface.

Context can be defined as "any information that can be used to characterise the situation of an entity" [20] and can be used to identify activities and events that have occurred in a smart home environment [21]. These context aware systems "provide relevant information and/or services to the user, where relevancy depends on the user's task" [22] and can be recorded by sensors, mobile devices and personal digital assistants [23]. Methods of acquiring context include sensing context, context that is gathered from sensors; deriving context, recording context in real time and explicitly gathering context that is provided by the user of the system [24]. Context may be gathered from different architectural layers including the network layer, middleware layer, application and service layer and user infrastructure layer [25].

AAL systems are said to be able "to prolong the time people can live in a decent way in their own home by increasing their autonomy and self-confidence" [26]. AAL may be able to provide assistance and support with activities of daily living [27] and provide assistance during the night to prevent trips and falls, help with disorientation and may calm a person who wakes up [4]. The types of assistance and support that may be provided include communication support that enables contact with friends, family and care providers [28] and reminiscence activities, "a range of activities and traditional tools aimed at stimulating thoughts, feelings and memories of times gone by" [29].

A Multi-Agent System is built up of several software agents; a software agent is defined as a "computer system that is situated in some environment and that is capable of autonomous action in this environment in order to meet its design objectives" [30]. A Multi-Agent system implements many software agents that interact together and can cooperate or compete to carry out complex tasks by exchanging specially formed messages. In the case of an AAL solution, the MAS may provide interventions through meaningful interactions with a person to aid them with carrying out activities of daily living. Examples of Multi-Agent smart environments are discussed by [31] and current directions for research in this area are Multi-intelligent software agents, tracking multiple residents, profiling multiple residents and multi agent negotiation. The different types of Multi-Agent programming languages that may be used was outlined by [32]. Examples include, declarative languages, that "are partially characterised by their strong formal nature, normally grounded on logic", Imperative languages, "less common, mainly due to the fact that most abstractions related to agent-oriented design are, typically, declarative in nature", Hybrid Approaches were declarative and imperative language features are combined. Examples of MAS research include an agent based model for supporting group emotions [33], an access control agent based security system [34] and an agent-based system for providing automated prompting [35]. The next section outlines related research and details how AALFI and associated MAS overcome shortcomings with the identified AAL systems.

Related research projects

Insufficient work has been devoted to a user's ability to understand the assistance that is being offered. If the subject's requirements change over time, the method for deploying the assistance is often not adapted to these new requirements. In comparison, AALFI can take into account changes in requirements so that the interaction methods may be further adapted. From the related research it is apparent that the primary method for carrying out interactions is visual. In contrast both visual and auditory modalities are provided for by AALFI. The subject may either interact with a visual interface through touch and reading messages or carry out interaction through a speech based interface, where simple commands are issued and simple messages spoken to the subject. The subject may not be supported by current AAL systems during the night when they are more vulnerable. AALFI has been compared to several research projects (Table 1) and a comparison of the similarities and differences follows.

The subject is able to interact with the MAS through AALFI either by means of touch or spoken auditory interaction. Intervention and feedback messages are displayed on the touch screen device or spoken; the method used to put forward the messages is adapted based on the subject's requirements profile. In comparison, the Multi-Modal pervasive framework [2] provides speech based interaction as it interprets commands that the subject speaks and carries out a particular action, the subject is able to write sentences that are recognized, touch an area on a map to get directions or speak words for actions to be carried out by the application. The application does not provide the person with meaningful feedback on the actions that are being carried out and it only provides assistance during the day.

The MAS developed in this work consists of 6 agents (GUI, data, sensor, intervention, profile and feedback). The GUI, intervention and feedback agents provide the MAS with the ability to interact with a subject either by presenting text and images on a touch screen device or speaking messages. In comparison the context framework [3] consists of three main agents for the handling of contextual information, the context collecting agent (CCA), context reasoning agent (CRA) and context management agent (CMA). The outlined context services do not provide a means to carry out user interaction as it is designed to be connected to intelligent devices and appliances and provide contextual data that details how the devices are being used.

A near field communications (NFC) interface [36] that allows a subject to select what they wish to eat during the day makes use of a NFC enabled mobile device and tags to

Table 1 Related research projects

Research	Feedback	Interface adaptation	Night/Day assistance	Interaction modalities
Multimodal pervasive framework for AAL [2]	No	Yes/Limited	Day	Visual
An intelligent home middleware system based on context awareness [3]	No	No	Day	Visual
Touch based user interface for elderly users [36]	No	No	Day	Visual
A multi-agent service framework for context aware elder care [16]	No	No	Day	Visual
Flexible architecture for AAL systems supporting adaptation of multi-model interfaces [37]	No	Yes/Limited	Day	Visual
NOCTURNAL [38]	No	Yes (different interface views)	Night	Visual/Auditory (Music)
Design and evaluation of a smart home voice interface for the elderly: acceptability and objection aspects [39]	No	No	Day	Auditory
Wireless sensor networks and human comfort index [40]	Yes (Subject to System)	No	Day	Visual
PUCK: an automated prompting system for smart environments: toward achieving automated prompting—challenges involved [41]	No	Yes/Limited	Day	Visual/Auditory (prompts to user)
RFID-driven situation awareness on TangiSense, a table interacting with tangible objects [42]	No	Yes (physical adaption of a table)	Day	Visual
AALFI	**Yes**	**Yes**	**Day/Night**	**Visual/Auditory**

recognize choices. This relies on the person correctly placing the mobile device over the desired tag and of course requires that the device will not be misplaced by the person. By comparison AALFI has been implemented on a touch screen device and the subject can carry out simple interactions through the touch screen interface or by speaking simple commands; the subject does not require the use of any other mobile devices.

A near field communications (NFC) interface [36] that allows a subject to select what they wish to eat during the day makes use of a NFC enabled mobile device and tags to recognize choices. This relies on the person correctly placing the mobile device over the desired tag and of course requires that the device will not be misplaced by the person. By comparison AALFI has been implemented on a touch screen device and the subject can carry out simple interactions through the touch screen interface or by speaking simple commands; the subject does not require the use of any other mobile devices.

A near field communications (NFC) interface [36] that allows a subject to select what they wish to eat during the day makes use of a NFC enabled mobile device and tags to recognize choices. This relies on the person correctly placing the mobile device over the desired tag and of course requires that the device will not be misplaced by the person. By comparison AALFI has been implemented on a touch screen device and the subject can carry out simple interactions through the touch screen interface or by speaking simple commands; the subject does not require the use of any other mobile devices.

A near field communications (NFC) interface [36] that allows a subject to select what they wish to eat during the day makes use of a NFC enabled mobile device and tags to recognize choices. This relies on the person correctly placing the mobile device over the desired tag and of course requires that the device will not be misplaced by the person. By comparison AALFI has been implemented on a touch screen device and the subject can carry out simple interactions through the touch screen interface or by speaking simple commands; the subject does not require the use of any other mobile devices.

The architecture of the multi-agent service framework for context-aware elder care (CASIS) [16] consists of device agents that are connected to smart furniture including smart tables, chairs, floors and home control networks. Linking to devices directly may cause issues in the future, if a new piece of furniture is added, a new agent will need to be developed and it is thought that having an agent for each piece of furniture may limit extensibility. In comparison, AALFI is not linked directly to the sensors, furniture or other devices; instead it consumes the generated data from these devices. CASIS uses context-aware information services to remind the person to take medicines and healthcare services that enable "healthcare professionals to get updated and aggregated bio data on the elder's health conditions". Many activities of daily living, support with night time activities and being able to differentiate between day and night activities can be offered by AALFI.

The next research project that has been considered is a Flexible Architecture for Ambient Intelligence Systems [37] that interacts with a subject through a virtual character, which mimics a relative or friend so that they can interact with a friendly face. A virtual character may have several complicating issues, the virtual character needs to be programmed and this may add to development time and the virtual character may require more processing power during interactions due to the rendering process. As highlighted by the authors, the virtual character is non-persistent; AALFI has persistence as key interventions and actions are remembered so that feedback may be presented to the subject. AALFI is touch screen based and provides a simple GUI that has large buttons and text that is of a large font and is clear. By implementing a simple interface, processing overheads may be reduced and the device that the interface runs on may not need to be that powerful.

AALFI makes use of a simple auditory interface to provide a person with access to intervention and feedback messages. The intervention messages detail something that the subject needs to correct, "the back door has been left open for 10 minutes please close the back door, or an action that they should carry out, "it is morning and it is recommended that you have breakfast". In comparison the Sweet-Home project [39] provides an auditory interface that allows the person to issue commands to control a smart home; communicate with the outside and to make use of shared electronic calendar. It was decided to concentrate on only providing simple key auditory interactions to a person to help prevent information overload and to keep auditory interactions simple so that confusion may be avoided. AALFI is similar to Sweet-Home in that both offer intervention type prompts to a person however meaningful feedback is not provided by the Sweet-Home auditory interface.

The Wireless sensor networks and human comfort index system [40] utilises user provided feedback and preferences to control environmental factors such as temperature and lighting. In comparison AALFI uses preferences to control how interactions are carried out through visual and auditory modalities and meaningful feedback is provided to the user that identifies issues with their activities that they themselves may need to correct.

AALFI offers a person simple prompts as intervention messages to suggest the person carries out a corrective action in response to detected events. In comparison PUCK [41] makes use of simple prompts to guide a person to carry out tasks and does not identify issues that may need to be corrected. AALFI is situational and contextually aware as contextual change events are processed, from this intervention messages are issued and feedback is generated.

The interventions and feedback messages are provided to a person through an adaptable interface with either a visual modality (a touch screen) or auditory modality (simple speech based interaction). In comparison the 'RFID-driven situation awareness on TangiSense [42], a table interacting with tangible objects' project makes use of RFID tags and adaptable tables (different functionality may be added and removed from a table) for the primary means of interaction and does not provide interaction through an auditory modality.

The last research project that has been considered is NOCTURNAL [38], a multi-agent system that provides assistance and support to older people during night through a bedside touchscreen interface [43] and does not provide assistance in any other location in the home, AALFI takes a different approach and allows the person to either leave the interface in one particular location or carry it to a different location so that assistance may be offered in key locations including the kitchen, living room, bedroom and WC. Meaningful pictures (Visual interaction) and calming music (Auditory interaction) are provided in response to detected events to help relieve agitation during the night, help to calm the persons and help them stay/return to sleep. AALFI complements the intervention assistance that is offered by the NOCTURNAL project by providing intervention assistance during the day, being aware of night time events and activities and providing feedback assistance that is based on these time periods and offering several additional interventions during the night designed to highlight any negative behaviours such as sitting up during the night in the kitchen or making use of the toilet at night. AALFI takes a different approach to assistance in that it provides text based messages that are designed to help encourage a person to carry out a task or corrective action in response to events that occur during the day and generate feedback during the day and night. Intervention type assistance is offered by NOCTURNAL during the night; AALFI provides intention assistance during the day and is aware of activities and events that occur during the night so that feedback assistance may be offered. Feedback is provided to a subject that details an identified trend from the previous events and corresponding interventions that may help the subject think about the activities and actions they are carrying out and may encourage the person to correct any recurring issues. In comparison, AALFI auditory interactions include speech recognition to recognize simple commands and speech synthesis to deliver messages and visual interactions through the use of textual messages, buttons and pictures. The next section details the Multi-Agent system and the associated Interventions and Feedback.

The multi-agent system, interventions and feedback

A Multi-Agent System was chosen for the implementation of AALFI over a centralized system as it is a more flexible and extendable methodology. The client device does not need to be powerful and may be a bedside touchscreen Tablet PC, for example. Seven agents have been implemented in the MAS and roles are outlined in Table 2. The current implementation of AALFI makes use of a 10 inch Windows 7 Tablet PC (full specification below[d]). The Tablet device was chosen as it fully supports JAVA, JADE and is portable and can be moved from room to room by the older person. In the future AALFI may offer further interface adaption based on the current location of the Tablet device.

Table 2 The multi-agent system agents

Agent	Role	Details
Sensor data agent	The sensor data agent is responsible for consuming and processing the sensor data and generating a sensor data message for the sensor agent	These two agents have been implemented as in the future the sensor data agent may be installed on a separate linked computer so that the data processing does not slow down the rest of the agent platform. This will allow AALFI to handle a greater volume of sensor data while helping to ensure the user experience through the interface is not affected by increased processing requirements.
Sensor agent	The sensor agent receives the sensor event messages and determines the sensor event message that is sent to the context agent.	The sensor agent has been implemented to receive sensor event data messages and determine what sensor event has occurred. This is important as without a properly formed sensor event message, the other agents in the MAS are not able to determine what has occurred and what needs to be carried out.
Context agent	The context agent determines how the context has changed and what has occurred in the environment.	Context that is processed including the time an event occurred, the type of event, how many times the event has occurred and the location of an event. Context is determined based on the sensors in the environment that have been triggered and how these correspond to the activity or event that has occurred.
Intervention agent	The intervention agent chooses the correct intervention for the event or activity that has been detected.	An intervention agent has been implemented for determining the correct intervention that should occur. This can include a textual message based intervention, playing calming music or displaying pictures. The intervention agent handles the intervention side of the assistance strategy; interventions correspond to activities and events that have just occurred.
Feedback agent	The feedback agent determines the appropriate feedback to provide to the person through the interface	The feedback agent is designed to offer the feedback side of the assistance strategy. Feedback is different to intervention assistance as it is formed based on historical activities, events, and offered interventions. For this reason feedback assistance functionally has been kept separate from the intervention functionally.
Graphical User Interface (GUI) agent	The GUI agent is responsible for choosing the correct interface features and functionality	The GUI agent controls and drives AALFI. This agent has been implemented to adapt the interface that the older person interacts with according to the assistance that is chosen and offered.
Profile agent	The profile agent manages and stores the current person interaction requirements profile.	The profile agent enables the people profile requirements to be set and updated. The profile requirements may be set by the administrator of AALFI prior to AALFI being used according to the older person's interaction requirements. The interaction requirements may be updated by the older person or a care provider so that changing requirements may be accounted for.

MAS architecture

Extra agents may be added when new functionally is added to the AAL. Computational resources may be shared amongst several computers over a network and therefore only the agents that control the adaptable interface need to be installed on the client device. The current revision of the MAS architecture is shown by Figure 1. This revision provides assistance through two interaction modalities: (i) a visual interaction modality where the person interacts through a touch screen device with text and pictures (ii) an auditory interaction modality where the subject is able to interact with the interface through speech recognition and the interface interacts with the subject through speech synthesis.

The architecture consists of 5 layers including the (1) Interaction, Communication and sensing layer (ICS) were sensing, control of actuators and devices and interactions occur, (2) the data layer were sensor data is captured from the sensors, agent action data is recorded and contextual data is stored, (iii) the decision and logging layer were the people profile is processed and the actions carried out by the agents is logged, (iv) information layer were relationships between the agents, environment and person are managed and appropriate interventions decided, (v) context layer were contextual changes are detected and managed. Information is exchanged by the agents between layers (6 – 9). The sensor and sensor data agents work together to process sensor event

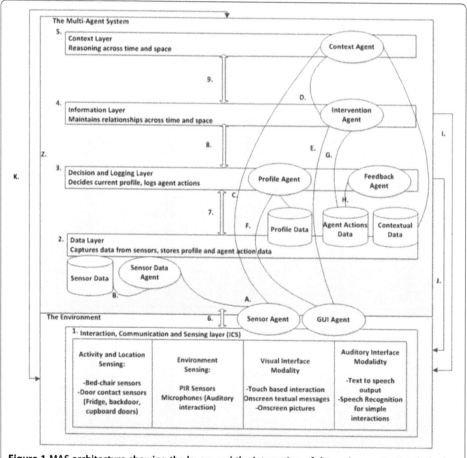

Figure 1 MAS architecture showing the layers and the interaction of the main agents. Details the key layers of the MAS architecture and shows the interactions that occur between the MAS agents.

data (A – B) and this results in a sensor event message being formed that contains the sensor type (PIR, bed-chair or door contact), time (in the format: yyyy-mm-dd hh:mm:ss) it was triggered and the event types (opening, closing and room visited) and the location of the sensor event (including the: bedroom, kitchen, main hall, Livingroom, Foodcupboard door, Fridgedoor...). The sensor event message (C) is sent to the context agent and this agent determines what has changed in the environment, for example if the back door has been opened and for how long it has been opened. The context agent sends a contextual event message is sent to the Intervention agent (D). Once the intervention agent receives this message, it determines the correct intervention to make to the person. This includes issuing a reminder to have meals at certain times of the day, alerting the person that the back door has been left open and during the night. The intervention message (F) is sent to the GUI agent, the appropriate method of putting forward the intervention is selected by the profile agent (F). Once the appropriate intervention has been selected, a record is stored (G) in the agent action data store. When feedback is requested by the person, this agent action data is analysed, patterns detected and appropriate feedback is selected (H). Interventions and feedback are presented to the person in the environment either with visual or auditory interactions (I) and (J). The MAS system is able to adapt the interventions that are provided to the person by tracking what the current contextual change, activity and what intervention has previously been issued. This is achieved by comparing the current event to the previous event throughout the current sensor event processing cycle. If the same event has previously occurred then how many times it has occurred and the time difference between the events is calculated. Events that logically follow each other (for example, door opening and door closing events) are recognised so that the context behind the event may be determined. For example, if the person is alerted that the back door has been opened for 10 minutes and did not close the door, the intervention issued for the door being open for 20 minutes would be different. This information is fed between layers (K) so that the most appropriate intervention is selected. The interface agent has been replaced with a GUI agent that offers more functionally and drives the interface during the multimodal interactions. The MAS consumes data from sensors that are located in the environment and these include bed-chair, door contact and PIR sensors as well as microphones for auditory interaction. The next section outlines the Multi-Agent system (MAS), what interventions and feedback are, and the underlying agent processes involved in forming the intervention and feedback messages.

Flexibility at the architectural level

The agents of the MAS detailed by Figure 1 display flexible characteristics that relate to context awareness and personalisation. Key agents of the MAS include the GUI Agent, Context Agent, Feedback agent and Intervention Agent.

The context agent flexibility relates to the ability to determine what has occurred in the environment and adapt the context message to the detected contextual changes. Without the flexibility to choose the correct contextual message, the MAS would not be able to determine the correct assistance to offer. The interaction methods chosen by the GUI Agent are flexible in that they can be further refined based on the currently selected profile. The profile represents the current older person's interaction requirements and these can be changed at any time to take into account a change of interaction preference or underlying interaction requirements relating to old age. The assistance offered by the

Feedback and Intervention agents are reliant on the underlying flexibility to adapt the assistance centred on what has occurred in the environment based on: the detected changes of context relating to a device, sensor or physical objects change of state such as for example a door being opened or closed; an activity the older person carries out such as being restless in bed (a pressure pad registers movement in the bed), using the WC (the older person enters the WC) or entering a room (the room state is detected to have changed from empty to occupied). During the night only a subset of the available interventions are offered such as for example a reminder to return to bed when the older person enters the kitchen, as previously discussed it is the flexible characteristics that enable a different intervention to be offered at different times during the day. The majority of actions the older person carries out during the night result in feedback assistance being generated and this assistance is only offered during the day. Without this flexibility both feedback and intervention assistance would be provided during the night and this may result in information overload and be detrimental to a good night's sleep.

Sequence of events for an intervention and receiving feedback

This subsection details the sequence of the agent processes for putting forward an intervention to the subject and giving the appropriate feedback, on demand. A sequence diagram (Figure 2) shows these agent processes.

Sensor data is stored in a sensor data repository; the sensor data agent retrieves this sensor data (1) and then sends a sensor data message to the sensor agent (2). Once this message has been received, the sensor agent sends a sensor event message to the context agent. The context agent determines how the context has changed, (3 – 5) and from this a context message is formed and sent to the interventions agent (6). The intervention agent receives this message and determines the appropriate intervention to make. Once an intervention has been determined an intervention message is sent to

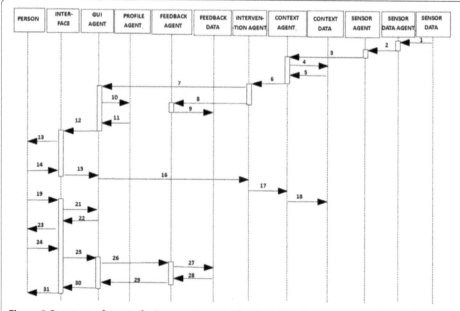

Figure 2 Sequence of events for interventions and feedback. Details the sequence of events for determining interventions and feedback assistance.

the GUI Agent (7) and a record of the intervention is kept by the feedback agent (8 – 9). Once the GUI Agent has received this message, it sends a profile check message to the profile agent (10 – 11), the profile details are then retrieved from the profile data store (not explicitly indicated in the figure). Once the correct profile has been selected, the GUI Agent chooses the appropriate interaction method and interface components to use, the interface is then adapted accordingly (12). The person is then able to interact with the interface (13). For example, the subject is told the back door is open, after a period of time the subject closes the back door and this generates an interface event (14) that is processed by the GUI agent (15). The GUI Agent ksends a message to the intervention agent that details the back door has been closed, resulting in a contextual change occurring (17) and this is recorded (18). If the subject chooses to receive feedback, they interact (19) with the touch screen device (visual interactions) or issue the keyword command 'feedback' (auditory interactions). The GUI agent provides feedback menu options to the person (21 – 22) and the person is then able to navigate through the available feedback using the touch screen device or listen to the feedback listening options. Once a choice has been made (25), the GUI Agent sends a message to the feedback agent to retrieve the feedback (26). The chosen feedback is gathered from the feedback data store (27 – 28) and the feedback message is sent to the GUI Agent (29). Depending on the current profile, the feedback will either be spoken to the person or displayed on the touch screen device screen (30). The person then receives the chosen feedback (31) and by carrying out the feedback activity, the person may be able to identify issues and correct these issues themselves. The following sections detail what an intervention and feedback is.

What is an intervention?

There are two types of interventions designed to help provide assistance and support with a wide range of events that may arise due to activities or actions that the person carries out and are designed to be simple and easy to follow so that the subject may not get confused. The two types of interventions are: (i) message intervention where information is conveyed to the user either through text to speech (Auditory modality) or a textual message displayed on a screen (visual modality) (ii) action intervention, using sound (an alarm, prompt or music) or visual stimulus (a light being turned on, picture and/or textual message being automatically displayed). The modality that is chosen to offer the current intervention is determined based on the older person interaction requirements and these requirements may be formed through carrying out research into the types of interactions that may be offered to an older person in an AAL scenario and are set through an internal 'profile check' process that is carried out before chosen assistance is offered.

The intervention process

The intervention process, detailed by Figure 3, shows the main agents that are responsible for determining the intervention (the Intervention agent), selecting the correct profile (Profile agent) and putting forward the intervention to the person (the Interface agent).

On receiving a contextual event message from the context agent (A), the intervention agent determines the appropriate intervention to make (B). Once this has been carried out, an intervention details message is formed (C) and this is sent to the GUI Agent

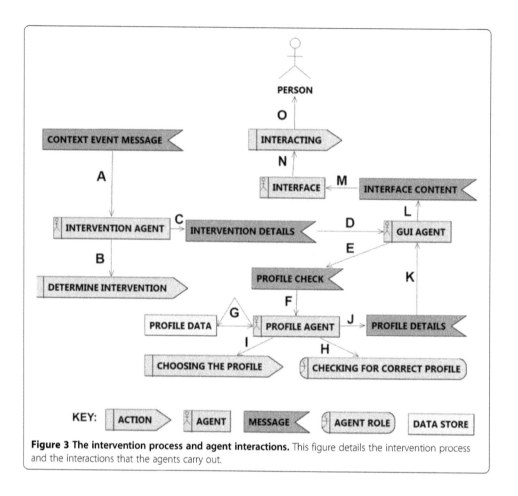

Figure 3 The intervention process and agent interactions. This figure details the intervention process and the interactions that the agents carry out.

(D). The GUI Agent sends a message to the profile agent (E) so that the appropriate interaction method may be chosen to put forward the intervention to the person. The profile agent receiving this message (F) and then retrieves profile data (G) chooses the correct profile (I) and checks the profile is correct (H). A profile message is sent back to the GUI Agent (J). The GUI Agent receives the profile message (K) and decides the appropriate interface content (L). The interface is adapted (M) and interaction can occur between the interface (N) and the person (O). The intervention is put forward to the person in a manner that they can understand as the interface is adapted according to the person's requirements profile. The following section provides details of feedback functionality.

What is feedback?

Feedback is designed to provide a user with a message that outlines a key trend or issue that has been detected from historical interventions that the MAS has carried out. Feedback may have a positive effect on a user's behaviour by outlining when good trends have been detected, for example if a subject has had a restful night's sleep, they will be issued with 'positive feedback'. In contrast, the feedback can draw the subject's attention to a recurring event or action that may need to be corrected; for example, if the person continually leaves the backdoor open.

- Feedback to the subject.

  Feedback is provided to the user when they push the feedback button (visual interaction method) or issue the keyword 'feedback' during auditory interaction. This may reduce information overload by allowing the person to choose when to receive feedback and not be automatically provided it by the MAS. The feedback is offered between the morning and evening. The feedback is not offered at night as it is though that it may disrupt a restful night's sleep.

- Feedback to the care provider/health professional.

  Feedback can also be made available to care provider and health professionals. This feedback would be more detailed and provide an insight into the activities that the person is carrying out and how the MAS is responding with interventions.

  The feedback complements the intervention functionality and may help the user to solve recurring issues themselves.

The feedback process

In order for the correct feedback to be identified and issued, every time an intervention occurs, a record is kept of when the intervention occurred, what the intervention was and how many times the intervention has been issued. Figure 4 shows the agents that are involved in the feedback process and shows how feedback is formed for 'restless sleep'.

When the user is detected to be restless the Sensor agent processes the bed sensor data associated with detecting restlessness (A), a sensor event is then sent to the context agent (B) – (C). When the Context agent has processed the sensor event message

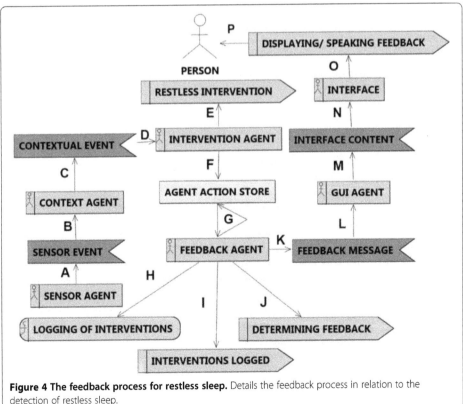

Figure 4 The feedback process for restless sleep. Details the feedback process in relation to the detection of restless sleep.

and determined the changes of context, it sends a contextual event message (D) to the Intervention. The intervention then carries out the appropriate intervention (E). Details of the intervention type, time and how many times it occurred are stored in an agent action data store (F). The Feedback agent retrieves the details of historical interventions. It logs the interventions (H) – (I) and from this log, it determines the appropriate feedback (J). A feedback message is generated (K), in this case the feedback is 'restless feedback' and is sent to the GUI Agent (L). The chosen feedback (M) is sent to the interface agent (N). Based on the current chosen profile, the appropriate interface content is chosen (P) and the interface adapted (O). The user is able to view or listen to the feedback with the interface (P) at any time during the day only, and not during the night.

Multi-agent process for adapting the interface

This sub section details the agent actions (Figure 5) that occur when the interface is adapted to put forward an intervention or feedback message to the older person.

A profile request is made (F) to the profile agent (G). The profile agent can either choose a visual profile (H) or an auditory profile (I) depending on the person's requirements. The chosen profile is sent to the GUI Agent as either (J) (Visual) or (K) (Auditory). These messages then either result in the display of interface content including textual messages, buttons for interaction and pictures (L) or when auditory interaction has been selected (M), speech output (text to speech) and speech recognition (persons issues simple commands). The visual interface features are displayed (N – P) or auditory prompts made (O – Q). The person is then able to interact visually (R) or through speech and sounds (S).

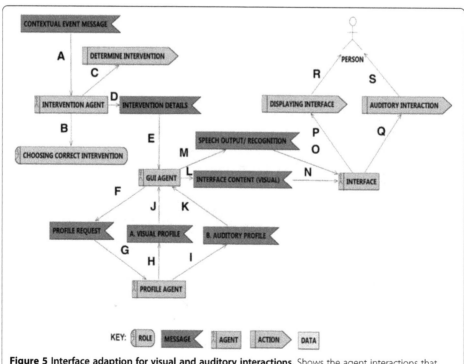

Figure 5 Interface adaption for visual and auditory interactions. Shows the agent interactions that occur for choosing appropriate visual and auditory interactions.

Adaption process explanation

The intervention agent receives a contextual event message (A) and from this it chooses the correct intervention (B) and determines the intervention to put forward to the person (C). The intervention details (D) are sent to the GUI Agent (E).

The next section details the adaptable multimodal interaction that may occur between AALFI and the older person.

Adaptable multimodal interaction

During the research phase of the project various interaction requirements were considered including those relating to visual interactions (sight, readability, navigation, control) and auditory (speech, issues relating to speech and language, effects conditions such as those which relate to a stroke) may affect the older persons ability to interact with the interface. It was decided to concentrate on specific requirements for a selection of possible users so that the prototype system could be implemented, demonstrated and evaluated. In the future further work may be carried out so that interaction issues that relate to a person's speech, other visual conditions and mobility may be accounted for and appropriate interactions offered and the layout of the GUI and GUI content may be further adapted by either the older person or care provider.

The visual interactions focus on those relating to putting forward the assistance to the person (including and not limited to the visual attributes of the interface including text size, pictures, font, size of interface...). Issues relating to navigation such as placement of buttons on the screen, size of buttons, position of interface elements and the difficulties that an older person may have with interacting with a computer interface have been considered and had an effect on the choice of device for AALFI, the design of the interface and the interaction functionality that is currently offered and may be offered in the future.

The adaption attribute is considered to be important for understanding the interventions and feedback. A user needs to be able to read and navigate the interface (visual interaction) or carry out speech based interaction and understand the messages that are being spoken (auditory interaction). The adaptable Multimodal interface that has been implemented is detailed by Figure 6 which shows 3 of the current adaptions that occur (A. small text, B. a transcript of auditory interactions and C. Large text).

In the future how the person is feeling may be used to further adapt how the interface is adapted and how interventions and feedback is offered to the older person. Biometric sensors may be used to measure the person's heart rate, moisture on the skin (sweat) and vocal stress (auditory interactions) to facilitate adaption according to how the person is feeling. The following sub section outlines the visual interaction that occurs.

Visual interaction

There are three forms of visual interaction; viewing intervention messages, viewing feedback messages and associated pictograms and viewing pictures that can be adapted based on the time of day. The types of interaction the user can make during visual interaction include navigating between the intervention, feedback and pictures functionality and alternating between the intervention/feedback messages and pictures. The user may further tailor the main interface (e.g., text size, buttons size) to their own

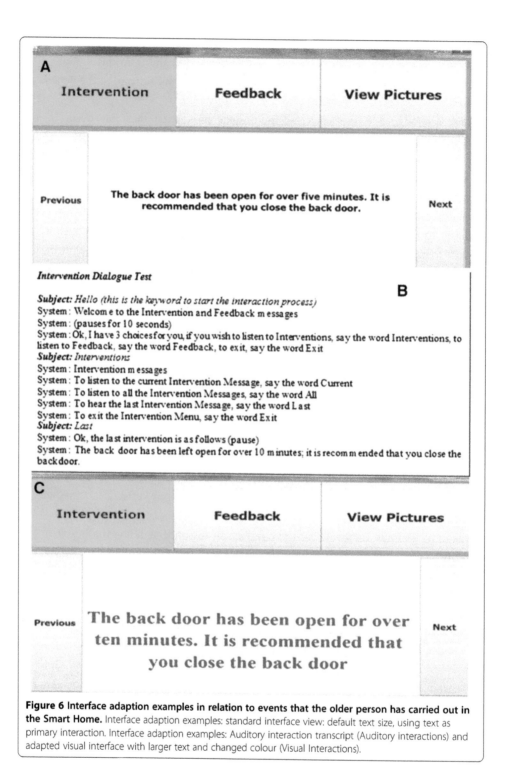

Figure 6 Interface adaption examples in relation to events that the older person has carried out in the Smart Home. Interface adaption examples: standard interface view: default text size, using text as primary interaction. Interface adaption examples: Auditory interaction transcript (Auditory interactions) and adapted visual interface with larger text and changed colour (Visual Interactions).

requirements and messages can be adapted so that the person is to navigate the interface and understand any feedback and intervention messages that are displayed.

Auditory interaction

When a profile has been set to auditory interaction, speech recognition is used to listen for a key word so that interaction can occur and simple commands be issued by the person, text to speech is used to output the relevant messages and menu options. The technologies used for the VoiceXML auditory interaction are detailed by Figure 7.

The VoiceXML menu that has been implemented provides simple voice based interactions. This comprises of: (i) Waiting Loop, the interface listens for a key word to be issued so that interaction may occur. Once the keyword has been issued, the person is welcomed to the voice menu and told what interactions that they can carry out. (ii) Main menu choices, the choices are: Listen to the feedback messages, listen to the intervention messages or exit the menu. (iii) Feedback menu, if the user has chosen to listen to feedback, they are asked if they wish to listen to the current feedback message, the last feedback message or listen to all the feedback messages. The user is also able to exit the feedback menu and return to the main menu (iv). Intervention menu, when the user has chosen to listen to interventions, they are able to listen to all the interventions, the current intervention, last intervention or exit to the main menu. (v) Exiting, if the user has chosen to exit the main menu, they are first asked if they wish to leave, on answering 'yes' the interaction interface is returned to the 'waiting loop'. If the person says 'no', the menu choices for the current menu are spoken to the person. In the past VoiceXML has primarily been used for banking and call centre interfaces and VoiceXML has undergone several revisions that have added to and improved functionary. The current implementation is designed to help validate the idea of having an auditory interaction modality as it currently does not leverage all the features of VoiceXML, however it provides a stepping stone for a future more advanced implementation that may offer different voices and be able to understand more words and phrases. The following sub sections outline sample dialogue between the interface (System) and the person (Subject) that occurs during auditory interaction.

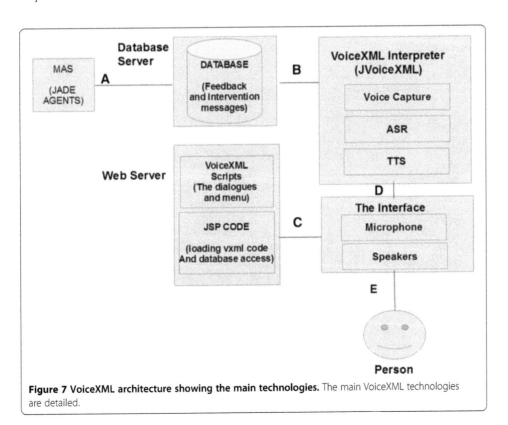

Figure 7 VoiceXML architecture showing the main technologies. The main VoiceXML technologies are detailed.

Interacting with care givers and health professionals

As previously outlined the interface is designed for the primary user, the older person. It was decided that a separate interface should be implemented to allow for the care providers, health professionals and older people to carry out simple changes to the interface adaption profile and the interface is shown by Figure 8.

The functionality that is offered includes changing the primary interaction profile, customizing the visual profile settings and adjusting the speed of the voice and further details are provided below.

- Change the primary interaction profile: There is a choice between visual, the GUI is displayed on a screen, buttons are displayed to allow navigation and textual messages and pictures are displayed and auditory, interactions occur through speech recognition (user to MAS Interface) and text to speech (MAS to user).
- Alter the visual profile settings: The text size of buttons, messages and other visual prompts may be changed so that the older person can read the messages and carry out effective navigation.
- Adapt the auditory settings (Figure 9): The speed of the computer generated voice may be altered to make it easier for the older person to understand what is being said. In the future the Voice may be changed from Male to Female depending on the person's preference and the sensitivity of speech recognition may be adjusted.

If an older person's requirements change over time, the interface adaption profile can be changed so that the person can continue to carry out and understand interactions. The next section details the three evaluations that were carried out to validate the underlying ideas, MAS and the Ambient Assisted Living Flexible Interface (AALFI).

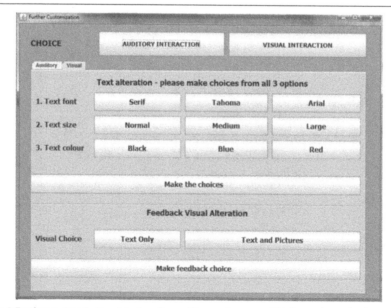

Figure 8 Further customization Interface for profile requirements. This figure shows the further customization interface.

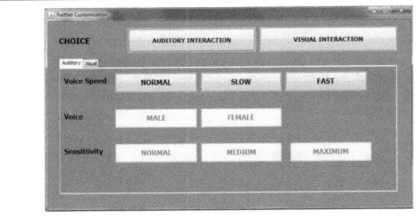

Figure 9 Spoken dialogue customization. Details the spoken dialogue customization.

Evaluation and results

Three evaluation exercises have been carried out including two with colleagues (outside the research team) to test the initial functionality and features and the third that took place at Age NI headquarters were the interface and ideas were evaluated during a workshop by potential stake holders. A scenario 'Meet Bob' was used to shape the research carried and the scenario is based on the real world sensor data that was processed during the evaluations. Details of the interventions and feedback messages are provided and there is a brief discussion on the utilised technology. The two evaluations conducted with colleagues are detailed and these first evaluations proved to be positive and laid the groundwork for the last evaluation that was conducted at the workshop. A final evaluation (Evaluation 4) was conducted across two workshop sessions and was attended by older people. This evaluation contributed to the validation of the interactions methods, the perceived flexibility of AALFI and the underlying MAS system and the current assistance strategies for assisting an older person in their own home.

The evaluation scenario

The scenario detailed below 'Meet Bob' was formed by analysing sensor data (Extract provided by Figure 10) gathered from a smart home during the course of several days.

"Location"	"SensorType"	"EventType"	"Datetime"
masterbedroom	bed-chair	out	2010-05-10 00:29:12
hall	pir	roomvisited	2010-05-10 00:29:16
downstairswc	pir	roomvisited	2010-05-10 00:29:32
hall	pir	roomvisited	2010-05-10 00:29:54
mainkitchen	pir	roomvisited	2010-05-10 00:30:00
mainkitchen	pir	roomvisited	2010-05-10 00:33:01
hall	pir	roomvisited	2010-05-10 00:33:13
downstairswc	pir	roomvisited	2010-05-10 00:33:21
downstairswc	pir	roomvisited	2010-05-10 00:34:58
hall	pir	roomvisited	2010-05-10 00:35:10
livingroom	pir	roomvisited	2010-05-10 00:35:17
masterbedroom	bed-chair	in	2010-05-10 00:35:39

Figure 10 Data extract for providing feedback for night time events (complementing the intervention type assistance offered by NOCTURNAL).

The Smart Home was single occupancy and the older person did not have any pets or visitors. The sensor data is consumed by the agents of the AALFI prototype so that it is possible to simulate a Smart Home scenario and observe the agents to see if they function as expected and provide the correct assistance and interface adaptions.

The resulting feedback for the sensor data extract (Figure 11) highlights the detected issue (using the WC several times during the night and offers a solution (not drinking before bed).

The sensor data extracts were used to build the scenario for the fictional older person 'Bob'. For each of the issues that Bob faces, there is corresponding sensor data from the Smart Home.

Scenario: "meet Bob"

A scenario is considered for the evaluations of AALFI were the daily and nightly activities of a fictional older person named Bob are detailed and issues that may be encountered are outlined. The scenario has four key parts: (1) the person, their circumstances and issues; (2) the environment; (3) Issues Day, provide an insight into the typical day of an older person; (4) Issues Night, offers an insight into the issues an older person may face during the night.

*(1) **The Person:** A fictional older person named **Bob** lives alone. He has several close friends and a son who visits several times a month. **Bob** is a keen baker and has an interest in history and genealogy. **Bob** has mild memory issues and has difficulty reading small text and therefore wears glasses. (2) **The Environment: Bob's** home, a single story dwelling has been fitted with several types of sensors including door contact sensors that are attached to the back, cupboard and fridge doors and these generate door opening and closing events. PIR sensors are located in the hall, kitchen, living room, WC, master and guest bedrooms and these generate 'room visited events'. Bed-chair pressure sensors have been placed in **Bob's** bed, generating bed-chair in and out events. These sensors are used together to detect changes of context in the environment. Touch screen interfaces are located in the kitchen and beside the bed in the living room and each touch screen has a microphone and speakers. (3) **Issues (DAY):** Due to several health issues **Bob** sleeps in a bed in the living room and does not sleep in the Master bedroom and on occasion **Bob** will have trouble waking and*

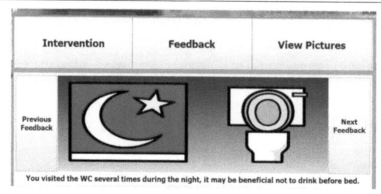

Figure 11 Feedback for WC use during the night.

*may spend most of the day in bed. During the course of a typical day, **Bob** may forget to close the back door and this can sometimes result in security issues occurring as in the past a stray dog has wandered in and made a mess of the kitchen. On occasion he will open fridge and cupboard doors and forget to close them, resulting in several food items spoiling and an increase in energy use. When **Bob** visits the downstairs WC, he sometimes forgets to flush the WC and wash his hands. **Bob** likes to keep in contact with his primary care contact on a Monday, Wednesday and Saturday so that they can arrange any activities and outline any issues that he is having. **Bob** may forget to eat regular meals during the day and this has led to increased weight loss. (4) **Issues (NIGHT) Bob** often goes to bed at 10:00 pm and during the night he usually has several restless periods were he moves about a lot in the bed. In the early hours of the morning he may sit up in bed and feel disorientated and distressed. If **Bob** gets up and leaves the bed, he will go to the kitchen. While **Bob** is in the kitchen he will sit for a long period of time and drink cups of tea. When **Bob** eventually returns to the bedroom and goes back to bed he will often awake again after a short period of time and have to get out of bed and go to the downstairs WC.*

Scenario: discussion

The target user of AALFI is an older person with mild cognitive issues such as forgetfulness and who is either short or long sighted. The 'issues (Night)' part of the scenario deals with the night time period and the activities that the person may require assistance with. Sensor data for the night time period has been analysed and common issues that older people may face during the night have been researched and this helps to determine the feedback that is offered the following day to highlight issues that occurred during the night. The 'issues (Day)' part of the scenario is designed to emulate a typical day that a person may have and show the types of activities that they can be supported; reminders to consume regular meals at set times during the day, identifying potential security and safety issues and reminding the person to carry out particular tasks.

Scenario: hardware and technology

AALFI and the associated MAS were installed on a 10 inch Touch Screen computer with speakers attached so that voice prompts could be heard over the background noise of the testing environment. During the introductory and background phases of the evaluation at the workshop, slides were presented using a projector. While workshop questionnaire 2 was completed, a live demo was carried out were the tablet was connected to the projector and the interface projected onto the screen. A microphone was used during the auditory modality demo and speakers were used to help the participants hear the auditory output. The speakers and microphone were required due to technical limitations with the Tablet hardware.

Scenario: intervention and feedback details

This section details the intervention (Table 3) and feedback (Table 4) messages that were utilised during the three evaluations.

The outlined intervention and feedback message triggers correspond to the real world sensor event data that was processed during the evaluation. The feedback detailed

Table 3 Intervention details

Trigger	Intervention	Details	Justification	Time period
A main door being opened (back or front)	Security Intervention	Warn person door is open, tell the person that the door is closed	The person may be living alone and may forget to close a door which may present a security risk	Day
	Time Intervention	Track the time the door is open to detect possible emergencies or forgetfulness	If the person leaves the door open for a long period of time, it may be due to them forgetting to close it or there could be an emergency	Day
Movement being detected in the living room Interventions	Living room interventions	Interventions which are tailored to tasks carried out in the living room. For example, watching TV, reading books and contacting friends and family	These living room interventions are tailored for day time tasks as the person s bed is located in the living room. Different Interventions are offered at night.	Day
Movement detected in the hall	Destination Intervention	Interventions that are designed to guide the person to a particular destination. For example, kitchen, WC or living room.	To guide the person to a destination during the day.	Day
Subject detected to be in the kitchen during the night (complements assistance offered by NOCTURNAL)	Reminder Interventions	This intervention is designed to remind the person that they should be asleep and that it is beneficial to return to bed.	Sitting up for long periods during the night in the kitchen may cause tiredness and this may have an effect on the person's daily routine and in extreme cases may lead to health issues.	Night

Table 4 Feedback message details

Trigger	Feedback	Details	Justification
Person detected to be restless several times during the night	You were detected to be restless last night and may not have got enough sleep	This feedback message is designed to draw the person's attention to their restlessness that occurred during the previous night.	Restlessness may lead to a lack of good quality sleep and this may have an adverse effect on the person both with their health and their daily routines.
Person leaving the back door open many times during a day	The backdoor has been left open several times, please remember that this may pose a security risk. During the winter, this feedback message will include a message regarding increased heating costs.	A security warning feedback message may help identify potential issues that may lead to the person being put at risk.	People who live alone may face an increased risk of burglaries and leaving the back and front door open for long periods of time may lead to these occurring. During the winter, heat may be lost through an open door and this can lead to increased heating Bobs.
Going in and out of the kitchen during the morning	As you have been in the kitchen several time this morning, please remember to have breakfast.	This feedback may encourage the person to consume breakfast is they have not done so when they view this feedback.	It may be important for a person to consume regular meals at the correct time. Therefore, during the morning if the person has been in and out of the kitchen several times, they will be given feedback that is designed to encourage the person to eat breakfast.
Leaving the fridge door open may times within a set time period	Leaving the fridge door open may increase energy use and lead to food spoiling.	This type of feedback is designed to encourage the person to ensure that they close the fridge door	Fridges may use a lot of energy and if the door is left open for long periods of time, this energy may increase.

(Table 4) complements the intervention assistance that NOCTURNAL provides with feedback assistance to help reinforce the issues that have been detected and encourage the older person to think about solutions that they may implement to overcome the issues.

AALFI contributing to the concept of flexibility

AALFI contributes to the concept of flexibility by offering (i) interaction strategies that can be tailored to an individual's preference, (ii) offering two types of assistance, (iii) the option to further adapt the interaction techniques to changing requirements and preferences, (iv) in the future, allowing others to access the assistance, (v) possibility of offering assistance to other groups of persons, (vi) adapting the assistance offered based on the time of day.

(i) A key concept of flexibility is tailoring the interaction method to an individual's specific requirements. AALFI allows for these preferences to be set up so that a person can choose between carrying out visual interactions (through the touch screen and reading assistance messages from the screen) or make use of auditory interactions (speaking to AALFI and listening to assistance messages). VoiceXML technologies are utilised which have previously only been used in call centre type applications. The auditory interactions mirror the visual interactions that an older person may carry out and allow them to receive the available assistance.

(ii) The assistance strategy is flexible, two types of assistance strategy are offered, intervention assistance for issues that require immediate attention and feedback assistance that details historical issues. The method of portraying the assistance is tailored to the message being put forward in that intervention assistance makes use of clear readable text based messages. For feedback assistance, a combination of text and pictures is used as the picture is thought to help encourage thought and reinforces the text portion of the message.

(iii) AALFI contributes to flexibility by allowing the interaction techniques to be further adapted based on the older persons changes of preferences as they at any time may choose to change from receiving visual interaction to auditory interaction; they are able to choose to receive both visual and auditory interactions at the same time or to choose only one type of interaction method. As an older person ages, their interaction requirements may change over time, AALFI allows for the older person requirements to be further adapted to take into account these changes so that they may continue to receive assistance. Who carries out these changes is also flexible as either the older person or primary care provider may make these changes at any time.

(iv) A feature that is being investigated as future work is to add flexibility to who can access AALFI. Currently only the older person has access to the assistance that is offered by AALFI. In the future a care provider, family member, friend or health professional may be given access to a tailored version of the assistance messages so that they are able to see how the older person is doing with regards to their health and wellbeing. AALFIs interfaces are designed in such a way that this will be relatively straightforward and the choice of JADE as the underlying MAS architecture allows for access to the assistance messages over a network and the wider internet. Interaction restrictions can be added so that only authorised users have access to the assistance messages and the level of detail contained in the message can be tailored to the person who is accessing them.

(v) Currently AALFI offers assistance to older people in their own home, however the underlying architecture is flexible as the assistance may be adapted so that non-older people such as children or persons with disabilities may receive assistance. This may be achieved by ensuring the sensor data that is consumed in a pre-set format. The interaction methods may then be adapted for these other groups of people.

(vi) The last way in which AALFI contributes to flexibility is that the assistance that is offered throughout the day is adapted to the current time of day, the situation and the message that needs to be forward to the person. For example, throughout the day the older person is given meal reminders on entering the kitchen, breakfast in the morning, lunch in the afternoon and dinner in the evening. However at night when the older person enters the kitchen, they are reminded of the importance of sleep and a suggestion is made that they return to bed. This flexibility ensures the assistance being offered is relevant to the current situation and that it has the desired effect on the older person's activities and behaviour.

Validation of perceived flexibility

AALFI has been demonstrated to 18 people, the first workshop was attended by health professionals, older person's and care providers, the second and third workshops were attended exclusively by older people. The participants were able to understand the assistance that was offered during the demonstrations and felt that the personalisation options were adequate for different older people. It is this heterogeneity of potential users being able to provide detailed feedback on the flexible features that has helped to validate the perceived flexibility of AALFI. The older people were also able to see how AALFI could be applied to different situations such as helping non older people. Full details of the workshops are presented in the results Section "Evaluation 1 and 2 details" below.

Evaluation 1 and 2 details

The first two evaluations were designed to validate the features and functionality of AALFI and the underlying MAS before carrying out validation with potential stake holders. This initial validation was considered to be important as it allowed for any underlying issues to be detected and solved. The participants consisted of 7 colleagues (outside the research team) from different research backgrounds and each had different experience and knowledge of computer interfaces, multi-agent systems and older person issues. By validating AALFI with participants from a broad range experiences, issues with features, functionally and ideas could be detected by participants who may not be an expert in a particular related research area. Each participant was allocated a 15 – 20 minute time slot and asked to complete a questionnaire to validate the usability of several key areas. These first two evaluation iterations conducted with colleagues were designed to help find any issues with the assistance being chosen in relation to scenario activities and events that are recognised from the corresponding sensor data and to discover any possible usability issues before carrying out evaluations with potential stake holders during the main evaluation conducted at the AGE NI workshop.

During the validation exercise participants were asked to view two demo videos that were recorded of AALFI consuming sensor data and offering intervention and feedback assistance in relation to the scenarios; the first related to the day part of the scenario and the second to the night part of the scenario and looking at the feedback that would be provided to an older person the following day. The video showed the interface interactions for four tasks: (1) View and navigate intervention messages, (2) View and navigate feedback messages, (3) Navigation of pictures and photos and (4) listening to calming music. After the videos had finished the participants were asked to complete the questionnaire to assess the usability of the interface for the following five areas: (1) Features and Functionality: Five questions were asked designed to measure the usability of the features and functionality of the interface in relation to reaching user goals, supporting the interface workflow, carry out frequently used tasks, level of required expertise to carry out tasks and how easy it is to use buttons; (2) Main Person Interface: Three questions were asked to determine the usability of the main interface and assessed the clearness of the interface layout and the effectiveness of directing the user to particular tasks; (3) Navigation: The participants were asked nine questions to assess the usability of the interface in relation to navigation, including how easy it to access and navigate the interface, the structure of the interface, clarity of buttons and any displayed text, whether the interface structure was clear and how easy it is to navigate the various parts of the interface; (4) Context and Text: This section of the questionnaire asked four questions dealing with the content of the interface and the text that is displayed. It accessed how appropriate text is, the terminology and language used, terms and the content of text. (5) Performance: The last three questions assessed the performance of the interface and concentrated on how the interface performed in relation to pauses, errors and readability issues and the configuration of the interface.

During the questionnaire phase of the validation exercise the participants were able to ask questions relating to the interface and functionally and see a live demonstration of particular interface functions. Once the questionnaire had been completed the interface was awarded an overall usability score of either very poor (less than 29), poor (between 29 and 49), moderate (between 49 and 69), good (between 69 and 89) and Excellent (more than 89). These usability scores are extracted from the chosen UX Design template [44] which was adapted for use in Evaluations one and two. The template was chosen as it was found to be effective for evaluating AALFI and it provided clear guidelines and a method to automatically calculate metrics relating to the usability.

Results: evaluation 1 and evaluation 2
This section details the results for Evaluation one Table 5 and (Figure 12) shows the total usability score given by each participant after the results for each question were checked and collated.

Results discussion
The results for the first evaluation were positive with a 'good usability' level being reached. Issues that were identified during the evaluation include the loudness of auditory music interaction and this highlights underlying issue with Tablet technology and the built in speakers. Text for the intervention messages was not centred and scroll

Table 5 Results from evaluation one and two

Question group	Group 1/Max rating (25)	Group 2/Max rating (15)	Group 3/Max rating (45)	Group 4/Max rating (15)	Group 5/Max rating (20)	Usability rating/Max overall rating (120)
Question group	25	15	45	15	20	120
Participant 1	22	13	37	12	18	102
Participant 2	20	12	33	10	11	86
Participant 3	25	15	41	15	19	115
Participant 4	25	15	44	14	19	117
Participant 5	24	15	37	14	15	105
Participant 6	22	13	42	15	18	110
Participant 7	21	12	34	13	16	96
Average usability rating for each question group	23	14	38	13	17	104
Usability rating (%)	92	93	84	87	85	87
Usability score						Good

bars had to be used and it was suggested that an older person may have difficulty scrolling the text. As a result of the evaluation the text size for all visual profiles was increased and the layout was improved so that textual messages could be displayed without a need for scroll bars. The Tablet was augmented with external speakers and a microphone so that AALFI and the MAS could be evaluated without being impacted by the Tablet computers technical limitations. The results are thought to be positive as the issues that were identified with text, message scrolling and layout were fixed and these improvements had not introduced any new usability issues. It was planned for this evaluation to fully test the expansion of the auditory modality that would allow for simple commands to be spoken to the interface and intervention and feedback messages to be read out to the person. However there were issues with the speech recognition and the microphone at the time of the evaluation and therefore this was not tested. These issues provided an opportunity to go back to the underlying code and identify ways to improve the speech recognition.

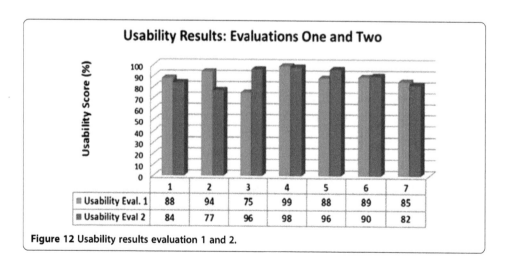

Figure 12 Usability results evaluation 1 and 2.

Evaluation and results: evaluation 3

The aim of the third evaluation were to evaluate all features and functionally of AALFI including the visual and auditory interaction modalities, providing a person with intervention and feedback messages, carrying out navigation of the interface and assessing potential stakeholders views on key ideas and issues. The evaluation was carried out during the day time period so that the day intervention and feedback assistance could be evaluated by the potential stake holders. During the live demo of AALFI, data sets from the scenarios were used to simulate the intervention and feedback assistance that would be offered and to show the interface adaptions that would occur. Feedback that is based on night time events was presented as the scenario data utilised during the live demo of AALFI included night time events and activities that were carried out by an older person.

Participant details and method for evaluation 3

During the course of the evaluation the participants were asked to complete two questionnaires, the first dealt with the underlying ideas behind the research and on their views on subject's related subjects. The second questionnaire was completed during a live demo of AALFI were the usability of the visual and auditory modalities were assessed. There were 11 participants at the workshop from a wide range of backgrounds including older people, health professionals, carers and subjects with Dementia (The results from the subjects with Dementia are not used as they were not expected and relevant approval was not in place; results from 9 participants are included in the evaluation).

Questionnaire 1: demographic details, thoughts on the research ideas and assistive technologies The participants were asked to complete a questionnaire to gather demographic information and assess their views on the research area and ideas. The demographic information included 3 pieces of information: (i) the participants age, this may be useful for determining if the participant falls within the target user group, (ii) gender, different genders may respond differently to visual and auditory interactions and may have different views on assistive technology, (iii) with whom the participant lives with, may be helpful for identifying future development opportunities such as multiple user occupancy. To help keep the evaluation process anonymous, the participants were not asked for their name, occupation or any other personally identifiable information. The participants were asked a number of questions to assess their views on 'assisted living' and their general attitude towards assisted technology. An area of assistance that has been considered is reminders to carry out activities and actions in response to detected events and changes of context. The participants were asked a number of questions to determine how forgetful they are during the day (to help assess the value of reminder based assistance) and how complex the feedback messages should be for visual and auditory interactions as the complexity may be important to ensure the subject is able understand the messages that are being conveyed. The last set of questions dealt with night time to help determine how the participants sleep and to gage the complexity of messages offered during this period of time. The live demo of AALFI was conducted in two parts to showcase the different interaction modalities and details follow.

Questionnaire 2: visual modality During the demo of the Visual Modality the participants were shown the interactions that occur for the intervention functionality (Figure 13); interventions messages were displayed and messages navigated by pressing the next and previous buttons. In total five messages were shown to the participants and each message corresponded to a detected event from the data.

Next the participants were shown the feedback functionality that includes a picture and text to represent the feedback that is being offered (Figure 14). Four feedback messages were shown to the participants and they were asked how useful they found feedback and to identity any usability issues. Once the feedback demonstration had been completed the participants were asked to listen to the auditory modality functionality demonstration were simple commands were issued to the interface and corresponding feedback and intervention message spoken by the interface.

Questionnaire 2: auditory modality The auditory evaluation was divided into two parts, the first dealt with the auditory interaction for interventions and the second with the auditory interaction for feedback. Simple commands were issued to AALFI to show participants how to initiate the interaction process and hear the intervention and feedback responses.

The demonstration was designed to emulate the functionally that is offered by the visual modality. The key words that were spoken to initiate an interaction include 'Hello' (to wake the interface from the 'waiting loop state'), 'Intervention' to load the intervention menu, 'Feedback', to listen to the feedback menu, 'Current' to listen to the current intervention of feedback menu, All to hear all feedback and intervention messages, 'Last' to listen to the last feedback and intervention message and 'Exit', depending on the current menu, this either exits to the first menu or returns AALFI to the waiting state.

This section provided an insight into the demonstration that was carried out during the workshop and details of the results for Questionnaire 1 and 2 follow.

Evaluation 3 results: Questionnaire 1

The results (Table 6) are interesting as it is apparent that older people may not be resistant to assistive technologies if they are useful and there is a clear benefit to the person.

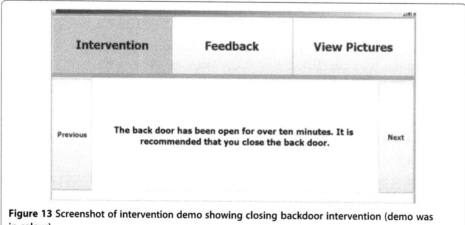

Figure 13 Screenshot of intervention demo showing closing backdoor intervention (demo was in colour).

Figure 14 Screenshot of the feedback part of the demo showing meal reminder (demo was in colour).

Support during the night may be beneficial as half the participants sleep quite badly, a quarter sleeps quite well and all the participants would make use of either visual or auditory interactions during the night. The offered feedback assistance can outline these issues with sleep and this may help an older person to think about why issues with sleep are occurring. This supports the current research idea to provide assistance during the day and provide feedback assistance based on night time events and activities. AALFI complements the research carried out by the successful completion of the NOCTURNAL project [38] were night time assistance was provided to subjects with dementia. The difficulties that an

Table 6 Questionnaire 1 results overview

Question details	Questionnaire one results			
1. Views on assistive technology.	(8/8) 100% would make use of assistive technology.			
2. When an assistive device would be used.	(0/8) 0% only use during the day	(1/8) 12.5% only use during night	(6/8) 75% would use during night and day	(1/8) 12.5% undecided
3. How forgetful the participants are.	(4/8) 50% are rarely forgetful.	(3/8) 37.5% are sometimes forgetful	(1/8) 12.5% are often forgetful.	
4. Determine views on complexity of visual interactions (Day).	(5/8) 62.5% favour basic visual interactions.	(3/8) 37.5% favour complex visual interactions.	(0/8) 0% would not use visual interactions.	
5. Participants views on auditory interactions (Day).	(3/8) 37.5% favour basic auditory interactions.	(3/8) 37.5% favour complex auditory interactions.	(2/8) 25% would not use auditory interactions.	
6. How the person sleeps during the night.	(0/8) 0% sleep very badly.	(3/8) 37.5% sleep quite badly.	(3/8) 37.5% sleep quite well.	(2/8) 25% sleep very well.
7. Complexity of night time visual interactions	(4/8) 50% favour basic visual interactions.	(3/8) 37.5% favour complex visual interactions	(1/8) 12.5% would not use visual interactions.	
8. Complexity of night time auditory interactions	(5/8) 62.5% favour basic auditory interactions.	(3/8) 37.5% favour complex auditory interactions.	(0/8) 0% would not use auditory interactions.	

older person may face during the night and the importance of night time events and activities are further discussed in [45] were they review research relating to night time assistance for an older person with dementia and the types of assistance that they may require including guidance to different locations using lights, playing calming music to assist with restlessness and determining why an older person may be awake. The majority of participants favour basic interactions during the day and night (Figure 15) and this result supports the idea to keep interactions simple

An idea that underpins the visual interactions that occur is to keep them as simple as possible so that an older person is able to understand the intervention and feedback messages that are being put forward to them.

In contrast to the complexity of visual interactions, the participants would favour basic auditory interactions during the night and complex auditory interactions during the day. This result is interesting as it shows that the auditory interactions during the day could be made more complex to allow for more features and functionality to be added. It was originally thought that carrying out auditory interactions during the night may cause an older person distress; however from this sample of results it is clear that this may not be the case and that auditory intervention during the night may be of benefit to an older person that is not able to carry out visual interactions. The results from this questionnaire were useful for finding out about potential stakeholders and the issues that they may face and how they view the complexity of interactions and the next section details the results for questionnaire 2.

Evaluation 3 results: Questionnaire 2

The results for questionnaire 2 are detailed by Table 7 and a majority of the participants thought the idea of making use of adaptable interfaces was very good and none thought it was quite or very poor.

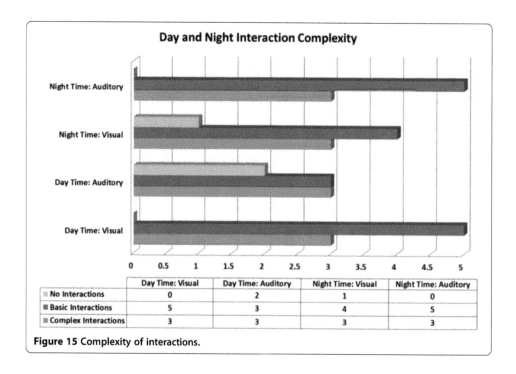

	Day Time: Visual	Day Time: Auditory	Night Time: Visual	Night Time: Auditory
No Interactions	0	2	1	0
Basic Interactions	5	3	4	5
Complex Interactions	3	3	3	3

Figure 15 Complexity of interactions.

Table 7 Questionnaire 2 results

Description	Results			
1. Views on the idea of an adaptive interface.	**(0/8) 0%** very poor	**(0/8) 0%** quite poor	**(3/8) 37.5%** quite good	**(5/8) 62.5%** very good
2. Appropriateness of adaptive interface for older people	**(1/8) 12.5%** thought it to be very appropriate.	**(0/8) 0%** to be inappropriate.	**(6/8) 75%** appropriate.	**(1/8) 12.5%** very appropriate.
3. What features they value in an adaptive interface (multiple answers accepted)[b]	**(5/8) 62.5%** value intervention feature.	**(4/8) 50%** value feedback feature.	**(7/8) 87.5%** value reminders feature.	**(1/8) 12.5%** value other features.
4. Which do they value most (feedback, interventions and reminders)	**(8/8) 100%** chose reminders.	**(0/8) 0%** chose feedback	**(0/8) 0%** chose interventions	
5. Usefulness of the voice operated interface	**(6/8) 75%** thought it was useful.	**(0/8) 0%** thought it was not useful	**(2/8) 25%** chose other	
6. Difficulty of using an adaptive interface	**(0/8) 0%** thought it was very difficult	**(3/8) 37.5%** thought it was difficult	**(4/8) 50%** thought it was quite easy	**(1/8) 12.5%** thought it was very easy

[b]For this question participants chose all that apply.

The results for the adaptive interface question are shown by (Figure 16), each of the answers from the questionnaire was rated with a score of 1 to 4 (1 being very poor, 4 being very good).

This was a very positive result as it helped to validate the underlying idea of implementing an AAL system were older people carrying out interactions with an Adaptive Interface.

AALFI provides intervention, feedback, reminder and picture display functionality and the results (Figure 17) show that intervention, feedback and reminders are considered to be useful and the picture functionality (classed as other) may be less useful. It is important to understand what potential stakeholders do value and this result will help to drive future work into advancing the functionality of AALFI.

Evaluation 4

Evaluation (EV-4) was carried out across two sessions which occurred on the dame day. The first session was attended by 4 participants and the second session by 6

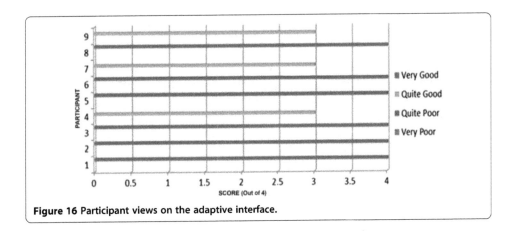

Figure 16 Participant views on the adaptive interface.

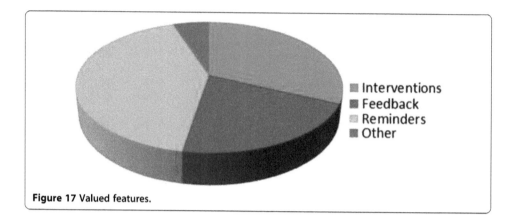

Figure 17 Valued features.

participants, the same questions and workshop format were followed at each session. All of the participants were of the target age for the research, over 60 years of age.

The participants were asked non-personally identifiable information including age; their gender; whether they live alone and if they live alone. In order to keep the results anonymous, the participants were not asked their name, address or anything else that could identify them.

The workshop questions and results are detailed in Table 8. These results represent the quantitative results as they allow for key research ideas, features and functionality to be measured.

The first four main questions assessed how the workshop participants view assistive devices and adaptive interfaces for themselves and for others such as friends and family. A score of 90% for question one was achieved and this is thought to be positive as it

Table 8 Quantitative results: evaluation 4 (EV-4) – (presented in a Thesis)

Question	Questionnaire one results (all results are out of 10)			
1. Will you use an assistive device?	Yes	No	Undecided	
	9	0	1	
2. When would you use an assistive device?	Day	Night	Both	
	0	1	9	
3. The idea and concept of the Adaptive Interface is...	Very good	Quite Poor	Poor	
	10	0	0	
4. For older people generally, the Adaptive Interface concept is...	Very Appropriate	Appropriate	Inappropriate	
	7	3	0	
5. In the Adaptive Interface, I would value...	Intervention	Feedback	Both	
	0	0	10	
6. Did you find the voice operated interface useful for people with sight problems?	Very Useful	Useful	Not Useful	
	8	2	0	
7. Which feature of the auditory interface would you improve?	Gender	Volume	Tone	N/A
	0	4	4	2
8. The method of receiving assistance that I prefer is...	Visual	Visual and text	Auditory Assistance	N/A
	1	5	3	1
9. Using the Adaptive Interface system would be...	Very easy	Quite easy	Quite difficult	Very difficult
	1x	5	3	1

shows that older persons will make use of assistive technology. For the second question, 90% of the participants answered that they would make use of an assistive device during the day and night, this validates the research ideas to provide assistance that deals with both the day and night time periods. 100% of participants thought that the concept of an adaptive interface was very good. For the next question, 70% of the participants thought that the adaptive interface was appropriate while 30% felt it was appropriate for older people. This result shows that when the older people themselves are going to use an assistive device they think it is very appropriate, however when they are thinking about friends and family making use of the interface, they have mixed feelings. Question 5 – 9 assessed specific features of AALFI that relate to the flexibility including the interaction method and the type of assistance that is offered in relation to the activities and actions an older person carries out and the resulting detected changes of context. With question 5, 100% said that they would make use of intervention and feedback assistance. This result validates offering two types of assistance to an older person and improves on previous assistance strategies were an older person is only offered intervention type assistance. Question 6 asked them to rate the usefulness of the voice operated interface with 80% thinking it was very useful and 20% that it was useful.

The result is positive as the participants were able to overlook the current limitations of the voice interface including the robotic voice and harsh tone. In order to aid further improvements of the voice interface, the participants were asked to choose which feature should be improved. 40% thought that the volume of the voice could be improved, 40% that the tone could be improved and 20% of the participants did not have an opinion. Question 8 assessed the participants preferred method of receiving assistance. A majority, 50% chose picture and text interactions (feedback), 10% chose text interactions (interventions) while 30% opted for auditory interactions. This shows that there may be scope to add pictures to the text interaction technique to further emphasise the assistance that is being offered. The last question was designed to gauge how easy to use the participants would find the adaptive interface. 10% felt that it would be very easy, 50% thought it would be quite easy while 30% though it would be quite difficult and 10% thought it would be very difficult. This result shows that overall a majority of older persons would find the adaptive interface easy to use, however there would need to be clear guidance and training provided so that an older person could get the most of the interface.

Qualitative results

This section details the qualitative results were the participants were asked to provide an opinion. **"Seems to open a whole range of useful interventions"**. This supports the use of intervention assistance and provides an insight into the types of interventions that an older person may like to see, including medication and reminder type assistance,

"I regularly take medication and sometimes I may forget to take the medication or take the wrong dose". "I currently live in a Fold and there have been occasions were a person has passed away or been unable to leave their bed and as the care taker does not check on residents during the weekend, this has gone undiscovered... would there be a way to alert a family member, friend or carer that a person has not left their bed in several hours". Currently AALFI is able to detect movement so that feedback assistance may be offered in relation to how well and older person sleeps, however this may be extended so that if an older person does not leave their bed in the morning, an alert could be sent to a family member, friend or care provider and outside assistance could be provided. The next statement is interesting as it represents a common view that an older person may not feel old and therefore may not think they need assistance at the current time, "Think it would be useful if they needed it later". From the discussions that was carried out it became apparent that older people may like to have the assistance installed in their home as early as possible, event after expressing this view several older people felt that having AALFI installed as early as possible would be of great benefit, "Having it installed early, getting used to it would mean "this was normal" not forced on me..." would allow for them to get to use to making use of it and to have time to learn about all the features and functionality, this would help overcome any current anxiety about assistive devise. The flexibility of the assistance strategies and interaction methods means that the older people may choose not to receive specific assistance and can further refine the interaction methods.

As previously discussed an underlying flexible characteristic of AALFI that may be explored further in the future is the ability to adapt the assistance based on the current sensor data. As long as the sensor data that has been gathered is of the correct format, AALFI may be able to consume it and offer the correct assistance. The participants at the workshop appreciated this future flexibility and would welcome assistance for other groups of people, "Could assistance be offered to people who are not old, but may have other problems or other disabilities...?"

"Not having to rely on family members..." "Give peace of mind to relatives as they may not be nearby. Be safer for the older person..." AALFI is flexible in that family members, care providers or friends may be given access to a subset of the assistance so that they are able to track the health and well-being off the older person and be given peace of mind.

"Lengthening the time of self-reliance..." "I can see were this would be of benefit for older independent people." "I would feel able to reflect on "oh I did not have a good night's sleep" The flexible nature of the assistance means it can both highlight recurring issues or provide support for events and activities as they occur in near real time. "Thought I was dreaming only..." "To recognise any issues needing to be addressed", This highlights the usefulness of feedback as a tool for drawing to the older person's attention recurring issues and this is reliant on the flexibility of the MAS to choose the correct assistance strategy.

"Not being dependant on glasses when one does not wear them 24 hours a day..." "Another voice when living alone and attracts attention in the first instance..."

These statements are thought to support the underlying flexibility to personalise the interaction method based on the older person's current interaction requirements and personal interaction preferences.

The results give a snapshot of the functionally and features that an older persons, health professionals and care providers value. In this case, with the group of people that completed the questionnaire, a particular functionality that was valued is reminders; however they also value interventions and feedback functionality. The current intervention messages contain several reminders, including a reminder to close the back door after a set period of time, having breakfast during the morning period and washing hands, however there is scope to expand the reminder capability to include other reminders such as getting up at a specific time and carrying out further activities of daily living. The result for the auditory voice interface was encouraging as the current implementation has several limitations including a unnatural monotone voice and on occasion is difficult to follow, the participants were able to look past these issues and determine that auditory/voice based interaction would be useful.

The implementation will be further refined in the future to overcome these issues and provide a more natural interaction method. The visual modality of the adaptive interface achieved a positive result as the majority of people found that they would not find the interface difficult to use and of the 3 who said it would be difficult, one said that they may find it less difficult over time. This result provides a basis for refinement to improve the usability of the visual modality. The next section provides a conclusion to this article.

Conclusions

The state of the art shows despite the intense and productive work in AAL there are still several underlying issues that can result in the assistance and support being provided to be inappropriate and not understood by the subject. For example, the systems do not provide the means to tailor the assistance and support to an individual's requirements and therefore the user may not understand the feedback.

An AAL system may provide assistance and support but not keep a record of what is occurring and the subject therefore does not get any meaningful feedback on what is occurring and may not be aware of any issues with the actions that they are carrying out. The system that has been developed provides a user with assistance and support that is tailored to their specific requirements. This will help to ensure that they are either able to read messages and interact with the interface during visual interaction or speak simple commands and hear simple prompts when auditory interaction is being used. Feedback can help the user identify and solve any recurring issues that have been identified with their actions or activities.

The flexibility displayed by AALFI encompasses the personalisation of the interactions in relation to the older person's requirements and changing requirements. The context aware characteristics that the MAS displays including the ability to choose the correct interactions, adapt the assistance offered in relation to the current time, activity carried out by the older person or the detected event and the number of times an event has occurred, help AALFI to provide flexible assistance and interactions. With this flexibility AALFI is able to provide the older person with the correct assistance, at the correct time and to adapt the interaction method for offering the assistance to the older person's requirements profile.

The research ideas, MAS and associated adaptable interface (AALFI) have undergone several steps of validation including a workshop with older people, care providers and health professionals. The workshop produced interesting results; older people are not afraid of technology and can appreciate it if it serves a meaningful purpose. The current interface and auditory interactions have been designed to be simple so that they are easy to understand, the participants felt that this was the correct route to take. Feedback and interventions are offered to the person during the day, while at night the MAS is aware of activities and events so that feedback may be offered the following day. AALFI complements the night-time assistance that is provided by NOCTURNAL with day time interventions, several new night time interventions and feedback assistance that is based on day and night time activities and events. Once the results were evaluated, it became apparent that even though the participants were not forgetful; they placed a high value on reminders and therefore when the current interventions are being revised and improved, more reminder interventions may be added. The comments, results and observations from the workshop will influence further development of the visual interface and refinement of the speech based interaction method.

Endnotes

[a]VoiceXML: http://www.w3.org/TR/voicexml21/.

[b]Carnegie Mellon University. CMU Sphinx. Open Source Toolkit For Speech Recognition. http://cmusphinx.sourceforge.net/wiki/research/.

[c]FreeTTS, http://freetts.sourceforge.net/docs/index.php.

[d]Windows 7, portable 10 inch Tablet PC, 32GB solid state hard drive, 2GB system memory, capacitive touch screen.

[e]Intervention Dialogue Test.

Subject: Hello (this is the keyword to start the interaction process).

System: Welcome to the intervention and feedback messages.

System: (pauses for 10 seconds).

System: Ok, I have 3 choices for you, if you wish to listen to interventions, say the word interventions, to listen to feedback, say the word feedback, to exit, say the word exit.

Subject: Interventions.

System: Intervention messages.

System: To listen to the current intervention message, say the word current.

System: To listen to all the intervention messages, say the word all.

System: To hear the last intervention message, say the word last.

System: To exit the intervention menu, say the word exit.

Subject: Current.

System: Ok, the current intervention is as follows (pause).

System: The back door has been left open for over 10 minutes; it is recommended that you close the backdoor.

[f]Feedback Dialogue Test.

Subject: Hello (this is the keyword to start the interaction process).

System: Welcome to the intervention and feedback messages.

System: (pauses for 10 seconds).

System: Ok, I have 3 choices for you, if you wish to listen to interventions, say the word interventions, to listen to feedback, say the word feedback, to exit, say the word exit.

Subject: Feedback.

System: Feedback messages.

System: To listen to the current feedback, say the word current.

System: To listen to all the feedback messages, say the word all.

System: To hear the last feedback message, say the word last.

System: To exit the feedback, say the word exit.

Subject: Last.

System: Ok, the last feedback message is as follows (pause).

System: Please remember that during the morning, breakfast is an important meal.

Competing interests
The authors declare that they have no competing interests.

Authors' contributions
JMcN has published papers in the area of Ambient Assisted Living in relation to helping older people carry out activities of daily living in their own home during the day and night. J has completed a PhD research project were a Multi-agent system, Ambient Assisted Living Flexible Interface (AALFI) and subsequent evaluations of AALFI, contributed to the research into supporting older people at home. JCA has carried out research in the areas of Ambient Assisted Living, Ambient Intelligence and Smart Environments and has been involved in many successful research projects including NOCTURNAL and AALFI. J has published many significant papers which have contributed to the knowledge and understanding of Ambient Intelligence and Ambient Assisted Living and has presided as editor over several successful Journals. MM has conducted research in diverse research areas including Computer Science, Artificial Intelligence and Ambient Assisted Living. M is Co-founder of the TRAIL Living lab and is a member of ENoLL- European Network of Living Labs. Research projects that M has contributed to, include COGKNOW, NOCTURNAL and AALFI. Maurice has published many noteworthy papers in the areas of Ambient Assisted Living and Artificial Intelligence. PMcC is a reader in computer science at the University of Ulster and has made substantial contributions to several research projects including COGKNOW, BRAIN, NOCTURNAL and AALFI, which have contributed to the knowledge and understanding relating to helping older people deal with the effects of ageing. P has published many notable papers in the areas of Ambient Assisted Living, Ambient Intelligence and Pervasive Computing which have furthered peoples understanding on how older people may be assisted and what assistance they may require. All authors have read and approved the final manuscript.

Acknowledgments
We wish to thank AGE NI who facilitated the workshop by inviting the participants, providing the workspace and looking after ourselves and the participants with ample sustenance. We acknowledge the participants at the workshop who gave up their valuable time to help evaluate the ideas behind AALFI and the visual and auditory interaction modalities.

Author details
[1]Department of Computer Science, Middlesex University, Hendon, London, UK. [2]School of Computing and Mathematics, University of Ulster Jordanstown, Shore Road, Newtownabbey, Belfast.

References
1. Busemeyer MR, Goerres a, Weschle S (2009) Attitudes towards redistributive spending in an era of demographic ageing: the rival pressures from age and income in 14 OECD countries. J Eur Soc Policy 19:195–212. doi:10.1177/0958928709104736
2. D'Andrea A, D'Ulizia A, Ferri F, Grifoni P (2009) A multimodal pervasive framework for ambient assisted living. Proc 2nd Int Conf PErvsive Technol Relat to Assist Environ - PETRA '09 1–8, doi: 10.1145/1579114.1579153
3. Chun-dong W, Xiu-liang M, Huai-bin W (2009) An Intelligent Home Middleware System Based on Context-Awareness. 2009 Fifth Int. Conf. Nat. Comput. IEEE, Tianjin, pp 165–169
4. Augusto JC, Carswell W, Zheng H et al (2011) NOCTURNAL Ambient Assisted Living. In: Keyson D, Lou MM, Streitz N et al (eds) Proc. Second Int. Conf. Ambient Intell, 7040th edn. Springer-Verlag, Berlin, Heidelberg, pp 350–354
5. Kartakis S, Stephanidis C (2010) A design-and-play approach to accessible user interface development in ambient intelligence environments. Comput Ind 61:318–328, 10.1016/j.compind.2009.12.002
6. Tamir DE, Mueller CJ (2010) Pinpointing usability issues using an effort based framework. 2010 IEEE Int. Conf. Syst. Man Cybern. IEEE, Istanbul, pp 931–938
7. Madiah M, Hisham S (2010) User-interface design: A case study of partially sighted children in Malaysia. 2010 Int. Conf. User Sci. Eng. IEEE, Shah Alam, pp 168–173
8. Wersenyi G (2010) Auditory Representations of a Graphical User Interface for a Better Human-Computer Interaction. In: Ystad S, Aramaki M, KronlandMartinet R, Jensen K (eds) Audit. Disp. SPRINGER-VERLAG BERLIN, HEIDELBERGER PLATZ 3, D-14197 BERLIN, GERMANY, pp 80–102
9. Bordini RH, Hubner JF, Woolbridge M (2007) The Jason Agent Programming Language. Program. Multi-Agent Syst. AgentSpeak using Jason. John Wiley and Sons, LTD, pp 31–68
10. Bellifemine F, Caire G, Poggi A, Rimassa G (2003) Jade-a white paper. EXP Search Innov 3:6–19
11. Pokahr A, Braubach L, Lamersdorf W (2005) Chapter 6 JADEX: A BDI REASONING ENGINE. In: Bordini R, Mehdi D, Jürgen Dix AEFS (eds) Multiagent Syst. Artif. Soc. Simulated Organ. Springer, US, pp 149–174
12. Augusto JC, Zheng H, Mulvenna MD et al (2011) Design and Modelling of the Nocturnal AAL Care System. In: Novais P, Preuveneers D, Corchado JM (eds) ISAm. Springer, Berlin Heidelberg, pp 109–116

13. Sebbak F, Mokhtari A, Chibani A, Amirat Y (2010) Context-aware ubiquitous framework services using JADE-OSGI integration framework. Mach. Web Intell. (ICMWI), 2010 Int. Conf. IEEE, Algiers, pp 48–53

14. Griss ML, Fonseca S, Cowan D, Kessler R (2002) SmartAgent: extending the JADE agent behavior model SmartAgent: extending the JADE agent behavior model

15. Hristova A, Bernardos AM, Casar JR (2008) Context-aware services for ambient assisted living: a case-study. Appl Sci Biomed Commun Technol 2008 ISABEL'08 First Int Symp, doi: 10.1109/ISABEL.2008.4712593

16. Jih W, Hsu JY, Wu CL et al (2006) A multi-agent service framework for context-aware elder care. AAMAS-06 Work. Serv. Comput. Agent-Based Eng, Hokkaido, Japan, pp 61–75

17. Butz A (2010) User Interfaces and HCI for Ambient Intelligence and Smart Environments. In: Nakashima H, Aghajan H, Augusto JC (eds) Handb. Ambient Intell. Smart Environ, 1st edn. Springer, USA, pp 535–558

18. Dumas B, Lalanne D, Oviatt S (2009) Multimodal interfaces: a survey of principles, models and frameworks. In: Denis L, Jürg K (eds) Hum. Mach. Interact. Springer, Berlin, Heidelberg, pp 3–26

19. Blumendorf M, Albayrak S (2009) Towards a Framework for the Development of Adaptive Multimodal User Interfaces for Ambient Assisted Living Environments. UAHCI '09 Proc. 5th Int. Conf. Access Human-Computer Interact. Part II. Springer-Verlag, Berlin, Heidelberg, pp 150–159

20. Abowd GD, Dey AK, Brown P et al (1999) Towards a better understanding of context and context-awareness. In: Gellersen H-W (ed) Handheld Ubiquitous Comput, 1707th edn. Springer Berlin, Heidelberg, pp 304–307

21. Cassens J, Kofod-Petersen A (2006) Using activity theory to model context awareness: a qualitative case study. Proc. 19th Int. Florida Artif. Intell. Res. Soc. Conf. AAAI Press. Citeseer, Florida, USA, pp 619–624

22. Dey AK (2001) Understanding and using context. Pers Ubiquitous Comput 5:4–7. doi:10.1007/s007790170019

23. Hong D, Chiu DKW, Shen VY (2005) Requirements elicitation for the design of context-aware applications in a ubiquitous environment. CEC '05 Proc. 7th Int. Conf. Electron. Commer, ACM, New York, NY, USA, pp 590–596

24. Mostefaoui GK, Pasquier-Rocha J, Brezillon P (2004) Context-aware computing: a guide for the pervasive computing community. Computerorg:39–48

25. Hong J, Suh E-H, Kim J, Kim S (2009) Context-aware system for proactive personalized service based on context history. Expert Syst Appl 36:7448–7457. doi:10.1016/j.eswa.2008.09.002

26. Steg H, Strese H, Loroff C et al (2006) Europe is facing a demographic challenge ambient assisted living offers solutions. Ambient Assist Living—European Overv Rep:1–85

27. Sun H, Florio VD, Gui N, Blondia C (2009) Promises and Challenges of Ambient Assisted Living Systems. Proc. 2009 Sixth Int. Conf. Inf. Technol. New Gener. 00. IEEE Computer Society, Las Vegas, NV, pp 1201–1207

28. Kleinberger T, Becker M, Ras E et al (2007) Ambient intelligence in assisted living: enable elderly people to handle future interfaces. Univers Access Human-Computer Interact Interact 4555(2007):103–112, doi: 10.1007/978-3-540-73281-5_11

29. Mulvenna M, Zhen H, Wright T (2009) Reminiscence Systems. In: Mulvenna M, Astell A, Zhen H, Wright T (eds) Proc. 1st Int. Work. Reminisc. Syst. CEUR-WS, Cambridge, pp 9–11

30. Wooldridge M, Fisher M, Huget M-P, Parsons S (2002) Model checking multi-agent systems with MABLE. Proc first Int Jt Conf Auton agents multiagent Syst part 2 - AAMAS '02 952, doi: 10.1145/544862.544965

31. Cook DJ (2009) Multi-agent smart environments. J Ambient Intell Smart Environ 1:51–55. doi:10.3233/AIS-2009-0007

32. Pokahr A, Braubach L (2009) A Survey of Agent-oriented Development Tools. In: El Fallah Seghrouchni A, Dix J, Dastani M, Bordini RH (eds) Multi-Agent Program. Springer, US, pp 289–329

33. Duell R, Memon ZA, Treur J (2012) Ambient Support for Group Emotion: an Agent-Based Model. In: Bosse T (ed) Agents Ambient Intell. - Achiev. Challenges Intersect. Agent Technol. Ambient Intell, 12th edn. IOS Press, pp 239–260

34. Dovgan E, Gams M (2012) An Access-Control Agent-Based Security System. In: Bosse T (ed) Agents Ambient Intell. - Achiev. Challenges Intersect. Agent Technol. Ambient Intell, 12th edn. IOS Press, pp 239–260

35. Das B, Narayanan C, Krishnan DJC (2012) Automated Activity Interventions to Assist with Activities of Daily Living. In: Bosse T (ed) Agents Ambient Intell. - Achiev. Challenges Intersect. Agent Technol. Ambient Intell, 12th edn. IOS Press, pp 137–158

36. Häikiö J, Wallin A, Isomursu M et al (2007) Touch-based user interface for elderly users. Proc. 9th Int. Conf. Hum. Comput. Interact. with Mob. devices Serv, ACM, New York, NY, USA, pp 289–296

37. Stefano P, Bonamico C, Regazzoni C, Lavegetto F (2005) 6 A Flexible Architecture for Ambient Intelligence Systems Supporting Adaptive Multimodal Interaction with Users. In: Riva G, Vatalaro F, Davide F, Alcaniz M (eds) Ambient Intell. IOS Press, The Netherlands, pp 97–120

38. McCullagh PJ, Carswell W, Mulvenna MD et al (2012) Nocturnal Sensing and Intervention for Assisted Living of People with Dementia. In: Lai D, Begg R, Palaniswami M (eds) Healthc. Sens. Networks - Challenges Towar. Pract. Appl. Taylor and Francis/CRC Press, Florida, USA, pp 283–303

39. Portet F, Vacher M, Golanski C (2011) Design and evaluation of a smart home voice interface for the elderly: acceptability and objection aspects. Pers Ubiquitous:1–18

40. Rawi M, Al-Anbuky A (2012) Wireless sensor networks and human comfort index. Pers Ubiquitous Comput:1–3. doi:10.1007/s00779-012-0547-9

41. Das B, Cook DD, Schmitter-Edgecombe M, Seelye A (2011) PUCK: an automated prompting system for smart environments: toward achieving automated prompting—challenges involved. Pers Ubiquitous Comput:1–15

42. Kubicki S (2011) RFID-driven situation awareness on TangiSense, a table interacting with tangible objects. Pers Ubiquitous Comput:1–6

43. Mulvenna M, Carswell W, McCullagh PP et al (2011) Visualization of data for ambient assisted living services. IEEE Commun Mag 49:110–117. doi:10.1109/MCOM.2011.5681023

44. Turner N (2011) A guide to carrying out usability reviews – UX for the masses. In: UX masses., http://www. uxforthemasses.com/usability-reviews/. Accessed 9 Feb 2012

45. Carswell W, McCullagh PJ, Augusto JC et al (2009) A review of the role of assistive technology for people with dementia in the hours of darkness. Technol Health Care 17:281–304, doi:10.3233/THC-2009-0553

8

A framework to integrate speech based interface for blind web users on the websites of public interest

Prabhat Verma[*], Raghuraj Singh and Avinash Kumar Singh

* Correspondence:
pvluk@yahoo.com
Computer Science and Engineering
Department, Harcourt Butler
Technological Institute, Kanpur,
208002, India

Abstract

Despite many assistive tools available for browsing the web, blind persons are not able to perform the tasks using internet that are done by persons without such disability. Even the futuristic social networking sites and other websites using the features of web 2.0 indicate a lesser accessible/responsible web. In this paper, we propose a framework, which can be used by the websites of public interest to make their important utilities better accessible and usable to blind web users. The approach is based on providing an alternate access system on the fly using one single website. The framework makes use of existing technologies like JavaScript, available speech APIs etc. and therefore provides a lightweight and robust solution to the accessibility problem. As a case study, we demonstrate the usefulness of the proposed framework by showing its working on a key functionality of the Indian Railways Reservation Website.

Keywords: Online TTS on web; Speech service; Speech interfaces; Accessibility; Usability; Navigability

Introduction

The original purpose of the World Wide Web was to be able to represent documents on different platforms and different user interfaces including text-based and auditory interfaces in a single computer network. It was then planned to convert each document into Braille [1]. Today, in 21st century, Internet is one of the biggest tools that have eased our life to a major extent. It has offered alternate ways of performing tasks which were otherwise tedious and time consuming. Thus, without requiring traveling a long distance and waiting in a queue for hours, one can access any information or can perform a task in seconds. Unfortunately, the benefits of this powerful tool are still away from the blind users who make the use of screen readers or similar assistive tools to surf the web. Findings of a study [2] reveal that accessing web content was "frustratingly difficult" for blind users, implying the need for availability of more accessible and usable web content and better assistive technology.

To get the status of web accessibility & usability among blind web users, we made a study on a group of 50 blind users at Adult Training Centre, National Institute of Visually Handicap, Dehradun, India during February, 2012. For this study purpose, we categorized web usage by a blind user into simple, intermediate and complex. A usage is simple if a blind user browses for some news article, e-book or collects information on some topic. Screen Readers may serve well for all such simple usages. Tasks like sending or receiving e-mails, performing simple queries like finding examination result of a student by entering his/her roll number may be considered as of intermediate complexity. Tasks like getting a travel ticket reserved or online shopping are of complex category because they require multiple form filling that may spread across several web pages in a complex structure.

The participants were comfortable in using normal keyboards for providing inputs to the computer. Screen Reader, JAWS was being used by them for web browsing and email. They admired JAWS and admitted that they were able to use internet only because of this software. However, they also told that sometimes they were not able to access all the components of a webpage using JAWS. Most often, they were not able to find where to click on the webpage and as a result not able to proceed further. They were also facing problems in selecting dates from the Calendar while form filling, accessing information from social networking sites like face-book, chatting etc. Thus using JAWS they were able to perform simple tasks e.g. news paper reading, general surfing, knowledge gathering, simple query etc. but they were not comfortable in performing complex tasks involving multiple form filling. Besides, JAWS is not a freeware and its cost is too high to be afforded by an average Indian individual. Thus, the web usage of the participants was limited to the institute laboratory only.

Above mentioned interaction with blind web users compelled us to think beyond the limitations of screen readers. We observed that while working for some web related task that involves multiple form-filling spread over many pages/interfaces, screen reader users have to face difficulties at several levels. In most of the cases, cursor control does not come automatically to the relevant form to be filled on next page. Instead, blind user may need to search or traverse along the general navigational structure of the webpage. Besides, JavaScript validation may also create problems. Most of the JavaScript validations work on the click event of submit button. It is not always easy to comply with the validation requirements using screen reader as user may have to search, among many fields, the one to be modified.

In this paper, some of these issues and challenges have been taken up. We propose a framework using which, dedicated speech based interface may be provided on an existing website of public interest by its owner for providing its important services to the blind users. Thus, a blind user can perform important tasks independently on such a website without using any assistive tool like screen reader.

Existing systems and related work

There have been two popular approaches among the researchers to address the issues related to speech based web access for blind user. The first approach employs a client based assistive tool (e.g. screen reader) to speak out the web content in some desired order. The other approach makes the use of online Text to Speech (TTS) service through a proxy server to convert and send the web data in mp3 or other format to the client where it is played by a browser plug-in. In both cases, a transcoder may be used to renders the web content after converting it to a more accessible form. Unfortunately, both the approaches do not provide perfect solution for the accessibility problem and suffer from their own limitations. Usability of the screen readers is mainly constrained by the complex structure/poor accessibility of web pages. The proxy server based approach may not be treated as reliable as they are maintained by a third party. Besides, they may not work on secure sites. Thus, there are many important web based tasks which, at present, cannot be performed satisfactorily by the blind user using any of the available assistive tools.

Screen readers

Various systems have been developed using approaches like content analysis, document reading rules, context summary, summary/gist based, semantic analysis, sequential information flow in web pages etc. But these systems have a number of issues which make them less usable. First, they are essentially screen readers or their extension. Second, they provide only browsing and do not support other applications like mail, form-filling, transaction, chat etc. A brief survey of some important Screen Readers is given here.

Some of the most popular screen-readers are JAWS [3] and IBM's Home Page Reader [4].

Emacspeak [5] is a free screen reader for Emacs developed by T. V. Raman and first released in May 1995; it is tightly integrated with Emacs, allowing it to render intelligible and useful content rather than parsing the graphics.

Brookes Talk [6] is a web browser developed in Oxford Brookes University in 90's. Brookes Talk provides function keys for accessing the web page. Brookes Talk reads out the webpage using speech synthesis in words, sentences and paragraph mode by parsing the web page content. It also uses some mechanism for searching the suitable results using search engines and supports a conceptual model of website too. It supports modeling of information on web page and summarizes the web page content.

Csurf [7] is developed by Stony Brook University. Csurf is context based browsing system. Csurf brings together content analysis, natural language processing and machine learning algorithm to help blind user to quickly identify relevant information. Csurf is composed of interface manager, context analyzer, browser object from tress processor and dialog generator. Csurf web browser uses the functionality of voice XML, JSAPI, freeTTS, Sphinx, JREXAPI, etc.

Aster (Audio system for technical reading) [8], developed by T. V. Raman, permits visually disabled individuals to manually define their own document reading rules. Aster is implemented by using Emacs as a main component for reading. It recognizes the markup language as logical structure of web page internally. Then user can either listen to entire document or any part of it.

Some researchers have also proposed to extract the web content using semantics [9].

Hearsay [10] is developed at Stony Brook University. It is a multimodal dialog system in which browser reads the webpage under the control of the user. It analyzes the web page content like HTML, DOM tree, segments web page and on the basis of this generates VoiceXML dialogues.

A Vernacular Speech Interface for People with visual Impairment named 'Shruti' has been developed at Media Lab Asia research hub at IIT Kharagpur, India. It is an embedded Indian language Text-to-Speech system that accepts text inputs in two Indian languages - Hindi and Bengali, and produces near natural speech output.

Shruti-Drishti [11] is a Computer Aided Text-to-Speech and Text-to-Braille System developed in collaboration with CDAC Pune and Webel Mediatronics Ltd, (WML) Kolkata. This is an integrated Text-to-Speech and Text-to-Braille system which enables persons with visual impairment to access the electronic documents from the conference websites in speech and braille form.

Screen reading software SAFA (Screen Access For All) [12] has been developed by Media Lab Asia research hub at IIT Kharagpur in collaboration with National Association for the Blind, New Delhi in Vernacular language to enable the visually disabled persons to use PC. This enables a person with visual impairment to operate PC using speech output. It gives speech output support for windows environment and for both English and Hindi scripts.

As far as general surfing is concerned, above mentioned screen readers are important and useful tool for the blind users. But, in case of complex tasks like information query, complex navigation, form-filling or some transaction, they do not work to the level of satisfaction. Some elements of websites that do not comply with the accessibility guidelines may be inaccessible to Screen Readers. Besides, they provide accessibility through abundant use of shortcut keys for which blind users have to be trained. Also, the screen readers need to be purchased and installed on the local machine which prevents them to use the internet on any public terminal.

Speech based web browsers

Prospects of Text-to-Speech (TTS) on web are gaining momentum gradually. At present, fetching mp3 on a remote web service is the only standard way for converting text to speech. APIs used for this purpose are proprietary and provide text to speech services, e.g. BrowseAloud [13] is a TTS service using which a web site can be speech enabled. Google Translate Service also has a TTS feature. Although many websites have provision of reading its contents, but it is limited to playing the content as a single mp3 file. There is no provision for interactive navigation and form filling in most of them [14].

WebAnywhere [14] is an open source online TTS developed at Washington University for surfing the web. It requires no special software to be installed on the client machine and, therefore, enables blind users to access the web from any computer. It can also be used as a tool to test the accessibility of a website under construction. WebAnywhere generates speech remotely and uses pre-fetching strategies designed to reduce perceived latency. It also uses a server side transformational proxy that makes web pages appear to come from local server to overcome cross-site scripting restrictions. On the client side, Javascript is used to support user interaction by deciding which sound to be played by the sound player.

Like screen readers, WebAnyWhere reads out the elements in sequential order by default. Although few shortcut keys are assigned to control the page elements, user has to make an assessment of the whole page in order to proceed further. In websites with poor accessibility design, user may be trapped during a complex navigation.

Although WebAnyWhere is a step forward in the direction of online installation-free accessibility, it has certain limitations: As the contents in WebAnyWhere are received through a third party, they may not be treated reliable. Fear of malware attacks, phishing etc. is associated with such access. Secure sites cannot be accessed using this approach as they allow only restricted operations on their contents. This is a major drawback since most of the important tasks like bank transaction, filling examination forms, using e-mail services etc. are performed over secure sites. These drawbacks compromise the usability of WebAnyWhere and limit it to an information access tool only.

ReadSpeaker Form Reader [15] is an online TTS service to website providers. It claims that it can help their customers/users in fill out online forms.

Task based approaches

Few websites e.g. State Bank of India (www.onlinesbi.com) offer key shortcuts to perform certain tasks e.g. fund transfer, check the balance etc. Fortunately these tasks are simple and limited to single page only. Still, no provision is made for speech synthesis assuming that Screen Reader will be used by the blind users.

There is a Framework, SICE [16] for developing speech based web applications that may provide specific functionality to blind users. The framework is based on VoiceXML specifications for developing web based interactive voice applications. Communications are made using VOIP (Voice Over Internet Protocol); therefore, user does not have the dependency on telephony interface as required by existing VoiceXML specifications. Unlike telephony, complex web data can be conveniently handled using customized two way dialogue based access system in a controlled way. The framework is more effective in developing speech based web access systems for dedicated functionalities rather than developing generalized speech interfaces. The drawback of the framework is that, being a heavyweight system, it requires huge investment on hardware and software on server side.

System design and architecture

Motivation

So far, researchers have been emphasizing on finding the generic solutions to the accessibility issues. Expectations from the web site owners or content providers have been limited to providing accessible contents that could be usable with screen readers. Being client side tools, Screen Readers most often fail to perform the task as the web author intentions may not be well understood by assistive tool. As a result, blind users fail to perform important tasks like reservation booking, tax deposition, bill payment, online shopping etc. We propose that for all such important utilities, accessibility solution could be automated on the server side by the website author/owner. Thus, there is a need to have an authoring tool which could provide an integrated solution for sighted and blind users using a single website.

Issues to be tackled are manifold. While surfing internet using a client based assistive technology like screen reader, blind user has to face problems in both intra webpage navigation and inter webpage navigation. The situation becomes worse in case of complex web pages. First, the website navigational structures need to be traversed on a webpage each time a screen reader user wishes to locate a relevant link. Besides, she may get stuck in-between when something goes wrong during the form validation on submit button of a form. Inter webpage navigational issues are primarily caused by possible multiple entry/exit points on related web pages. After submitting a form on webpage, control may not reach to the relevant form or link on the next page. As a result, visually disabled user has to search the relevant form or link sequentially. Efforts have been made to tackle the issue using some semi-automatic client based approaches e.g. Curf [7] uses a context based approach to reach to the most relevant link on the next page. Unfortunately, these approaches do not serve our purpose.

Our proposed framework is inspired by online TTS Systems like WebAnywhere, BrowseAloud, ReadSpeaker form reader etc.. Working of a client-based tool, IMacro [17] has equally inspired us to automate the user activity, rather from server side in our case. Although IMacro is not an assistive technology, as it has been used to automate bulk form filling on client machine, our idea is to provide a similar functionality to client from server side.

Feasibility analysis

Although, direct speech enabling of public websites seems to be the best strategy in terms of usability and accuracy with which blind users can interact with complex form elements, it has not been a popular approach in industry. There are certain fears that must be overcome to make the approach feasible in general. First and most prominent one is that web authors need to create two documents for everything they write, which is obviously an overhead. The issue is tackled as follows: Is it possible to send the text in speech (mp3) form to the blind user from the same webpage that caters the other users? If so, overheads of maintaining two copies of same webpage can be eliminated.

The other fear is related with the hardware cost to maintain the speech server and other interfaces. A lightweight solution is imperative in terms of hardware and software architecture. Meeting these two requirements can make direct speech enabling the websites a feasible solution.

Design goals and decisions

The goal of this work is to design a framework which will facilitate the owner of website to provide a speech interface to its important services for the blind users. The framework should be based on providing an alternate access system on the fly on the same website so that the overheads involved are minimal. It should be scalable i.e. can be expanded for additional functionalities over time. Accessibility, Usability and Navigability should be enhanced considerably. Access time/Usage time for a given task should be reduced. Instances of confusion or indecisiveness during navigation should be eliminated completely. The system should be able to run for secure connections or at least in a mix of secure and insecure connection with extra measures of security through providing restricted access to the alternate speech based system.

Local installations should not be required. Thus, user should be able to access and use the website from any public terminal. However, it should seamlessly work with screen reader like JAWS if available, without any conflict. Speech synthesis for the text on the web and voice feedback for keyboard operations as a prerequisite for a blind user to use the web should be provided.

The conceptual architecture

To provide an alternate interface for blind users on websites of public interest with the goals stated in previous section, a framework has been designed by us that make use of

JavaScript and dynamic contents to improve the accessibility and usability through their power of controlling the tasks on the user computer [18]. The framework is inspired by WebAnyWhere, discussed in previous section with two notable differences: First, in the proposed system, the speech based interface shall be provided by the first party i.e. the owner of the website rather than by a third party as is the case with WebAnyWhere. Second, our predefined task based approach enforces strict ordering of elements to be spoken and this ordering is priory known to the server. The framework is based on the "attach on request" concept. Thus, it makes the use of one single site to provide the speech based interface on the fly without affecting its normal course for the sighted users.

SpeechEnabler is the core of this framework. It is implemented as a web server plug-in. The *SpeechEnabler* acts like a macro recorder which records and saves the sequence of page/form elements (hereafter called 'the active nodes') to be visited to perform a given task in the form of executable code on the server. Thus, on the website to be speech enabled for some functionality, the web author has to simply emulate the form (s) filling along the webpage(s) in the desired sequence. The *SpeechEnabler* records the active nodes with their order of traversal in the form of a macro. A key shortcut is designated on the home page of the original site to make a request for accessing the functionality by the blind users. On user request through the designated key shortcut for the task, the macro on the server is run; attaching the client side JavaScript code on the response page(s) on the fly. As a result, a logical chain is created among active nodes, which is known to both client and server. In addition, it attaches the sever side interface with the speech server, which is responsible to send the text of the form elements to the client in the form of MP3 file. A pre-fetching technique is used to minimize latency. Speech feedbacks for user key strokes during form filling is handled locally at client machine by JavaScript. The complete process has been described pictorially in Figures 1 and 2.

JavaScript has a remarkable ability of modifying a node in the document structure on the fly. On trigger of the macro as a result of user request, the process creates the response page(s) on the fly attaching a unique ID to each relevant element in the order of the traversal to perform the task. For example, if there are eight active nodes to be traversed on the first page, IDs from 101 to 108 will be assigned to them. Similarly, in the next (second) page, if there are five active nodes to be traversed, IDs from 201 to 205 will be assigned to them and so on. Fixation of IDs to the active nodes in this way

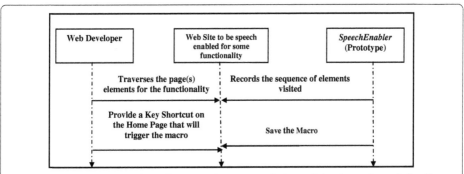

Figure 1 Interactions during the website creation: on an existing website, it requires a little effort to make a functionality speech enabled using *SpeechEnabler.*

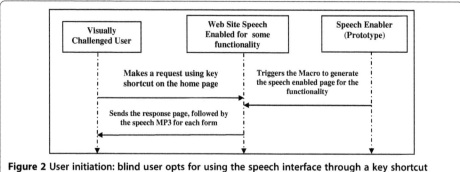

Figure 2 User initiation: blind user opts for using the speech interface through a key shortcut request from the home page.

ensures the strict ordering of traversal to perform the task and also in pre-fetching the next element to be spoken out. Assignment of IDs also helps in making the focus to an active node which is found to be the source of error during form validation.

Interactions of user with the host server and speech server are shown using the conceptual architecture in the Figure 3. Initially, *SpeechEnabler* contains the application logic (order of traversal among active nodes for the functionality, saved in macro) and speech services (logic to forward the speech request to the speech server) as shown through interaction labeled (a) in the Figure. User request to use the functionality is sent using the designated key shortcut on the homepage. As a result, the relevant macro of the *SpeechEnabler* is run. *SpeechEnabler* handles the application logic on its own by preparing the response page on the fly and forwards the speech requests to the speech server. This fact is shown using interaction labeled (b) in the Figure. Once the page is loaded, command and control is taken by the web browser through the JavaScript code of the page for generating speech output through the speech server for the element in focus. Speech server converts the content of the speech service request forwarded by the browser into the speech MP3 and streams it to the user as part of response. This process is shown through interaction labeled (c) in the Figure.

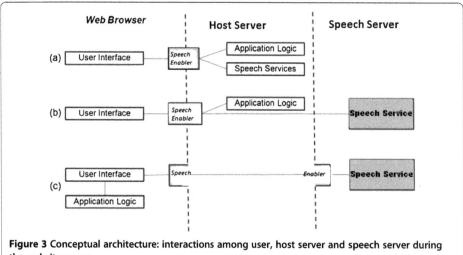

Figure 3 Conceptual architecture: interactions among user, host server and speech server during the website usage.

In the proposed system, the order of the page/form elements to be focused and spoken is made definite and predefined. The speech server sends the speech mp3 for each active form element. Arrived mp3 file is played for currently focused form element on the user machine using a browser plug-in player and the user is prompted to enter their details. Meanwhile, speech for the next element in the order is pre-fetched. Focus to the next element in the form is made by the down arrow key press which, at the same time, generates an event on which the pre-fetched speech for the element currently focused is played. Thus, user may control the traversal along the active page elements using up or down arrow keys. On pressing the submit button in a form, user control is directed to the relevant form on the next page which is again known priory. Component diagram of the complete System is depicted in Figure 4.

Implementation aspects

The prototype system has been implemented by us using Java programming language. It has 3-tier architecture: a client i.e.; web browser which is Java enabled. The client also includes speech plug-in for browser to play the sound. User Interface Object consists of HTML pages with JavaScript functions and applets. Blind Users' requests are routed through the key shortcuts that invoke the underlying applet. The Server component includes a HTTP server, an RMI Server, an RMI registry, html pages,

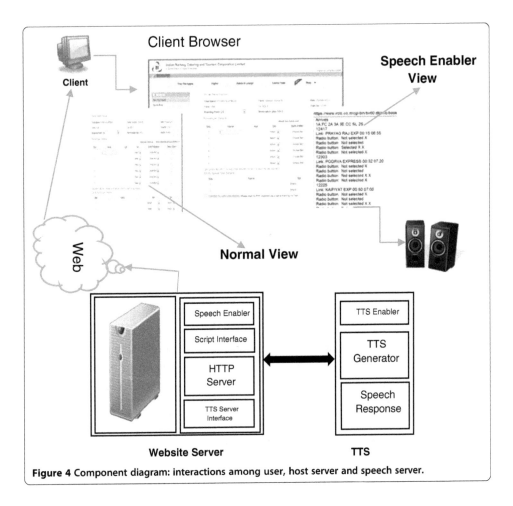

Figure 4 Component diagram: interactions among user, host server and speech server.

Applet classes etc. Apache Tomcat Server has been used as web (HTTP) Server. RMI Server is mainly used to implement the function of *SpeechEnabler*. Free Festival Text to Speech (TTS) System has been used for producing speech. At client side, MP3 is played by Adobe Flash Player. A model application is developed using the prototype system for a functionality which has been described in the next section.

Case-study: Indian railways website

Indian Railways, being fully State controlled, is a major means of local transport in India. At present, Indian Railways provides various services viz. enquiry, online reservation, tour planning & management and hotel booking through its exclusive website, i.e. www.irctc.co.in. Prior to this service being operational, the travelers had to physically visit the reservation centers to avail the reservation and other services. They had to wait in long queues to get the services. Now, as a convenient choice, a user can avail the service promptly, without making any physical movement, through online access to the Indian Railways Website. A large number of persons are taking advantage of this facility every day.

Unfortunately, this facility is not being availed by approximately seven million visually disabled in the country due to lack of any suitable interface available on the website for them. As compared to their sighted counterparts, they are in more need of such a facility that could empower them by avoiding their physical movement to get the service at a reservation centre. To take care of security related issues at high priority and to prevent various malpractices & abuses made by agents or others, the site owners have imposed various types of restrictions for using the website or its database. This prevents the use of third party approaches like 'WebAnyWhere' to access the site through speech.

The website has several noted instances of inaccessibility where a screen reader user may get trapped during a task e.g. *Book a Berth*. If this task could be done by providing a separate dialogue based system accessible from the homepage of the Indian Railways website, it would be more than worth making effort for providing such an interface.

Navigation related issues

If the Indian Railways website, stated above is observed, it will be revealed that each web page is divided into many frames. To perform a task e.g. Book a Berth may not be a problem to a sighted person as s/he can always locate the link of interest to proceed forward. But, for a blind user, using a screen reader, it may take long time to locate the required link as the screen reader will speak out the links in sequential order including those belonging to general navigational structure. For example, to book a ticket, after login on the first page, focus would not automatically go to "Plan my Travel" form on the next page (Figure 5). The situation is even worst on next page. It is really difficult to reach to "List of Train" frame (Figure 6) traversing along general navigational structure and "plan my Travel" links.

Further, structure of website may also create confusion and situation of indecision. Some frames are inaccessible to the screen readers. For example, after submitting the train and class details, the Train details and availability appears just above the previous form "List of Trains" which is inaccessible to the screen reader (Figure 7).

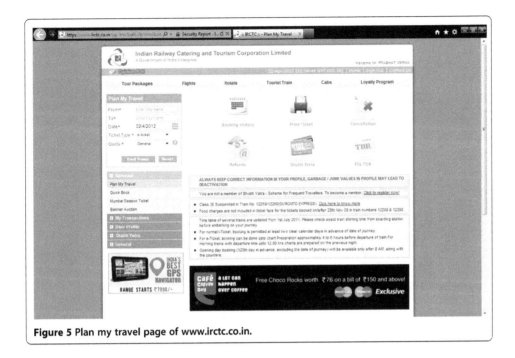

Figure 5 Plan my travel page of www.irctc.co.in.

Even some information pertaining to table data may not be semantically co-related since screen reader speaks out all the table headings followed by all the table data. For a big table, it becomes difficult to remember that which data belongs to what heading.

On "Ticket Reservation" page (Figure 8), speech equivalent for *captcha* is not provided which prevents a blind user to proceed further.

A blind user may accidently click a link or picture of an advertisement which may take him/her away from his website of interest.

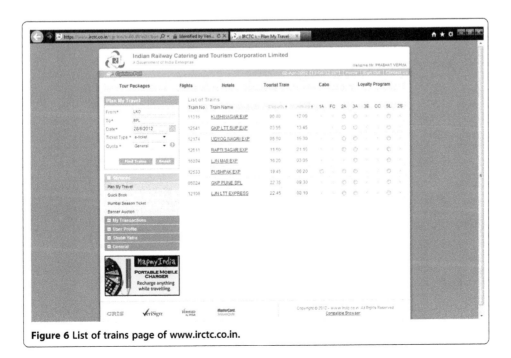

Figure 6 List of trains page of www.irctc.co.in.

Figure 7 Berth availability page of www.irctc.co.in.

Identify the key functionalities of the website

The first step is to identify the key functionalities on the Indian Railways website, which should be made accessible and usable through a speech based interface. The functionalities may be speech enabled in a phased manner: more important first. To begin with, *Book a Berth* is a heavily used functionality on the site. Thus, it a good start point to make this functionality speech enabled.

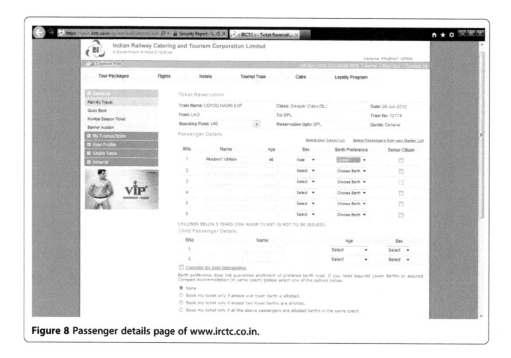

Figure 8 Passenger details page of www.irctc.co.in.

Speech enabling the book a berth functionality

The task *Book a Berth* is fairly complex as a user requires visiting at least Nine different web pages including two pages from a third party (i.e., Bank: to make payment). Each page has several links. Thus, after submitting a form on each page, user has to find the next page element of interest on his/her own as the control does not automatically redirect to the next desired page element. To speech enable the task *Book a Berth* as per our plan, the order of traversal of the active nodes is recorded by the *SpeechEnabler* in a macro on the host server. User request through the designated key shortcut triggers the relevant macro on the server. On the response page, *SpeechEnabler* assigns a unique ID to each active node in sequential order and adds the JavaScript code to establish a close chain among these active nodes. On the server side, it attaches the necessary code to interact with speech API. The response page is sent to the user along with the speech mp3 in sequential order of the active nodes.

The working of the speech enabled functionality *Book a Berth* may be demonstrated using the following *scenario*. Here, it is assumed that the blind user makes the use of down arrow keys to focus the next active nodes after filling the value for the current input.

(i) Home Page (Figure 9).
- a. Blind user presses the designated Functionality Key shortcut for *Book a Berth*
- b. Control transfers to "Login Form" on the left frame.
- c. System speaks: User Name, Text Box.
- d. Blind user enters his user name in the text box currently in focus, listens speech feedback for key-presses made by him/her.
- e. System speaks: Password, Text Box.
- f. User enters his Password, listens his key presses in the text box currently in focus.

Figure 9 Home page of www.irctc.co.in.

g. System speaks: Login, Submit Button.

h. On user click, Control transfers to linked page at "Plan My Travel" Form.

(ii) Plan My Travel Page (Figure 5).

a. System speaks: From, Text Box.

b. User enters the code for Source Station, listens his key presses in the text box currently in focus.

c. System speaks: To, Text Box.

d. User enters the code for Destination Station, listens his key presses in the text box currently in focus.

e. System speaks: Date, Date Table Object.

f. System speaks the Headers (Month name) from each table of months,

g. User clicks the month name in the table header currently in focus.

h. System speaks each date of the selected Month table sequentially.

i. User clicks the desired date in the table currently in focus.

j. System speaks: Ticket Type, Option Button.

k. System speaks options for Ticket Type, sequentially.

l. User clicks the desired Ticket Type in the Option Button currently in focus.

m. System speaks: Quota, Option Button.

n. System speaks options for Quota, sequentially.

o. User clicks the desired Quota Type in the Option Button currently in focus.

p. System speaks: Find Trains, Submit Button.

q. On user click, Control transfers to linked page at "List of Trains" Page.

(iii) List of Trains Page (Figure 6).

a. System speaks: List of Trains, Option Button.

b. System speaks options for Trains and berth availability.

c. User clicks the desired Train & Class in the Option Button currently in focus.

d. On user click, Control transfers to the page having "Train Details".

(iv) Train Details Page (Figure 7).

a. System speaks: Availability, Table with Links.

b. System speaks the table data sequentially for date, availability and Link for "Book."

c. User clicks the "Book" link on the desired date currently in focus.

d. Control transfers to the "Passenger Details" page

(v) Passenger Details Page (Figure 8).

a. System speaks: Name, Text Box.

b. User enters his name, listens his key presses in the text box currently in focus.

c. System speaks: Age, Text Box.

d. User enters his Age, listens his key presses in the text box currently in focus.

e. System speaks: Sex, Option Box.

f. System speaks the Options

g. User selects his Sex, currently in focus.

h. System speaks: Berth Preference, Option Box.

i. System speaks the Options,

j. User selects his Berth Preference, currently in focus.

k. System speaks: Senior Citizen, Checkbox.

l. User checks if eligible, the checkbox currently in focus.

m. System speaks: Verification Code, Text Box.

n. System speaks the code.

o. User enters each character of the code in the text box currently in focus after listening it.

p. System speaks: Go, Submit Button.

q. On user click, Control transfers to linked page at "Ticket Details" Page.

(vi) Ticket Details Page (Figure 10).

a. System speaks the details of the ticket.

b. System Speaks: Make Payment, Submit Button.

c. On user click, Control transfers to the "Make Payment" Page

(vii) Make Payment Page (Figure 11).

a. System speaks: Types for Payments, Option Button.

b. System speaks each available payment type

c. User clicks the preferred type currently under the focus.

d. System speaks: Options available, Radio Button.

e. System speaks the available options for the type of payment selected by the user.

f. User selects the preferred option under focus. Control transfers to the bank page for payment.

System assessment and performance analysis

In this paper we have outlined an alternative approach for addressing the issue related to usability of the websites of public interest. There are instances of important tasks like the one described by us as a case study, which are difficult to be performed by blind users using any of the existing web surfing tools. The proposed framework will provide workable and robust solutions to such complex

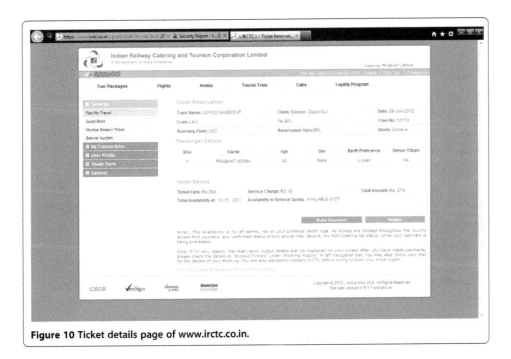

Figure 10 Ticket details page of www.irctc.co.in.

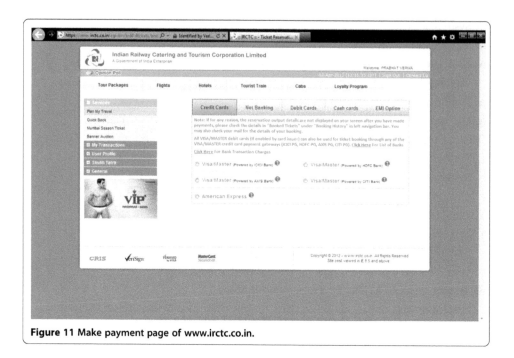

Figure 11 Make payment page of www.irctc.co.in.

tasks. Thus, a blind user can perform the task on any available public terminal conveniently.

An assessment of the framework has been performed by us on its early prototype with 5 blind web users. All the participants were adult males and already using the screen reader JAWS for web surfing. They were assigned the task of performing 'book a berth' first on the Indian Railways website using screen reader JAWS and then on the dummy speech-enabled Railways Reservation Website designed and created by us for testing purpose using the prototype framework. General structure of this dummy website is similar to the original one. However, JavaScript form validations are provided at individual field level. Since there was no actual provision for online payment on our dummy site, we could test the functionality 'Book a Berth' up to *filling Passenger details*. This was acceptable since most of our noted cases of indecision/confusion occur within this span of form filling.

Using screen reader on the Indian Railways website, none of the participants could complete the task without assistance. Four participants got stuck on the 'Plan my Journey' page. Only one participant could reach up to 'List of Trains' page where he could not locate the train details using screen reader. Participants were then asked to perform the same task on our speech-enabled dummy website for railway reservation. All the participants completed the task without difficulty. In fact, they were amazed by the simplicity and ease with they could perform this tedious task.

Overall results of this evaluation can be summarized as follows:

- *Usability* is visibly enhanced as all the participants could perform the task without difficulty.
- *Time* taken to perform 'Book a Berth' functionality is considerably reduced as compared to screen reader JAW.

- Due to chaining concept among related forms/fields and JavaScript validations on the individual field level, all the points of confusion and indecision during navigation are eliminated. Thus, *Navigability* is enhanced.

However, an exhaustive assessment of the framework with target group is still to be made that would be possible only after the System is developed completely.

Conclusions and future directions

In this paper, we highlighted the need and importance of direct speech-enabling the heavily used public websites for making their important services usable to the blind users and presented a framework for this purpose. These services may be accessed by blind users on any public terminal without having the need for any local installation. The approach is based on providing an alternate access system on the fly from one single site. The framework makes use of existing technologies like JavaScript, available speech APIs etc. Therefore, it provides a lightweight and robust solution to the accessibility problem. A future enhancement in the framework may be suggested where all the page elements except for the active nodes are 'locked' thus allowing blind users only to traverse along the active nodes in a definitive order.

Traditionally, an industry criterion for making investment on a project has been determined by the number of use cases offered by the aimed product. Thus, working at such a micro level may not gain due importance. Our work is primarily addressed to the responsible owners of the big websites meant for public usage that are accessed heavily. A little effort on their part could help blind users to a great extent. Thus, owners of the websites of public interest should come forward to add provisions for dedicated speech based interfaces for blind users.

All websites are not accessed equally on the Web. Therefore, it seems important that the websites which account for heavy traffic are made better accessible [19]. Public utility website owners should feel a greater sense of responsibility in providing feasible, error free and workable functionality from the point of view of blind users rather than leaving them to struggle with their screen readers. Usability, in its best form, at least for the most important functionalities, must be incorporated by the owners of these websites at the time of design itself. Other functionalities may be added up on the need basis in an incremental way.

It is hoped that the goal of achieving the benefits of internet to all including visually disabled users as desired by its original propagators can be achieved to some extent by providing the speech based dedicated functionalities on important websites of public interest.

Competing interests
The authors declare that they have no competing interests.

Authors' contributions
PV conceived of the study and its design. AKS participated in the design of the study and in drafting the diagrams. RRS reviewed and revised the whole manuscript. All authors read and approved the final manuscript.

Authors' information
Prabhat Verma works as Asst. Professor in CSE Department, Harcourt Butler Technological Institute, Kanpur. He has about 13 Years experience in academics. He did his Ph. d. in Computer Science and Engineering from Uttarakhand Technical University, Dehradun in January 2013, M. Tech. in Computer Science and Engineering from U. P.

Technological Institute, Lucknow in 2008 and B. E. in Computer Technology from Barkatullah University, Bhopal in 1992. His interests include Object Oriented Systems, Human Computer Interaction, and Web Technology.
Raghuraj Singh works as Professor in CSE Department, Harcourt Butler Technological Institute, Kanpur. He has about 22 Years experience in academics. He did his Ph.d. in Computer Science and Engineering from U. P. Technical University, Lucknow in 2006, M. S. in Software Systems from B.I.T.S. Pilani in 1997 and B. Tech. in Computer Science and Engineering from Kanpur University, Kanpur in 1990. He has graduated five Ph.D. students. His interests include Software Engineering, Artificial Intelligence, and Human Computer Interaction.
Avinash Kumar Singh has worked as a Research Fellow in CSE Department, Harcourt Butler Technological Institute, Kanpur. He has completed M. S. in Software Systems from BITS, Pilani in 2013 and Master in Computer Application from IGNOU, New Delhi in 2008. His interests include Brain Computer Interaction, Machine Learning, and Robotics.

Acknowledgements
The authors would like to thank the University Grant Commission, New Delhi, Uttarakhand Technical University, Dehradun and Adult Training Centre, National Institute of Visually Handicap, Dehradun for providing their support for the research work.

References
1. Steinmetz R, Nahrstedt K (2004) Multimedia applications. X media Publishing Series, Springer. ISBN 3540408495, 9783540408499
2. Enabling Dimensions (2002) Usage of computers and internet by the visually disabled: issues and challenges in the Indian context, findings of a study conducted by enabling dimensions, January 2002, New Delhi. http://www.enablingdimensions.com/downloads
3. Freedom Scientific. http://www.freedomscientific.com/ access date 18.02.2012
4. Harper S, Patel N (2005) Gist summaries for visually disabled surfers. In: ASSETS'05: Proceedings of the 7th international ACM SIGCCESS conference on Computers and accessibility, New York, NY, USA, 2005. pp 90–97
5. EMACSPEAK. http://emacspeak.sourceforge.net/smithsonian/study.html
6. Zajicek M, Powel C, Reeves C (1999) Web search and orientation with brookestalk. In: Proceedings of tech. and Persons with disabilities Conf. 1999. (CSUN'99), Los Angeles
7. Mahmud J, Borodin Y, Ramakrishnan IV (2007) Csurf: A context-driven non-visual web-browser. In: Proceedings of the International Conference on the World Wide Web (WWW'07), Banff, Alberta, Canada, May 08-12, 2007
8. Raman TV (1998) Audio system for technical reading, Ph.D. Thesis. Springer. ISBN 3-540-65515-8
9. Huang A, Sundaresan N (2000) A semantic transcoding system to adapt web services for users with disabilities. In: Fourth International ACM Conference on Assistive Technologies, November 13-15, 2000, Virginia, ACM-SIGCAPH. Published by ACM
10. Ramakrishnan I, Stent A, Yang A (2004) Hearsay: enabling audio browsing on hypertext content. In: Proceedings of the 13th International Conference on World Wide Web (2004). ACM Press, pp 80–89
11. Media Lab Asia http://medialabasia.in/index.php/shruti-drishti
12. Screen Access For All (SAFA) http://punarbhava.in/index.php?option=com_content&view=article&id=919&Itemid=291 access date 18.02.2012
13. Aloud Browse http://www.browsealoud.com access date 18.02.2012
14. Bigham J, Prince C, AND Ladner R (2008) WebAnywhere: a screen reader on-the-go, W4A2008 -Technical, April 21–22, 2008. Co-Located with the 17th International World Wide Web Conference, Beijing, China
15. Read Speaker. http://www.readspeaker.com/readspeaker-formreader/ access date 22.09.2013
16. Verma P, Singh R, Singh A (2011) SICE: an enhanced framework for design and development of speech interfaces on client environment, 2011. Int J Comp Appl (0975 – 8887) 28:3
17. Internet Macros. http://www.iopus.com/imacros/ access date 22.09.2013
18. Bigham J, Ladner R (2007) Accessmonkey: a collaborative scripting framework for web users and developers, in W4A2007 technical paper May 07–08, 2007. Co-Located with the 16th International World Wide Web Conference, Banff, Canada
19. (2012) WebInsight. http://webinsight.cs.washington.edu/accessibility/ access date 18.02.2012

9

ColShield: an effective and collaborative protection shield for the detection and prevention of collaborative flooding of DDoS attacks in wireless mesh networks

I Diana Jeba Jingle[1*] and Elijah Blessing Rajsingh[2*]

* Correspondence: dianajebajingle@
gmail.com; elijahblessing@karunya.edu
[1]Department of Computer Science
and Engineering, LITES, Thovalai,
India
[2]KSCST, Karunya University,
Coimbatore, India

Abstract

Wireless mesh networks are highly susceptible to Distributed Denial-of-Service attacks due to its self-configuring property. Flooding DDOS attack is one form of collaborative attacks and the transport layer of such networks are extremely affected. In this paper we propose *ColShield*, an effective and collaborative protection shield which not only detects flooding attacks but also prevents the flooding attacks through clever spoof detection. *ColShield* consists of Intrusion Protection and Detection Systems (IPDS) located at various points in the network which collaboratively defend flooding attacks. *ColShield* detects the attack node and its specific port number under attack. In order to reduce the burden on a single global IPDS, the system uses several local IPDS for the collaborative mitigation of flooding attacks. The evaluation of *ColShield* is done using extensive simulations and is proved to be effective in terms of false positive ratio, packet delivery ratio, communication overhead and attack detection time.

Keywords: Collaborative; Bandwidth; Traffic; Timer; IPDS; Spoofing

Introduction

Wireless mesh networks (WMN) has a wired-cum-wireless semi-centralized infrastructure that allows an end host to easily join the network and communicate with any host by exchanging packets. WMN uses a high speed back-haul network that can transmit packets at high bandwidth in large range. WMN consists of gateways that optimize the network performance and integration with other wireless networks, intermediate mesh routers that are stationary and mesh clients that are mobile. The mesh routers must be synchronized [27] as it is the optimal feature of WMN. These mesh routers operate as bridging points in inter-network and can be integrated with other wireless devices. However, the mobility and self-configuring property of wireless mesh networks (WMN) makes the attackers to prevent the internet's service to legitimate users by flooding excess amount of messages to the corresponding server thereby forming a Denial of Service (DoS) attack. The main objective of DoS attacks is either to completely tie up certain resources or to bring down an entire network so that the legitimate users are not able to access service(s).

DoS attackers mainly use IP spoofing as a moderator for launching flooding attacks. Such spoof-based flooding attacks can be traced easily if launched by a single attacker. The most sophisticated type of DoS attack is the flooding attack [28] that occurs at all the layers of WMN [11]. In case, if multiple attackers are collaboratively involved in launching flood packets at the victim, it will lead to a Distributed Denial of Service attack which is one form of collaborative flooding attack. The collaborative flooding DDoS attacks [42] are spread by natural distributed processing architecture of the network. It normally floods the mesh clients and the intermediate mesh routers using hierarchal control points [37] to congest the WMN traffic communication. Collaborative flooding DDoS attacks exploits the huge resource asymmetry between the internet and the victim. Collaborative flooding attacks can bring the entire network down and they are very hard to detect because the attack is distributed. Also it is impossible to trace the attacker. The attackers use a large number of machines to collaboratively flood packets simultaneously at the victim. These machines are ready to participate in the attack and are called as compromised machines [31] or zombies. To avoid these issues, this paper focuses on spoof-based collaborative detection of collaborative flooding DDoS attacks.

Intrusion detection systems [34] can be used to detect such collaborative flooding attacks; however, they may have a high incidence of false alarms. Current rules-based and anomaly-based intrusion detection systems detect intrusions either by matching patterns of network and users activities with pre-defined rules or they define the normal profile of system usages and then look for deviation. These approaches have their consequences and drawbacks. The former is well suited for known intrusions but it cannot detect new intrusions. The latter relies on deviation from normal usage and sometimes fails to detect well known intrusions. This paper presents an effective intrusion protection and detection system (IPDS) that detects and prevents collaborative flooding attacks against clever spoofs at the mesh client level. *ColShield* comprises of a distributed two-level architecture with group of local IPDS at the mesh router level and a single global IPDS at the gateway router level. All these IPDS collaboratively involve in protecting the source network from collaborative flooding of DDoS attacks. This informative paper aims to be an opening to a research that could hopefully end up with a mechanism to prevent flooding attacks.

This paper proceeds as follows. Section Related work summarizes the related work. Section The proposed system describes the architecture and operation of *ColShield* system and its metrics and algorithms. Section Performance results presents the simulations [29] we conducted to evaluate *ColShield*. Finally Section Conclusion concludes the paper.

Related work

DDoS attacks are quite advanced and powerful methods to attack a network system and to make it either unusable to the legitimate users or downgrade its performance. They are increasingly mounted by professional hackers in exchange for money and benefits. Yet there seems to be no silver bullet to the problem. This survey examines the possible solutions to this problem and analyzes the feasibility of those approaches. Based on the analysis of existing solutions, we proposed a desirable solution to defend collaborative flooding of DDoS. *Firecol* [1] uses Intrusion Prevention Systems (IPS) which form virtual protection rings around the hosts to defend flooding attacks collaboratively by exchanging selected traffic information. However, FireCol cannot detect the specific port under attack. SACK^2 [2] detects SYN flood attacks [5] against skillful spoofs. It does by identifying the victim server and the TCP port being attacked by exploiting the behavior of the SYN/ACK-CliACK pair. SACK^2 has low and controllable false positive and false negative rates as well as short detection delay. However, SACK^2 can detect only SYN flood attacks against skillful spoofs. TVA [24] uses capabilities to discard unauthorized traffic floods on a single autonomous system. TVA achieves high throughput, but the problem is TVA stores all capability information of each user on routers and a router with limited number of queues may not be able to protect all the legitimate users.

DWARD [13] autonomously detects and filters attack traffic from legitimate traffic by dropping the excess traffic by limiting the traffic rate to and from the victim thereby reducing the overload at the victim. But DWARD cannot detect attack traffic until connection buffer fills up thereby causing increased time delay to detect an attack and it causes more communication overhead. DARB [4] uses an active probing detection method and a TTL based rate-limit counteraction method to detect and filter SYN flooding attack [26] traffic accurately and independently on the victim side. DARB consumes more amount of the victim's bandwidth and causes computation overhead for both detecting and counteracting methods. Ge Zhang et al. [8] proposes a priority mechanism for blocking attacks on SIP proxies caused by external processing. But this mechanism causes time delay [41] and decreased throughput when SIP proxies interact with external servers. Haidar Safa et al. [9] proposed CDMS that is implemented at the edge routers of spoofed IP address' networks to defend the victim. CDMS also a communication protocol is used to encourage collaboration between various networks to protect each other. This mechanism is very efficient and it prevents the routers from being overloaded. However this mechanism causes time delay to detect and filter an attack. Sudip Misra *et al.* [20] proposed DLSR which uses the concept of Learning Automata (LA) and prevents the server being overloaded with excess amount of illegitimate traffic from crashing and keeps the server functioning. However DLSR cannot effectively differentiate valid user's IP address and spoofed user's IP address and it also causes excess time delay to detect and filter an attack. Patrick P.C. *et al.* [17] proposes an online early detection algorithm based on the statistical CUSUM method for detecting signalling DoS attacks on wireless networks in a timely manner. This approach does not detect the attack traffic that has a spoofed IP address and causes signaling load on the control plane. This mechanism detects signaling DoS attacks by monitoring inter-setup time samples and blocks both benign and malicious traffic when the signaling load reaches a threshold. Supranamaya Ranjan et al. [22] proposed DDoS-Shield to detect the attack packets that overwhelm the system resources such as bandwidth. DDoS Shield consist of a suspicion assignment mechanism that examines requests belonging to every session (TCP,UDP,ICMP) and assigns suspicion values to sessions and a DDoS-resilient scheduler that schedules the sessions based on the values assigned to the sessions and decides which session to be forwarded and when. The scheduler also performs rate-limiting. DDoS shield improves the victim's concert by consuming less memory for buffering requests and responses. However DDoS Shield consumes more processing time and cannot produce good throughput.

Joseph Chee Ming Teo et al. [14] proposes a group key agreement protocol to protect heterogeneous networks against DoS attacks. But it causes more communication overhead in heterogeneous networks. Wei Chen et al. [23] proposes a storage-efficient data structure and a change-point detection method to distinguish complete three-way TCP handshakes from incomplete ones. This mechanism leads to large memory consumption. Sungwon Yi et al. [15] introduced a two-level cache Content Addressable Memory (CAM) to dynamically detect and quarantine the unresponsive TCP flows [18]. But it leads to large memory comsumption. Dimitris Geneiata et al. [7] proposed a two-part bloom filter based monitor to detect and filter flooding attacks against proxy servers. The monitor's main task is to record the state of any incoming session in 3 different filters and the filter is indexed through a hash function. This mechanism uses an alarming system to trigger an alarm and report if any entries in the filter exceed the threshold value. This mechanism is very efficient and cost-effective and causes reduced time delay to detect an attack. However, hashing of entries in the filters leads to computation overhead and more CPU utilization. Dimitris Geneiatakis et al. [6] proposes a new header to overcome signaling DoS attacks in SIP servers. But the scheme uses a pre-shared key which when explored leads to password-based attacks and also it is vulnerable to man-in-the-middle attacks. It is observed in [9] that collaborative flooding attacks (DDoS) depend heavily on IP spoofing; therefore clever IP spoof detection might contribute to solving the problem. A common way for preventing IP spoofing is by using ingress and egress filters on firewalls [19]. But it fails in wireless networks where legitimate packets could have topologically incorrect addresses. In this paper, we have introduced a spoof-based collaborative detection of collaborative flooding attack (DDoS).

The proposed system

The ColShield system

The *ColShield* system (Figure 1) uses a semi-centralized architecture maintaining a group of local IPDS that is installed near the local routers and a global IPDS that is installed

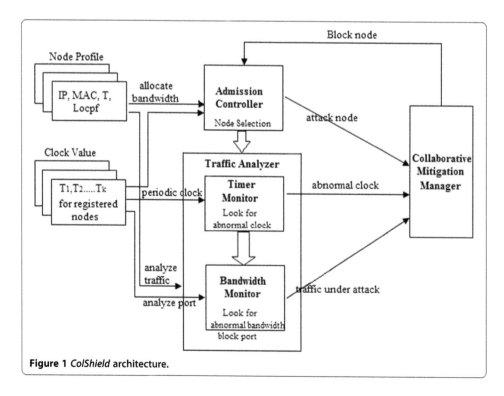

Figure 1 *ColShield* architecture.

near the gateway router. This paper focuses on spoof-based collaborative detection of collaborative flooding DDoS attacks. The *ColShield* system consists of four main components which mutually involve in mitigating collaborative flooding DDoS attacks. The Figure 1 shows the architectural view of the *ColShield* system. The ColShield components are described as follows: The *admission controller* is responsible for allocating initial bandwidth for each node using a bandwidth allocation algorithm. The *admission controller* accepts the node that completes the registration process successfully. The nodes have to initially register with the network by sending few confidential information. At the end of registration process, the *admission controller* allocates a bandwidth b_n and a bandwidth validity time, i.e., *TTL* for each node. The *traffic analyzer* component comprises of two components namely the *timer monitor* and the *bandwidth monitor*. The *timer monitor* maintains the clock values [21,25] being sent periodically by each node. These clock values are compared with the threshold value. The nodes that match the threshold value are forwarded to the *bandwidth monitor* for analyzing the traffic abnormalities. Finally, the *admission controller*, the *timer monitor* and the *bandwidth monitor* altogether informs the *collaborative mitigation manager* about their observation in abnormalities of each node. The *collaborative mitigation manager* decides whether to accept or to reject the node and its traffic. However, since the entire traffic cannot be possibly monitored altogether by a single global IPDS component, we promote the usage of multiple IPDS components for efficient detection and filtering of the attack.

The global IPDS maintains a node profile which consist of the following information namely the client node's IP address, the client node's MAC address, the client node's timer value, the client node's location proof information [30], the client node's allotted bandwidth and the TTL value. The global IPDS also maintains a local profile which consists of the IP address of the local IPDS, the total number of client nodes connected to it and its neighboring local IPDS. The local IPDS maintains a profile which consists of the timer values of each client node, the number of flows within each client node, its corresponding port number and the corresponding client node to which the flow is being transmitted or received.

Clever spoof detection

IP spoofing [10] is the main gateway for collaborative DoS attacks [9] which is considered as a most complex attack in which the attackers create raw IP packets with valid IP and TCP headers. An attacker might spoof a single source address or multiple source addresses. It is a difficult task for the listener to detect and filter the spoofing attacks with multiple source addresses than detecting spoofing attacks with single source address. Spoofing attacks can be prevented by using network ingress filters [3,12,16] and egress filters in proper network locations. *IP Security* (IPsec) also provides an excellent defense against IP spoofing, but this protocol generally cannot be required because its deployment is currently not suitable to work with wireless mesh networks [32]. Filtering does not solve the problem of collaborative flooding of DoS attacks and it is a quite challenging task to block spoofing attacks with multiple source addresses. Hence clever spoof detection is necessary to mitigate collaborative DoS attacks. The clever spoof detection process is depicted in Figure 2 and it is carried out in two phases. The admission controller initiates the detection process in phase 1 (Algorithm 1) and timer manager completes the detection process in phase 2 (Algorithm 2). During phase 1, the

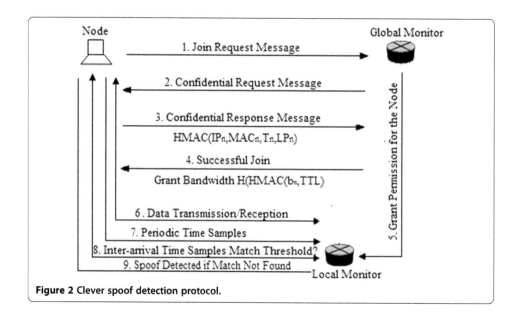

Figure 2 Clever spoof detection protocol.

bandwidth allocation is done for each node and in phase 2, the inter-arrival time samples are monitored for each node. We monitor the inter-arrival time samples at each node in order to detect the presence of IP spoofing in wireless mesh networks thereby providing a way to mitigate collaborative flooding attacks.

Admission controller

We model the backbone of the wireless mesh network (WMN) R as a directed graph $G = (V, E)$ where V represents the set of client nodes in the network and E represents set of directed links. $V = N + M$ where $N = n_1, n_2, \ldots n_r$ is the set of registered nodes in the network and each client node $n \notin N$. M is the set of monitor nodes in the network and it is represented as $M = G_m + \{L_m\}$ where G_m represents the global IPDS and L_m represents the local monitor. The network consists of a group of intrusion protection and detection systems (IPDS) with a single global IPDS, G_m and a cluster of local IPDS L_m. Each client node n before it joins a network has to send a join request message, R_j (n) to the global IPDS G_m. The G_m requests a confidential message $REQ_c(n)$ to client node n to prove its identity. The client in turn replies with its confidential message $RES_c(n)$ to the G_m. The confidential reply message consists of four pieces of information namely, IP address of the client node IP_n, MAC address of the client node MAC_n, Timer value of the client node $z_n(t_i)$ and LP_n, the location proof information [33] of the client node which refers to the actual distance of the client node n from the global IPDS G_m. $z_n(t_i) = z_n(t_c) + K_{sec}$ where $z_n(t_c)$ is the client node's current time and K_{sec} is the client node's secret key. The length of the secret key K_{sec} is 16 bits and its initial value is obtained by adding the least significant 8 bits of IP address with the least significant 8 bits of MAC address along with a 16 bit random number. These 32 bits are hashed into a 16 bit secret key value which forms the length of K_{sec}. The subsequent values of K_{sec} is incremented by 1 bit from the initial value every t_i time interval. The LP_n value is obtained by adding the client node's current distance from the global IPDS D_n with the client node's current available time $z_n(t_c)$. Thus if a client node wants to prove its identity, the IP_n, MAC_n and LP_n values should match $z_n(t_i)$. The G_m by checking the validity of confidential information, replies with a successful join and grants a bandwidth b_n along with TTL to the client node n. TTL is the bandwidth validity period for client node n. The client node after receiving the bandwidth becomes a part of the network. In this phase, the initial stage of spoof detection is done.

Algorithm 1: *Bandwidth Allocation Algorithm*

$Input:$ $set\ of\ client\ nodes\ n\ that\ have\ not\ yet\ registered.$
  $i.e., n \notin N.$
$Output:$ $bandwidth\ allocation\ b_n\ for\ client\ node\ n.$
$Step\ 1:$ $Client\ node\ n\ sends\ a\ join\ request\ message\ R_j$
  $to\ G_m\ .$
$Step\ 2:$ $The\ G_m\ asks\ for\ confidential\ request\ message$
  $REQ_c\ from\ client\ node\ n.$
$Step\ 3:$ $Client\ node\ n\ replies\ with\ a\ confidential\ response$
  $RES_c\ to\ the\ G_m.$
$Step\ 4:$ $If\ IP_n, MAC_n, LP_n \Rightarrow z_n(t_i)\ then\ return\ true(n)$
  $i.e., client\ node\ n\ is\ not\ spoofed.$
$Step\ 5:$ $If\ IP_n, MAC_n, z_n(t_i), LP_n \Rightarrow true(n) then$
  $grant(H(HMAC(b_n, TTL))$
$Step\ 6:$ $Client\ node\ n\ successfully\ joins\ the\ network.$
  $Now\ n \in N.$

Traffic analyzer

Each *ColShield* IPDS analyzes the traffic within its detection window range. The traffic analyzer consists of two components of which the timer monitor completes the spoof detection process and the bandwidth monitor [35] initiates the flood detection process (Algorithm 3). The timer monitor involve in checking the periodic timer values of each mesh client node. Each mesh client node after joining the network is under the control of the local IPDS. The registered mesh client node, in order to prove its identity to the local IPDS sends periodic timer values to its local IPDS, i. e., L_m. The timer values are the inter arrival time samples of each mesh client node being sent periodically. The local monitor checks the validity of the client node by comparing whether the subsequent inter-arrival timer values match the threshold. The local IPDS concludes the client node as abnormal if the inter-arrival timer values did not match the threshold value by which spoofed node is detected. The timer monitor is described by a timer function,

$$q_n = \max(E(z_n(t)), z_n(t_i)) \tag{1}$$

where $E(z_n(t)$ is the determined threshold value for node n and $z_n(t_i)$ is the actual real-time timer value of node n to be compared with. If $z_n(t_i) = E(z_n(t))$ then $q_n = 0$ and the timer value of node n is benign. If $z_n(t_i) \neq E(z_n(t))$ then the timer value of node n is suspected to be malicious and has to undergo a condition check to confirm the attack. $z_n(t_i)$ values can exceed within an upper limit α and a lower limit β where

α and β are pre-specified constant parameters and $\alpha = \beta = 1$. If the value of $z_n(t_i)$ is greater than $E(z_n(t))$ then the $z_n(t_i)$ value for node n is considered to be malicious if it exceeds the α value. (i.e.) $z_n(t_i) + \alpha = E(z_n(t))$. Likewise, if the $z_n(t_i)$ value is less than $E(z_n(t))$ then the $z_n(t_i)$ value for node n is considered to be malicious if it exceeds the β value. (i.e.) $z_n(t_i) - \beta = E(z_n(t))$. The local IPDS L_m monitors the periodic time samples of all nodes at a given time slot t_i. For a node n the actual real-time timer values is given as,

$$\sum_{\substack{i=1 \\ n \in N}}^{r} z_n(t_i) = \sum_{\substack{i=1 \\ n \in N}}^{r} (z_n(t_i) - \beta) \| (z_n(t_i) + \alpha) \quad (2)$$

$z_n(t_i)$ value can be further expressed as,

$$\sum_{\substack{i=1 \\ n \in N}}^{r} A z_n(t_i) \geq \sum_{\substack{i=1 \\ n \in N}}^{r} z_n(t_i) \leq \sum_{\substack{i=1 \\ n \in N}}^{r} B z_n(t_i) \qquad (3)$$

where, $\displaystyle\sum_{\substack{i=1 \\ n \in N}}^{r} A z_n(t_i) = \sum_{\substack{i=1 \\ n \in N}}^{r} (z_n(t_i) - \beta)$ and $\displaystyle\sum_{\substack{i=1 \\ n \in N}}^{r} B z_n(t_i) = \sum_{\substack{i=1 \\ n \in N}}^{r} (z_n(t_i) + \alpha)$.

The bandwidth monitor has the responsibility to monitor the bandwidth consumption of each client node. During this phase, the local IPDS involve in detecting flooding attacks. The bandwidth monitor categorizes the traffic flow as normal and abnormal. The traffic is said to be normal if the amount of bandwidth consumption adhere to the limit and abnormal traffic consumes a higher bandwidth than the limit. The bandwidth consumption in the sense includes the bandwidth consumed by a single node, per-node per-flow bandwidth and per-node multiple-flow bandwidth. We consider the bandwidth allocation for the global and local IPDS to be stable and predefined. Our aim is to allocate bandwidth for each client node $n \notin N$ and to monitor whether each client node utilizes their allotted bandwidth. Let I_u be the bandwidth update interval which is the time between the last bandwidth allocation and current bandwidth reallocation for each client node. Each client node is permitted to utilize only their allotted bandwidth. Nodes failing to use b_n might have been deviated to $b_{n'}$. The deviation of b_n and $b_{n'}$ must not exceed ϖ. The local IPDS checks whether the fraction of bandwidth allotted for each client node is normal. The local IPDS does this by using the formula, $b_n \leq B_r / N$ where B_r is the total bandwidth allotted to the mesh client nodes in the network. The local IPDS checks whether the fraction of bandwidth utilized per-flow during a single time interval by each client node is within the allotted bandwidth. The per-node per-flow bandwidth is given by, $b_{nf} \leq b_n / C_n$ where C_n is the number of flows established between a mesh client node and another. The local IPDS also checks whether the fraction of bandwidth consumption for all flows per-node during subsequent time intervals. The per-node multiple-flow bandwidth is given by,

$$\sum_{\substack{1 \leq t \leq r \\ 1 \leq f \leq k}} b_{nft} \leq b_n / C_n \qquad (4)$$

where f represents the number of flows established between a mesh client node and another node and t represents the time interval of the allotted bandwidth. If any abnormalities were found, the local IPDS detects the attacker node and its port number.

Algorithm 2: *Timer Monitor Algorithm*

$Input: Timer\ values\ of\ each\ clientnode\ z_n(t_i)$
$\qquad i = 1 \ldots k\ and\ n \in N$
$Output: Boolean\ value\ true(n)\ or\ false(n)$
$Timer\ function: q_n = \max(E(z_n(t)), z_n(t_i))$

1. $\forall_{\substack{i=1\ldots r \\ n \in N}} If\ z_n(t_i) = E(z_n(t))\ then$
2. $\qquad return\ true(n)$
3. $Else\ if\ z_n(t_i) \neq E(z_n(t))\ then$
4. $\qquad If\ z_n(t_i)) < E(z_n(t))\ then$
5. $\qquad\qquad q_n = E(z_n(t))$
6. $\qquad\qquad If\ Az_n(t_i) = E(z_n(t))\ then$
7. $\qquad\qquad\qquad return\ true(n)$
8. $\qquad\qquad Else$
9. $\qquad\qquad\qquad return\ false(n) => spoof\ detected$
10. $\qquad\qquad Endif$
11. $\qquad Else\ if(z_n(t_i)) > E(z_n(t))\ then$
12. $\qquad\qquad q_n = z_n(t_i)$
13. $\qquad\qquad If\ Bz_n(t_i) = E(z(t))\ then$
14. $\qquad\qquad\qquad return\ true(n)$
15. $\qquad\qquad Else$
16. $\qquad\qquad\qquad return\ false(n) => spoof\ detected$
17. $\qquad\qquad Endif$
18. $\qquad Endif$
19. $Endif$

Algorithm 3: *Bandwidth Monitor Algorithm*

$Input: Set\ of\ registered\ client\ nodes\ n \in N$
$\qquad b_n, bandwidth\ fraction\ allotted\ to\ node\ n.$
$Output: Boolean\ value\ true(n)\ or\ false(n)$

$Step\ 1: If\ b_n \leq B_r/N \rightarrow true(n)\ then\ go\ to\ step\ 4.$

$Step\ 2: If\ b_n \leq B_r/N \rightarrow false(n) then\ go\ to\ step\ 3.$

$Step\ 3: If\ dev(b_n, b_n') \leq \varpi \rightarrow true(n)\ then\ go\ to\ step\ 4\ 4$

$\qquad Else\ go\ to\ step\ 6.$

$Step\ 4: If\ b_{nf} \leq b_n/C_n\ then\ return\ true(n)$

$\qquad Go\ to\ step\ 5$

$Step\ 5: If\ \sum_{\substack{1 \leq t \leq r \\ 1 \leq f \leq k}} b_{nft} \leq b_n/C_n\ then\ r\ eturn\ true(n)$

$Step\ 6: return\ false(n) \Rightarrow flood\ detected$

Collaborative mitigation

We focus on spoof-based collaborative mitigation of collaborative flooding DDoS attacks (Algorithm 4) [36]. All the local IPDS and the global IPDS collaboratively involve in mitigating the flooding attacks (Algorithm 5). The local IPDS L_m executes the bandwidth monitoring algorithm for detecting the attacker client node. Once it detects the attacker client node, it first blocks the port number under attack and then blocks the future traffic to and from the specified port number. It then informs the neighboring local IPDS NL_m about the

Attacker IP Address	ALERT Message

Figure 3 ALERT message format.

attacker client node by sending an ALERT message which contains the IP address of the attacker client node and an ALERT message which is depicted in Figure 3. Now the local IPDS along with its neighbors inform the global IPDS about the attacker. When the global IPDS receives the ALERT message, it blocks future traffic to and from that client node under attack and revokes the allotted bandwidth from that client node. Now the client node under attack is released from the network and it cannot communicate with the nodes in the spoofed network. Thus flooding attack is collaboratively mitigated in this phase. Again if the released node wishes to join the network, it has to re-register and obtain new bandwidth from the network. The attacker in any case cannot bypass the bandwidth monitor test and thus it fails which leads to repeated re-registration process. The effectiveness of *ColShield* lies with the traffic analyzer which aims at analyzing abnormal traffic from the client nodes. Our paper focuses on detecting spoof-based collaborative flooding attacks (i. e., detecting collaborative flooding attacks that occur through IP spoofing). *ColShield* can detect 85% of spoofed nodes and once spoofing attacks are detected, collaborative flooding attacks are easily detected and mitigated because collaborative flooding attacks don't have much effect on spoof free nodes.

Algorithm 4: *Collaborative Mitigation Algorithm*

$Input:$ f_n, $incoming$ $traffic$ $flow$ at $node$ n
   $z_n(t_i)$, the $periodic$ $timer$ $values$
   $i = 1 \dots r$ and $n \in N$
$Output:$ $DDoS$ $free$ $network$
$Step$ $1:$ If $z_n(t_i) \rightarrow false(n)$ $then$
$Step$ $2:$ $L_m \rightarrow block$ (IP_n, P_n)
$Step$ $3:$ $Else$ if $f_n \rightarrow false(n)$ $then$
$Step$ $4:$ $L_m \rightarrow block$ (f_n)
$Step$ $5:$ $signal(alert(L_m(n))) \rightarrow recv(NL_m)$
$Step$ $6:$ $signal(alert(L_m(n), NL_m(n))) \rightarrow recv(G_m)$
$Step$ $7:$ $G_m \rightarrow block$ (n)
$Step$ $8:$ $G_m \rightarrow remove$ (n)
$Step$ $9:$ $Endif$
$Step$ $10:$ $Endif$

ColShield metrics

ColShield maintains the following metrics:

1) *Traffic flow metric:* This metric helps to calculate the total number of communications taken place in the network when we install the ColShield system in the network. The total traffic flow at the global IPDS is given by,

$$f(G_m) = \sum_{m=1}^{i} f_{out}(L_m) \tag{5}$$

where $f_{out}(L_m)$ is the sum of all outgoing traffic flow coming out from all the local IPDS. All mesh client nodes has to pass through the local IPDS to send and receive messages. Therefore, the total traffic flow at the local IPDS is obtained by adding the total incoming and outgoing traffic flow at each mesh client node. The total traffic flow at the local IPDS is given by,

$$f(L_m) = \sum_{n \in N} f_{in}(n) + \sum_{n \in N} f_{out}(n) \tag{6}$$

where $f_{in}(n)$ is the client node's incoming traffic and $f_{out}(n)$ is the client node's outgoing traffic. The total traffic flow at the mesh client nodes is given by,

$$f(n) = \sum_{c=1}^{i} f_c(n) + \sum_{d=1}^{i} f_d(n) \tag{7}$$

where $f_c(n)$ is the client node's control flow traffic and $f_d(n)$ is the client node's are the control flow traffic and data flow traffic at the mesh client nodes.

The control flow traffic at the mesh client node n is given by,

$$f_c(n) = f_{cin}(n) + f_{cout}(n) \tag{8}$$

where $f_{cin}(n)$ is the client node's incoming control flow traffic and $f_{cout}(n)$ is the client node's outgoing control flow traffic. The data flow traffic at the mesh client node n is given by,

$$f_d(n) = f_{din}(n) + f_{dout}(n) \tag{9}$$

where $f_{din}(n)$ is the incoming data flow traffic at the client node and $f_{dout}(n)$ is the outgoing data flow traffic at the client node. The total number of control messages exchanged between the mesh clients, the local IPDS and the global IPDS are required to calculate the communication overhead.

2) *Throughput metric:* The proposed system guarantees a minimum throughput of λ and all client nodes should adhere within this throughput. i.e.,

$$\sum_{n \in N} b_n \leq \lambda \tag{10}$$

The throughput is affected by the fraction of bandwidth allocated to each client node. The client nodes for which the bandwidth is allocated through the bandwidth allocation protocol are considered for achieving wireless mesh network throughput.

3) *Bandwidth allocation metric:* b_n is the fraction of bandwidth allotted to each client node $n \in N$ and $B_r = B - B_{mb}$ where B is the total bandwidth allotted to the network, B_{mb} is the bandwidth allotted for the local and global IPDS and B_r is the bandwidth allotted to each mesh client nodes who joins the network. The bandwidth constraint is given by,

$$b_n \leq B_r / N \tag{11}$$

4) *Bandwidth deviation metric:* The bandwidth deviation metric is given by,

$$dev(b_n, b_{n'}) \leq \varpi \tag{12}$$

Each client node is allotted a bandwidth b_n within the network and they are permitted to utilize only their allotted bandwidth. Nodes failing to use b_n might

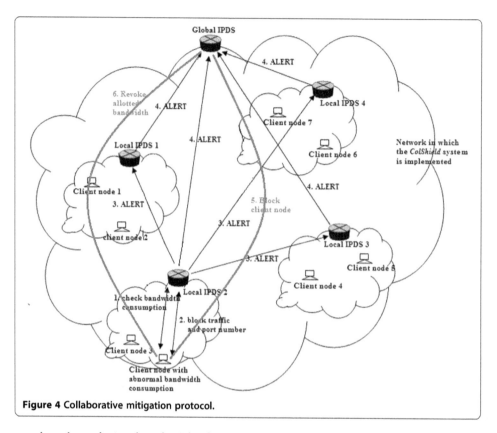

Figure 4 Collaborative mitigation protocol.

have been deviated to $b_{n'}$. The deviation of b_n and $b_{n'}$ must not exceed ϖ whose value is 0.1. If the deviation exceeds ϖ then it leads to rejection of that client node.

Performance results

We used NS-2 simulator for implementing WMN model for security [37,38] against collaborative flooding attack (DDOS). The model is adapted from the IEEE 802.11b/g based adhoc network including the mesh clients that are mobile and backbone mesh routers that are stable. The hierarchical architecture of the WMN was implemented using administrative domain (AD) cluster design. In the model, a gateway router was statically assigned as global IPDS and the local routers are statically assigned as local IPDS while the client nodes are enabled using random waypoint wireless model as mesh clients. In addition, the gateway router is assigned as back-bone router. The adhoc network security standard IEEE802.11i was used for simulation due to the ongoing standardization of WMN security. We have compared the performance of *ColShield* with *FireCol*. We use the following metrics for evaluating the performance of *ColShield*: 1) false positive ratio 2) detection time 3) packet delivery ratio and 4) communication overhead 5) average throughput 6) bandwidth consumption and 7) registration overhead.

1) *Packet delivery ratio (PDR):* It is the ratio of the total number of packets delivered to the mesh client to the total number of packets received at the local IPDS. The local IPDS delivers those packets that wins the timer manager protocol and the bandwidth monitor protocol. Figure 5 shows the packet delivery ratio of *ColShield* with respect to the percentage of local IPDS. The PDR is reasonably good and does not affect the performance of the network.

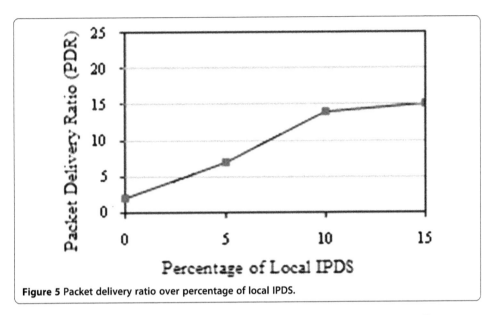

Figure 5 Packet delivery ratio over percentage of local IPDS.

2) *False positive ratio:* The false positive rate is the amount of legitimate traffic wrongly detected as malicious. Since each IPDS store the full TCP connection information, it can have false rates. However, this will not affect the final detection behavior. Figure 6 shows the false positive rates of *FireCol* and *ColShield* with respect to the percentage of local IPDS. The false positive ratio is roughly increased to 5% which is acceptable and does not affect the final detection results.

3) *Attack Detection Time:* The attack detection time is the delay between the attack occurs and when it is detected. The detection of flooding attack [39,40] is based on detection of increase in a client node's clock inter-arrival times. Figure 7 shows the detection delay for *FireCol* and *ColShield*. The *ColShield* can detect the start of the attack within one detection time interval and end of an attack within two detection time periods. The proposed method can achieve more accurate detection with a shot latency. When the percentage of local IPDS increases, the attack detection time is less.

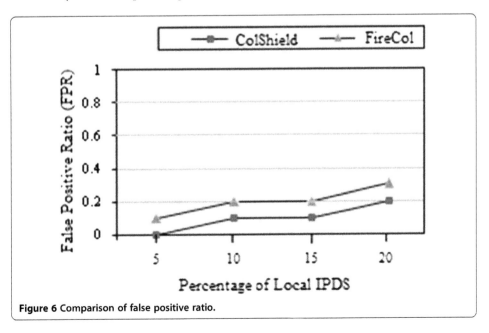

Figure 6 Comparison of false positive ratio.

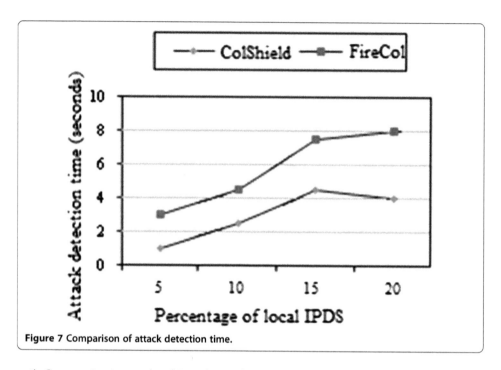

Figure 7 Comparison of attack detection time.

4) *Communication overhead:* It is the total number of control messages exchanged between the mesh clients, the local IPDS and the global IPDS. Compared to the mesh client level and the gateway router level, the maximum number of communications take place at the mesh router level. The communication overhead is obtained by summing up the total traffic flow at the global IPDS and the local IPDS. The communication overhead for *ColShield* is depicted in Figure 8. The figure shows the percentage of data messages and control messages being transmitted in the wireless mesh network. Only 20% of control messages are exchanged within the system which is comparetively less than the total number of data packets exchanged in the system. The communication overhead does not affect the performance of the network.

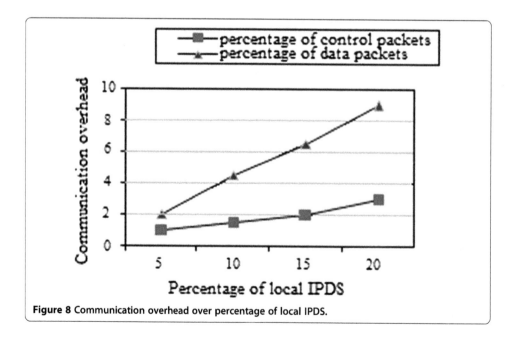

Figure 8 Communication overhead over percentage of local IPDS.

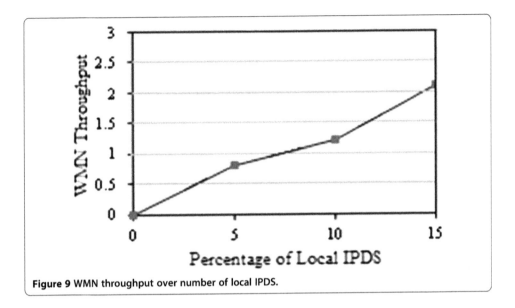

Figure 9 WMN throughput over number of local IPDS.

5) *WMN throughput*: It is defined as the sum of the data delivered to all the client nodes in the network in a given time unit (seconds). The throughput is affected by the fraction of bandwidth allotted to each client node in the network. Figure 9 shows the WMN throughput with respect to the percentage of local IPDS. The client nodes that obtain bandwidth through the bandwidth allocation process are eligible for achieving WMN throughput.

6) *Attack detection ratio:* It is the rate at which the spoofing attacks and the flooding attacks are detected. When the network size increases the percentage of local IPDS increases which leads to the increase in attack detection ratio. Once the spoofing attacks are detected, the flooding attacks are detected easily in a timely manner. Figure 10 shows the attack detection ratio of the *ColShield* system with respect to the percentage of local IPDS in the WMN. The attack detection ratio calculates the

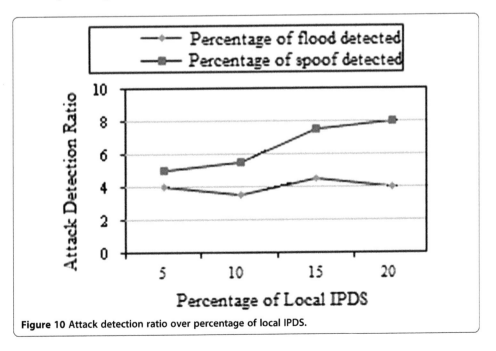

Figure 10 Attack detection ratio over percentage of local IPDS.

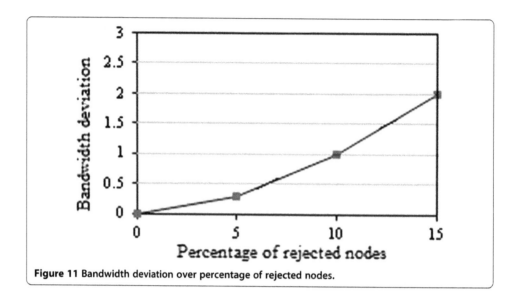

Figure 11 Bandwidth deviation over percentage of rejected nodes.

percentage of spoofing attack detected by the system while running the bandwidth allocation process and the timer monitor protocol. The attack detection ratio also calculates the percentage of flooding attacks detected by the system while running the bandwidth monitor protocol. The attack detection ratio for spoofing attack and flooding attack is reasonably good which is the goal of the *ColShield* System.

7) *Bandwidth deviation:* It is the fraction of deviated bandwidth from the allotted bandwidth. Figure 11 shows the percentage of bandwidth deviation with respect to the percentage of rejected nodes. The percentage of rejected nodes increases when they cross the threshold value ϖ. It is strictly followed that nodes that have a bandwidth deviation beyond the threshold value are rejected.

8) *Registration overhead:* The number of communications and the number of computations required by a client node during the registration process determines the registration overhead (Figure 12). A single client node communicates four messages to complete the registration process. But each node requires X-OR computations for a single timer value to complete the registration process, which is reasonable. The

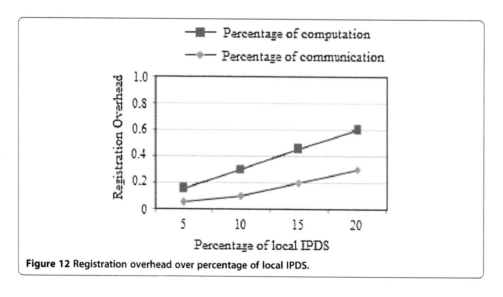

Figure 12 Registration overhead over percentage of local IPDS.

computations are required in all phases to continually monitor the registration of client nodes, to allocate bandwidth as well as to analyze traffic and to effectively mitigate spoof-based collaborative flooding attacks. The computation overhead can be balanced by placing reasonable number of local IPDs in the network. As the number of local IPDS increases in the network, the computation overhead is tolerated to 60%.

ColShield effectiveness relies on the collaboration between different IPDS. The *ColShield* cannot be enabled on all routers. The IPDS are routers that perform detection and forward messages to the neighboring routers and the global IPDS. An IPDS communicates with neighboring IPDS only for signaling collaborative information. Thus only 20% of communication overhead is caused in the network which does not affect the performance of the network.

Conclusion

In this paper, we propose an effective flood detection and prevention architecture, *ColShield* to detect flooding attacks and also report the specific victim client node and port being attacked. *ColShield* does not give any chance for an attacker to evade the detection. The time taken to detect the start of an attack is less than one detection interval and the time taken to detect the end of an attack is less than two detection intervals. Through simulations, it is demonstrated that *ColShield* is the fastest and most accurate detection method compared with *FireCol*.

Competing interests
The authors declare that they have no competing interests.

Authors' contributions
I.Diana Jeba Jingle carried out the studies on wireless mesh networks and distributed denial-of-service attacks, designed the architecture and algorithms, carried out the simulation experiments and drafted the manuscript. Elijah Blessing Rajsingh provided full guidance and support to prepare the manuscript. All authors read and approved the final manuscript.

Authors' information
I. Diana Jeba Jingle is the Assistant Professor of Loyola Institute of Technology and Sciences, India. She reveived her Bachelor of Engineering degree in Information Technology from Sun College of Engineering and Technology, Anna University, India in 2006. She received her Master of Engineering degree in Computer Science from Francis Xavier Engineering College, Anna University, India in 2008. Currently she is pursuing her Ph.D in Karunya University, Coimbatore, India. Her research interests lie in the area of Wireless Networks, Mobile Ad-hoc Networks and network security and specifically focus on denial-of-service characterization, detection and defense, IP spoofing defense. She is a member of CSI. Elijah Blessing Rajsingh is the Professor and Director for the Department of Computer Science and Engineering of Karunya University, India. He received his Master of Engineering degree with Distinction from the College of Engineering, Anna University, India. He received the Ph. D degree in Information and Communication Engineering from the College of Engineering, Anna University, India in 2005, focusing on Security in Wired and Wireless Networks. He is the member of IEEE. He has very strong research background in the areas of Network Security, Mobile Computing, Wireless & Ad hoc Networks, Parallel and Distributed Computing. He is an Associate Editor for International Journal of Computers & Applications, Acta Press, Canada and member of the editorial review board for International Journal of Cases in E Commerce as well as for Information Resources Management Journal, Idea Group Publishers, USA. He is the recognized guide for Ph.D students of Karunya University and is guiding students in their doctoral programme. He has published a number of papers in well-referred international journals and conferences.

Acknowledgement
We would like to thank the reviewers for their valuable comments.

References
1. François J, Aib I, Boutaba R (2012) Firecol: a collaborative protection network for the detection of flooding Ddos attacks. IEEE/ACM Trans Networking 20(6):1828-1841
2. Sun C, Hu C, Liu B (2012) SACK2: effective SYN flood detection against skillful spoofs. IET Inf Secur 6(3):149–156

3. Shevtekar A, Anantharam K, Ansari N (2005) Low rate TCP denial-of-service attack detection at edge routers. IEEE Commun Lett 9(4):363-365

4. Xiaoa B, Chenb W, Hec Y (2008) An autonomous defense against SYN flooding attacks: detect and throttle attacks at the victim side independently. J Parallel Distr Comput 68:456–470

5. Cert Advisory Ca-1996-21 (1996) TCP SYN Flooding and IP Spoofing Attacks". CERT CC. https://www.cert.org/historical/advisories/CA-1996-21.cfm?

6. Geneiatakis D, Lambrinoudakis C (2007) A lightweight protection mechanism against signaling attacks in a SIP-based VoIP environment". Telecommun Syst 36(4):153–159

7. Geneiatakis D, Vrakas N, Lambrinoudakis C (2009) Utilizing bloom filters for detecting flooding attacks against SIP based services. J Comput Secur 28(7):578–591

8. Zhang G, Fischer-Hübner S, Ehlert S (2010) Blocking attacks on SIP VoIP proxies caused by external processing". Telecommun Syst 45(1):61–76

9. Safa H, Chouman M, Artail H, Karam M (2008) A collaborative defense mechanism against SYN flooding attacks in IP networks. J Netw Comput Appl 31(4):509–534

10. Mopari IB, Pukale SG, Dhore ML (2009) Detection of DDoS attack and defense against ip spoofing. In: Proceedings of the International Conference on Advances in Computing, Communication and Control, ICAC3'09, Mumbai, Maharashtra, India, PP, pp 489–493

11. Khalil I, Bagchi S, Shroff NB (2008) Mobiworp: mitigation of the wormhole attack in mobile multihop wireless networks. J Ad Hoc Netw 6:344–362

12. Ioannidis J, Bellovin S (2002) Implementing Pushback: Router-Based Defense Against Dos Attacks. In: Proc. NDSS

13. Mirkovic J, Reiher P (2005) D-WARD: A Source-End Defense Against Flooding Denial-Of-Service Attacks. IEEE Trans Dependable Secure Comput 2(3):216-232

14. Chee J, Teo M, Tan CH, Ng JM (2007) Denial-of-service attack resilience dynamic group key agreement for heterogeneous networks". Telecommun Syst 35(3–4):141–160

15. Saxena N, Denko M, Banerji D (2010) A hierarchical architecture for detecting selfish behaviour in community wireless mesh networks. J Comp Commun 548–555

16. Ferguson P, Senie D (2000) Network Ingress Filtering: Defeating Denial Of Service Attacks That Employ IP Source Address Spoofing. Internet RFC 2827

17. Lee PPC, Bu T, Woo T (2009) On the detection of signaling Dos attacks On 3G/Wimax wireless networks. J Comput Netw 53(15):2601–2616

18. Yi S, Deng X, Kesidis G, Das CR (2008) A dynamic quarantine scheme for controlling unresponsive TCP sessions. Telecommun Syst 37(4):169–189

19. Misra S, Dhurandher SK, Rayankula A, Agrawal D (2010) Using honeynodes for defense against jamming attacks in wireless infrastructure-based networks. J Comput Electr Eng 36(2):367–382

20. Misra S, Krishna PV, Abraham KI, Sasikumar N, Fredun S (2010) An adaptive learning routing protocol for the prevention of distributed denial of service attacks in wireless mesh networks. Comput Math Appl 60(2):294–306

21. Jana S, Kasera SK (2010) On fast and accurate detection of unauthorized wireless access points using clock skews. IEEE Trans Mob Comput 9(3):449–462

22. Ranjan, Swaminathan R, Uysal M, Nucci A, Knightly E (2009) DDoS-Shield: DDoS-Resilient scheduling to counter application layer attacks. IEEE/ACM Trans Networking 17(1):26–39

23. Chen W, Yeung D-Y (2006) Throttling spoofed SYN flooding traffic at the source". Telecommun Syst 33(1–3):47–65

24. Yang X, Wetherall D, Anderson T (2008) TVA: A DoS-limiting network architecture. IEEE/ACM Trans Networking 16(6):1267-1280

25. Jana S, Kasera SK (2010) On fast and accurate detection of unauthorized wireless access points using clock skews. IEEE Trans Mob Comput 9(3):449-462

26. Wang H, Zhang D, Shin KG (2002) Detecting SYN flooding attacks". In: Proceedings of IEEE INFOCOM, vol 23, pp 1530–1539

27. Granelli F, Doron E, Wool A (2009) IEEE 802.11s Wireless Mesh Networks: Challenges and Perspectives. In: Proceedings of Lecture Notes of the Institute for Computer Sciences, Social Informatics and Telecommunications Engineering (LNICST), vol 13, pp 263–271

28. Fallah MS (2010) A puzzle-based defense strategy against flooding attacks using game theory. IEEE Trans Dependable Secure Comput 7(1):5–19

29. Mirkovic J, Hussain A, Fahmy S, Reiher P, Thomas RK (2009) Accurately measuring denial of service in simulation and testbed experiments. IEEE Trans Dependable Secure Comput 6(2):81–95

30. Kuo S-P, Kuo H-J, Tseng Y-C (2009) The beacon movement detection problem in wireless sensor networks for localization applications. IEEE Trans Mob Comput 8(10):1326–1338

31. Gao D, Reiter MK, Song D (2009) Beyond output voting: detecting compromised replicas using HMM-based behavioral distance. IEEE Trans Dependable Secure Comput 6(2):96–110

32. Fabio Martignon A, Stefano Paris B, Antonio Capone B (2009) Design and implementation of mobisec: a complete securityarchitecture for wireless mesh networks. J Comput Netw 53:2192–2207

33. Huang D-W, Lin P, Gan C-H (2008) Design and performance study for a mobility management mechanism (WMN) using location cache for wireless mesh networks. IEEE Trans Mob Comput 7(5):546-556

34. Hwang K, Cai M, Chen Y, Qin M (2007) Hybrid Intrusion detection with weighted signature generation over anomalous internet episodes. IEEE Trans Dependable Secure Comput 4(1):41-55

35. Chen S, Song Q (2005) Perimeter-based defense against high bandwidth DDOS attacks. IEEE Trans Parallel Distrib Syst 16(6):526-537

36. Ehud D, Avishai W (2010) WDA: a web farm distributed denial of service attack attenuator. J Comput Netw 1037–1051

37. Muogilim OE, Loo K-K, Comley R (2011) Wireless mesh network security: a traffic engineering management approach. J Netw Comput Appl 34(2):478–491

38. Dong J, Ackermann K, Nita-Rotaru C (2009) Secure group communication in wireless mesh networks. J Ad Hoc Netw 7:1563–1576

39. Noh S, Jung G, Choi K, Lee C (2008) Compiling network traffic into rules using soft computing methods for the detection of flooding attacks. J Appl Soft Comput 8:1200–1210
40. Li L, Su-Bin S (2008) Packet track and traceback mechanism against denial of service attacks. J China Univer Posts Telecommun 15(3):51–58
41. Li Q, Trappe W (2006) Reducing delay and enhancing dos resistance in multicast authentication through multigrade security. IEEE Trans Inf Forensics Sec 1(2):190–204
42. Liu Q, Yin J, Leung VCM, Cai Z (2013) FADE: forwarding assessment based detection of collaborative grey hole attacks in WMNs. IEEE Trans Wirel Commun 12(10):5124–5137

10

Color Directional Local Quinary Patterns for Content Based Indexing and Retrieval

Santosh Kumar Vipparthi[*] and Shyam Krishna Nagar

* Correspondence:
Santu155@gmail.com
Department of Electrical
Engineering, Indian Institute of
Technology BHU, Varanasi, India

Abstract

This paper presents a novel evaluationary approach to extract color-texture features for image retrieval application namely Color Directional Local Quinary Pattern (CDLQP). The proposed descriptor extracts the individual R, G and B channel wise directional edge information between reference pixel and its surrounding neighborhoods by computing its grey-level difference based on quinary value $(-2, -1, 0, 1, 2)$ instead of binary and ternary value in 0°, 45°, 90°, and 135° directions of an image which are not present in literature (LBP, LTP, CS-LBP, LTrPs, DExPs, etc.). To evaluate the retrieval performance of the proposed descriptor, two experiments have been conducted on Core-5000 and MIT-Color databases respectively. The retrieval performances of the proposed descriptor show a significant improvement as compared with standard local binary pattern LBP, center-symmetric local binary pattern (CS-LBP), Directional binary pattern (DBC) and other existing transform domain techniques in IR system.

Keywords: Content based image retrieval (CBIR); Multimedia retrieval; Local patterns; local ternary patterns (LTP); Directional Binary Patterns (DBC)

Introduction

With the radical expansion of the digitization in the living world, it has become imperative to find a method to browse and search images efficiently from immense database. In general, three types of approaches for image retrieval are, text-based, content-based and semantic based. In recent times, web-based search engines such as, Google, Yahoo, etc., are being used extensively to search for images based on text keyword searching. Here, any image needs to be indexed properly before retrieving by text-based approach. Such an approach is highly tiresome and also unrealistic to handle by human annotation. Hence, more efficient search mechanism called "content based image retrieval" (CBIR) is required. Image retrieval has become a thrust area in the field of medicine, amusement and science etc.. The search in content based approach is made by analyzing the actual content of the image rather using metadata such as, keywords, tags or descriptions associated with an image. Hence, system can filter images based on their content would provide better indexing and return more accurate results. The effectiveness of a CBIR approach is greatly depends on feature extraction, which is its prominent step. The CBIR employs visual content of an image such as color, texture, shape and faces etc., to index the image database. Hence these features can be further classified as general (texture, color and shape) and domain specific (fingerprints, human faces) features. In this paper, we mainly focused on low-level features; the feature extraction method used in this paper is an effective way of integrating low-level features into whole. Widespread literature survey on CBIR is accessible in [1-4].

The concept of color is one of the significant feature in the field of content-based image retrieval (CBIR), if it is maintained semantically intact and perceptually oriented way. In addition, color structure in visual scenery changes in size, resolution and orientation. Color histogram [5] based image retrieval is simple to implement and has been well used and studied in CBIR system. However, the retrieval performance of these descriptors is generally limited due to inadequacy in discrimination power mainly on immense data. Therefore, several color descriptors have been proposed to exploit special information, including compact color central moments and color coherence vector etc. reported in the literature [6,7].

Texture is one of the most important characteristic of an image. Texture analysis has been extensively used in CBIR systems due to its potential value. Texture analysis and retrieval has gained wide attention in the field of medical, industrial, document analysis and many more. Various algorithms have been proposed for texture analysis, such as, automated binary texture feature [8], Wavelet and Gabor Wavelet Correlogram [9,10], Rotated Wavelet and Rotated Complex Wavelet filters [11-13], Multiscale Ridgelet Transform [14] etc.. In practice texture features can be combined with color features to improve the retrieval accuracy. One of the most commonly used method is to combining texture features with color features; these include wavelets and color vocabulary trees [15] and Retrieval of translated, rotated and scaled color textures [16] etc..

In addition to the texture features, the local image features extraction attracting increasing attention in recent years. A visual content descriptor can either be local or global. A local descriptor uses the visual features of regions or objects to describe the image, where as the global descriptor uses the visual features of the whole image. Several local descriptors have been described in the literature [17-29], where the local binary pattern (LBP) [17] is the most popular local feature descriptor.

The main contributions of the proposed descriptor are given as follows. (a) A new color-texture descriptor is proposed, it extracts texture (DLQP) features from an individual R, G and B color channels. (b) To reduce the feature vector length of the proposed descriptor, the color-texture features were extracted from horizontal and vertical directions only.

The organization of this paper is as follows, In Section "Introduction", introduction is presented. The local patterns with proposed descriptor are presented in Section "Local patterns with proposed Descriptor". Section "Experimental results and discussions", presents the retrieval performances of proposed descriptor and other state-of-the art techniques on two bench mark datasets (Corel-5000 and MIT-Color). Based on the above work Section "Conclusions" concludes this paper.

Local patterns with proposed Descriptor

The concept of LBP [17], LTP [21] and DBC [29] has been utilized to extract texture features (DLQP) from individual color channels (R, G and B) to generate a new color-texture feature called CDLQP.

Local binary patterns (LBP)

The concept of LBP was derived from the general definition of texture in a local neighborhood. This method was successful in terms of speed and discriminative performance [17].

In a given 3×3 pixel pattern, the LBP value is calculated by comparing its center pixel value with its neighborhoods as shown below:

$$LBP_{N,R} = \sum_{i=0}^{N-1} 2^i \times f_1(p_i - p_c) \tag{1}$$

$$f_1(x) = \begin{cases} 1 & x \geq 0 \\ 0 & x < 0 \end{cases} \tag{2}$$

where N stands for the number of neighbors, R is the radius of the neighborhood, p_c denotes the grey value of the centre pixel and p_i is the grey value of its neighbors.

The LBP encoding procedure from a given 3×3 pattern is illustrated in Figure 1.

Local ternary patterns (LTP)

The local ternary pattern (LTP) operator, introduced by Tan and Triggs [20] extends LBP to 3-valued codes called LTP.

$$f_2(x, p_c, \tau) = \begin{cases} +1, & x \geq p_c + \tau \\ 0, & |x - p_c| < \tau \\ -1, & x \leq p_c - \tau \end{cases} \Bigg|_{x=(p_i - p_c)} \tag{3}$$

where, τ is user-specified threshold.

After computing local pattern LP (LBP or LTP) for each pixel (i, j), the whole image is represented by building a histogram as follows:

$$H_{LP}(l) = \sum_{i=1}^{N_1} \sum_{j=1}^{N_2} f_2(LP(i,j), l); l \in \left[0, \left(2^P - 1\right)\right] \tag{4}$$

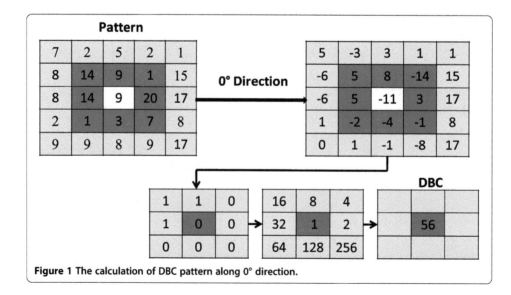

Figure 1 The calculation of DBC pattern along 0° direction.

$$f_2(x, y) = \begin{cases} 1 & x = y \\ 0 & else \end{cases} \tag{5}$$

where the size of input image is $N_1 \times N_2$.

Directional binary code (DBC)

The directional binary code (DBC) was proposed by Baochang et al. [30]. DBC encodes the directional edge information as follows.

In a given an image I, the first-order derivative is calculated, $\dot{I}(g_i)$ along 0°, 45°, 90° and 135° directions. The detailed calculation of DBC in red color channel along 0° direction is shown in Figure 1.

$$I'(g_i) = I(g_c) - I(g_i); \quad i = 1, 2, 3, 4 \tag{6}$$

The directional edges are obtained by,

$$\hat{I}_\alpha^{DBC}(g_c) = f_4\left(I'\left(g_j\right)\right); \quad j = (1 + \alpha/45) \, \forall \alpha = 0^\circ, 45^\circ, 90^\circ \text{ and } 135^\circ \tag{7}$$

The DBC is defined ($\alpha = 0°, 45°, 90°$ and $135°$) as follows:

$$DBC\left(I(g_c)\right)|_\alpha = \left\{ \hat{I}_\alpha^{DBC}(g_c); \hat{I}_\alpha^{DBC}(g_1); \hat{I}_\alpha^{DBC}(g_2); \ldots \ldots \hat{I}_\alpha^{DBC}(g_8) \right\} \tag{8}$$

Proposed descriptor

Color Directional Local Quinary Pattern (CDLQP)

In this section, the procedure to generate a new color-texture feature (CDLQP) descriptor is explained. Let I_i be the ith plain (color space) of the image (e.g., Red color component from the "RGB" color space), where $i = 1,2,3$. The DLQP feature is computed independently from each (R, G and B) color channels.

For a given image I, the first-order derivatives of 0°, 45°, 90° and 135° directions are calculated using Eq. (6).

The directional edges were obtained by Eq. (9). The local quinary values were obtained by Eq. (10).

$$\hat{I}^{i\left(\begin{smallmatrix}DLQP\\\alpha\end{smallmatrix}\right)}(g_c) = f_5\left(I'\left(g_j\right)\right); \quad j = (1 + \alpha/45) \forall \alpha = 0^\circ, 45^\circ, 90^\circ \text{ and } 135^\circ \tag{9}$$

$$f_6(p_c, \tau_2, \tau_1) = \begin{cases} +2, & p_c \geq \tau_2 \\ +1, & \tau_1 \leq (p_c) > \tau_2 \\ 0, & -\tau_1 > (p_c) < \tau_1 \\ -1, & \tau_2 < (p_c) \leq -\tau_1 \\ -2, & p_c \leq -\tau_2 \end{cases} \tag{10}$$

where, τ_2, τ_1 are the upper and lower threshold parameter respectively.

The Nth-order CDLQP is defined ($\alpha = 0^\circ, 45^\circ, 90^\circ$ and 135°) as follows:

$$CDLQP^{(i),N}\left(I(g_c)\right)|_\alpha = \left\{ \hat{I}_\alpha^{(i)DLQP}(g_c); \hat{I}_\alpha^{(i)DLQP}(g_1); \hat{I}_\alpha^{(i)DLQP}(g_2); \ldots \ldots \hat{I}_\alpha^{(i)DLQP}(g_8) \right\} \tag{11}$$

DLQP is a quinary (−2, −1, 0, 1, 2) pattern, which is further converted into four binary patterns such as, two upper patterns (UP) and two lower patterns (LP). The detailed representation of these four patterns is shown in Figure 2. Finally, the whole image is represented by building a histogram supported by Eq. (12).

$$H^i{}_{CDLQP|_\alpha}(l) = \sum_{j=1}^{N_1} \sum_{k=1}^{N_2} f_7\big(CDLQP(j,k)|_\alpha, l\big); \quad l \in [0, 511] \tag{12}$$

where

$$f_7(j,k) = \begin{cases} 1, & \text{if } j = k \\ 0, & \text{if } j \neq k \end{cases}$$

The size of the input image is $N_1 \times N_2$.

In this brief, to reduce the feature vector length color-texture features were extracted from horizontal and vertical directions only.

The details of the proposed color-texture descriptor is given as follows. The steps for extracting 0° degree information is shown in Figure 1. Figure 2 and Eq. (10) explain the procedure to calculate the quinary pattern. The generated quinary pattern is further coded into two upper (A & B) and two lower (C & D) binary patterns which are shown in Figure 2. The two upper (A & B) patterns were obtained by retaining 2 by 1 and replacing 0 for −2, −1, 1 and 0 for A pattern. Likewise, pattern B was obtained by retaining 1 by 1 and replacing 0 for other values. A similar procedure was followed for other two lower patterns.

From the Figure 2, "-11, 3, −14, 8, 5, 5, −2, −4, −1" texture information are obtained when first-order derivative applied in 0° direction. Further, the derivatives are coded in to quinary pattern "-2, 1, −2, 2, 2, 2, −1, −2, −1" using upper and lower thresholds ($\tau_1 = 2$ & $\tau_2 = 1$). Finally, the quinary pattern was converted into four binary patterns (two UP and two LP). The entire operation was applied on individual color channels to generate color-texture features.

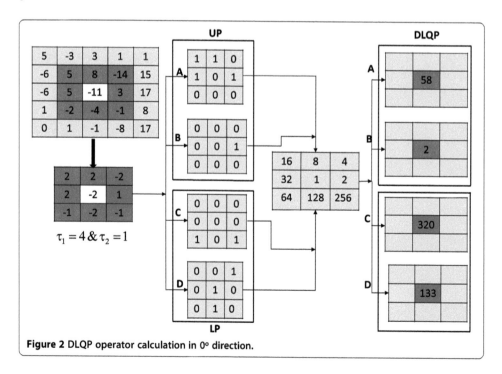

Figure 2 DLQP operator calculation in 0° direction.

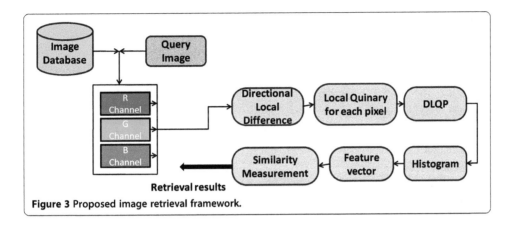

Figure 3 Proposed image retrieval framework.

Proposed system framework for image retrieval

Figure 3 illustrates the proposed image retrieval system frame work and algorithm for the same is given below.

Algorithm: The proposed algorithm involves following steps

Input: Image; Output: Retrieval Result

1. Separate RGB color components from an image.
2. Calculate the directional edge information on each color space.
3. Compute the local quinary value for each pixel.
4. Construct the CDLQP histogram for each pattern.
5. Construct the feature vector.
6. Compare the query image with images in the database using Eq. (16).
7. Retrieve the images based on the best matches.

Query matching

The retrieval performance of any descriptor not only depends on feature extraction approach, but also on good similarity metrics. In this paper four types of similarity distance measures are used as discussed below:

$$Manhattan \ or \ L_1 \ city-block \ Distance: D(Q,T) = \sum_i \left| f_i(Q) - f_j(T) \right| \tag{13}$$

$$Euclidean \ or \ L_2 \ Distance: D(Q,T) = \left(\sum_i \left| f_i(Q) - f_j(T) \right|^2 \right)^{1/2} \tag{14}$$

$$Canberra \ Distance: D_s(Q_m, T_m) = \sum_{i=1}^{Lg} \frac{\left| f_{T_m,i} - f_{Q_m,i} \right|}{\left| f_{T_m,i} + f_{Q_m,i} \right|} \tag{15}$$

$$d_1 \ Distance: D(Q,T) = \sum_{i=1}^{Lg} \left| \frac{f_{T,i} - f_{Q,i}}{1 + f_{T,i} + f_{Q,i}} \right| \tag{16}$$

where Q is query image, Lg is feature vector length, T is image in database; $f_{I,i}$ is i^{th} feature of image I in the database, $f_{Q,i}$ is i^{th} feature of query image Q.

Advantages of proposed methods

1. A new color-texture descriptor is proposed, it extracts texture (DLQP) features from an individual R, G and B color channels.
2. To reduce the feature vector length of the proposed descriptor, the color-texture features were extracted from horizontal and vertical directions only.
3. To verify the retrieval performances of CDLQP, two extensive experiments have been conducted on Corel-5000 and MIT-Color databases respectively.
4. The retrieval performances show a significant improvement nearly 10.78% in terms of ARP on Corel-5000 database and 9.12% improvement on MIT-Color database in terms of ARR as compared with LBP.

Experimental results and discussions

In image retrieval, various datasets are used for several purposes; these includes Corel dataset, MIT dataset and Brodtz texture dataset etc.. The Corel dataset is the most popular and commonly used dataset to test the retrieval performance, MIT-Color dataset used for texture and color feature analysis and Brodtz dataset used for texture analysis. In this paper, to verify the retrieval performances of the proposed descriptor Corel-5000 and MIT-Color datasets are used respectively.

In these experiments, each image in the database is used as the query image. The retrieval performance of the proposed method is measured in terms of recall, precision, average retrieval rate (ARR) and average retrieval precision (ARP) as given in Eq. (17) - Eq. (21) [26]

The recall is defined for a query image I_q is given in Eq. (17).

$$R(I_q, n) = \frac{1}{N_G} \sum_{i=1}^{|DB|} |\delta(f_3(I_i), f_3(I_q))| \, Rank(I_i, I_q) \leq n| \tag{17}$$

where, N_G is the number of relevant images in the database, 'n' is the number of top matches considered, $f_3(x)$ is the category of 'x', $Rank(I_i, I_q)$ returns the rank of image I_i (for the query image I_q) among all images in the database ($|DB|$).

$$\delta(f_3(I_i), f_3(I_q)) = \begin{cases} 1 & f_3(I_i) = f_3(I_q) \\ 0 & Otherwise \end{cases} \tag{18}$$

Similarly, the precision is defined, as follows:

Table 1 The retrieval performances of the proposed method (PM) and other existing methods on Corel-5000 database in terms of ARP and ARR

Database	Performance (%)	Methods							
		CS-LBP	BLK-LBP	LBP	LTP	DBC	DLExP	LTrPs	PM
Corel-5000	ARP	32.96	45.75	43.62	49.05	50.52	48.72	48.79	**54.40**
	ARR	13.99	20.29	19.22	21.40	22.19	21.05	21.86	**23.13**

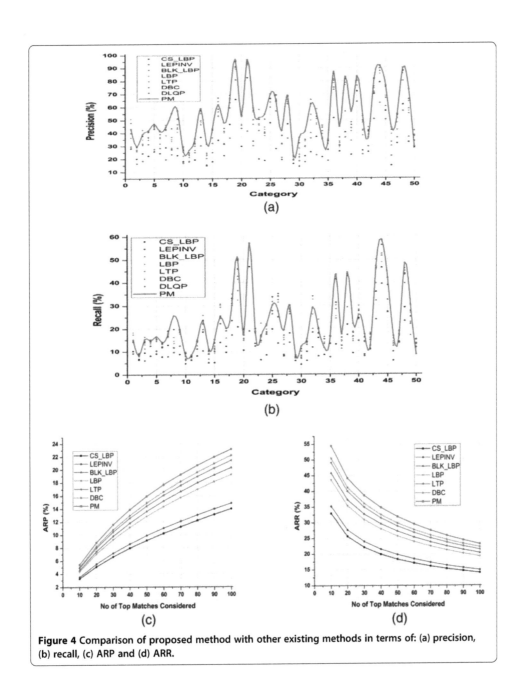

Figure 4 Comparison of proposed method with other existing methods in terms of: (a) precision, (b) recall, (c) ARP and (d) ARR.

$$P(I_q, n) = \frac{1}{n} \sum_{i=1}^{|DB|} |\delta(f_3(I_i), f_3(I_q))| Rank(I_i, I_q) \leq n| \tag{19}$$

The average retrieval rate (ARR) and average retrieval precision (ARP) are defined in Eq. (20) and Eq. (21) respectively.

Table 2 The retrieval results of the proposed method on Corel-5000 database with different distance measures in terms of ARP and ARR

Performance	Distance measure			
	L1	Canberra	L2	d_1
ARP (%)	50.02	37.72	54.11	**54.40**
ARR (%)	20.54	14.86	22.98	**23.13**

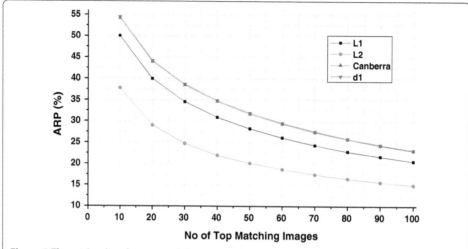

Figure 5 The retrieval performance of the proposed method with different distance measures in terms of ARP on Corel-5000 database.

$$ARR = \frac{1}{|DB|} \sum_{i=1}^{|DB|} R(I_i, n) \Bigg|_{n \leq N_G} \tag{20}$$

$$ARP = \frac{1}{|DB|} \sum_{i=1}^{|DB|} P(I_i, n) \tag{21}$$

where, $|DB|$ is the total number of images in the database.

Where N_1 is the number of relevant images (Number of images in a group), N_C is a number of groups and N_2 is Total number of images to retrieve. The results obtained are discussed in the following subsections.

Experiment on Corel-5000 database

To verify the performances of the proposed descriptor the Corel 5000 database [30] is used. It comprises 5000 images of 50 different categories; each category has 100 images, either in size 187×126 or 126×187. The Corel database is a collection of various contents ranging from natural images, animals to outdoor sports. In this experiment the retrieval performances of the proposed descriptor is calculated in terms of precision, average retrieval precision (ARP), recall, average retrieval rate (ARR). Table 1 illustrates the retrieval performances of the proposed descriptor on Corel-5000 database in terms of ARP and ARR. Figure 4(a) and (b) shows category wise retrieval

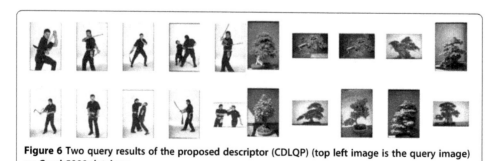

Figure 6 Two query results of the proposed descriptor (CDLQP) (top left image is the query image) on Corel-5000 database.

Figure 7 Example images from MIT-Color database, one image from each category.

performance of the proposed method with other existing methods. Figure 4(c) and (d) shows entire database retrieval performance on Corel-5000 dataset. Table 2 illustrates retrieval performance of the proposed descriptor with different distance measures. From Figure 4, it is observed that the proposed method shows less retrieval performance on categories 1, 25, 26, 27 and 50 as compared to the other existing methods. The reason behind this is, the categories 1, 25, 26, 27 and 50 contain the distinct color information within the categories. However, the overall (average) performance of the proposed method shows a significant improvement as compared to the existing methods in terms of precision, recall, average and average retrieval rate on Corel-5 K database. From Table 1 and Figure 4 it is evident that the proposed method outperforms than other existing methods on Corel-5000 database. From the Table 2 and Figure 5 it is clear that d_1 distance measure show better retrieval rate than other existence distance measures. From this experiment it is observed that the proposed descriptor shows 10.78% improvement as

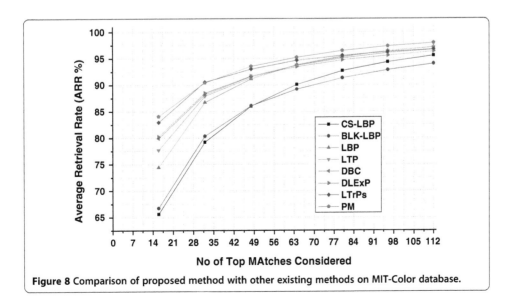

Figure 8 Comparison of proposed method with other existing methods on MIT-Color database.

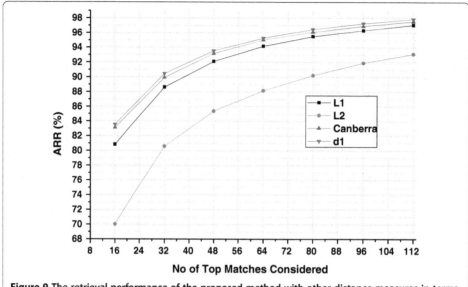

Figure 9 The retrieval performance of the proposed method with other distance measures in terms of ARR on MIT-Color database.

compared to LBP. The query result of the proposed method on Corel-5000 database is shown in Figure 6 (top left image is the query image). Finally, from above discussion and observations it is clear that the proposed descriptor show a significant improvement as compared to other existing methods in terms of their evaluation measures on Corel-5000 database.

Experiment on MIT-Color database

In this experiment, we first demonstrate about MIT-Color dataset [31]. Further, we describe the retrieval performances of the proposed descriptor. MIT-Color dataset consists of 40 different textures with size 512×512. Further, these textures are divided into sixteen 128×128 non-overlapping sub images, thus creating a database of 640 (40×16) images. The sample images of this database are shown in Figure 7. The retrieval performance of the proposed descriptor and other state-of-the-art techniques are shown in Figure 8. From the Figure 8 it is clear that the proposed descriptor has shown significant improvement around 9.12% as compared to LBP in terms of ARR. From Figure 9 it is clear that d_1 distance measure show better retrieval rate than other existence distance measures. From these observations it is concluded that the proposed

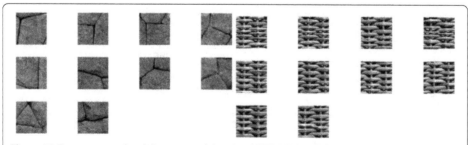

Figure 10 Two query results of the proposed descriptor (CDLQP) (top left image is the query image) on MIT-Color database.

descriptor yields better retrieval rate than other state-of-art techniques. Further, the query result of the proposed descriptor on the MIT-Color database is shown in Figure 10 (top left image is the query image).

Conclusions

A novel evaluationary color-texture descriptor namely Color Directional Local Quinary Pattern (CDLQP) is proposed for image retrieval application. CDLQP extracts the texture features from individual R, G and B color channels using directional edge information in a neighborhood with gray-level differences between the pixels by a quinary value instead of a binary and ternary one. The extensive and comparative experiment has been conducted to evaluate our color-texture features for IR on two public natural databases namely, Corel-5000 and MIT-Color dataset. Experimental results of the proposed descriptor CDLQP show a significant improvement as compared to other state-of-the art techniques in IR system.

Competing interests
All authors declare that they have no competing interests.

Authors' contributions
All authors VSK and NSK work together in conception, implementation, write and apply the proposed methods in this paper then they read and approved the final manuscript.

Authors' informations
Santosh Kumar Vipparthi was born in 1985 in India. He received the B.E and M.Tech degrees in Electrical, Systems Engineering from Andhra University, IIT-BHU, India in 2007 and 2010 respectively. Currently he is pursuing the Ph.D. degree in the Department of Electrical Engineering at Indian Institute of Technology BHU, Varanasi, India. His major interests are image retrieval and object tracking.
Shyam Krishna Nagar was born in 1955 in India. He received the Ph.D degree in Electrical engineering from Indian Institute of Technology Roorkee, Roorkee, India, in 1991. He is currently working as Professor in Department of Electrical Engineering, Indian Institute of Technology BHU, Varanasi, Uttar Pradesh, India. His fields of interest are includes digital image processing, digital control, model order reduction and discrete event systems.

References
1. Rui Y, Huang TS (1999) Image retrieval: Current techniques, promising directions and open issues. J Vis Commun Image Represent 10:39–62
2. Smeulders AWM, Worring M, Santini S (2000) A. Gupta, and R. Jain, Content-based image retrieval at the end of the early years. IEEE Trans Pattern Anal Mach Intell 22(12):1349–1380
3. Kokare M, Chatterji BN, Biswas PK (2002) A survey on current content based image retrieval methods. IETE J Res 48(3):261–271
4. Ying L, Dengsheng Z, Guojun L, Wei-Ying M (2007) A survey of content-based image retrieval with high-level semantics. Elsevier J. Pattern Recognition 40:262–282
5. Swain MJ, Ballar DH (1991) Indexing via color histograms. Proc. In: 3rd Int. Conf. Computer Vision, Rochester Univ., NY., pp 11–32
6. Pass G, Zabih R, Miller J (1997) Comparing images using color coherence vectors. In: Proc. 4th. ACM Multimedia Conf, Boston, Massachusetts, US, pp 65–73
7. Stricker M, Oreng M (1995) Similarity of color images. In: Proc. Storage and Retrieval for Image and Video Databases, SPIE, pp 381–392
8. Smith JR, Chang SF (1996) Automated binary texture feature sets for image retrieval. In: Proc. I EEE Int. Conf. Acoustics, Speech and Signal Processing, Columbia Univ., New York, pp 2239–2242
9. Moghaddam HA, Khajoie TT, Rouhi AH, Saadatmand MT (2005) Wavelet Correlogram: A new approach for image indexing and retrieval. Elsevier J. Pattern Recognition 38:2506–2518
10. Moghaddam HA, Saadatmand MT (2006) Gabor wavelet Correlogram Algorithm for Image Indexing and Retrieval. In: 18th Int. Conf. Pattern Recognition, K.N. Toosi Univ. of Technol., Tehran, Iran., pp 925–928
11. Subrahmanyam M, Maheshwari RP, Balasubramanian R (2011) A Correlogram Algorithm for Image Indexing and Retrieval Using Wavelet and Rotated Wavelet Filters. International Journal of Signal and Imaging Systems Engineering 4(1):27–34
12. Kokare M, Biswas PK, Chatterji BN (2007) Texture image retrieval using rotated Wavelet Filters. Elsevier J Pattern recognition letters 28:1240–1249
13. Kokare M, Biswas PK, Chatterji BN (2005) Texture Image Retrieval Using New Rotated Complex Wavelet Filters. IEEE Trans. Systems, Man, and Cybernetics 33(6):1168–1178

14. Gonde AB, Maheshwari RP, Balasubramanian R (2010) Multiscale Ridgelet Transform for Content Based Image Retrieval. IEEE Int. Advance Computing Conf, Patial, India, pp 139–144

15. Subrahmanyam M, Maheshwari RP, Balasubramanian R (2012) Expert system design using wavelet and color vocabulary trees for image retrieval. International Journal of Expert systems with applications 39:5104–5114

16. Cheng-Hao Y, Shu-Yuan C (2003) Retrieval of translated, rotated and scaled color textures. Pattern Recognition 36:913–929

17. Ojala T, Pietikainen M, Harwood D (1996) A comparative study of texture measures with classification based on feature distributions. Pattern Recognition 29(1):51–59

18. Ojala T, Pietikainen M, Maenpaa T (2002) Multiresolution gray-scale and rotation invariant texture classification with local binary patterns. IEEE Transactions on Pattern Analysis and Machine Intelligence 24(7):971–987

19. Guo Z, Zhang L, Zhang D (2010) Rotation invariant texture classification using LBP variance with global matching. Pattern Recognition 43(3):706–719

20. Zhenhua G, Zhang L, Zhang D (2010) A completed modeling of local binary pattern operator for texture classification. IEEE Transactions on Image Processing 19(6):1657–1663

21. Tan X, Triggs B (2010) Enhanced local texture feature sets for face recognition under difficult lighting conditions. IEEE Tans Image Proc 19(6):1635–1650

22. Subrahmanyam M, Maheshwari RP, Balasubramanian R (2012) Directional local extrema patterns: a new descriptor for content based image retrieval. Int J Multimedia Information Retrieval 1(3):191–203

23. Subrahmanyam M, Maheshwari RP, Balasubramanian R (2012) Local Tetra Patterns: A New Feature Descriptor for Content Based Image Retrieval. IEEE Trans Image Process 21(5):2874–2886

24. Subrahmanyam M, Maheshwari RP, Balasubramanian R (2012) Local Maximum Edge Binary Patterns: A New Descriptor for Image Retrieval and Object Tracking. Signal Processing 92:1467–1479

25. Subrahmanyam M, Maheshwari RP, Balasubramanian R (2012) Directional Binary Wavelet Patterns for Biomedical Image Indexing and Retrieval. Journal of Medical Systems 36(5):2865–2879

26. Vipparthi S, Nagar SK (2013) Directional Local Ternary Patterns for Multimedia Image Indexing and Retrieval. Int J Signal and Imaging Systems Engineering. Article in press

27. Takala V, Ahonen T, Pietikainen M (2005) Block-Based Methods for Image Retrieval Using Local Binary Patterns. LNCS 3450:882–891

28. Marko H, Pietikainen M, Cordelia S (2009) Description of interest regions with local binary patterns. Pattern Recognition 42:425–436

29. Baochang Z, Zhang L, Zhang D, Linlin S (2010) Directional binary code with application to PolyU near-infrared face database. Pattern Recognition Letters 31:2337–2344

30. Corel-5000 Corel image database, [Online]. Available: http://www.ci.gxnu.edu.cn/cbir/Dataset.aspx

31. MIT Vision and Modeling Group, Vision Texture, [Online], Available: http://vismod.media.mit.edu/pub/

11

Smart card based time efficient authentication scheme for global grid computing

Jaspher Willsie Kathrine Gnanaraj[1*], Kirubakaran Ezra[2] and Elijah Blessing Rajsingh[3]

* Correspondence:
meet.katee@gmail.com
[1]Department of Information
Technology, Karunya University,
Coimbatore, Tamilnadu, India
Full list of author information is
available at the end of the article

Abstract

Decentralization in every walk of life has resulted in the development of Global Grid networking. Data sharing and access depends on their availability, capability, cost and user requirements. One of the needs for a secure Grid Environment is a strong authentication for users. Since Authentication is the entry point into every network, a novel smart card based authentication scheme has been proposed. The proposed authentication scheme utilizes the biometric data embedded in a smart card along with the ID and password of the user. The Time efficient performance of the proposed scheme in comparison with the existing Secure Socket Layer based authentication scheme is discussed. The attacks which the proposed scheme is able to withstand are also discussed.

Keywords: Grid computing; Authentication; Authorization; Biometric

Introduction

Grid computing involves sharing heterogeneous resources which are located in geographically distributed places belonging to different administrative domains [1]. Grid data sharing is not file exchange but rather access to computers, software, data and other resources. Grid involves the creation of a dynamic Virtual Organization (VO). Each virtual organization comprises of users and their resources and any other services (S) joined by a common goal [2]. Each of the user or resource is available from different administrative domains (DO). Each user/resource have their own trust policy which requires a local to global and global to local mapping of the access policies as discussed in [3].

The basic security for the Globus Toolkit (GT 4) is the Grid Security Infrastructure (GSI) [4,5]. It depends on the Public Key Infrastructure (PKI), X.509 Proxy certificates and Transport Layer Security (TLS) for authentication. GSI involves third party verification for authorization. The GT framework is based on the Open Grid Services Architecture (OGSA) which uses the Secure Socket Layer (SSL) based on TLS. The GSI security is secure enough but has scalability problems [5].

The existing authentication schemes are based on the user name and the password and certificates which are generated by a secure Certificate Authority (CA) [5]. The existing authentication schemes belong to two factor authentication scheme which involves user name/password and some cards like those used in Banks. The Security for the Grid Environment is deployed in the middleware which is used to access the grid network. Examples of Grid middleware are UNICORE (Uniform Interface to Computing Resources) [6], Globus [6], Legion [7] and Gridbus [8].

In [9] a Four-Factor based Biometric Authentication has been proposed. But the addition of location does not guarantee the avoidance of insider attack. The proposed authentication scheme optimizes the security of a grid environment by adding more features like biometric data in a smart card for optimal authentication.

User authentication has been in discussion for a long time to enhance the security of any system at the entry level itself. Many methods such as password based systems, ID based systems, and etc. have been used. A hash-chain based remote user authentication in which all the passwords are encoded is given in [10]. In all the initial remote based authentication systems, a verifier table is to be placed in the server side which becomes a problem if the server is compromised.

In this paper the remote based authentication system which is very much suited for the Grid Environment is considered. Based on the existing remote authentication systems, an enhanced system is designed. In order to avoid maintaining a verifier table Hwang et al., proposed a non-interactive smart card based scheme without verifier tables [11]. A finger print based remote user authentication scheme was proposed in [12]. This scheme was found to be vulnerable to masquerade attacks and many other attacks [13,14]. In [15-17], the biometric data itself is taken as a key for encryption/decryption. The secret data is extracted by using the biometric template as the key. The biometric data is to be stored in the server side and used for comparison. But for effective Biometric authentication, the process is to be done in the client side [18] to avoid any problem due to the server being compromised [19]. In [20], the method has been optimized with the matching being done in the server side. But the server does not store any biometric data in its database thereby protecting the privacy of the user.

The method in [20] provides a three factor authentication which is password – something the user knows; smart card – something the user has; biometrics – something the user is. A further enhancement to this type of authentication is to add a fourth factor thereby providing a four factor authentication [21]. The fourth factor can be the addition of location of the user – someplace the user is. The military data sharing requirements take into consideration the place in which the user is positioned so as to find the location of any valid/invalid user. So, the sensitive areas of application require security with some amount of privacy preservation. Section three gives an overview of the existing authentication systems in grid computing. Section four discusses the proposed security framework with reduced stages for authentication of a grid user.

Existing security framework for grid

A Grid Environment is created by means of using general-purpose grid software libraries known as middle ware. The Grid environment is based on a layered architecture as shown in Figure 1.

From the Figure 1, the security features are seen in the middleware portion of the grid layer. The existing security solution uses Open Grid Services Architecture (OGSA) architecture [22]. This security feature used in GT is also used in Virtual Organization Membership Services (VOMS) [23] for the purpose of authorization also. The OGSA architecture uses GSI which in turn depends on the certificate based SSL for authentication and WS-Secure Conversation message transport and confidentiality. The existing

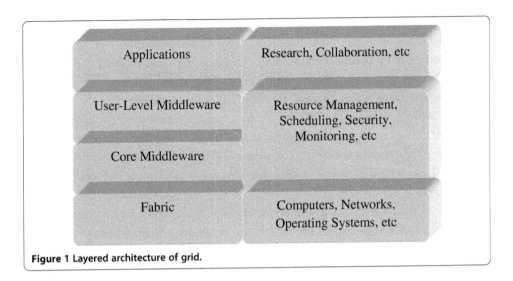

Figure 1 Layered architecture of grid.

system based on OGSA and GSI have some basic security solutions for solving the authentication and authorization criteria. The scalability, heterogeneity and increase in attacks have led to the need of a new security framework which is based on the existing architecture with additional features to tackle the day to day attacks. The next section discusses about the proposed authentication scheme.

Proposed authentication system

The proposed authentication scheme has three phases such as the Registration phase, the Login phase and the Mutual Authentication phase. An additional password change phase is added to ensure that the user can change his/her password when required. In each phase distinct operations are defined for the user and the server. The proposed authentication methodology is shown in Figure 2.

In the Registration phase, based on the details provided by the user along with the inputs given by the server, the smart card data is stored and given to the user through a secure medium. Only during the Login and the mutual authentication phase is the user and the server authenticated to each other. Once the mutual authentication is a

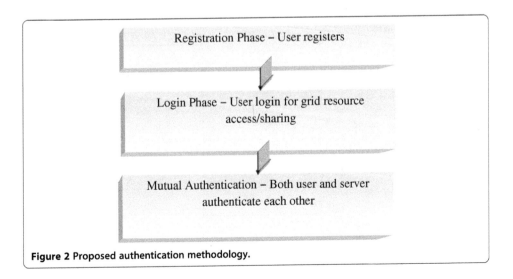

Figure 2 Proposed authentication methodology.

success, then the user can go on to the next operation involved in the data transaction. The triple DES along with any other light-weight encryption algorithm can be used. The process flow of the proposed authentication scheme is shown in Figure 3.

During the initialization phase, the server stores both the asymmetric and symmetric key in its database. Once a user requests for registration, the server accepts the user's hashed password in a secure way. This way assures that the server does not know the actual data and neither is data stored openly in any database within the server. The validity of the user is checked based on the comparison of the hashed data rather than the original data. This method of storage makes sure that the user's data is not lost under any circumstance.

All the hashed data are stored in the Registration/Authentication server's database and the encrypted data required for the further use of the user is stored in the smart

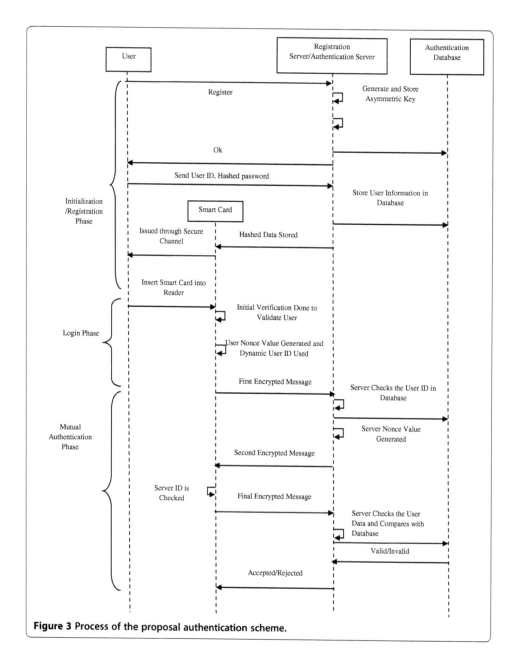

Figure 3 Process of the proposal authentication scheme.

card and sent to the user. The user then uses the smart card for further access to the Grid environment. The smart card does the initial validation of the user and then forwards the user data to the server, where further authentication is the done. In the proposed scheme, both the user and the server validate each other and hence it is complete mutual authentication. Only when the user and the server both satisfy the validation criteria then the data transfer occurs. If the user validation does not succeed it is rejected or the user is requested to start the authentication from the beginning of the login phase. The next section gives the detailed explanation of each phase of the proposed authentication system.

Details of the authentication scheme

This authentication scheme involves three factors, using a smart card which holds the data of what the user is i.e., the biometric data (B), what the user knows i.e., the password (PW), Identifier (ID) and the data that the user has i.e., smart card. This scheme has three phases such as Registration Phase, Login phase and a mutual authentication phase. The added features are the dynamic User ID (CID) and the dynamic server ID (SID). The Registration/Authentication server is configured to support symmetric and asymmetric encryption and decryption. In grid a client at one scenario can be the server at the next instant since it has to satisfy a need. Hence this system should be in such a way that each user is able to identify the requestor of the resource by his/her credentials. The notations used in this paper are given in Table 1.

Registration phase

During the registration phase, the user tries to register for a grid membership within a Virtual Organization (VO). During the membership registration, the user is given a particular Identifier (ID_i). The user registers his/her biometric data (B_i) which maybe a fingerprint or an iris template. The user also selects a random number r and a password (PW_i).

The following are the series of steps done in the server:

a. Server generates public-private key pair (p_k, s_k) for asymmetric encryption/decryption.
b. Server generates a secret key x for symmetric encryption/decryption.
c. Both (x, s_k) are kept secure in the server.

Table 1 Notations used in this paper

S	Server
U_i	User
S_{ID}	Identity of server S_i
ID_i	Identity of user U_i
B_i	Biometric data of U_i
(PW_i)	Password of U_i
h(.)	One-way hash function
x	The master secret key
(p_k, s_k)	Public-private key pair
$\oplus$	The exclusive-OR operation
$\parallel$	Message concatenation
R	Random number generated by U_i
n_u	Nonce value generated by U_i
n_s	Nonce value generated by the server S_i

The operations done at the user side are:

a. The user records his/her user Identifier (ID_i)
b. The user records the biometric template (B_i)
c. The user selects a random string r and password (PW_i)

The user computes $SB_i = \delta\,(B_i) = h(r \oplus h(B_i))$. The value of SB_i is sent to the server securely along with the one-way hash function h(.) of the Password and the identifier (ID_i) of the user. The server receives (ID_i , $h(PW_i)$,SB_i) through a secure channel. By using the values sent by the user, the server computes, y_i such that,

$$y_i = E_x(ID_i \| h(PW_i) \| SB_i) \quad (1)$$

where E_x (.) represents the symmetric encryption using the secret key x The server stores the user's password (PW_i) and the related identifier (ID_i) of the user and the calculated y_i. The operations continued in the server side are:

a. Server computes $K = h(ID_i \| x)$
b. Server stores (K, $h(.)$, p_k) in the smart card.
c. Server sends smart card to the user securely.

Once the user receives the smart card, a few entries are to be stored in it along with the data already available in the smart card i.e., y_i.

The following operations are done to confirm the registration:

a. The user enters the biometric data which can be an iris data /fingerprint B_i
b. The user encrypts the random number r with PW_i such that $E_{pW_i}(r)$ is obtained.
c. $E_{pW_i}(r)$ is stored in the smart card.
d. $SB_i = \delta\,(B_i) = h(r \oplus h(B_i))$ is stored in the smart card.

Login phase

A user U_i is allowed to enter the grid environment using his/her smart card. The user enters his/her Password (PW)' and does a biometric scan denoted by B_i^*. The user's smart card retrieves the random value "r" from $E_{pW'}(r)$ by using the password (PW)' entered by the user U_i. The smart card computes $SB_i^* = \delta\,(SB_i') = h(r \oplus h(B_i'))$. This value is compared with the already stored value of $SB_i = \delta\,(B_i) = h(r \oplus h(B_i))$ to confirm if the user is the same. Then the smart card generates a nonce value "n_u" and computes $M = (K \oplus n_u)$. Then CID_i is calculated such that, $CID_i = h\,(ID_i \| n_u)$.

Then value of C_0 is computed such that,

$$C_0 = E_{p_k}(M \| CID_i \| y_i \| u) \tag{2}$$

Where $E_{p_k}(.)$ denotes the encryption function using the server's public key. "u" is the random value selected by the user during login time. To ensure the liveliness of the user, a nonce value is added in the value of C_0 along with the already existing random values to add more security. C_0 is sent to the server.

Mutual authentication phase

Once C_0 is received by the server, the server does the following operations,

a. Server decrypts C_0 using its private key s_k
b. Server computes "n_u^*" such that $n_u^* = M \oplus K$ where $K = h(ID_i \parallel x)$. The server uses the ID_i obtained from y_i.
c. The validity of the user is checked by using the Identifier ID_i to the one received by the server. By using the value of n_u^* the value of CID_i^* is calculated.
d. Then the value of CID_i^* is compared with the value of CID_i to check if $CID_i = CID_i^*$.
e. Also the value of ID_i can be verified with the ID stored in the ID table for the users at the server end. A comparison of ID's is done to make sure that verification is done correctly even when the Server ID table is corrupted.
f. The remaining terms of C_0 i.e., (h (PW_i) $\parallel$ SB_i) is retained for future reference.

Server computes a values of C_1 such that

$$C_1 = E_u(N \parallel SED \parallel S_{ID} \parallel v) \tag{3}$$

Where S_{ID} = Server's identity and v is the random number chosen by the server and u is the random number selected by the user and sent in C_0. The server generates a nonce value "n_s" and computes $N = (K \oplus n_s)$. From the value of n_s, the value of the symmetric key u is generated. Server ID $SED = h(S_{ID} \parallel n_s)$. The dynamic ID and n_s is used to make sure that the data was not tampered during transmission. Server sends C_1 to the user U_i.

In the User Side, the following operations are done,

a. The smart card decrypts C_1 using the random value of u.
b. The value of S_{ID} is checked for valid server ID. The smart card computes SED^* $= h(S_{ID} \parallel n_s^*)$ using its nonce value n_s^*. Smart Card computes "n_s^*" such that $n_s^* = N \oplus$ K where $K = h(ID_i \parallel x)$.
c. Then SED^* is calculated by using the value of the generated n_s^* and $ID_{i.}$, i.e., SED^* $= h(S_{ID} \parallel n_s^*)$. If $SED^* = SED$, then the server is valid and the data has not been tampered with.

The smart card calculates the following value

$$C_2 = E_v (h (PW))' \parallel SB_i' \tag{4}$$

The server decrypts C_2 using v and calculates the value of y_i^* from the values sent in C_2. If $y_i^* = y_i$, the server matches the values of the password and the biometric template to confirm the authenticity of the user.

If an attacker is to attack, he/she has to deduce the random and the nonce values which makes the attack much difficult. The value of SB_i^* in C_2 is compared with SB_i of y_i. If the value match is within a threshold range then the user is confirmed valid. The three phases are considered for computing the cost since they will be used repeatedly. Once all the steps have been completed successfully, it is clear that mutual authentication of both the user and the server is done for login of the user. The server secret number v can be used as a session key material and h (v) can be used as a session key which is shared with the server.

Password change phase

The user U_i is authenticated by using the Password (PW') used initially for login process. Once authenticated, the user is prompted to enter the new password. Once the new password (PW") is entered, the $y_i = E_x (ID_i \parallel h(PW_i) \parallel SB_i)$ value of $h(PW_i)$ is replaced with the value of $h(PW_i")$. An intimation of the password change is given to the server and it replaces the old password for the user identifier with the new password. Thereby the user is allowed to further login by using the new password.

Implementation of the proposed authentication scheme

In this section, the performance and functionality of the proposed authentication scheme is analysed and comparison has been made with the existing SSL based Authentication used in the OGSA framework of Globus Toolkit.

The biometric matching is not done mostly in the smart card in proposed scheme but rather in the remote server without losing the privacy of the biometric data. Any light-weight public-key cryptosystem can be used for the encryption and decryption process. The total time taken for the execution of the proposed algorithm is purely based on the crypto-algorithm selected for the process of encryption and decryption.

In our proposed Scheme, Advanced Encryption Standard (AES) based on block cipher is used. Also Rivest Cipher 4(RC4) algorithm which uses stream cipher can be used. RSA of 1024 bits [24] is used for the Asymmetric Encryption. The AES algorithm used here has a key length of 128 bits and RC4 algorithm of 128 bit key length can be used. The time taken for execution of the SSL based authentication in milliseconds (ms) is shown in Table 2. The algorithm is executed for an input of 10 users each of a 26 kB biometric finger print image. MD5 scheme has been used for hashing.

Performance analysis of initial/registration phase

A simple Grid environment was created and the security algorithm was implemented for 10 users. A simple hosting environment has been created as presented by [25]. In a Microsoft .NET platform and J2EE application server as an administrative server, the hosting environment has been implemented for 10 connected users. The time taken for

Table 2 Total time taken for registration and authentication

User	Time taken for each access-proposed scheme (ms)	Time taken for registration and authentication-SSL based scheme (ms)
1	710.32	553
2	710.76	612
3	565.58	550
4	555.95	518
5	604.90	549
6	719.52	594
7	710.11	617
8	570.58	553
9	591.16	525
10	606.35	550

execution of the Initial/Registration phase and the login and mutual phases were calculated. The resistance of the security algorithm to attacks has been analysed in the next section through the equations. Based on the time factor criteria, the implementation of the proposed algorithm is based on the following system configuration of Processor Speed – 2.13 GHz, RAM size 3.00 GB, System Type – 32-bit OS. The implementation has been done in Java. The time taken for the Initial process and authentication of each user is shown in Table 2.

The Table 2 gives the time taken for each user for the initial registration and access in to the grid environment. The Figure 4 is the corresponding chart for Table 2. From the graph it is clear that the time taken for initial registration of a user using smart card is marginally more than the existing SSL based scheme. The Table 3 shows the time for each user login and authentication. It is the time taken for a single access into the grid network. The corresponding graph is shown in Figure 5. From the graph it is clear that the time for each access is very less when compared to the time taken for the SSL based authentication. Table 4 gives the total time taken for the users as they increase in entering into the grid environment. The Figure 6 gives the corresponding graph for the Table 4. From Table 4 it is clear that the time for the combined registration and access is more in the initial phase due to the collection of biometric data and the smart card distribution. The Figure 6 is the graph for Table 4.

In Table 5, the time taken for each access of user login is given. The Figure 7 is the corresponding graph for Table 5. The Figure 7 shows that the total time for each user login is very less when compared to that of the SSL based authentication scheme. It is clear from the collected data, that though the time for initial operation is more for from the Figures 5 and 7, it is clear that even though the registration phase of each user is more, the time taken for each access is much lesser than the time taken for execution of the SSL scheme. This increase in time during initial stages is very much compensated during each user access. It is clear from the data collected that the selection of the encryption algorithm used for encryption influences the time taken for completion of the execution of the process. Lightweight algorithms like Camellia [26] in place of AES algorithm and Elliptic Curve Cryptography in place of RSA algorithm can also be considered for usage.

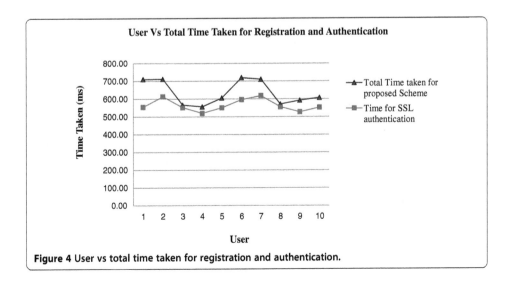

Figure 4 User vs total time taken for registration and authentication.

Table 3 Time taken for each grid access

User	Time taken for each access-proposed scheme (ms)	Time taken for each access-SSL based scheme (ms)
1	70.77	553
2	71.33	612
3	72.28	550
4	68.64	518
5	70.75	549
6	72.92	594
7	68.82	617
8	82.65	553
9	72.56	525
10	70.38	550

The next section gives a brief discussion on the security analysis of the proposed authentication scheme.

Security analysis of the proposed authentication scheme

In this section, the security and performance analysis of the proposed authentication scheme are presented. The attacks which are withstood by the proposed scheme of authentication are explained.

ID-theft attack

As in equation $C_0 = E_{p_k}(M\|CID_i\|y_i\|u)$, a dynamic user ID named as CID_i is created by the smart card based on the nonce value n_u instead of using the user's own ID. This helps to withstand the ID-theft attack and also preserves the privacy of the user.

Clock synchronization and replay attack problem

In [27], the problem in timestamp based authentication is given as replay attack due to the transmission delays in an unpredictable network. Even though the networks are fast

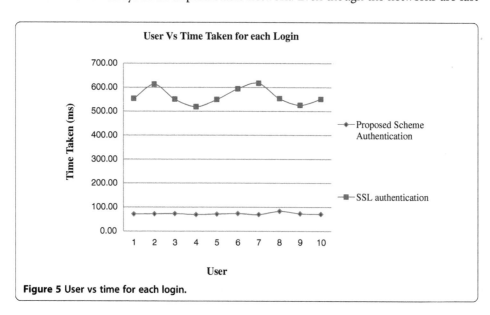

Figure 5 User vs time for each login.

Table 4 Initial time taken for SSL based and proposed scheme

No. of users	Total time for no. of users - SSL based (sec)	Total time for no. of users - proposed scheme (sec)
1	0.55	0.64
2	1.17	1.56
3	1.72	2.20
4	2.23	2.82
5	2.78	3.49
6	3.38	4.29
7	3.99	5.08
8	4.55	5.71
9	5.07	6.40
10	5.62	7.08

the speed may vary based on the geographical and political distribution. To avoid using of timestamps, a nonce value n_u is used each time the user sends his/her data and a nonce value n_s is also used by the sever to proclaim the server's validity. Since a nonce value such as n_u and n_s in equations $C_0 = E_{p_k}(M \| CID_i \| y_i \| u)$ where $M = (K \oplus n_u)$ and $C_1 = E_u (N \| SED \| S_{ID} \| v \| pos_s)$ where $N = (K \oplus n_s)$ can be used only once, and not repeated, the user/server can be safeguard themselves from replay attacks.

Modification attack

Each authentication message in from equation (1), (2), (3) and (4) include a one-way hash function along with an encryption algorithm. The hash value in each equation requires a nonce value or a random value. Even if the attacker gets hold of each of these equations the decryption part and breaking the hash function is not possible. If the attacker has the value of $h(PW_i)$, to find the password, the attacker needs find an equivalent of the hash function by trying each password. This attack is difficult because the attacker has to first break into the encrypted data $C_0 = E_{p_k}(M \| CID_i \| y_i \| u)$. The

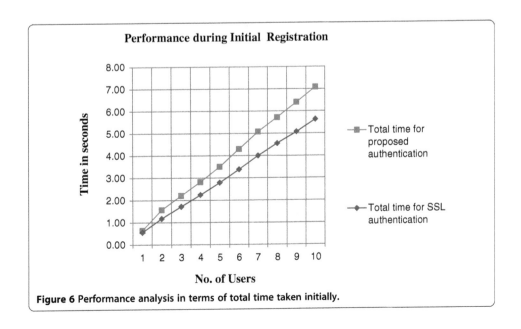

Figure 6 Performance analysis in terms of total time taken initially.

Table 5 Time for access of all the 10 users

Users	Total time for each access-proposed scheme (sec)	Total time for each access-SSL based (sec)
1	0.07	0.55
2	0.14	1.17
3	0.21	1.72
4	0.28	2.23
5	0.35	2.78
6	0.43	3.38
7	0.50	3.99
8	0.58	4.55
9	0.65	5.07
10	0.72	5.62

attacker then needs to send the correct dynamic ID using the nonce. For an attacker to get all the values correct is impossible which makes modification attack difficult. Without knowing the actual data of these two values, the original data cannot be modified. Modification of the equations will be noted by the legitimate user and server and since all the messages are linked, it makes modification attack harder.

Mutual authentication

At the end of the mutual authentication phase, both the server and the client authenticate each other thereby establishing mutual authentication. During each phase, of the equations C_0, C_1 and C_3, the user and server check the validity of each other using the values of CID, SED, M, N. If the server has any doubt in the validity of the user, the message C_2 can be asked to be resent.

Man-in-the-middle attack

An attacker A who tries to do a man-in-the middle attack needs to know the decryption keys u, v and r in each message signal else its message will be discarded by the server or the client.

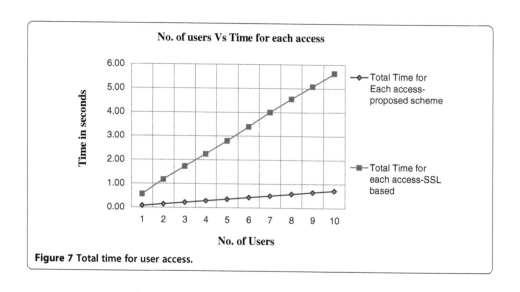

Figure 7 Total time for user access.

Security of the stored data on the smart card

The smart card holds the value of $(ID_i, y_i, h(.), p_k)$ where, $y_i = E_x(ID_i \parallel h(PW_i) \parallel SB_i)$. If the smart card is compromised, the data it provides is not easily accessible to the attacker. Without knowing the matching password and the ID of the user, the attacker cannot move further along the authentication phase. Knowing the public key of the server complicates matters since the attacker has to find the encryption algorithm and a matching value of C_0 to send to the server. Furthermore, the hash function has to be broken in order to get the secret data. The biometric data is stored in the open for anyone to copy it. It is stored in the form of a template combined with a random string which needs to be found to get the data. Thus the data stored in the smart card is secure.

Conclusion and future work

The proposed authentication scheme has provided an enhanced security with an optimal overall time taken for the operation. The authentication scheme can be made more secure by using a triple DES algorithm but it increases the security criteria and also increases the overall time taken for authentication. By increasing the security during the authentication phase itself we can try to minimize any other malicious insider attacks and also reduce external attacks. The increase in time during registration is one-time value and hence it is not considered as a disadvantage. The biometric data used for authentication can also be used in the consecutive authorization process thereby lessening the database space utilized by reusing the data used in authentication. The AES, RC4 algorithm can be replaced by any other light weight encryption algorithm like camellia. Further study has to be done by using different combination of algorithms. The data's used for authentication can also be used for authorizing the user for a resource access.

Competing interests

The authors declare that they have no competing interests.

Author's contributions

GJWK, analyzed the requirement of the security for Grid Computing, designed the framework, conducted the experiment and drafted the manuscript. EK gave full support in conducting the experiment and assisted in draft work and revised the manuscript. EBR contributed by reviewing the work done and in revising the content of the manuscript. All authors read and approved the final manuscript.

Acknowledgement

The authors wish to thank Karunya University for the support by providing infrastructure for carrying out the simulation. The authors thank the senior professors and the industrial experts for providing valuable suggestions to improve the quality of the research paper.

Author details

[1]Department of Information Technology, Karunya University, Coimbatore, Tamilnadu, India. [2]SSTP Systems, Bharat Heavy Electricals Limited, Trichy, Tamilnadu, India. [3]School of Computer Science and Technology, Karunya University, Coimbatore, Tamilnadu, India.

References

1. Foster I (2002) A three point checklist. GridToday 1(6):1–4, July publication
2. Foster I, Kesselman C, Tuecke S (2001) The anatomy of the grid: enabling scalable virtual organizations. Int J High Perform Comput Appl 15(3):200–222
3. Zhou Q, Yang G, Shen J, Rong C (2005) A scalable security architecture for grid, Sixth International Conference on Parallel and Distributed Computing, Applications and Technologies., pp 89–93
4. Bendahmane, Essaaidi M, El Moussaoui A, Younes A (2009) Grid computing security mechanisms: state-of-the-art, International Conference on Multimedia Computing and systems ICMS '09., pp 535–540
5. Von W (2005) Globus toolkit version 4 grid security infrastructure: a standards perspective., Available at: http://www.globus.org/toolkit/docs/4.0/security/GT4-GSI-Overview.pdf, Accessed: January 2011

6. Almond J, Snelling D (1999) UNICORE: uniform access to supercomputing as an element of electronic commerce. Future Generat Comput Syst 613:1–10

7. Andrew S, Grimshaw W, Wulf A (1997) The legion vision of a worldwide virtual computer. Commun ACM 40 (1):39–45

8. Buyya R, Venugopal S (2004) The gridbus toolkit for service oriented grid and utility computing: an overview and status report, Proceedings of the first IEEE International Workshop on Grid Economics and Business Models., pp 19–66, ISBN 0-7803-8525-X

9. Jaspher Willsie Kathrine G, Kirubakaran E (2011) Four-factor based privacy preserving biometric authentication and authorization scheme for enhancing grid security. Int J Comput Appl 30(5):13–20

10. Lamport L (1981) Password authentication with insecure communication. Comm ACM 24(11):770–772

11. Hwang T, Chen Y, Laih CS (1990) Non-interactive password authentication without password tables. IEEE Conference on Computer and Communication Systems 1:429–431

12. Lee JK, Ryu SR, Yoo KY (2002) Fingerprint-based remote user authentication scheme using smart cards. Electron Lett 38(12):554–555

13. Chang CC, Lin IC (2004) Remarks on fingerprint-based remote user authentication scheme using smart cards. ACM SIGOPS Operating System Rev 38(4):91–96

14. Lin CH, Lai YY (2004) A flexible biometrics remote user authentication scheme. Comput Stand Interfac 27(1):19–23

15. Uludag U, Pankanti S, Prabhakar S, Jain AK (2004) Biometric cryptosystems: issues and challenges. Proc IEEE Special Issue on Multimedia Security for Digital Rights Management 92(6):948–960

16. Dodis Y, Ostrovsky R, Reyzin L, Smith A (2004) Fuzzy extractors: how to generate strong keys from biometrics and other noisy data. Advances in cryptology-eurocrypt 2004. Lect Notes Comput Sci 3027:523–540

17. Juels A, Wattenberg M (1999) A fuzzy commitment scheme. In: Proceedings of the 6th ACM Conference on Computer and Communications Security., pp 28–36

18. Sutcu Y, Li Q, Memon N (2007) Protecting biometric templates with sketch: theory and practice. IEEE Transactions on Information Forensics and Security 2(3):503–512

19. Chen CM, Ku WC (2002) Stolen-verifier attack on two new strong-password authentication protocol. IEICE Transactions on Communications E85-B(11):2519–2521

20. Fan C-I, Lin Y-H (2009) Provably secure remote truly three-factor authentication scheme with privacy protection on biometrics. IEEE Transactions on Information Forensic and Security 4(4):933–945

21. Trammell DD (2008) Four-factor authentication., Available at: http://blog.dustintrammell.com/2008/11/21/four-factor-authentication/#more-160, Accessed: January 2011

22. Foster I et al The open grid services architecture, version 1.5., Available at: http://www.ogf.org/documents/GFD.80.pdf, 2006, Accessed: January 2011

23. Alfieria R et al (2005) From gridmap-file to VOMS: managing authorization in a grid environment. Futur Gener Comput Syst 21:549–558

24. Coffey N (2012) Comparison of ciphers., Available at: http://www.javamex.com/tutorials/cryptography/ciphers.shtml, Accessed: January 2012

25. Foster I, Kesselman C, Nick JM, Tuecke S (2002) Grid services for distributed system integration. Journal Computer 35(6):37–46

26. Moriai S, Kato A, Kanda M (2005) Addition of camellia cipher suites to transport layer security., Available at: http://tools.ietf.org/pdf/rfc4132.pdf, Accessed: January 2012

27. Gong L (1991) Security risk of depending on synchronized clocks. ACM Operating System Review 26(1):49–53

12

Generating metadata from web documents: a systematic approach

Hsiang-Yuan Hsueh[1][*], Chun-Nan Chen[2] and Kun-Fu Huang[3]

* Correspondence:
chyhsueh@itri.org.tw
[1]Computational Intelligence
Technology Center, Industrial
Technology Research Institute,
Taiwan, R.O.C
Full list of author information is
available at the end of the article

Abstract

In this paper, a mechanism generating RDF Semantic Web schema from Web document set as the semantic metadata is proposed. Analyzing both the structural and un-structural content of Web documents, semi-structured Web documents can be conceptualized as resource objects with inter-relationships in RDF diagram. Technically, hyperlinks, basic annotations, and keywords in web documents will be properly analyzed, and corresponding RDF schema will be generated following the mechanism and rules proposed in this paper. It is expected that with the semantic metadata of document sets on the Web being systematically translated instead of manually edited, the semantic operation on the Web, such as semantic query or semantic search, will be possible in the future.

Keywords: Semantic web, Resource description framework, Metadata

Introduction

With the popularity of Internet and World Wide Web (WWW, Web), the size of documents on the Web grows dramatically. It is indeed that content on the Web has become the dominant resource to users for problem solving purposes.

However, the utilizing and query of such information resource is a challenge. Owing to the semi-structured nature of documents on the Web, people could not get the contents or documents what they really need from the search and query processes on the Web. Typically, the semi-structured documents can only be "navigated" by user. It is almost impossible for a web document to be semantically understood by machine without preprocessing.

It is obvious that the main reason Web cannot be precisely queried by users is the lack of semantic metadata of web documents. One typical and well-known solution for users to utilize the web document is Internet Search Engines. It tried to acquire all available web documents on the Web, parse the documents, and generate semantic layer of documents with form of some factors or data structures, such as term frequency (TF), inverted document frequency (IDF), inverted index, or PageRank, etc. However, the semantic layers in the Search Engine are limited, since they are usually designed for full-text information retrieval process. Users may need more advanced retrieval functionalities, such as attribute-based or arithmetic-based query (e.g. Finding all documents describing Ubuntu operating system newer than Ubuntu 8.04), which cannot properly provided by Search Engines.

One of the solutions to enable the ability for web documents utilized like a database is the generating of "schema" of web documents. There must be a plenty of approaches to express the Web with more schema-like manners. The dominant approach is the utilization of Semantic Web standard [1]. The main goal of Semantic Web is to play the role of extension of Web so that information can be linked together at the semantic level and interpreted by machine [2]. In other words, the core of Semantic Web is to provide schema-model-like metadata of web documents, Resource Description Framework (RDF) [3], so that information implicitly embedded in web document set can be operated and queried semantically.

The limitation of Semantic Web standard is the popularity. Currently, the Semantic Web still cannot be widely adopted on the Web, since a large number of un-structure web documents available on the Internet contain texts in natural language that can only be read by human beings. To be properly handled by machine automatically, providing corresponding schema of web documents is the most straightforward way for content providers and developers so that data service providers such as Internet Search Engine can understand semantic of web documents with efficient way. However, for content providers and developers, it is almost impossible to generate such metadata manually. The schema of web document can only be declared and edited by publishers using < meta > tags or other modern annotation methods, such as Open graph [4], microformat [5], or microdata [6], etc. Even when RDF has been recognized as the future standard for schema-model of web documents, publishers must edit and publish the RDF manually. The case will be even worse because RDF must be created and edited following underlying eXtensible Markup Language (XML) syntax. For publishers of Web resource, it is indeed a time-consuming work. It is also impossible to ask publishers of all web documents currently available on Internet to provide the corresponding RDF schema. While some solutions such as [7,8] claims that generating useful annotations as metadata from unstructured web documents is possible, there is still no scalable and semi-automatic solutions to generate semantic metadata of web documents based on the semantic related to the topic implicitly embedded in the content and relationships of web documents.

In this paper, we propose a systematic mechanism generating RDF Semantic Web schema from web document set as the corresponding schema-model-like semantic metadata. By analyzing the structure and content of Web objects in the web document set, they can be conceptualized as resource objects with inter-relationships in RDF diagram. It is also expected that when the semantic metadata of document sets on the Web being systematically translated instead of manually edited, the semantic-ready web documents will be more popular on the web since the Semantic Web standard can be adopted by content providers and developers. The semantic operation on the whole Web, such as semantic query or semantic search, will be therefore possible in the near future. Both content developers and data service providers will be benefit from the web environment with rich semantic natures.

The remainder of this paper is organized as follows. In Section "Literature review", we briefly introduce the related works about the Semantic Web engineering. Section "Solution to generate metadata from Web documents" describes our proposed approach that generates semantic metadata of web documents based on the actual content and relationships of web documents. This approach will then be demonstrated and discussed with the illustrative example in Section "Feasibility study and discussion". Finally, Section "Conclusion" concludes this paper and discusses some future applications.

Literature review

Utilizing Web with semantic manners is always a big challenge. Some solutions and approaches had proposed in order to generate the semantic information of semi-structured web documents, such as:

A. Search Engine: All search engine vendors provide internal semantic layers in their own search engine architectures for full-text information retrieval purposes. For example, the solutions of Google extract information about links and the content of documents by means of keywords. Google's solution also emphasizes the "quality" of links using PageRank model [9]. However, as we discussed in Section "Introduction", such internal semantic layer can be applied for full-text search. Some advanced query mechanisms are not widely supported.

B. Annotation Standards: On the other hands, there are some standards, such as OpenGraph, microformats, and microdata, proposed as extension of Hyper Text Markup Language (HTML) so that the semantic information can be embedded in the web documents as form of HTML elements or attributes. However, such elements or attributes are typically applied to annotate the data pieces in the web document. It is not suitable for "modeling" the web document sets or other textbases.

In order to modeling the web document sets or other textbases with form of schema model, it is potential that Semantic Web Standards can be applied. The Semantic Web is the next-generation Web that can be understood and be processed directly by machine. The scenario of Semantic Web deployment is that the information sources on the Web bring the metadata as semantic in a well-defined format for machine to operate, so that it is possible to support the integrated and uniform access to information sources and service as well as intelligent applications for information processing on the Web [10].

Technically, the Resource Description Framework (RDF) specification, which has become the recommended standard from World Wide Web Consortium (W3C) at 1999, is the most dominant enabler of Semantic Web. RDF is actually the "semantic model" of Web. In the model, any assertions about propositions can be created with simple language [11]. By such simple and formal language, everything on the Web can be treated as individual "resource" with a set of "properties". Concepts about resources can be modeled as the "object-property-value" triple.

Modeling the semantic information embedded among resources on the Web, it is possible for operation of Web documents with more semantic manners. For example, users can perform some attribute-oriented or arithmetic-based query on the whole Web, such as *"ALL documents published by W3C"*. The Web, which is currently the largest pool of information resource, can be utilized by users with more effective way by applying proper schema-model-like metadata layer on the Web.

Currently, there are some practical works addressed on the construction of metadata layer on the whole Web and create the user interface to users for querying the Semantic Web by indexing all available schemas on Internet. For example, the Swoogle [12] is a search engine for semi-structured knowledge information. The knowledge can be expressed by either RDF or Web Ontology Language (OWL) [13]. The search engine periodically acquires the knowledge files available on the Web. Users can perform search operations to query the knowledge repository managed by Swoogle. On the other hand, Sindice [14] is another project for Semantic search on the Web. It maintains the index to Semantic Web pages available on the Web. Users can perform semantic search based on either keywords or SPARQL [15]. However, the main problem of evolution of current semantic search engine is the insufficiency of Semantic Web resources on the Web. Nowadays, only a few portions of Web resources are created or maintained following the Semantic Web standard. It is not easy for users to acquire enough results that can be utilized for problem solving purposes.

As for the related works about enabling the Semantic Web and RDF as metadata of information resource, many studies have concentrated on enabling the ability of querying heterogeneous information resources using Semantic-Web-related approaches. For example, Jiang et al. [16] propose an architecture of exposing relational data source to the Semantic Web applications with SPARQL from the object-oriented perspective. Data source from relational database will be properly mapped to corresponding ontology from object-oriented perspective and make run-time translation efficiently. Then the Semantic Web applications can use SPARQL to query the ontologies and retrieve the knowledge back. On the other hand, Chen et al. [17] establish the database-to-ontology mapping functions. With these functions, it will be clarified whether SPARQL can support migration from relational database to semantic ontology, which is expressed by RDF. Once RDF as semantic layer is built, all applications can use SPARQL to search information in RDF data. Database application could be properly migrated as Semantic Web application by replacing SQLs with SPARQL queries.

Yet another category of studies have focused on looking for the translation mechanism to Semantic-Web-enabled information resource from traditional information sources. For example, Krishna [18] introduces a conversion of relational model databases into RDF formats. And the method from de Laborda [19] is to extract the semantic information of a relational database and transform it into Semantic Web metadata including RDF. On the other hand, D2RQ project [20] provides a mapping between relational database schema and Semantic Web concepts. D2RQ takes a relational database schema as input and presents the corresponding RDF interface of as output.

Furthermore, some studies provide solutions for generating RDF as annotations from information resources. For example, [7,8] provide mechanisms using either knowledgebase or natural language processing (NLP) technologies to annotate the content of Web page, and express the whole annotation map by RDF. However, the annotations in previous works are not enough for semantic search operations, since 1) the linguistic annotation, such as annotation of "part of speech" around the data pieces of the web document, cannot satisfy users, because users tend to get the answer about the questions which motivate users to search on the Web, and 2) semantic extraction of unstructured content using language grammars/parsers is not scalable.

There are also some studies focused on the conceptualization of Web documents. For example, Gu et al. [21] proposed a description method to express the structural content of Web pages using RDF. The structured parts in Web documents can then be conceptualized using RDF diagram. However, the conceptualization solutions totally based on structural information, such as < meta > tags, hyperlinks, or Resource Description Framework-in-attributes (RDFa) [22] information, still have some bottle-necks for semantic search operations. The most drawback is that the semantic and information that users want to query are often not available in the structural information of Web document sets. Analyzing the hyperlinks or other information cannot imply that users can query the Web document set with more semantic manners. For unstructured content, the human computing is the only way to be applied if users are interested in the semantic of such content.

In summary, RDF is indeed a useful data model to express semi-structured Web document sets. It has been widely adopted in many Semantic-Web-related literatures. However, there are still neglects for systematic or semi-automatic mechanism to generate the data model of Web information resources based on both the content and structure of Web document sets so that content publishers can maintain the semantic and users can utilize the information resource effectively.

Solution to generate metadata from Web documents

This paper proposed a mechanism for constructing Semantic Web with bi-directional approach: For content providers and developers, it is necessary to generate the schema-model-like metadata as semantic information of web resource/documents they maintained; Data service providers such as search engine vendors can acquire and maintain the semantic information on the whole Web so that it is possible for semantic search including attribute-oriented or arithmetic-based query operations. Table 1 discussed the design choice of proposed solution:

Figure 1 illustrates the proposed solution to generate the corresponding schema of Web site.

Table 1 Design choice of solution

Approach	Pros and cons
Top-down	Using traditional search engine index as semantic layer ●→**Pros:** No need for content providers and developers to generate semantic information. Search engine will discover the semantic information ●→**Cons:** Current search engines do not support advanced operations
Bottom-Up	Users provided annotations for data pieces in web documents ●→**Pros:** For users it is easier to annotate data pieces, there are specifications and standards for users to follow. ●→**Cons:** The annotations in the web documents may not relate to the topic or semantic of web documents because anything in the web document can be annotated. For data service providers it might not be useful for semantic engineering.
Bi-directional	●→**Pros:** It is easier for data service providers to provide semantic search schemes because schema of available web document can be collected easier due to the popularity ●→**Cons:** Systematic approach to generate schema is required to motivate the content providers and developers generating schema of web documents they maintained

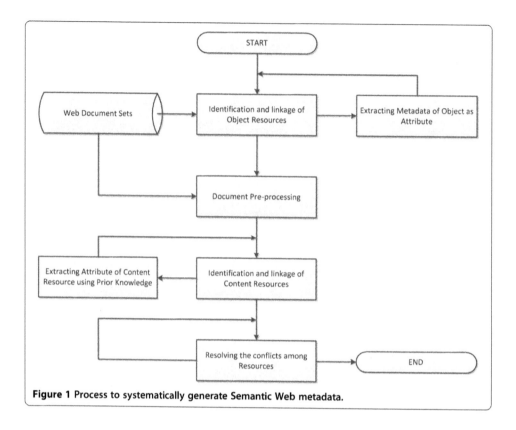

Figure 1 Process to systematically generate Semantic Web metadata.

It is indeed that the bi-directional approach is a feasible choice for adoption of Semantic Web standards. The main goal of this work is to generate Semantic Web metadata, which is expressed by RDF, of a Web site or other Web document sets systematically. In this article, two types of resource in the Web can be obtained and expressed in RDF:

- Object Resource: The real object, such as files, can be identified as "resources" in RDF.
- Content Resource: On the other hand, some objects or concepts which are appeared in content of documents can also be identified as "resources" in RDF.

To achieve the goal, the following steps are necessary to extract semantic information from Web document set:

Step 1   Identification and linkage of Object Resources

The first step involves the identification of object resources based on file structure and hyperlinks. The object resources can be identified based on URL and hyperlink. For any Web document set, the set of Web resource with inter-relationship information can be obtained and expressed as a preliminary RDF diagram using a crawler-like algorithm, as shown in the following Figure 2:

```
Function travel_document(document d) begin

    Recognize that d as a visited object resource;

    Add a node dc is a child node of d; /* the node dc is a pseudo node represents the inter-relationship */

    For each document d' which d hyperlink to begin

        If the type of dc is NOT defined then begin

            Add a property rdf:type of dc which is a "type object" rdf:bag;

        end;

        Add relationship from d to d' with form of property of dc;

        if d' has not been visited begin

        travel_document(d');

    end;

    end;

end.

Function MAIN(Web document set S) begin /* S is input of web document set for discovering schema */

    while there exists a document d in set S not be visited begin

    travel_document(d);

    end;

end.
```

Figure 2 Algorithm to generate relationships among object resources.

Basically, the structural relationships among object resources can be established by traversal of Web document set via hyperlink. It should be noted that:

1) There might be no semantic relationships among resources which have structural interrelationships.
2) For any web document set, one or more "entry points" might be available. That is, the documents can be considered as one or more tree structures conceptually. Documents (nodes) will be connected by hyperlinks (edges) in tree structures.

Step 2 Extracting metadata of Object Resource as Attributes of Object Resource

This step is responsible for extracting the metadata of object resource. Minimally, such metadata information includes the basic file information, such as file size and file authors, and the content information, such as MIME type or character encoding information which can be defined in < meta > fields in a Web document. It is indeed that the metadata must be translated as the properties of an object resource.

Step 3 Document Pre-processing

Typically, the content resources, which reflect some objects or concepts, are embedded in the content of object resource. In order to extract valuable information, the un-structured Web documents must be pre-processed so that the information embedded in documents can be handled automatically. Theoretically, all noun terms are potential content resources which can reflect some objects or concepts. In this article, however, for simplicity consideration, the information to be extracted only includes the keywords and the terms, which are already the representatives of extracted objects preliminary RDF diagram. For keyword extraction, there are many approaches to extract the keywords from Web documents. The most common way is the weighting approaches, such as TF-IDF factor, to determine the set of keywords of one document by calculating the "weight" of a term in a document. By this step, a set of terms are extracted as the potential representatives of content objects.

Step 4 Identification and linkage of Content Resources

In this step, content resources will be generated according to the relationships among extracted terms from previous step and preliminary RDF diagram. The following algorithm shown in the Figure 3 refines the preliminary RDF diagram using extracted term set:

Basically, the terms extracted as keywords will be considered as potential "content resource" in the step, since a keyword, such as "W3C" or "Linux", often reflects some physical objects or concepts. In this step, the inter-relationship among object resources and content resources will be preliminarily connected. It is then the semantic relationship among Web resources and concepts.

Step 5 Extracting Attributes of Content Resources

For each object resource R begin

  For each extracted term T from R begin

    If the term is the representative of an object resource R' OR a content resource R' then begin

      Add relationship from R to R' such that R' is a property of R;

    else begin

      Recognize that T is a newly-added object resource R';

      Set that T is representative of R';

      Add relationship from R to R' such that R' is a property of R;

    end;

  end;

end.

Figure 3 Algorithm to generate relationships among content resources.

In this step, the attributes of content resources must be extracted. The method to extract the attribute name about certain concept is out of the scope of this article. There are many approaches to extract attribute information of one concept from Web document automatically. Some common ways include the solution to extract attribute from structural part of Web document, or solutions using prior knowledge to determine the potential attribute with attributes of certain concept [23]. For any attribute of one concept to be extracted from Web document, it must be defined as the attribute of the corresponding content resource reflect the concept. After the step is done, all available resources, attributes, and inter-relationships will be extracted and expressed on the RDF graph.

Step 6 Resolving the conflicts among resources

Different from database resource, the Web document set cannot be normalized in order to keep the data consistency and storage minimization. There might be redundant or even conflict resource or attribute items in the Web document set. For example, some documents indicated that the newest kernel version of Linux is "3.2", while some out-of-date documents still said that the newest kernel version is "2.6.18". Strategically, to resolve the conflict among resource can be systematically done by the following procedure, as shown in Figure 4.

The first sub-step involves the resolution of linguistic conflicts in the RDF diagram, which might occur in resources identifications, attribute names, or even the values. Using thesauri or other prior knowledge, the conflict, such as synonym or homonym, must be eliminated first. For example, if two web documents represents identical attribute name with different value:

- *D(A): {Keyword = "Ubuntu", CurrentVersion = "8.04"}*
- *D(B): {Keyword = "Ubuntu", CurrentVersion = "12.04"}*

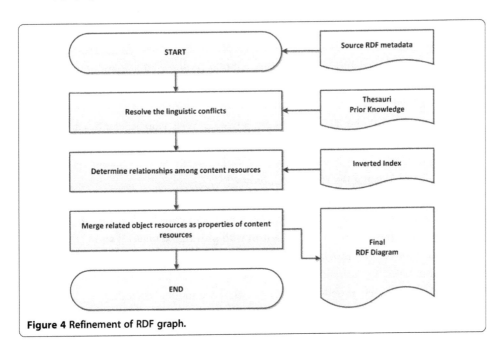

Figure 4 Refinement of RDF graph.

From the prior knowledge, the *CurrentVersion* attribute value in A must be ignored.

Next, the inter-relationships among content resources should be identified. In this article, the inter-relationship can be modeled by the "similarity" of two resources. Since the content resources come from the "keywords" extracted from documents, "keywords" should be representatives of content resources. The similarity of any two content resources X and Y can be calculated by the probability of co-occurrence of two representative and conflict-free keywords. The relationships among two content resources can be recognized if the similarity value exceeds some threshold:

$$Similarity(X, Y) = \frac{P(X \cap Y)}{P(X \cup Y)} \geq \varepsilon$$

The last sub-step is responsible to annotate the relationship from content resources to object resources. The semantic of such relationship is to identify "ALL real objects which are related to some concepts". Strategically, in this sub-step, all object resources related to a content object can be merged as a "Bag" property of the content object. Like an inverted index, it is therefore possible for users to query about resources relevant to some concepts. After the conflicts are resolved, the final RDF diagram which represents the metadata of Web document set can be obtained.

Feasibility study and discussion

In this section, a set of experiments are applied to demonstrate the feasibility of proposed mechanism to translate a Web document into corresponding RDF model. We also discuss some lesson learned in this section.

Considering the Web document D = http://www.w3.org/News/2011#entry-9116. From the web document, it can be obtained that D is actually an anchor section of Web document http://www.w3.org/News/2011 and contains a News paragraph about Cascading Style Sheets (CSS). The keyword set extracted from D is *{CSS, W3C}*. D has linked to Web document set *{D1, D2, D3, D4, D5, D6, D7}*. Partial RDF diagram of D can be visualized as shown in Figure 5:

Please note that in this case, only the semantic directly related to D is shown in the graph and only one content resource *{CSS}* is visible as illustrative demonstration in the graph. Semantic relationships about another content resource *{W3C}* are not shown here.

The translated XML document of the RDF is shown in Figure 6:

It should be noted that the all resources in Semantic Web will be identified using Uniform Resource Identifier (URI), which may be denoted as Universal Resource Locator (URL) or Universal Resource Name (URN). For example, the content resource "CSS" can be identified using the URN *"urn:object:CSS"*.

Since the feasibility of proposed mechanism is basically certified, in order to demonstrate the advantage of proposed mechanism, we apply a set of illustrative experiments to compare the effectiveness of proposed mechanism with previous studies [7] and [21].

The Extractiv project [7] provided a knowledge-engineering-based mechanism to generate the annotation for "contents in web documents". The basic principle is similar to the microdata approach proposed in HTML 5: To annotate according to known ontology and prior-knowledge. The Figure 7 illustrates the semantic information of a web document Z = http://www.ubuntu.com generated from Extractiv project:

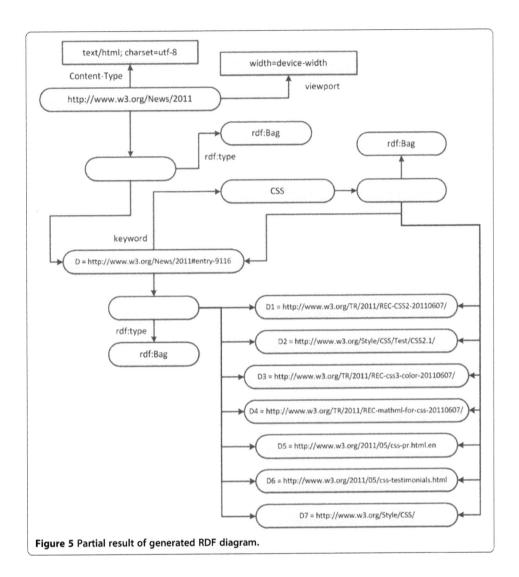

Figure 5 Partial result of generated RDF diagram.

In the generated semantic information, users can easily obtain some types of "entities" in some location of the document. However, the main drawback of such solution is the requirement of inventing extremely rich prior knowledge. For example, the Extractiv system must understand that "Ubuntu is an Operating System". The generation process will be failed if no knowledgebase or ontology presented. On the other hand, the generated semantic information is not always useful for users. For instance, the fact that "2012 is an instance of DATE-TIME" might not be helpful for users with question answering purposes.

On the other hand, there are indeed some studies, such as [21], try to introduce approaches describing semantic of the web document based on the structural metadata. The Figure 8 shows partial RDF diagram of D using approach in [21]:

It is obvious that the generated RDF in [21] is based on 1) the structural relationships among object resources, and 2) the structural metadata in < meta > tags that can be easily acquired from the web document. However, the unstructured semantic information, which might be more valuable for users, cannot be extracted and expressed in the RDF diagram by such approach. The query on < meta > tag information such as

```xml
<?xml version="1.0"?>
<rdf:RDF xmlns:rdf="http://www.w3.org/1999/02/22-rdf-syntax-ns#" xmlns:rs="http://www.w3.org/News/2011">
 <rdf:Description rdf:about="http://www.w3.org/News/2011">
  <Content-Type>text/html; charset=utf-8</Content-Type>
  <viewport>width=device-width</viewport>
  <rs:recource>
   <rdf:Bag>
    <rdf:li rdf:resource="http://www.w3.org/News/2011#entry-9116" />
    <!-- Declaration of other object resources are omitted -->
   </rdf:Bag>
  </rs:recource>
 </rdf:Description>
 <rdf:Description rdf:about="http://www.w3.org/News/2011#entry-9116">
  <rdf: keyword rdf:resoutce="urn:onject:CSS" />
  <rs:recource>
   <rdf:Bag>
    <rdf:li rdf:resource="http://www.w3.org/TR/2011/REC-CSS2-20110607/" />
    <rdf:li rdf:resource="http://www.w3.org/Style/CSS/Test/CSS2.1/" />
    <rdf:li rdf:resource="http://www.w3.org/TR/2011/REC-css3-color-20110607/" />
    <rdf:li rdf:resource="http://www.w3.org/TR/2011/REC-mathml-for-css-20110607/" />
    <rdf:li rdf:resource="http://www.w3.org/2011/05/css-pr.html.en" />
    <rdf:li rdf:resource="http://www.w3.org/2011/05/css-testimonials.html" />
    <rdf:li rdf:resource="http://www.w3.org/Style/CSS/" />
   </rdf:Bag>
  </rs:recource>
 </rdf:Description>
 <rdf:Description rdf:about="urn:onject:CSS">
  <rs:recource>
   <rdf:Bag>
    <rdf:li rdf:resource="http://www.w3.org/TR/2011/REC-CSS2-20110607/" />
    <rdf:li rdf:resource="http://www.w3.org/Style/CSS/Test/CSS2.1/" />
    <rdf:li rdf:resource="http://www.w3.org/TR/2011/REC-css3-color-20110607/" />
    <rdf:li rdf:resource="http://www.w3.org/TR/2011/REC-mathml-for-css-20110607/" />
    <rdf:li rdf:resource="http://www.w3.org/2011/05/css-pr.html.en" />
    <rdf:li rdf:resource="http://www.w3.org/2011/05/css-testimonials.html" />
    <rdf:li rdf:resource="http://www.w3.org/Style/CSS/" />
   </rdf:Bag>
  </rs:recource>
 </rdf:Description>
 <!-- Declaration of other content resources are omitted -->
</rdf:RDF>
```

Figure 6 The XML expression of generated RDF diagram.

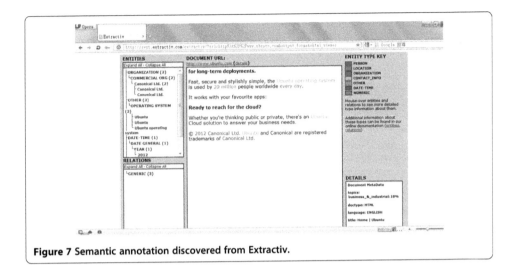

Figure 7 Semantic annotation discovered from Extractiv.

"Finding all documents with UTF-8 character encoding" might not be helpful for users with question answering purposes.

It is indeed that the proposed mechanism has some advantages compared to previous approaches. As for the application and adoption of proposed mechanism, it is potential to be the core technology of Semantic Web search engine based on Semantic Web or RDF [24,25]. The main characteristic of such search engine is to provide a semantic layer in the search engine so that users can perform semantic search operation based on semantic layer. With such automatically-generated RDF as metadata of Web document set, it is therefore possible for query operations on Web document sets with more semantic manner. For example, when users want to query about all documents about "CSS", it is easy to acquire the result set {D, D1, D2, D3, D4, D5, D6, D7} from the semantic description of the RDF graph. Under such scenario, combining the current keyword-based information retrieval technology in finding potential semantic

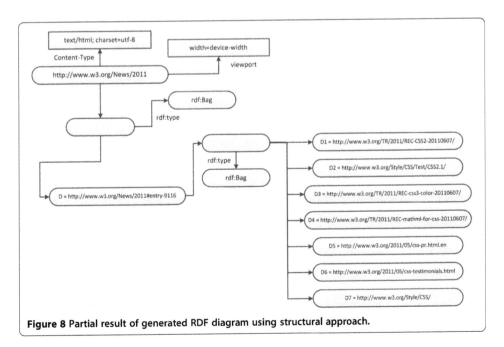

Figure 8 Partial result of generated RDF diagram using structural approach.

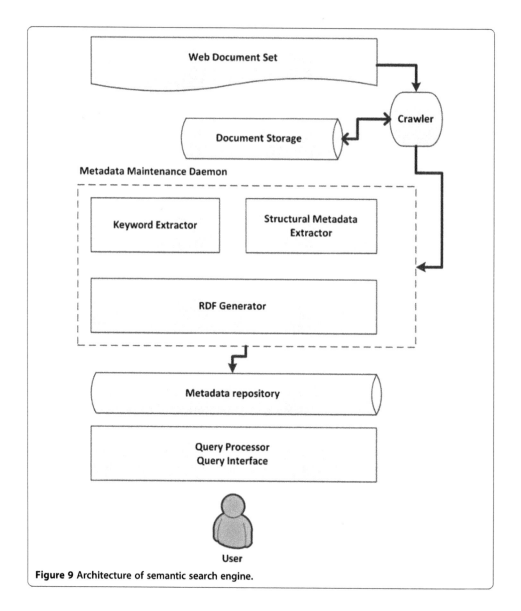

Figure 9 Architecture of semantic search engine.

information and formulating in RDF schema is a potential key technology for current search engine to seamlessly enable the semantic search functions.

As for the implementation of RDF generator in semantic search engine on Semantic Web, a referential architecture can be illustrated as shown in Figure 9. It should be noticed that in this article, the bi-directional approach is recommended that content providers and developers should be responsible for generating of RDF schema of web documents they maintained. However, implementation of RDF generator in semantic search engine is still required because the popularity of "schema-ready" web documents will highly depend on the willing of content providers and developers to generate the RDF schema with either manually or systematically approaches.

The main goal of semantic search engine illustrated is to provide a metadata repository, where the metadata with RDF form is automatically generated and maintained, as semantic layer for users to perform semantic query. In the referential architecture, the goal will be achieved by maintenance daemon. There are at least five modules included in the daemon:

- Crawler: For any Internet search engine, a crawler will be necessary to perform as backend service to acquire available Web resource.
- Structural Metadata Extractor: The module is utilized to extract structural information from Web document set created by crawler. Any structured and analyzable part of Web documents will be extracted and transformed into metadata, which described the structure information of the Web document set. In other words, the module is the extractor of object resources and performing the Step 1 and Step 2 of the proposed mechanism.
- Keyword Extractor: The module is responsible to extract semantic of content in Web documents. Based on keyword extraction methods, keywords reflecting certain concepts can be extracted from the content of Web documents. In other words, the module is the extractor of object resources and performing the Step 3 to Step 5 of the proposed mechanism.
- RDF Generator: The module is responsible for generating of RDF metadata, which will be physically expressed by extensible markup language (XML) or other formats, from extracted semantic and structural information. On the other hand, the module must reconcile the heterogeneity and conflicts come from metadata of different Web documents. In other words, the module is the extractor of object resources and performing the Step 6 of the proposed mechanism. In this module, external prior knowledge or thesauri might be necessary.
- Query Processor and Interface: The module is actually a human-machine interface. Users' intension must be properly expressed using some query formats such as SPARQL or XQuery [26] that can query the metadata repository directory. The processor will execute and return the query result back to users. In the module, a ranking mechanism based on the nature of Semantic Web, which is out of the scope of this article, might be necessary in order to determine the relevance of results to users' intension.

In summary, the Table 2 provides discussion and comparisons with other methods which are illustrated in Section "Literature review".

Table 2 Discussion and comparisons with other methods

Approach	Discussion and comparisons
Search Engine for Semantic Web [12,14]	The search space depends on the acquirable schema or other semantic information. No discussions for generating semantic information from semi-structured documents.
Middleware handling heterogeneity [16,17] Schema Translation from database [18-20]	The middleware or translator can map or convert schema between structured data sources and Semantic Web schema. It is infeasible on the cases of semi-structured or even un-structured data resources.
Schema generation from document based on knowledge engineering [7,8]	Current schemes can generate either linguistic or semantic annotation of data pieces in web documents using prior-knowledge or NLP technologies. It is not suitable for "modeling" the web document sets or other textbases. For problem-solving or topic search purposes, the solutions are not sufficient.
Schema generation from document based on structural part of document [21]	The structure-based approaches generate RDF only based on structural part of document. Such solution is simple to implement, while the generated RDF might not be helpful for users for question solving purposes.

Conclusion

In this paper, we propose a six-step systematic mechanism generating RDF Semantic Web schema from Web document set as the corresponding schema-model-like semantic metadata. In our approach, different from previous studies and solutions, both structural information and content information are analyzed using prior knowledge. Schema-model-like semantic information can therefore be generated systematically from our mechanism. By analyzing strategies for link and concept extraction, Web resources can be conceptualized as resource objects with inter-relationships in RDF schema diagram. We also demonstrate the feasibility of proposed mechanism using an illustrative case study. It is also expected that the proposed mechanism is general applicable. First, it is feasible to be the core technology of next-generation search engine. In this article, we discuss the architecture of semantic search engine on Semantic Web based on RDF and the proposed mechanism. With the semantic meta-data of document sets on the Web being systematically translated instead of manually edited by either content providers or data service providers, the semantic operation on the whole Web, such as semantic query or semantic search based on certain semantic layer, will be possible in the near future. Furthermore, it is applicable as one of important module in web document development software. Many data service providers, such as Google rich snippet project [27], encourage content providers publish web document with rich semantic. The proposed mechanism is a feasible way for content providers develop semantic information systematically and semi-automatically. The reputation of such web document is expected to be basically certified and admired.

As for the future directions, the most important work is to enrich the schema of the web documents. It is indeed that in the schema, "keyword" might not be the only content resource to be extracted although in this article the scope is limited in keywords. It is recommended that the RDF schema will be more completed by integrating other categories of "semantic-like content", such as annotations, tags, or other acquirable properties.

Competing interests

The authors declare that they have no competing interests.

Authors' contributions

H-YH designed, conceptualized, and evaluated the solutions proposed in this article. C-NC and K-FH identified the innovation of proposed solution in this article by collecting and reviewing all available previous studies. All authors drafted the manuscript. H-YH refined the manuscript iteratively and did the final revision. All authors read and approved the final manuscript.

Author details

[1]Computational Intelligence Technology Center, Industrial Technology Research Institute, Taiwan, R.O.C. [2]Chunghwa Telecom Laboratories, Taiwan, R.O.C. [3]Information & Communication Research Lab, Industrial Technology Research Institute, Taiwan, R.O.C.

References

1. (2010) Semantic Web, http://www.w3.org/standards/semanticWeb
2. Raimbault T (2010) Overviewing the RDF(S) Semantic Web. Proceedings of International Conference on Computational Intelligence and Software Engineering (CiSE 2010). IEEE Press, Wuhan, China, pp 1–4
3. (2004) Resource Description Framework (RDF), http://www.w3.org/RDF
4. (2012) Open Graph (Facebook Developers), https://developers.facebook.com/docs/opengraph
5. (2012) About Microformats, http://microformats.org/about
6. (2011) HTML5.1 Nightly: A vocabulary and associated APIs for HTML and XHTML, http://www.w3.org/html/wg/drafts/html/master/Overview.html
7. (2011) Extractiv Project, http://www.extractiv.com/

8.   Mukhopadhyay D, Kumar R, Majumdar S, Sinha S (2007) A New Semantic Web Services to Translate HTML Pages to RDF. Proceedings of 10th International Conference on Information Technology (ICIT 2007). IEEE Press, Orissa, India, pp 292–294

9.   Brin S, Page L (1998) The Anatomy of a Large-Scale Hypertextual Web Search Engine. Computer Networks and ISDN Systems 30(1–7):107–117

10. Decker S, Mitra P, Melnik S (2000) Framework for the Semantic Web: An RDF Tutorial. IEEE Internet Computing 4(6):68–73

11. Agarwal PR (2012) Semantic Web in Comparison to Web 2.0. Proceedings of 3rd International Conference on Intelligent Systems, Modelling and Simulation (ISMS). IEEE Press, Kota_Kinabalu, Malaysia, pp 558–563

12. Finin T, Ding L, Pan R, Joshi A, Kolari P, Java A, Peng Y (2005) Swoogle: Searching for knowledge on the Semantic Web. Proceedings of the 20th national conference on Artificial intelligence (AAAI 2005). AAAI Press, Pittsburgh, Pennsylvania, USA, pp 1682–1683

13. (2004) Web Ontology Language (OWL), http://www.w3.org/2004/OWL

14. Oren E et al (2008) Sindice.com: A Document-oriented Lookup Index for Open Linked Data. International Journal of Metadata, Semantics and Ontologies 3(1):37–52

15. (2008) SPARQL Query Language for RDF, http://www.w3.org/TR/rdf-sparql-query

16. Jiang H, Ju L, Xu Z (2009) Upgrading the relational database to the Semantic Web with Hibernate. Proceedings of International Conference on Web Information Systems and Mining (WISM 2009). IEEE Press, Shanghai, China, pp 227–230

17. Chen Y, Yang X, Yin K, Ho A (2008) Migrating Traditional Database-based Systems onto Semantic Layer, Proceedings of International Conference on Computer Science and Software Engineering (CSSE 2008), 4. IEEE Press, Wuhan, Hubei, China, pp 672–676

18. Krishna M ( ) Retaining Semantics in Relational Databases by Mapping them to RDF. Proceedings of the 2006 IEEE/WIC/ACM international conference on Web Intelligence and Intelligent Agent Technology (WI-IAT 2006). IEEE Press, Hong Kong, China, pp 303–306

19. de Laborda C (2006) Bringing Relational Data into the Semantic Web using SPARQL and Relational OWL. Proceedings of the 22nd International Conference on Data Engineering Workshops (ICDE 2006). IEEE Press, Atlanta, GA, USA, p 55

20. Bizer C (2004) D2RQ - Treating Non-RDF Databases as Virtual RDF Graphs. Proceedings of the 3rd International Semantic Web Conference (ISWC2004). Hiroshima, Japan

21. Gu Y, Dan L (2010) Web resources description model based on RDF. Proceedings of 2010 International Conference on Computer Application and System Modeling (ICCASM 2010), pp V9-222-V9-225

22. (2008) RDFa1.1 Primer: Rich Structured Data Markup for Web Documents, http://www.w3.org/TR/xhtml-rdfa-primer/

23. Nakane F, Otsubo M, Hijikata Y, Nishida S (2008) A basic study on attribute name extraction from the Web. Proceedings of IEEE International Conference on Systems, Man and Cybernetics (SMC 2008). IEEE Press, Singapore, pp 2161–2166

24. Jin Y, Lin Z, Lin H (2008) The Research of Search Engine Based on Semantic Web. Proceedings of International Symposium on Intelligent Information Technology Application Workshops (IITAW 2008). IEEE Press, Shanghai, China, pp 360–363

25. Priebe T, Schlager C, Pernul G ( ) A Search Engine for RDF Metadata. Proceedings of 15th International Workshop on Database and Expert Systems Applications (DEXA 2004). IEEE Press, Zaragoza, Spain, pp 168–172

26.   (2011) XQuery 1.0: An XML Query Language, Secondth edn, http://www.w3.org/TR/xquery

27. (2012) Rich snippets (microdata, microformats, and RDFa), http://support.google.com/webmasters/bin/answer.py?hl=en&answer=99170

13

Designing a collaborative visual analytics system to support users' continuous analytical processes

Dong Hyun Jeong[1*], Soo-Yeon Ji[2], Evan A Suma[3], Byunggu Yu[1] and Remco Chang[4]

*Correspondence: djeong@udc.edu

[1] Department of Computer Science and Information Technology, University of the District of Columbia, 4200 Connecticut Avenue NW, 20008 Washington, DC, USA
Full list of author information is available at the end of the article

Abstract

In recent, numerous useful visual analytics tools have been designed to help domain experts solve analytical problems. However, most of the tools do not reflect the nature of solving real-world analytical tasks collaboratively because they have been designed for single users in desktop environments. In this paper, a complete visual analytics system is designed for solving real-world tasks having two integrated components: a single-user desktop system and an extended system suitable for a collaborative environment. Specifically, we designed a collaborative touch-table application (iPCA-CE) by adopting an existing single-user desktop analytical tool (iPCA). With the system, users can actively transit from individual desktop to shared collaborative environments without losing track of their analysis. They can also switch their analytical processes from collaborative to single-user workflows. To understand the usefulness of the system for solving analytical problems, we conducted a user study in both desktop and collaborative environments. From this study, we found that both applications are useful for solving analytical problems individually and collaboratively in different environments.

Keywords: Visual analytics; Collaborative visual analysis; Analysis process; Table-top environment

1 Introduction

Collaboration in real-world analysis can be regarded as a process of working together or sharing decision-making to develop a joint strategy or answer for the given complex tasks. Since collaboration is beneficial for solving complicated tasks, domain experts often work together to solve analytical problems in a collaborative setting [1]. However, it has been known that real-world analysts typically perform both individual and group tasks, and as a result must frequently transition between single-user and multi-user collaborative workflows during the course of their analysis [2,3]. Despite this fact, most visual analytics solutions have been designed either as standalone single-user applications or as purely collaborative systems, and very few analytical tools have been developed that cohesively support both activities.

Although data analysis is often considered to be a stand-alone task, previous research has shown that analysis of empirical data in collaborative environments is important and should be considered when developing visualization applications [4,5]. While collaborative analytics can occur in a variety of interaction modalities, we focus specifically on collaboration using a multi-touch table. Specifically, a complete visual analytical system is designed for solving real-world tasks ought to have two integrated components: a single-user desktop application and an extended system suitable for a collaborative environment. Specifically, an existing single-user desktop analytical tool for exploring data using principal component analysis (called iPCA [6]) is adapted into a collaborative touch-table application (called iPCA-CE [7]). Extending an existing desktop application into a collaborative touch-table environment introduces unique technical challenges. The inherent differences between mouse and touch-based interaction require that the user interface must be redesigned, and limitations may also be imposed by factors such as system performance. However, despite the costs of converting an existing application into a new interaction modality, we believe that supporting both single-user and collaborative work in an integrated fashion provides important benefits for real-world analysis.

With the iPCA and iPCA-CE applications, analysts can perform their analytical tasks by switching back and forth between sign-user desktop and collaborative visual analytics environments. As a result, the system parameters and analytical findings for these tools are tightly integrated so that analysts may seamlessly transition without losing track of the analysts' analysis process. To support the sharing of analytical results (i.e. findings), which many experts consider it to be the purpose of collaboration [2], we defined an XML-based format for managing the findings from analyses, which can "follow" the user as they transition between single-user and collaborative contexts. In a single-user desktop environment, we performed a user study to see the effectiveness of iPCA for solving analytical tasks, and creating and sharing findings in a single-user desktop environment. To understand how participants cooperate and share their findings for solving analytical tasks in a collaborative environment, we conducted an additional user study with a varying number of available workspaces in a collaborative environment.

This paper is organized as follows. First, we discuss the previous research in collaborative visualization that is relevant to our approach. In Section 3, we represent our viewpoint to support analysts' continuous analytical processes in different environments. In Section 4, we provide an overview of our visual analytics tools and outline the technical challenges involved with extending an existing application for deployment in a collaborative environment. Next, in Section 5, we then describe the improvements made to our applications to support the sharing of analytical processes. In Sections 6 and 7, we report the user study that was performed to understand users' analytical processes in a desktop and collaborative environment, respectively. Finally, in Section 8, we discuss future work and conclude the paper.

2   Previous work

Collaborative visualizations have a long history. Coleman et al. [8] described four general reasons why collaborative visualization is compelling as (1) experts' knowledge can be available any time and at any place, (2) this expertise can be transferred to others, improving the local level of knowledge, (3) based on the supported accessibility, visualization products can be reviewed and modified as they are produced, reducing turn-around time, and (4) remote accessibility can reduce the need to relocate the expertise physically.

Grimstead et al. [9] reviewed 42 collaborative visualization systems in terms of five attributes: number of simultaneous users, user access control, communication architecture, type of transmitted data, and user synchronization. They found that a synchronous system, in which all collaboration takes place simultaneously, has the benefits of bringing groups of individuals together over a distance, bridging the knowledge gaps between them, and building their knowledge structure concurrently. However, they noted that a synchronous system is still limited, in that people have to be in front of computers at the same time. In an asynchronous collaborative visualization system, collaboration occurs at different times. If people are in different time zones and different places, an asynchronous collaborative system might be beneficial, since important knowledge can be shared with others at their own convenience [10].

Mark and Kobsa [11] performed an empirical study to understand the differences between group and individual behavior within collaborative information visualization environments. They found that a group solves the given questions more accurately and spends less time doing so. However, it is still unknown what features should be supported within a collaborative data analysis system on a touch-table in order to reliably gain these benefits. Ma [12] discussed existing web-based collaborative workspaces in terms of sharing high-performance visualization facilities, visualizations, and findings, and noted that sharing visualization resources will eventually provide support for collaborative workspaces. Despite the numerous collaborative visualization systems that have been developed, it is still unclear how these systems should be designed, though some guidelines have been suggested. Heer and Agrawala [13] provided design considerations for asynchronous collaboration in visual analytics environments. Additionally, in a review of existing applications in terms of controlling the visualization, Johnson [14] outlined challenges and suggested guidelines for the design of synchronous collaborative visualizations. However, none of these guidelines address how analytic processes might be extended across both single-user and collaborative modalities, as we focus on in this paper.

In a co-located collaborative environment, numerous studies [15-17] have been performed to understand users' collaborative analytical processes and how best to design useful collaborative visualization or visual analytics systems. Notably, Isenberg [16] proposed design guidelines for designing an efficient collaborative environment. Robinson [15] also provided design guidelines for collaborative synthesis supporting visual analytics tools. Although most of these studies are designed to understand users' analytical processes, they focus on single co-located environments. However, in our study, we observed that a collaborative environment imposed several limitations on the users' analytical processes (see Section 5 for details). These results guided us to think differently about creating and supporting a continuous analytical process, namely by combining both a single-user desktop environment and a collaborative environment into a complete, integrated system.

It is this combination of single-user and collaborative environments that set this work apart from similar research on collaborative visual analytics systems. For example, Cambiera [16] is a visual analytics solution which supports collaborative searching through large text document collections on a touch surface. In addition to searching through documents, this system is capable of tracking the findings from analyses and maintaining awareness of collaborators' work. However, while Cambiera might support both environments, it is mainly designed for table-top collaborations and does not allow analysts to migrate their findings between collaborative and single-user contexts. Additionally, Forlines and Lilien [18] converted a single-user, single-display molecular visualization into a collaborative multi-display system. Each display is intended for the group as a whole, and there seems to be no consideration or ability for a user to break away from the collaborative environment, perform individual analysis within an isolated workspace, and then return to the collaborative environment to share their results. They provide a separate tablet PC that is used to make more accurate selections than is possible on their touch table. Although they do speculate that each user could have their own tablet, these personal interfaces serve only for making selections in the collaborative space, not conducting individual analyses.

Likewise, a very closely related system for conducting geospatial analysis utilizes tablet PCs to allow users to issue commands to the collaborative environment [19]. Interestingly, they theorize that their single shared display might discourage individuals from exploring, while providing individuals their own personal interfaces might make them more comfortable exploring their own ideas in private before sharing them with collaborators. Indeed, our work builds on this speculation, examines the issues involved, and provides a mature implementation that supports and encourages this behavior. Overall, to the best of our knowledge, there is no visual analytics tool has been mainly designed to support both single and collaborative environments. Most visual analytics tools are designed to work in a single desktop environment. Therefore, they need to be modified or rebuilt to make them work in a collaborative environment. Since modifying or rebuilding existing visual analytics tools requires additional time and efforts, web-based technology is commonly adopted to build collaborative visual analytics spaces [12]. In this paper, we explain how our visual analytics tools (iPCA and iPCA-CE) are designed to support both environments with emphasizing some technical considerations how to overcome technical limitations of supporting the environments (see Section 4.4).

3   Users' analytical processes

Based on understanding existing literature of collaborative environments, we suggest that users' analyses should not be isolated in one environment (i.e. desktop or collaborative environments). An individual user performs a data analysis and compiles a list of findings in a desktop environment. When enough interesting results are found, the user meets with other analysts in a collaborative environment to discuss and share these findings. After sharing findings with each other, the users then work together interactively to perform a collaborative group analysis. Afterwards, the users then take the findings from the collaborative analysis back into a single-user setting for individual analysis and validation. This process then continuously repeats.

In here, we developed an informal model for general analytical process that should be supported and maintained to allow analysts to switch back and forth between single-user and collaborative workflows. As illustrated in Figure 1, we believe that analysts perform four distinct sharing processes: (a) asynchronous self-sharing in the desktop environment, (b) synchronous sharing in a collaborative environment, and (c, d) two asynchronous transitional sharing processes between the desktop and collaborative environments. All four sharing processes can be supported by passing the finding parameters between users and applications. Processes (a) and (b) form continuous loops within each

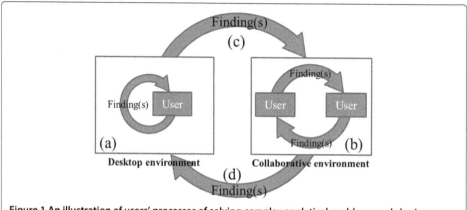

Figure 1 An illustration of users' processes of solving complex analytical problems and sharing analysis results (findings). It shows four users' processes including **(a)** asynchronous self-sharing in a desktop environment, **(b)** synchronous sharing in a collaborative environment, and **(c, d)** asynchronous transitional sharing processes between environments.

environment, while processes (c) and (d) form a global loop through which the entire analysis process iterates over time. By providing support for all four sharing processes, we form an integrated visual analytics system which reflects the analytical processes carried out by real-world experts.

The illustration of users' processes of solving complex problems and sharing analysis results (findings) has been presented as a poster [7] at the visualization conference (VisWeek 2010). Visualization experts' opinions were positive to our idea of preserving users' continuously analysis process in different environments instead of isolating them in one environment. Some of them commented that providing two visual analytics tools is good for performing collaborative and single-user analytical processes, especially when solving difficult analytical problems.

4   System overview

Although supporting collaboration when solving real-world analytical tasks is important, most visual analytics tools have been designed as single-user desktop systems [7,20]. Since we believe that user-friendly visualizations in a collaborative environment enable users to find results more accurately, we chose to extend a known and useful application to work in a collaborative touch-table environment. Multi-touch surfaces support a rich set of interactions that allow multiple users to work together to solve complex analytical problems interactively. We selected the Interactive Principal Component Analysis (iPCA) application, which has been shown to be an effective and easy to use desktop visualization for analysing data sets and interactively exploring the parameters of principal component analysis [6]. Figure 2 shows a system overview showing iPCA and iPCA-CE with an analysis of the Glass dataset, which is a publicly available scientific result from the UCI Machine Learning Repository [21].

With the system, a single user performs an analysis with iPCA (Figure 3A) and multiple users collaborate with the extended collaborative application (iPCA-CE) (Figure 3B). Since the collaborative application is an extended version of the desktop application, both

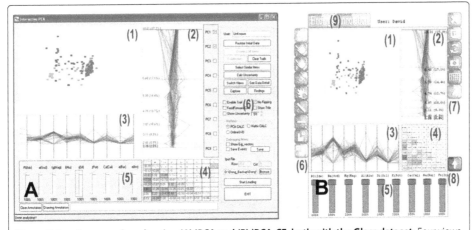

Figure 2 A system overview showing (A) iPCA and (B) iPCA-CE, both with the Glass dataset. Four views (1 ~ 4) and a set of sliderbars (5) are shown in both applications. Buttons and menus (6) in iPCA were converted to several touchable buttons (6 and 7). In iPCA-CE, the sliderbars can be expanded and collapsed by pressing the toggle button (8), and tab buttons (9) were added to access users' findings and annotations. Both applications support manipulating and changing the scale of the projected data items.

applications support similar user interaction techniques (selection, manipulation, zooming, etc.) to perform interactive data analysis [6]. Therefore, the users can perform a smooth transition with their findings from one environment to another.

4.1 Principal component analysis

Principle Component Analysis (PCA) is a mathematical procedure widely used for high dimensional data analysis. PCA is a powerful tool capable of reducing dimensions and revealing relationships among data items. It has been viewed as a "black box" approach that is difficult to grasp for many of its users because the coordinate transformation from original data space into eigenspace makes it difficult for the user to interpret the underlying relation [22]. PCA projects a dataset to a new coordinate system by determining the eigenvectors and eigenvalues of the dataset. It involves a calculation of a covariance matrix of the dataset to minimize the redundancy and maximize the variance. With the covariance matrix, the eigenvectors and eigenvalues are calculated. The eigenvectors are unit eigenvectors (lengths are 1). Once the eigenvectors and the eigenvalues are calculated, the eigenvalues are sorted in descending order. This gives us the components in order of significance. The eigenvector with the highest eigenvalue is the most dominant

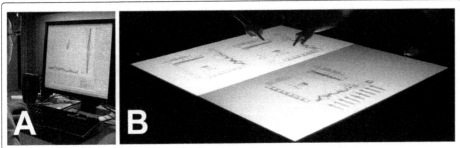

Figure 3 Performing visual anlaytical tasks with iPCA and iPCA-CE. (A) A single user is performing an analysis of the Glass dataset (214 × 9 matrix) using iPCA. **(B)** Multiple users are interactively collaborating on a multi-touch table using iPCA-CE.

principle component of the dataset (PC1). A detailed explanation about PCA can be found in [22,23].

4.2 iPCA

iPCA (Figure 2A) is designed (1) to help the user understand the complicated black-box operation of principal component analysis [22] and (2) to allow the user to analyse complex data sets interactively [6]. Specifically, it focuses on assisting the user in better understanding and utilizing PCA for analysis by visualizing the results of principal component analysis using multiple coordinated views and a rich set of user interactions. The application is designed primary for use on a standard desktop computer. Since our primary goal of this study is to design a collaborative visual analytics system to support a continuous analysis process, the system has been upgraded to support annotation techniques (see Section 5 for detail).

The application consists of four views: Projection view (Figure 2A-1), Eigenvector view (Figure 2A-2), Data view (Figure 2A-3), and Correlation view (Figure 2A-4). In the Projection view, all data items are projected based on the first and second principal components by default. The Eigenvector view displays the calculated eigenvectors and eigenvalues in a vertically projected parallel coordinate view. The distances between the eigenvectors in the parallel coordinate view vary based on their eigenvalues, separating the eigenvectors based on their mathematical weights. The Data view shows the original data points in parallel coordinates. The Correlation view represents Pearson-correlation coefficients and relationships between variables as a matrix of scatter plots and values. Pearson-correlation coefficient provides a value between +1 and -1 by measuring the linear correlation between two variables. If the value is close to 1, the two variables maintain a positive correlation. Otherwise (close to -1), the two variables preserve a negative correlation. All views are closely connected, such that if the user changes the elements in one view, its corresponding results are updated in other views (brushing & linking). This interactivity allows the user to infer relationships between the coordinated spaces (see the paper [6] for details).

4.3 iPCA-CE

iPCA-CE (Figure 2B) is an extension of iPCA designed specifically for use in a collaborative touch-table environment [24]. Each workspace in iPCA-CE displays the same four views as iPCA. However, the system provides the capability to create multiple workspaces within the application, each of which can be used independently. We deployed iPCA-CE on a multi-touch display system designed by the Renaissance Computing Institute (RENCI) (http://www.renci.org). It provides a 46″ × 42″ work surface using two high resolution projection displays.

Due to differences between desktop and collaborative environments, iPCA-CE is designed to support multi-touch input. From our previous study with iPCA [6], only important and frequently used interaction features were replicated as touchable buttons in iPCA-CE. A total of 16 touchable buttons and 2 tab buttons were designed for interaction in iPCA-CE: nine buttons for interacting with represented data items (Figure 2B-6), six buttons for controlling the application (Figure 2B-7), one toggle button (Figure 2B-8) for expanding and collapsing the slider-bars panel, and two tab buttons (Figure 2B-9) for managing annotations and findings.

To support users managing and sharing their findings, annotation techniques are added to both applications. A detailed explanation about these annotation techniques is included in Section 5.

4.4 Technical challenges

Creating a collaborative tabletop visual analytics system based on a single-user desktop counterpart is not without technical challenges. These challenges involved with the transitioning of a single-user, single-touch system to a multi-user, multi-touch environment include performance limitations, differences in rendering mechanisms, and differences in user input modalities. Here, we present the most significant challenges in detail and describe our solutions for overcoming them.

4.4.1 *Performance*

With a few exceptions, multi-threaded operation is not usually required for desktop-based visual analytics applications since all interactions are based on single mouse input. However, in a collaborative environment, multiple processes and threads are necessary to manage the display and listen for incoming touch events. By utilizing a multi-process and multi-threaded architecture, iPCA-CE becomes significantly more complex than iPCA. However, this architecture allows the application to take advantage of a multi-core CPU to support non-interrupted real-time interactivity for multiple users.

In the development of the collaborative system, it is important to use two concurrent processes, one of which utilizes individual threads. The multi-touch engine runs in its own process, which detects finger touches on the table and sends input event messages to the client application via TCP/IP. In the iPCA-CE process, the input thread receives messages from the multi-touch engine and adds them to a queue. The content of each of these messages is relatively simple, but describes the position of a user's touch, as well as the state of the touch (finger-down, finger-drag, etc.). A separate thread then processes the queue to determine its relevance to updating the iPCA-CE interface. For instance, multiple (false) touches will be condensed into one single touch by this thread to reduce unnecessary computation. Finally, the rendering thread receives update requests based on the processed queue. It then renders the visual interface and, if necessary, performs principal component analysis on the underlying data.

4.4.2 *Rendering mechanisms*

The rendering mechanism for iPCA-CE differs significantly from the desktop version since iPCA-CE needs to support multiple interfaces for multiple users. While iPCA utilizes a single OpenGL context, iPCA-CE needs to create multiple "virtual" contexts, one for each of the interfaces. The general architecture of the iPCA-CE interface is based on the Pad++ metaphor [25], in which each interface is called a "portal".

However, unlike Pad++, the portals in iPCA-CE are not always axis-aligned. Since a multi-touch table is inherently without orientation, we wanted the iPCA-CE interface to be usable by all users standing around the table, regardless of their positions. To that end, each of the portals needs to be rotatable on demand so that it can be appropriately oriented to its user's position around the table. The rendering mechanism for each iPCA-CE portal is therefore based on a hierarchical structure of geometries (such as a line, a dot, or a polygon), each referenced by the coordinates of its parent portal. As the user rotates or resizes a portal, each geometry will update its global coordinates to reflect the change.

This low-level change to the rendering mechanism affects the implementation of several features in iPCA-CE. For instance, a screen capture of a user's hand-drawn annotations can no longer be accomplished by copying a rectangular frame buffer because the portal might not be axis-aligned. The operation now requires two steps, one to render the portal in an axis-aligned manner using an additional back buffer, and the second operation to capture the image.

4.4.3   Input modalities

In traditional mouse-based interaction, the user can move a mouse over a visual element to highlight the element (such as to display its label) without the use of the mouse buttons. In a multi-touch environment that utilizes infrared refraction and reflection to detect a user's touch, there is no way to discern the difference between mouse-over and mouse-drag (holding down a mouse button and moving the mouse) because both operations require the user's finger to be touching the surface of the table .

One method for overcoming this inherent difference is to use a multitude of gestures to describe each possible operation. However, given the number of features in iPCA-CE, creating a gesture for each feature will inevitably confuse the user and steepen the learning curve, thereby lowering the usability of the system. We therefore take a "low-tech" approach by creating buttons along the borders of each portal (see Figure 2B). The majority of the features in iPCA-CE can be performed by activating or toggling these buttons. However, for the user's convenience, a few popular gestures that have been widely adopted by multi-touch devices (such as the iPhone) have been incorporated into the iPCA-CE interface. These gestures include resizing, zooming, and rotation by using two fingers simultaneously. During our user study, we observed that these gestures were intuitive for participants and did not introduce usability concerns during their analyses.

4.5   Integration

Together, iPCA and iPCA-CE form an integrated toolset which allows analysts to switch back and forth between the two visualizations on separate hardware without losing track of their current analysis tasks. While single-user analysis could technically be performed on the touch-table using the collaborative application, this might not be as effective and productive as using the standalone desktop application. Since experts often prefer to work alone and switch their analysis process into a collaborative group activity only when necessary [3], it is important to provide both applications, using hardware appropriate for the type of interaction required by each. Since iPCA and iPCA-CE applications support a continuous analysis process that permits analysts to switch back and forth between desktop and collaborative environments, users can export findings and system parameters back and forth between applications, allowing them to transition from single-user to collaborative contexts without losing track of their current analytical process.

In Section 5, we describe users' analytical processes when managing and sharing analytical findings within and between iPCA and iPCA-CE.

5   Sharing analytical processes

In a collaborative environment, it is easier to share findings and communicate ideas than on a single-user desktop computer, but it may be more difficult to perform individual analyses due to interference [26]. Consequently, analysts may continuously switch back and forth between desktop and collaborative workflows (see Figure 1(c-d)). Based on this model, we improved the iPCA and iPCA-CE applications to support this continuous analysis process. We suggest that providing support for managing and sharing findings is as important as providing useful analysis tools because the users' end goal is to discover evidence that supports their hypotheses.

5.1   Managing findings

A finding from visual analysis procedures may be represented as a screenshot, which shows what was found during the analysis, and may include an annotation, which explains in more detail what the screenshot represents. In iPCA and iPCA-CE, both screenshots and annotations are used to manage users' findings. The applications provide two methods for providing annotations: text and drawing. Text-annotation is an indirect approach for explaining the details of a user's finding. Drawing-annotation allows users to directly indicate important elements or features visually on-screen. In iPCA, both methods of annotation are performed using a keyboard and mouse. However, in iPCA-CE, annotations needed to be supported differently because all interactions are initiated by finger touches. Therefore, a virtual keyboard is displayed for text-annotation, and a drawing tool is used for drawing-annotation. Figure 4 shows examples in which users utilize these annotation tools to indicate their findings in iPCA and iPCA-CE.

Findings are stored in an XML format (see Figure 5) similar to the P-Set model [27]. However, since our design philosophy does not require us to track all of a user's exploration procedures, we simply describe each finding with parameter sets. The parameter sets are similar to the sets defined in the P-Set model, though defined specifically for our visual analytics system. Sets represent interactive operations (such as selection and deletion), view, sliderbar control, text- and drawing-annotations, and a final result. Since

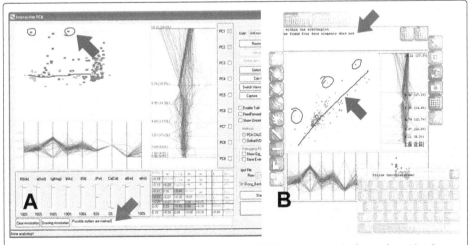

Figure 4 Annotation examples in (A) iPCA and (B) iPCA-CE. Text-annotation (red arrows) contains data inputted using either a desktop keyboard (iPCA) or a virtual keyboard (iPCA-CE). Drawing-annotation (blue arrows) allows users to directly annotate onto the display using a drawing tool controlled by a mouse (iPCA) or finger touches (iPCA-CE).

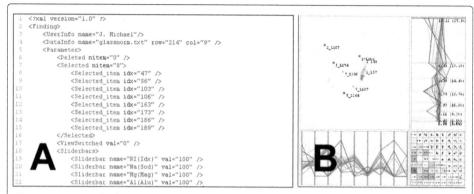

Figure 5 An example of (A) an analytical finding defined in an XML format and (B) a screenshot of the final result. A user has selected eight possible outliers during the analysis, which are highlighted in the screenshot.

users' findings can easily be recreated with the parameter sets, it is an important and useful feature for sharing findings with others. Each finding is identified by the user's name and a timestamp.

Figure 6 shows how findings are managed. In iPCA, all findings are listed chronologically in a separate window, and the user is provided with buttons for updating or deleting findings in the list (see top of Figure 6A). A finding is created using the current view and annotations and added to the list by selecting a button in the main window. In iPCA-CE, however, the differences in display and interaction require that findings be managed differently than the desktop applications. Findings are managed within a tabbed window activated by a button above each workspace (see bottom of Figure 6A). Each finding is represented as a screenshot thumbnail identified with the user's name and timestamp. Findings are created by touching a capture button in the workspace, and findings can be moved into the workspace for updating via a simple drag-and-drop operation. Since multiple users can use iPCA-CE simultaneously, each user has their own storage space (i.e. directory or folder) to manage findings.

5.2   Sharing findings

Asynchronous self-sharing occurs in most single user desktop applications (see Figure 1a). In iPCA, the user can continuously create findings and track the history of their analysis by viewing the previously created findings (see Figure 6B). Previously saved findings can

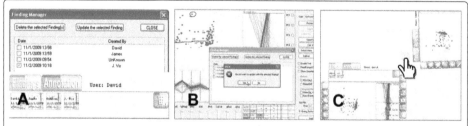

Figure 6 Interacting with findings. (A) Management of findings in iPCA (top) and iPCA-CE (bottom). Findings are displayed chronologically and are identified by a timestamp and the creator's name. **(B)** Updating the workspace with a previously created finding in iPCA. **(C)** The user performs a drag & drop operation to pass a finding from the original workspace (bottom left) to the other collaborator's workspace (top right) in iPCA-CE.

be displayed, allowing the user to track the history of the analysis and continuously update previous findings based on recent results.

Transitional sharing from the desktop application to the collaborative environment represents the process by which the results from a single user's analysis are made public for the rest of the group (see Figure 1c). If the user wants to take their findings from iPCA into a collaborative setting, the XML file can be transmitted over the network and imported into iPCA-CE.

Synchronous sharing in the collaborative environment provides users with the capability of viewing others' findings to gain the understanding of collaborators' analytical processes (see Figure 1b). This type of sharing allows users to work together simultaneously to find new analytical results. This is analogous to traditional procedures for sharing analysis results, such as preparing presentation slides or written reports to present and discuss in a group meeting. This is accomplished in iPCA-CE by dragging findings directly from one workspace to another (see Figure 6C). Using this direct passing operation, collaborators can easily become aware of each other's analytical processes and results, although they each still maintain an individual workspace for performing their analyses. Since this sharing operation should be subject to the agreement of the collaborator, a confirmation window is displayed to ask for permission to accept the finding being shared by another.

Transitional sharing from the collaborative environment back to the desktop application (see Figure 1d) has not been considered in many previous collaborative visual analytics systems. However, we believe this is an important method for users to further investigate interesting results that were shared during the collaborative session. Thus, it is also possible to export the findings of collaborative analysis from iPCA-CE as an XML file for transmission over the network to iPCA. To understand the sharing processes, we performed user studies in two different environments. In following sections, we described how we performed the studies and what we found.

6   Understanding users' analytical processes in a single-desktop environment

Although it has been found that the initial version of iPCA is superior to SAS/INSIGHT for solving analytical questions [6] from the within-subjects user study, the effectiveness of the updated version of iPCA for solving analytical tasks, and creating and sharing findings in single-desktop environments has not been clearly determined. To understand the users' analytical processes as well as the effectiveness of capturing and sharing findings with iPCA, we performed a user study. In the study, we asked participants to capture their findings with utilizing text- and drawing-annotations. This study was conducted under the approval (protocol number: 325298-1) by the institutional review board (IRB) at the University of the District of Columbia.

6.1   Study design and procedure

About 10 participants joined to the study (eight male and two female). Four participants were undergraduate students, five were graduate students, and one was a faculty. Each participant was asked to solve the five task questions, which were:

- What is the most striking outlier(s) you can find? An outlier is a point that does not fit the overall patterns of the dataset.

- Find a dimension that most and least affects the PCA outputs in the Projection View using the first and second principle components.
- Find two dimensions that maintain a highly positive and negative correlation.
- How does removing the first dimension affect the PCA results using the first and second principle components? List as many observations as possible.

The order of the questions was counter-balanced to avoid learning effect. Prior to beginning the task questions, participants were given a tutorial how to use the system. In addition, a plenty of time was given to make them feel comfortable about using the application. For the tutorial session, the Iris dataset [21] (150 data items × 4 dimensions) was used. All participants were allowed to solve each task question in maximum five minutes. For the task questions, the Wine dataset (179 data items × 13 dimensions) was used. They were requested to find and record evidence using both the text and drawing annotation methods supported by the application. During the study, all participants' time-stamped interactions were captured by built-in functions of the system and saved automatically into log files.

Overall task completion time and their findings were evaluated by analysing the recorded interaction logs and the captured findings. After solving each task question, a post-task questionnaire was given for tracking their personal opinions about the task and the tool for solving the task. At the end of the study, their personal factors of ease of use and usefulness of the system were asked using a 5-point Likert scale, with higher numbers corresponding to more positive ratings. In addition, they were asked to provide their personal qualitative feedback about the application.

6.2 Study results

Although half of the participants are new to visualization, approximately 72% of the participants answered correctly. About 78% of the participants mentioned that iPCA was very or somewhat useful for solving the all task questions. From the study, we noticed that most participants spent relatively large amount of time by trying to find correct answers through interaction with dimensions (specifically for the task 3 and 4).

After the evaluation, post-evaluation questionnaire was given as,

- Does iPCA help you understand the dataset better?
- Do the 4 views (Projection, Eigenvector, Data, and Correction view) allow you to perform a better analysis on the dataset?
- Is the manipulation (by using the Dimension Slider and the Control options) useful for understanding the dataset and solving the task questions?
- Would the ability to interactively alter the data help you explore what-if scenarios?
- Overall, how well do you understand PCA? (why? and why not?)

As shown in Figure 7, about 88% of the participants answered positively to the post-evaluation questions except the last question. In answering how well the participants understood PCA, most participants indicated that they understood PCA well. Three participants claimed that they did not fully understand PCA because of the limited amount of time (about less an hour). From their comments, we can assume that if we perform a long-term evaluation [28], it might be possible to determine the usefulness of iPCA for understanding PCA. When asking how useful and easy of iPCA for

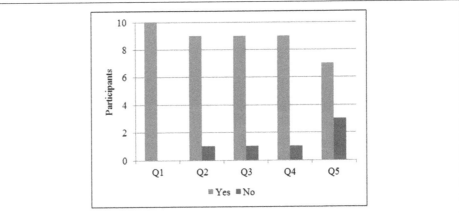

Figure 7 Post-evaluation results. Most participants answered positively to all post-evaluation questions. For the question 5, three participants pointed out that they did not fully understand PCA because of time limitation.

solving analytical questions, most participants answered positively. Seven participants ($M = 4.2, SD = 0.92$) answered iPCA was "very easy" and "easy" to use and eight participants ($M = 4.5, SD = 0.85$) mentioned iPCA was "very useful" and "useful" for solving the given analytical task questions.

6.3 Discussion

Since interaction is somewhat related to users' reasoning [29], we can assume that our participants' performance in using iPCA is attributed solely to the interface design and the set of interactions. We believe that interaction plays a significant role in solving analytical task questions by understanding PCA deeply. Unfortunately, we are not able to isolate the specific factor(s) that plays a major role in determining the participants' performance due to the multiple coordinated views, the interactions, or others. We simply believe that the interactions play a significant role in that the user' direct and continuous manipulation with PCA is rewarded with immediate visual feedback.

We found that the single desktop application (i.e. iPCA) is good for understanding data, identifying anomalies, and sharing their findings. By analysing log files, we found that most participants tend to create findings and track the history of their analysis by checking the previously created findings. They created about three ± two findings on average when completing each given task. Participants commented that the supported annotation techniques in iPCA are useful and efficient to manage and share their findings. However, we found that they prefer not to share findings since iPCA does not support a direct sharing mechanism over the network. From this study, we found that single desktop environments have advantages for providing private working environments that help users concentrate on solving analytical problem themselves without getting interrupted by other people. However, this approach includes a limitation as:

- It is difficult to work together collaboratively with others in single desktop environments because of limited shared space.

7   Understanding users' analytical processes in a collaborative environment

To overcome the limitations of sharing ideas, parallelizing efforts, and performing discussion and consensus building in single-user desktop environments (see Section 2), numerous studies on collaborative visualization have been performed. However, a limited number of studies have been performed to find limitations in a collaborative environment, such as our multi-touch table, especially when solving analytical problems. Based on our understanding of user behaviors when solving complex analytical problems, along with the results of studies of real-world analysts [2,3], we performed an additional user study with the collaborative iPCA-CE application in single, double, and multiple workspaces. This study was conducted under the approval (protocol number: 09-11-04) by the institutional review board (IRB) at the University of North Carolina at Charlotte.

7.1   Study design

A total of 12 graduate students participated in the study (nine male, three female). Eight participants had limited experience using a multi-touch table, and four of them had no experience. The experiment required two participants to work together to solve a given task. The study used a within-subjects design with three conditions, corresponding to the number of available workspaces (see Figure 8):

- Single: The two participants shared a single workspace.
- Double: Each participant had their own personal workspace.
- Multiple: Participants were allowed to create as many workspaces as they desired.

The order of the conditions was counterbalanced across the study to eliminate ordering effects.

7.2   Study procedure

Prior to beginning each condition, participants were given a tutorial about the tool they were about to use which instructed them on basic functionalities. Similar to the study in desktop environments, the Iris dataset was used for the tutorial session. Participants were given sufficient time to familiarize themselves with the task and user interface. For each condition, participants were asked to find the most striking outlier(s) in one of the following datasets: the E.Coli dataset (336 data items × 7 dimensions), the Forest Fire dataset (517 data items × 11 dimensions) and the Glass dataset (214 data items × 9 dimensions). They were instructed to have a discussion with their partner to justify their findings, and were requested to find and record evidence using both the text and drawing annotation methods provided by the application. Participation in the study took approximately one hour.

Figure 8 These pictures show people performing multiple collaborative data analyses in iPCA-CE.
(A) People are working together by looking at the same tool and results within a single workspace, **(B)** working together, but in different workspaces (one workspace per each person), and **(C)** working with several workspaces (more than two workspaces possible per each person).

During the study, all interactions on the multi-touch table were recorded internally using screen capture software. In addition, participants' interactions were video captured using a high-definition camera facing down from the ceiling and their verbal communications were audio recorded. Additionally, all participants' time-stamped interactions were captured by built-in functions of the system and saved automatically into log files. Based on the interaction logs and recordings, we calculated the following task performance measures from their analysis: (1) overall task completion time, (2) verbal communication time spent discussing or justifying findings, and (3) number of findings discovered. After each condition, participants completed a post-condition questionnaire in which they were asked to report the condition's ease of use and intuitiveness. They were also asked to rate how well they were able to understand the data and how well they were able to communicate with their partner. All ratings were on a 5-point Likert scale, with higher numbers corresponding to more positive ratings. At the end of the study, participants were asked to specify their preferred condition for solving problems and indicate which condition they felt best facilitated communication and sharing ideas with others. They were also asked to provide qualitative feedback describing the advantages and disadvantages of each condition.

7.3 Study results

7.3.1 Task performance

Each of the task performance measures was treated with a repeated measures ANOVA testing the within-subjects effect of workspace condition. The analysis for task completion time ($M = 531.57sec., SD = 254.76$) was not significant, $p = .19$. Time spent in verbal communication ($M = 211.64sec., SD = 182.82$) was also not significant, $p = .72$. The analysis for the number of findings discovered was significant, $F(2, 10) = 15.67, p < .01, \mu_p^2 = .76$. We conducted post-hoc analysis using paired-sample t-tests with a Bonferroni corrected significance value of $\alpha = 0.17$ to reduce error in multiple comparisons. Participants using a single workspace ($M = 2.33, SD = 1.03$) discovered fewer findings than those using a double workspace ($M = 5.83, SD = 2.32$), $p < .01$, or multiple workspaces ($M = 5.17, SD = 2.14$), $p < .01$. The double workspace and multiple workspace conditions were not significantly different, p = .42. Figure 9(A-B) shows the results for the task performance measures. These results indicate that in a collaborative system, providing each user with their own personal workspace (or multiple workspaces) allows them to better perform an analysis task, although the task completion time and time spent communicating were not affected.

7.3.2 Post-condition ratings

Each of the post-condition ratings (1-5) was treated with a repeated measures ANOVA testing the within-subjects effect of workspace condition. Although none of the results were significant, the application was rated highly for ease of use ($M = 4.03, SD = 0.41$), $p = .63$, and intuitiveness ($M = 4.03, SD = 0.64$), $p = .80$. The participants also responded that they could understand the data moderately well, ($M = 3.86, SD = 0.59$), $p = .91$, and found it easy to communicate with their partner ($M = 4.17, SD = 0.52$), $p = .33$. Figure 9(C-D) shows the distribution of participant ratings. Interestingly, there was an outlier that rated the single workspace condition negatively on several measures.

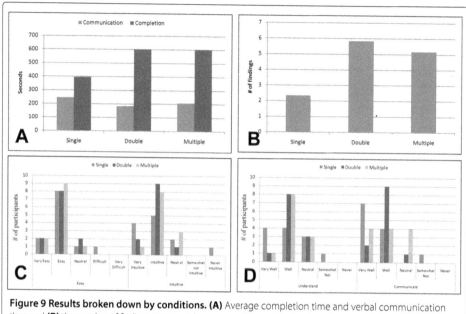

Figure 9 Results broken down by conditions. (A) Average completion time and verbal communication time and **(B)** the number of findings across workspace conditions. Distribution of participant ratings for **(C)** ease of use and intuitiveness and **(D)** abilities to understand data and communicate ideas with a partner.

This is because this participant had contradictory ideas about the analysis procedure as compared to his/her partner. We will discuss this in more detail later (see Section 7.4).

7.3.3 Preferences and qualitative feedback

With regards to overall preferences for solving problems, four participants preferred double workspaces, and eight participants preferred multiple workspaces. No participants indicated a preference for the single workspace condition. These preferences are consistent with our results indicating that they were able to discover fewer findings when using a single workspace. However, when asked which condition they preferred for communicating and sharing ideas, half of the participants preferred a single workspace, with the remaining six split evenly between the multiple and double workspace conditions. This indicates that a single shared workspace may be effective for communicating findings since users are looking at the same visual representation of the data. When reviewing participants' qualitative feedback, we found that most participants pointed out that the multi-touch table interactions were helpful in understanding the data. However, the overall feedback we received for this collaborative visual analytics application was very positive.

7.4 Discussion

During the course of the study, we observed that participants continuously communicated their ideas in the single workspace condition because they needed to have an agreement before performing an action in their shared workspace (see Figure 8A). In the single workspace condition, we found that interference [26] sometimes occurred between collaborators because their desired working areas are overlapped. We also observed that when one participant was interacting with the single shared workspace, the partner would observe these interactions and try to think of new ideas or strategies. This pattern of collaboration is alternated continuously as the participants exchanged roles. However, we also noticed that when partners had different ideas of how to solve a problem, collaborating in a shared workspace became difficult.

Overall, four participants mentioned that although a collaborative environment is useful to share ideas and findings, it is difficult to perform visual analysis simultaneously. For example, in the double and multiple workspace conditions (see Figure 8B and 8C), one participant pointed out that he felt like he was racing his partner to discover more findings. Participants suggested that they would also like to have an isolated workspace (such as a desktop environment) for solving analytical problems. Additionally, though all recruited participants were healthy and of average fitness, most participants mentioned that standing in front of the multi-touch table for long periods of time was difficult due to fatigue.

From this study, we found that collaborative environments have advantages for solving analytical problems, especially when sharing ideas and findings. However, this approach has several limitations, such as:

- It is difficult to collaborate in a shared workspace when users' ideas conflict.
- Interference between collaborators may cause difficulty in forming new ideas or strategies.
- Users become fatigued when standing at a multi-touch table for long periods of time.

In light of both the advantages and limitations of collaborative environments, we suggest that users' analyses should not be isolated in one environment. As shown in Section 3, the developed informal model for the general analytical process should be supported and maintained to allow analysts to switch back and forth between single-user and collaborative workflows. An individual user performs a data analysis and compiles a list of findings in a desktop environment. When enough interesting results are found, the user meets with other analysts in a collaborative environment to discuss and share these findings. After sharing findings with each other, the users then work together interactively to perform a collaborative group analysis. Afterwards, the users then take the findings from the collaborative analysis back into a single-user setting for individual analysis and validation. This process then continuously repeats.

iPCA and iPCA-CE applications support a continuous analysis process that permits analysts to switch back and forth between desktop and collaborative environments. Users can export findings and system parameters back and forth between applications, allowing them to transition from single-user to collaborative contexts without losing track of their current analytical process. As shown in Figure 1, we defined that sharing findings between the two different environments is performed as asynchronous transitional sharing processes. However, synchronous sharing between the two environments can be supported depending on how applications are designed. In such case, it is important to support isolating users if they want to work themselves. The two applications are available publicly online at the URL http://www.knowledgeviz.com/iPCA/.

8 Conclusion and future work

Although many useful visual analysis applications have been developed to assist users in understanding complicated relationships in large data sets, they are mostly limited desktop applications designed for single users. Collaborative visual analytics environments have also been developed, which allow users to work together to solve complex analytical problems. However, on their own, neither of these two modalities entirely reflects the continuous analytic processes carried out by real world experts. In this paper, we presented an integrated visual analytics toolset composed of a single-user desktop application and a collaborative touch-table system. Based on the consideration of sharing findings, we presented an informal model for the general analytical process that occurs as analysts switch back and forth between single-user and collaborative environments. By following this model, both the desktop and collaborative applications support this continuous analysis process.

Since the exact processes for sharing ideas and analysis findings is still unclear, there is much work to be done in understanding the knowledge sharing process in collaborative environments. In the future, it will be necessary to perform an expert evaluation of sharing analysis results between the single-user and collaborative environments. These results will provide guidelines for designing visual analytics systems that accurately reflect the analytical processes carried out by real-world experts.

Competing interests
The authors declare that they have no competing interests.

Authors' contributions
DJ carried out the implementation of the system and usability studies and drafted the manuscript. SJ participated in the first usability study and performed the statistical analysis of the study result. ES and BY participated in analyzing the study results and helped to draft the manuscript. RC conceived of the study, and participated in it design and coordinating. All authors read and approved the final manuscript.

Acknowledgements
This work was partially supported by US Army Research Office (ARO) grant W911NF-13-1-0143.

Author details
[1]Department of Computer Science and Information Technology, University of the District of Columbia, 4200 Connecticut Avenue NW, 20008 Washington, DC, USA. [2]Department of Computer Science, Bowie State University, 14000 Jericho Park Rd., 20715 Bowie, MD, USA. [3]Institute for Creative Technologies, University of Southern California, 12015 Waterfront Drive, 90094 Playa Vista, CA, USA. [4]Department of Computer Science, Tufts University, 419 Boston Ave, 02155 Medford, MA, USA.

References
1. Pike WA, Stasko J, Chang R., O'Connell TA (2009) The science of interaction. Inf Visualization 8(4):263–274. doi:10.1057/ivs.2009.22
2. Chin G. Jr., Kuchar OA, Wolf KE (2009) Exploring the analytical processes of intelligence analysts. In: Proceedings of the SIGCHI Conference on Human Factors in Computing Systems. CHI '09. ACM, New York, NY, USA. pp 11–20. doi:10.1145/1518701.1518704
3. Fink GA, North CL, Endert A, Rose S (2009) Visualizing cyber security: usable workspaces. In: Visualization for Cyber Security, 2009. VizSec 2009. 6th International Workshop On. IEEE. pp 45–56. doi:10.1109/VIZSEC.2009.5375542
4. Carlbom I, Hsu WM, Klinker G., Szeliski R, Waters K, Doyle M, Gettys J, Harris KM, Levergood TM, Palmer R, Palmer L, Picart M, Terzopoulos D, Tonnesen D, Vannier M, Wallace G (1992) Modeling and analysis of empirical data in collaborative environments. Commun ACM 35(6):74–84. doi:10.1145/129888.129893
5. Ekanayake J, Pallickara S, Fox G (2008) A collaborative framework for scientific data analysis and visualization. In: Collaborative Technologies and Systems, 2008. CTS 2008. International Symposium On. IEEE. pp 339–346. doi:10.1109/CTS.2008.4543948
6. Jeong DH, Ziemkiewicz C, Fisher BD, Ribarsky W, Chang R (2009) ipca: An interactive system for pca-based visual analytics. Comput Graph Forum 28(3):767–774
7. Jeong DH, Suma EA, Butkiewicz T, Ribarsky W, Chang R (2010) A continuous analysis process between desktop and collaborative visual analytics environments. In: IEEE Visual Analytics Science and Technology. IEEE. pp 231–232
8. Coleman J, Goettsch A, Savchenko A, Kollmann H, Kui W, Klement E, Bono P (1996) Teleinvivotm: towards collaborative volume visualization environments. Comput Graphics 20(6):801–811
9. Grimstead IJ, Walker DW, Avis NJ (2005) Collaborative visualization: a review and taxonomy. In: Proceedings of the 9th IEEE International Symposium on Distributed Simulation and Real-Time Applications. DS-RT '05. IEEE Computer Society, Washington, DC, USA. pp 61–69. doi:10.1109/DISTRA.2005.12. http://dx.doi.org/10.1109/DISTRA.2005.12
10. Marchese FT, Brajkovska N (2007) Fostering asynchronous collaborative visualization. In: Proceedings of the 11th International Conference Information Visualization, IV '07. IEEE Computer Society, Washington, DC, USA. pp 185–190. doi:10.1109/IV.2007.52. http://dx.doi.org/10.1109/IV.2007.52

11. Mark G, Kobsa A (2005) The effects of collaboration and system transparency on cive usage: An empirical study and model. Presence 14(1):60–80

12. Ma K-L (2007) Creating a collaborative space to share data, visualization, and knowledge. SIGGRAPH Comput Graph 41(4):4–144. doi:10.1145/1331098.1331105

13. Heer J, Agrawala M (2008) Design considerations for collaborative visual analytics. Inf Visualization J 7:49–62

14. Johnson G (1998) Collaborative visualization 101. ACM SIGGRAPH - Comput Graphics 32(2):8–11

15. Robinson AC (2008) Collaborative synthesis of visual analytic results. In: Visual Analytics Science and Technology, 2008. VAST '08. IEEE Symposium On. IEEE. pp 67–74. doi:10.1109/VAST.2008.4677358

16. Isenberg P (2009) Collaborative information visualization in co-located environments. PhD thesis, University of Calgary, Calgary, Canada

17. Wigdor D, Jiang H, Forlines C, Borkin M, Shen C (2009) Wespace: The design development and deployment of a walk-up and share multi-surface visual collaboration system. In: Proceedings of the SIGCHI Conference on Human Factors in Computing Systems, CHI '09. ACM, New York, NY, USA. pp 1237–1246. doi:10.1145/1518701.1518886

18. Forlines C, Lilien R (2008) Adapting a single-user, single-display molecular visualization application for use in a multi-user, multi-display environment. In: Proceedings of the Working Conference on Advanced Visual Interfaces, AVI '08. ACM, New York, NY, USA. pp 367–371. doi:10.1145/1385569.1385635

19. Forlines C, Esenther A, Shen C, Wigdor D, Ryall K (2006) Multi-user, multi-display interaction with a single-user, single-display geospatial application. In: Proceedings of the 19th Annual ACM Symposium on User Interface Software and Technology, UIST '06. ACM, New York, NY, USA. pp 273–276. doi:10.1145/1166253.1166296

20. Mahyar N (2014) Supporting sensemaking during collocated collaborative visual analytics. PhD thesis, University of Victoria

21. Bache K, Lichman M (2013) UCI Machine Learning Repository. http://archive.ics.uci.edu/ml

22. Jolliffe IT (2002) Principal component analysis. 2nd edn.. Springer Verlag, New York. doi:10.1007/b98835 (http://www.springer.com/us/book/9780387954424)

23. Jeong DH, Ziemkiewicz C, Ribarsky W, Chang R (2009) Understanding principal component analysis using a visual analytics tool. In: Technical Report, Charlotte, Charlotte Visualization Center at UNC Charlotte, USA

24. Jeong DH, Ribarsky W, Chang R (2009) Designing a PCA-based collaborative visual analytics system. IEEE Visualization Workshop on Collaborative Visualization on Interactive Surfaces (CoVIS) 09, pp. 24-27

25. Bederson BB, Hollan JD (1994) Pad++: a zooming graphical interface for exploring alternate interface physics. In: Proceedings of the 7th Annual ACM Symposium on User Interface Software and Technology, UIST '94. ACM, New York, NY, USA. pp 17–26. doi:10.1145/192426.192435

26. Tse E, Histon J, Scott SD, Greenberg S (2004) Avoiding interference: how people use spatial separation and partitioning in sdg workspaces. In: Proceedings of the 2004 ACM Conference on Computer Supported Cooperative Work, CSCW '04. ACM, New York, NY, USA. pp 252–261. doi:10.1145/1031607.1031647

27. Jankun-Kelly TJ, Ma K-L, Gertz M (2007) A model and framework for visualization exploration. IEEE Trans Vis Comput Graph 13(2):357–369

28. Shneiderman B, Plaisant C (2006) Strategies for evaluating information visualization tools: Multi-dimensional in-depth long-term case studies. In: Proceedings of the 2006 AVI Workshop on BEyond Time and Errors: Novel Evaluation Methods for Information Visualization, BELIV '06. ACM, New York, NY, USA. pp 1–7. doi:10.1145/1168149.1168158

29. Dou W, Jeong DH, Stukes F, Ribarsky W, Lipford HR, Chang R (2009) Recovering reasoning processes from user interactions. IEEE Comput Graph Appl 29(3):52–61. doi:10.1109/MCG.2009.49

14

Task context-aware e-mail platform for collaborative tasks

Masashi Katsumata

Correspondence: katumata@nit.ac.jp
Department of Computer and
Information Engineering, Nippon
Institute of Technology, 4-1
Gakuendai, Miyashiro-machi,
Minamisaitama-gun, Saitama, Japan

Abstract

E-mail communication has become an essential part of collaborative tasks in enterprises. However, when conventional e-mail applications are used for collaborative tasks, problems with task-related resources management arise. In this paper, we present a task context-aware e-mail platform that helps users to send e-mails quickly and efficiently. This platform also automatically extracts data from reply e-mail messages. It enables users to automatically classify task-related information and user support services using a task context model. The task context model is built based on ontology as a semantic representation of the associations between task and task-related e-mail processes. This paper describes the design and implementation of this system on the basis of the task context model. To verify the efficacy of the prototype system, we conducted experiments that demonstrate the systems effective task awareness and user support services.

Keywords: Task context; Ontology; Collaborative task; E-mail platform

Introduction

E-mail-based communication has become an essential part of collaborative tasks in enterprises. E-mail communication is required for organizational tasks in order to achieve effective task management and for reuse of e-mail messages and their related resources (such as schedules, attached files, and contact lists). Knowledge workers can efficiently search and use e-mail messages and the corresponding resources by organizing these messages according to individual tasks [1,2]. Thus, multi-tasking knowledge workers often set up automatic filtering into folders or manually move e-mail messages into folders. Recently, enhanced conventional task-management systems and task-centric mail clients have been used for this purpose. Further, several research studies that support the discovery of e-mail messages and the related resources by adding metadata to e-mails and the related resources have been conducted [2-6].

In this paper, we present a task context-aware e-mail platform that helps users to send e-mails quickly and efficiently. This platform also automatically extracts data from the e-mail messages returned in reply. In order to realize the concept of this platform, we introduce the task context model as an ontology-based semantic representation of the conceptual associations between a task and the task-related e-mail process. By using the task context model, the system can provide a context-aware service for mail form composition and mail data extraction. To verify the feasibility of the concept of this platform, we built a prototype system. We also describe the system's effective task awareness and user support services evidenced in the experimental results.

The remainder of this paper is organized as follows. First, we give an overview of related work. Then, we present the features of the task context model and discuss the design of the task context-aware e-mail platform. To verify the feasibility of the concept underlying this platform, we present a prototype implementation and discuss its effective task awareness and user support services evident in experimental results obtained. Finally, we conclude our paper and outline future research directions.

Related work

In using e-mail for organizational work, a vast amount of task-related information has to be handled. Therefore, much research has been done in the area of task-related management support in the past few years.

TaskMaster [3] enhances e-mail clients and enables them to function as task-management systems by managing resources such as e-mail messages and file attachments for each task. In addition, a useful user interface with both browsing and operating resources is also provided. This system makes it easy to search through the resources of a task. TV-ACTA [4] provides prestructured containers that are created inside the e-mail folder hierarchy to support personal information management. Specialized subfolders called "Components" within each ACTA Activity automatically organize and present information appropriate for aspects of the activity at hand. ACTA is designed to create a more efficient personal information management environment with the ultimate goal of providing context metadata for machine learning and automation techniques.

KASIMIR [7] and OntoPIM [8] are ontology-based personal task-management systems. These systems provide semi-automated functions for retrieving and registering task-related information within e-mail messages according to an ontology-based model. Activity Explorer [4] supports knowledge workers with context switching and resource rediscovery by organizing and integrating resources, tools, and people around the computational concept of a work activity. However, the support functions of the systems presented above do not apply to reusing of the managed data for tasks.

Eklund and Cole [9] and Brendel and Krawczyk [10] used ontology to model e-mail-related attribution information (such as group, project, and member), and proposed a system that provides a user interface with visualized and grouped formal concept analysis that can be used to search for various types of task-related information. Topika [11] enhances an existing e-mail client to provide suggestions about relevant shared spaces such as Wikis. The system facilitates the transition management of a user's collaborative activities to appropriate collaboration tools.

These systems are all primarily concerned with improving the management of and the search for task-related information. In contrast, our primary goal is to provide support for reuse of managed data according to a user's role.

Design of the task context-aware e-mail platform

Task context model

We created an ontology-based semantic representation model that represents the conceptual associations between a task and e-mail processes. We call this the task context model. The task context-aware e-mail platform performs services for users based on this task context model. The model relates the conceptual associations between a task and an e-mail process to physical context entities (such as e-mail messages, attached files, group members, and mail form items). In the task context model, task-related e-mail messages and resources, called task context data, are handled as a task unit. The files created and schedule data for the given task are also handled as task context data. In addition, this platform provides a service that automatically retrieves the task-related resources contained in e-mail messages. The operation of this service is considered later in this paper. These task context data are utilized in the user support service to accomplish tasks.

The semantic representation of the task context model is based on the Resource Description Framework (RDF) [12]. RDF is a collection of triples, each of which consists of a resource, a property, and a literal. A set of such triples is called an RDF graph. Figure 1 shows a sample task context model represented by an RDF graph.

The task context concept represents the role of managing task-related resources. In addition, on the assumption that it is used within an organization, the task context concept represents the relationship among task-related resources that are frequently used in collaborative work. The task context is represented as a property of a "Task" resource. We define the conceptual associations of the task context's attribution as follows: Task is "Subject", task context is "Predicate", and the value of the task context denotes "Literal". In the task context model, task contexts are classified as entities such as files, schedules, participants, memos, and mail form items. Further, we define the conceptual mail procedure in collaborative task. We call this "Action". The Action concept represents mail procedures that frequently occur in collaborative task e-mail communications. We consider the following three Actions for collaboration tasks:

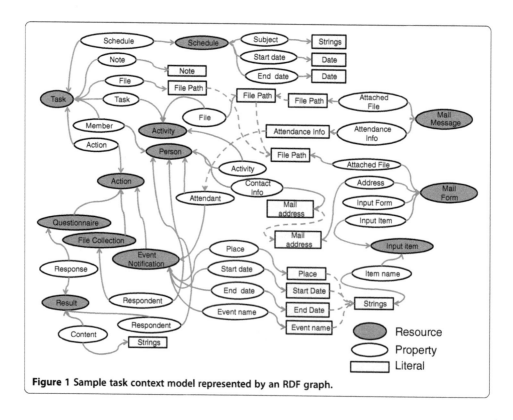

Figure 1 Sample task context model represented by an RDF graph.

1. Event Notification. A mail procedure concept that has the objective of attendance confirmation for an event being held in an organization.
2. Questionnaire Request. A mail procedure concept that has the objective of soliciting questionnaire requests and responses.
3. File Collection. A mail procedure concept that notifies that a file is to be collected and obtains an attached file in response.

Task context management

The task context model manages the task context's property and its value for each task. This property represents a task-related file, member, contact information, and schedule data, as shown in Figure 1. The value of the task context is automatically retrieved from an e-mail message on the basis of the task context model when the e-mail arrives on the mail server implemented in our study (see Figure 2).

Figure 3 shows how task context is assigned to property in the task context model. When the task owner registers the task for group work in the client, RDF/XML formatted data based on the task context model are automatically generated and managed by the task context server. The upper part of Figure 3 shows the RDF model of the task context model, and the lower part shows the task context data that are generated according to the task context model. The figure also shows how this model can concurrently handle multiple tasks such as "meeting" and "lab party".

Service for e-mail process

The aims of the task context-aware e-mail platform are to support 1) the composition of e-mail forms and 2) the extraction of the data contained in reply e-mails. The support for creating e-mail forms is provided when a task owner creates an e-mail form

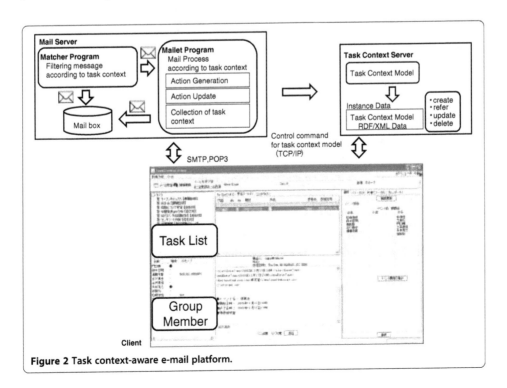

Figure 2 Task context-aware e-mail platform.

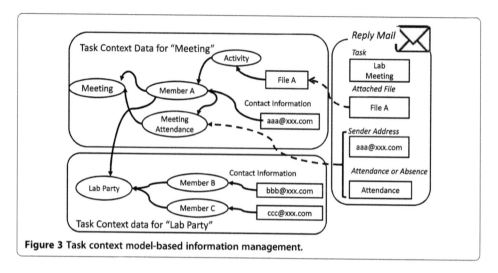

Figure 3 Task context model-based information management.

for a task request and a task member creates an e-mail form in reply to a task request. On the other hand, the support for the extraction of data contained in a reply e-mail is provided when a task owner receives a reply mail from a task member. In this paper, the user support service is intended for three actions: Event Notification, Questionnaire Request, and File Collection. The user support service in the e-mail process provides a service that supports both the creation of e-mail forms and organization and retrieval of data from reply e-mails for these mail actions.

Implementation

System overview

We implemented a prototype system that executes a service for task members on the task context-aware e-mail platform. The prototype system comprised the following three systems: task context server, mail server, and mail client (see Figure 2). The task context server manages the task context (e.g., file path, schedule, and contact information) and its value, which is generated according to the RDF/XML data format. In the task context server, task context is managed under each task. We implemented a task context server that can connect to the mail server and the mail client. The task context server can accept a request command (create, refer, update, and delete) from the mail server and client via TCP/IP. On accepting a request command, the task context server can update the task context model using the Jena application programming interface [13]. The mail server is built on Apache James [14]—a mail application platform that enables users to write custom application programming code for e-mail processing. Apache James provides e-mail filtering through a function called Matcher and provides e-mail processing through another function called Mailet. We introduced extended e-mail headers to realize the service (see Table 1). After Matcher refers to the extended e-mail headers, Mailet can be executed according to the purpose of these extended e-mail headers.

The client can connect to both the mail server and the task context server. In addition to general e-mail operations, the client provides a user interface that manages the task context data. The e-mail message submitted by the client is automatically added to the extended e-mail header. In our prototype system, the client displays a structured mail form by referring to the extended e-mail header. The client can also

Table 1 Types of extended mail headers

Header name	Role
X-Task-Name	Indicates the name of the task
X-Task-Owner	Indicates the task owner
X-Action-Model-Type	Indicates the request generating the Action and the type of Action
X-Action-Update-Type	Indicates the request updating the state of Action and the type of Action
X-Action-Retrieve-Type	Indicates the request retrieving the task context data and the type of Action

receive other e-mail messages in accordance with RFC2822 [15]. The client's user interface comprises six main areas—task member, file, calendar, task, message, and form. The prototype system was implemented in Java, using Apache James to run the mail application platform and to handle XML messages.

E-mail form composition service

When a task owner selects the type of Action on the client, an e-mail form for the selected Action is displayed. In the e-mail form for the Action, task-related data are provided as a list of suggestions of possible inputs. Consequently, the task owner spends less time typing and querying for information related to the task. When the task client receives an e-mail from the task owner, the reply form is displayed by referring to the extended e-mail header X-Action-Model-Type.

The displayed input fields on the reply form are the elements of the Action type corresponding to "reply mail form composition," as shown in Table 2. A task member can type the value according to the displayed input field on the reply form.

Data extraction service

When the mail server receives an e-mail according to the type of Action, the contents of the reply e-mail are automatically retrieved as the task context. In the task context server, the retrieved task context data are managed as RDF/XML formatted data that are based on the conceptual model for Action. When the task context server receives a reply e-mail, the value of the task context in Action is updated, and the state of Action is displayed on the client's state panel. Thus, the task owner can confirm the state of the task intuitively without checking each reply e-mail. Automated processes such as the generation or updating of Action are performed via Mailet according to the value of the extended mail header.

Table 2 Services for action type

Function	Event notification	Questionnaire request	File collection
Request mail form composition	Schedule form (Start date, End date, Place, Event name)	Questionnaire form (Support form composition)	File name and stored folder name
Request mail form composition	Attendance form (Yes, No)	Questionnaire form (reply form)	Selection of attached file
Automated extraction	Attendance data	Questionnaire response data	Attached file

The process of generation of an Action instance is depicted in Figure 4. When the mail server receives an e-mail from the task owner, Matcher program determines Mailet program according to the value of extended e-mail header. Mailet program generates a task context model according to the given Action on the task context server. When the mail server receives the reply e-mail message from the task member, the Matcher program refers to the extended e-mail header X-Action-Update-Type, and Mailet program updates the state of Action. Mailet program updates the value of state by referring to the text element in XML format contained in the body part of the e-mail message. The above procedure is also followed for reply e-mails from other task members and updates to the value of the attendance for Action. The attendance data and the questionnaire data can be written to a Comma Separated Value (CSV) file on the assumption that task context data might be used by a spreadsheet application (e.g., Microsoft Excel). In the case of File Collection, files are automatically renamed according to a predefined file name from the attached file in the task member's reply e-mail.

Evaluation

Experimentation overview

We conducted an experiment to verify the efficacy of our platform in which we obtained qualitative data compiled from 13 university students (male, 21–22 years old). The prototype system was set up in our laboratory. One of the 13 students was elected as the task owner, and the others as task members. We conducted the experiment according to the following procedure. First, the task owner notified the task members about a group meeting for a research report. On receiving the e-mail about a group meeting, task members replied to the e-mail stating attendance of meeting to the task owner. After the group meeting, the task owner requested completed questionnaires from the task members and the meeting report for a research presentation. The task owner then checked and confirmed that reply e-mails were received from the task members. Further, he gathered or added up the data in the messages within the reply e-mail.

The experiment was divided into two sessions: using a conventional e-mail platform and using our prototype system. The two sessions were administered sequentially. During the conventional e-mail platform session, the procedures for the experiment were held over the first four weeks. In the next four weeks, the procedures for the experiment using the prototype system were held. In this experiment, we made the following assumptions:

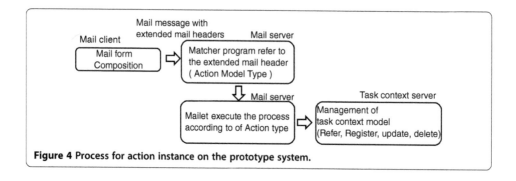

Figure 4 Process for action instance on the prototype system.

1. Conventional e-mail system scenario
   (a) Task owner's usage condition and work
   (i) The e-mail addresses of the task owner and task members are registered in the e-mail client.
   (ii) The date of the group meeting is provided to the task members.
   (iii) Indication of attendance confirmation, questionnaire request, and deadline of the research report are handled by e-mail, and the task owner checks the reply e-mails.
   (b) Task member's usage condition and work
   (i) The reply e-mail is created in response to the task owner's request e-mail.
2. Proposed e-mail system scenario
   (a) Task owner's usage condition and work
   (i) Each group member's e-mail address is registered in the proposed system.
   (ii) The scheduled date for the group meeting is registered in the scheduler of the client system.
   (iii) Indication of attendance confirmation, questionnaire request, and deadline of the report are handled by e-mail. Collecting the content for the reply e-mail is performed by the user support service in the proposed system.
   (b) Task member's usage condition and work
   (i) A reply e-mail is created in response to the task owner's request e-mail.

Experimental results

This section presents the experimental results obtained in order to verify the efficacy of the prototype system and its provision of the service that indicates the task context according to the user's role. By means of an experiment, we realized our concept using a prototype system. Then, we investigated the results of the questionnaire regarding the prototype system's superiority compared with the conventional e-mail client (Mozilla Thunderbird).

Table 3 shows the results of the questionnaire in terms of task awareness for the following user support services: Event Notification, Questionnaire Request, File Collection, and Task context management.

We describe the concern of task awareness for user support services below.

Awareness of task

The task owner was rated more than 4.0 on average for each category (Event notification, Questionnaire Request, File Collection). We believe that this assessment of the user support service for the task owner was given a high evaluation because of the automated function for the task owner. In checking attendance for meeting, the

Table 3 Results of the questionnaire about usage of the prototype system

Action type	Task owner		Task member	
	Awareness of task	Awareness of task-related resources	Awareness of task	Awareness of task-related resources
Event notification	4.75	4.75	4.5	4.3
Questionnaire request	4	5	4.7	4
File collection	4.5	4.75	4.8	4.27

following opinion was obtained: "It is good because of the possibility to check the state of the task on the client".

The task member rates were more than 4.5 on average. Hence, it appears that task members could easily notice newly arrived tasks. Because task information is managed in the task context server, it pushes new task information to the user's client automatically. We think that the assessment of the work necessary for the reply e-mail attained a high valuation.

Awareness of task-related resource

The task owner was rated more than 4.75 on average for each category. Thus, it appears that our prototype system reduced the number of search operations for task-related information compared with the conventional e-mail system. Our prototype system provides an automated function for the task owner. The automated function (implemented in the Mailet program) extracts the context data from the reply e-mail message. The task owner can thus check the task-related resources in each panel shown in Figure 2. These reasons strongly substantiate the high rating obtained from the task owner. We found that the user interface view for the task owner was effective for organizing task-related information. Moreover, we also found that the burden of operation for organizing task-related information decreased when performing user support service.

The task member rates were more than 4.2 on average for each category. To provide the context data for a given task, we implemented task context view panel on the client shown in Figure 2. Therefore, task members could easily confirm the task schedule on the calendar panel. For each category, the results confirmed a high valuation in terms of awareness of service functionality for a given task.

Conclusions

In this paper, we described the design and implementation of a task context-aware e-mail platform for collaborative tasks. In order to provide a task context-aware service for task members, we introduced a task context model that represents conceptual associations between a task and the related mail process. Using the prototype system, we confirmed that the task context-aware platform executed the required services on the basis of the task context model. An operational experiment conducted enabled us to obtain insightful comments that can help to improve the prototype system for practical use from the point of view of an actual user environment. In future work, we will further develop the prototype to support more tasks.

The prototype system was deployed and evaluated in the relatively small confines of our laboratory, resulting in only a limited number of tasks and e-mail messages being handled among group members. Therefore, to validate our concept, we will expand the prototype system uses to larger organizations.

Competing interests

The author declares that he has no competing interests.

References

1. Krämer J-P (2010) PIM-Mail: Consolidating Task and Email Management. Extended Abstracts on Human Factors in Computing Systems. Proceedings of the 28th of the international conference extended abstracts on Human factors in computing systems, ACM, New York, pp 4411–4416

2. Ducheneaut N, Bellotti V (2001) Email as a Habitat. In: An Exploration of Embedded Personal Information Management, ACM Interactions, 8., pp 30–38

3. Bellotti V, Ducheneaut N, Howard M, Smith I (2003) Taking Email to Task: The Design and Evaluation of a Task Management Centered Email Tool. In: Proceedings of the SIGCHI Conference on Human Factors in Computing Systems. ACM, New York, pp 345–352

4. Bellotti V, Thornton JD, Chin A, Schiano D, Good N (2007) TV-ACTA: Embedding an Activity-Centered Interface for Task Management in Email. In: Proceedings of the Conference on Email and Anti-Spam

5. Geyer W, Muller MJ, Moore MT, Wilcox E, Cheng LT, Brownholtz B, Hill C, Millen DR (2006) Activity explorer: activity-centric collaboration from research to product. IBM Syst J 45:713–738

6. Cozzi A, Farrell S, Lau T, Smith BA, Drews C, Lin J, Stachel B, Moran TP (2006) Activity management as a web service. IBM Syst J 45:695–712

7. Grebner O, Ong E, Riss UV (2008) KASIMIR—Work Process Embedded Task Management Leveraging the Semantic Desktop. In: Proceedings of Multikonferenz Wirtshaftsinformatik, Workshop Semantic Web Technology in Business Information Systems., pp 715–726

8. Lepouras G, Dix A, Katifori T, Catarci T, Habegger B, Poggi A, Ioannidis Y (2006) OntoPIM: From Personal Information Management to Task Information Management. In: Proceedings of SIGIR Workshop on Personal Information Management., pp 78–81

9. Eklund P, Cole R (2002) Structured Ontology and Information Retrieval for Email Search and Discovery. In: Hacid M-S, Raś ZW, Zighed DA, Kodratoff Y (eds) ISMS2002, 2366. Proceedings of the 13th International Symposium on Methodologies for Intelligent Systems (ISMIS 2002), Lyon, France, pp 75–84

10. Brendel R, Krawczyk H (2008) E-mail User Role Identification Using OWL-Based Ontology Approach. In: Proceedings of the 1st International Conference on Information Technology., pp 18–21

11. Mahmud J, Matthews T, Whittaker S, Moran TP, Lau T (2011) Topika: Integrating Collaborative Sharing with Email. In: Proceedings of the SIGCHI Conference on Human Factors in Computing Systems. ACM, New York, pp 3161–3164

12. Candan KS, Liu H, Suvarna R (2001) Resource description framework: metadata and its applications. ACM SIGKDD Explorations Newsletter. ACM, New York, 3(1):6–19

13. Jena API https://jena.apache.org/

14. Apache James Project http://james.apache.org

15. Resnick P (2001) Internet Message Format. RFC Editor

Provably secure attribute-based encryption with attribute revocation and grant function using proxy re-encryption and attribute key for updating

Takeru Naruse[1*], Masami Mohri[2†] and Yoshiaki Shiraishi[3†]

* Correspondence:
naruse.takeru@nitzlab.com
[†]Equal contributors
[1]Nagoya Institute of Technology, Nagoya, Japan
Full list of author information is available at the end of the article

Abstract

Ciphertext-Policy Attribute-Based Encryption (CP-ABE) is suitable for data access control on a cloud storage system. In CP-ABE, the data owner encrypts data under the access structure over attributes and a set of attributes assigned to users is embedded in user's secret key. A user is able to decrypt if his attributes satisfy the ciphertext's access structure. In CP-ABE, processes of user's attribute revocation and grant are concentrated on the authority and the data owner. In this paper, we propose a ciphertext-policy attribute-based encryption scheme delegating attribute revocation processes to Cloud Server by proxy re-encryption. The proposed scheme does not require generations of new secret key when granting attributes to a user and supports any Linear Secret Sharing Schemes (LSSS) access structure. We prove that the proposed scheme is secure against attack by unauthorized users and Cloud Server.

Keywords: Cryptographic cloud storage; Ciphertext-policy attribute-based encryption; Attribute revocation and grant; Proxy re-encryption

Background

Sharing of data on a cloud storage has a risk of information leakage caused by service provider's abuse. In order to protect data, the data owner encrypts data shared on the cloud storage so that only authorized users can decrypt.

Ciphertext-Policy Attribute-Based Encryption (CP-ABE) [1,2] is suitable for data access control in the cloud storage system. The authority manages the attributes in the system. The data owner chooses an access structure and encrypts message under the access structure. The set of attributes assigned to users is embedded in his secret key. A user is able to decrypt a ciphertext if his attributes satisfy the ciphertext's access structure.

There are user's attribute revocation and grant in CP-ABE. In simple processes of user's attribute revocation, when his attributes are revoked, the data owner re-encrypts the shared data so that revoked user cannot decrypt. Then, the authority redistributes new secret keys so that other users can decrypt. In simple processes of user's attribute grant, the authority generates a new secret key. These simple processes are concentrated on the data owner and the authority.

Some attribute revocable CP-ABE schemes have been proposed [3-5]. Yu et al. [3] proposed a scheme combining CP-ABE with proxy re-encryption. The authority can delegate re-encryption and secret key update to proxy servers. However, this scheme has a limitation in access policy because it can only express "AND" policy. Hur et al. [4] proposed a scheme using key encryption keys (KEKs). A service provider distributes KEKs to each user. The service provider re-encrypts a ciphertext by an attribute group key. Then, he encrypts attribute group key by using KEKs so that authorized user can decrypt. As the number of system users has increases, the number of KEKs also increases and management becomes complicated. Liang et al. [5] proposed a scheme using user information (UI). UI is generated by Revocation Tree and Revocation List. An authorized user can decrypt ciphertexts by using secret key and UI. In this scheme, users whose attributes are revoked lose the access rights to all shared data by attribute revocation processes.

Moreover, in these schemes [3-5], the authority needs to generate a new key when granting attribute to users.

In this paper, we propose a CP-ABE scheme delegating attribute revocation processes to Cloud Server by proxy re-encryption and meets the following requirements.

1) *Support any Linear Secret Sharing Schemes (LSSS) access structure.* In existing schemes, there are following three expression methods of the access structure: tree, vector and matrix.

   The schemes using tree (for example the schemes of [1,4]) are not given the security proof under the standard model because they use hash functions for encryption.

   The schemes using vector whose elements are combined by AND condition are given the security proof under the standard model (for example the scheme of [3]) but they cannot perform flexible access control because only "AND" can be used for decryption conditions.

   By using matrix, for example a LSSS matrix, it is possible to use "AND" and "OR" for decryption conditions, that is, it is possible to perform a fine-grained access control and give the security proof under the standard model [2,5]. However, the revocation function is not shown in [2], and the scheme of [5] can revoke the only specified users but cannot revoke the only specified attributes.

2) *Revoke the only specified attribute (attribute level user revocation).* In the scheme of [5], users whose attributes are revoked lose the access rights to all shared data. To perform a fine-grained access control of shared data, it is desirable to revoke the only specified attributes. The schemes of [3,4] meet this requirement.

3) *Does not require the generation of new secret key when granting attribute to user.* In the way that the authority generates a new secret key and sends the key to a user every time it grants attributes to a user, the calculation amount of the authority is large in the case attributes are frequently granted. To avoid focusing the process of user's attribute grant in the authority, we enable cloud servers to update user's secret key. As far as we know, there is no scheme that meets this requirement.

We prove that the proposed scheme is secure under the standard model. We define attack model 1 as attack by unauthorized users and attack model 2 as attack by Cloud Server. We prove the proposed scheme is IND-CPA secure in the standard model against each attack model.

Methods

Preliminaries

Bilinear Maps

Let G_1, G_2 be two cyclic groups of prime order p. Let P be a generator of G_1. A bilinear map is a map $e : G_1 \times G_1 \rightarrow G_2$ with the following properties:

1) Bilinearity: for all $P, Q \in G_1$ and $a, b \in Z_p$, we have $e(aP, bQ) \rightarrow e(P, Q)^{ab}$.
2) Non-degeneracy: $e(P, P) \neq 1$.
3) Computability: There is an efficient algorithm tocompute $e(P, Q)$ for all $P, Q \in G_1$.

Linear Secret Sharing Scheme (LSSS)

Definition 1 (Linear Secret Sharing Schemes (LSSS) [2,6]) A secret-sharing scheme Π over a set of parties $\mathcal{P}$ is called linear (over Z_p) if

1) The shares for each party form a vector over Z_p.
2) There exists a matrix an M with l rows and n columns called the share-generating matrix for Π. For all $i = 1, ..., l$, te i'th row of M we let the function ρ defined the party labeling row i as $\rho(i)$. When we consider the column vector $v = (s, r_2, ..., r_n)$, where $s \in Z_p$ is the secret to be shared, and $r_2, ..., r_n \in Z_p$ are randomly chosen, then Mv is the vector of l shares of the secret s according to Π. The share $(Mv)_i$ belongs to party $\rho(i)$.

Suppose that Π is an LSSS for the access structure $\mathbb{A}$. Let $S \in \mathbb{A}$ be any authorized set, and let $I \subset \{1, 2, ..., l\}$. Then, there exist constants $\{\omega_i \in Z_p\}_{i \in I}$ such that, if $\{\lambda_i\}$ are valid shares of any secret s according to Π, then $\sum_{i \in I} \omega_i \lambda_i = s$. Futhermore, there these constants $\{\omega_i\}$ can be found in time polynomial in the size of the share-generating matrix M [6].

Decisional Parallel Bilinear Diffie-Hellman Exponent Assumption

Choose a group G_1 of prime order p according to the security parameter. Let $a, s, b_1, ..., b_q \in Z_p$ be chosen at random and $P \in G_1$ be a generator of G_1. If an adversary is given $\vec{y} =$

$$P, sP, aP, ..., a^q P, \quad , a^{q+2} P, ..., a^{2q} P$$

$$\forall_{1 \leq j \leq q} \; s \cdot b_j P, (a/b_j)P, ..., (a^q/b_j)P, \quad , (a^{q+2}/b_j)P, ..., (a^{2q}/b_j)P$$

$$\forall_{1 \leq j,k \leq q, k \neq j} (a \cdot s \cdot b_k/b_j)P, ..., (a^q \cdot s \cdot b_k/b_j)P$$

it must remain hard to distinguish $e(P,P)^{a^{q+1}} \in G_2$ from a random element in $R \in G_2$.

An algorithm $\mathcal{A}$ that outputs $z \in \{0, 1\}$ has advantage ϵ in solving decisional *q-parallel* BDHE in G_1 if

$$\left| \Pr\left[\mathcal{A}\left(\vec{y}, T = e(g,g)^{a^{q+1}s} \right) = 0 \right] \right.$$

$$\left. - \Pr\left[\mathcal{A}\left(\vec{y}, T = R \right) = 0 \right] \right| \geq \epsilon$$

We say that the (decision) *q-parallel* BDHE assumption holds if no polytime algorithm has a non-negligible advantage in solving the decisional *q-parallel* BDHE problem [2].

System Model and Definition

Model

There are four entities in the proposed scheme as follows.

User: The user downloads the shared data from Cloud Server.

Data owner: The data owner encrypts the shared data then uploads to Cloud Server.

Authority: The authority manages attributes in the system and publishes the parameters used for encryption. It generates a secret key that user's attributes are embedded and PRE keys used for re-encryption and updating secret key. The authority is trusted party.

Cloud Server: Cloud Server stores shared data. It re-encrypts encrypted shared data and update secret key by using PRE keys received from the authority. Similar to previous schemes [3,4], we assume Cloud Server to be curious-but-honest. That is, it will honestly execute the tasks assigned by legitimate parties in the system. However, it would like to learn information of encrypted shared data as much as possible.

Algorithm Definition

Our proposed scheme is composed of 8 algorithms: Auth.Setup, DO.Enc, Auth.Ext, U.Dec, Auth.ReKeyGen, C.ReEnc, C.ReKey, C.AddAtt.

Auth.Setup: The setup algorithm takes as input the security parameter and attribute universe description. It outputs the public parameters PK, master secret key MSK and the keys for granting an attribute J.

DO.Enc: The Encryption algorithm takes as input the public parameters PK, an LSSS access structure $\mathbb{A}$, and a message $\mathcal{M}$. It outputs a ciphertext CT.

Auth.Ext: The key extraction algorithm takes as input the master key MK, and a set of attributes S. It outputs a secret key SK and t_{ID}.

U.Dec: The decryption algorithm takes as input a secret key SK for a set S and a ciphertext CT for an access structure $\mathbb{A}$. If the set of attributes S satisfies the access structure $\mathbb{A}$, it outputs a message $\mathcal{M}$.

Auth.ReKeyGen: The re-encryption key generation algorithm takes as input the master key MK and a set of attributes γ for update. It outputs the redefined master key MK', the redefined public parameters PK', and the PRE (Proxy Re-Encryption) keys rk.

C.ReEnc: The re-encryption algorithm takes as input an attribute y for update, the ciphertext component D_i and a PRE key list RKL_y. It outputs the re-encryption ciphertext component D_i'.

C.ReKey: The key regeneration algorithm takes as input an attribute w for update, the secret key component K_w and the PRE key list RKL_w. It outputs the updated secret key component K_w'.

C.GrantAtt: The attribute grant algorithm takes as input an attribute v, the key for granting an attribute J_v, t_{ID} and the PRE key list RKL_v. It outputs secret key component K_v and redefines the key for granting an attribute J_v'.

Security Definition

We prove that unauthorized users and Cloud Server cannot decrypt ciphertext CT that was encrypted by the proposed scheme. Since we assume Cloud Server is honest, we do not consider active attacks from Cloud Server by colluding with unauthorized or revoked users. We define two attack models and security models as follows.

Attack Model 1 In this model, we assume an attack by unauthorized users. Security in this model is defined with the following game.

-Init. The adversary A submits the challenge access structure $\mathbb{A}$ to the challenger C.

-Setup. The challenger C runs setup algorithm and gives the public parameters PK to the adversary A.

-Phase1. The adversary can issue following query.

- Ext query : The adversary A submits a set of attributes S where S does not satisfy the access structure $\mathbb{A}$ to the challenger. The challenger C gives secret key corresponding S.
- Add query : The adversary A submits a set of attributes S' where $S \cup S'$ does not satisfy the challenge access structure $\mathbb{A}$. The challenger C gives the secret key component K_x corresponding to S'.

-Challenge. The adversary A submits two equal length messages M_0, M_1. The challenger flips a random coin b, and encrypts M_b under $\mathbb{A}$. The challenger gives ciphertext CT to the adversary A.

-Phase2. Phase1 is repeated.

-Guess. The adversary A outputs his guess b' of b.

The advantage of an adversary A in this game is defined as $\Pr\left[b' = b\right] - \frac{1}{2}$.

Definition 2 A ciphertext-policy attribute-based encryption scheme is secure if all polynomial time adversaries have at most a negligible advantage in the above game.

Attack Model 2 In this model, we assume an attack by Cloud Server. Security in this model is defined with the following game.

-Init. The adversary A submits the challenge access structure $\mathbb{A}$ and version number ver^* to the challenger C.

-Setup. The challenger C runs setup algorithm and gives the public parameters PK and PRE key and the keys for granting an attribute J to the adversary A.

-Phase1. The adversary can issue following query.

- K_x query : The adversary A submits a set of attribute S. The challenger C gives secret key component K_x corresponding to S to the adversary A.

-Challenge. The adversary A submits two equal length messages M_0, M_1. The challenger flips a random coin b, and encrypts M_b under $\mathbb{A}$. The challenger gives ciphertext CT to the adversary A.

-Phase2. Phase1 is repeated.

-Guess. The adversary A outputs his guess b' of b.

Definition 3 A ciphertext-policy attribute-based encryption scheme is secure if all polynomial time adversaries have at most a negligible advantage in the above game.

Our Scheme

Overview

The proposed scheme is based on Waters's scheme of CP-ABE [2]. Water's scheme supports any LSSS access structure. We apply the idea of attribute revocation shown in [3] to the proposed scheme. In the proposed scheme, the attribute key is included in the ciphertext and secret key to delegate attribute revocation processes to Cloud Server. The attribute key is master key components corresponding to each attribute in the system. When user's attributes are revoked, the authority re-defines the attribute keys, and generates PRE keys for updating the attribute keys. Cloud Server re-encrypts ciphertext and updates secret key by updating attribute key by using PRE key. Each attribute is associated with version number for updating attribute key.

Cloud Server keeps user list UL, re-encryption key list RKL and the key for granting an attribute to secret key J. UL records user's *ID*, user's attribute information, secret key components, t_{ID}. t_{ID} is a random number that randomize each secret key to prevent users' collusion attack. t_{ID} should "bind" components of one user's key together so that they cannot be combined with another user's key components[2]. RKL records update history of attribute (version number) and PRE keys.

When granting attributes to users, Cloud Server generates user's secret key components correspond to granting attribute from t_{ID} and J, and sends secret key component to the user. The user joins secret key component to own secret key. Thus, it is possible to grant attributes to users without generation of new secret key by the authority.

Algorithm

Auth.Setup(*U*) The setup algorithm takes as input the number of system attributes *U*. It first chooses a group G_1 of prime order p, a generator $P \in G_1$. It then chooses random group elements $Q_1, ..., Q_U \in G_1$ that are associated with the *U* attributes in the system. In addition, it chooses two random $\alpha, a \in Z_p$, and random $Att_1, ..., Att_U \in Z_p$ as the attribute key.

The public parameters are

$$PK := \ < P, e(P,P)^\alpha, aP, Q_1, ..., Q_U, T_1 = Att_1 P, ..., T_U >$$

The master key is $MK := \ < \alpha, Att_1, ..., Att_U >$.

The keys for granting an attribute are $J := \ < \{x, J_x = 1/Att_x\}_{1 \le x \le U} >$.

DO.Enc $(PK, (M, \rho), \mathcal{M})$ The Encryption algorithm takes as input the public parameters *PK*, an LSSS access structure (M, ρ), and a message $\mathcal{M}$. The function ρ associates rows of M to attributes. Let M be an $l \times n$ matrix. It first chooses a random vector $\vec{v} = (s, y_2, ..., y_n) \in Z_p$. For $i = 1$ to l, it computes $\lambda_i := \vec{v} \cdot M_i$. It then chooses random $r_1, ..., r_l \in Z_p$ and outputs the ciphertext

$$CT := \ < C, C', (C_1, D_1), ..., (C_l, D_l) > =$$

$$< Ke(P,P)^{\alpha s}, sP, \left(\lambda_1(aP) - r_1 Q_{\rho(1)}, r_1 T_{\rho(1)} \right), ..., \left(\lambda_l(aP) - r_l Q_{\rho(l)}, r_l T_{\rho(l)} \right) >$$

with (M, ρ).

Auth.Ext (MK, S) The key extraction algorithm takes as input the master key *MK*, and a set of attributes *S*. It first chooses a random $t_{ID} \in Z_p$. It then outputs t_{ID} and the secret key

$$SK := < K, L, \forall x \in S \; K_x > =$$

$$< \alpha P + t_{ID}(aP), t_{ID}P, \forall x \in S \; (t_{ID}/Att_x)Q_x > .$$

U.Dec (SK, CT) The decryption algorithm takes as input a secret key SK for a set S and a ciphertext CT for access structure (M, ρ). Suppose that S satisfies the access structure and let I be defined as $I = \{i : \rho(i) \in S\}$. Then, let $\{\omega_i \in Z_p\}_{i \in I}$ be as set of consistants such that if $\{\lambda_i\}$ are valid shares of the secret s according to M, then $\sum_{i \in I} \omega_i \lambda_i = s$.

The decryption algorithm first computes

$$\frac{e(C', K)}{\prod_{i \in I} \left(e(C_i, L) e(D_i, K_{\rho(i)}) \right)^{\omega_i}} =$$

$$\frac{e(P, P)^{\alpha s} e(P, P)^{ast_{ID}}}{\prod_{i \in I} \left(e(P, P)^{ta\lambda_i \omega_i} \right)} = e(P, P)^{\alpha s}.$$

It can then decrypt the message $\mathcal{M} = C/e(P, P)^{\alpha s}$.

Auth.ReKeyGen(MK, γ) The re-encryption key generation algorithm takes as input the master key MK and a set of attributes γ for update. For each $x \in \gamma$, it chooses random $Att'_x \in Z_p$ as the new attribute key, and computes $T'_x := Att'_x P$, $rk_{x \to x'} := \frac{Att'_x}{Att_x}$. It then replaces each Att_x of the master key component with Att'_x, and each T_x of public parameter with T'_x. It outputs the redefined the master key MK', the redefined public parameters PK', and the PRE keys $rk := \{x, rk_x\}_{x \in \gamma}$.

C.ReEnc$(y(=\rho(i)), D_i, RKL_y)$ The re-encryption algorithm takes as input an attribute y $(=\rho(i))$ for update, the ciphertext component D_i and a PRE key list RKL_y. It first checks version of attribute y. If y has the latest version, it outputs $\perp$ and exit. Let $Att_{y^{(n)}}$ be defined as an attribute key of the latest version of attribute y. It computes $rk_{y \mapsto y^{(n)}} := rk_{y \mapsto y'} \cdot rk_{y' \mapsto y''} \cdots rk_{y^{(n-1)} \mapsto y^{(n)}} = Att_{y^{(n)}}/Att_y$. Then, it outputs the re-encrypted ciphertext component $D'_i := rk_{y \mapsto y^{(n)}} \cdot D_i = \left(Att_{y^{(n)}}/Att_y \right) \cdot r_i Att_y P = r_i Att_{y^{(n)}} P$.

C.ReKey $(w, K_{w,ID}, RKL_w)$ The key regeneration algorithm takes as input an attribute w for update, the secret key component K_w and the PRE key list RKL_w. It first checks version of attribute w. If w has the latest version, it outputs $\perp$ and exit. Let $Att_{w^{(n)}}$ be defined as the attribute key for the latest version of attribute w. It computes $rk_{w \leftrightarrow w^{(n)}} := rk_{w \leftrightarrow w'} \cdot rk_{w' \leftrightarrow w''} \cdots rk_{w^{(n-1)} \leftrightarrow w^{(n)}} = Att_{w^{(n)}}/Att_w$. It then outputs the updated secret key component $K'_w := rk_{w \leftrightarrow w^{(n)}}^{-1} \cdot K_w = (Att_w/Att_{w^{(n)}}) \cdot (t_{ID}/Att_w)Q_w = (t_{ID}/Att_{w^{(n)}}) Q_w$.

C.GrantAtt (v, J_v, t_{ID}, RKL_v) The attribute grant algorithm takes as input an attribute v, the key for granting an attribute J_v, t_{ID} and the PRE key list RKL_v. It first checks version of attribute v. Let $Att_{v^{(n)}}$ be defined as the attribute key for the latest version of attribute v. It first computes $rk_{v \leftrightarrow v^{(n)}} := rk_{v \leftrightarrow v'} \cdot rk_{v' \leftrightarrow v''} \cdots rk_{v^{(n-1)} \leftrightarrow v^{(n)}} = Att_{v^{(n)}}/Att_v$. It then outputs secret key component for $K_v := t_{ID} \cdot rk_{v \leftrightarrow v^{(n)}}^{-1} \cdot J_v = t_{ID} \cdot (Att_v/Att_{v^{(n)}}) \cdot (1/Att_v)Q_v = (t_{ID}/Att_{v^{(n)}})Q_v$ and redefines the key for granting an attribute $J'_v := rk_{v \leftrightarrow v^{(n)}}^{-1} \cdot J_v = (1/Att_{v^{(n)}})Q_v$.

We show the flow of our scheme in Fig 1. In Fig 1, γ denotes a set of user u's attributes which are revoked and β denotes a set of attributes that granting to user u.

Security Proof

We prove that unauthorized users and Cloud Server cannot decrypt ciphertext CT that was encrypted by using the proposed scheme.

Security Proof in the Attack Model 1

Theorem 1 Suppose the decisional q-*parallel* BDHE assumption holds and a challenge matrix of size is $l^* \times n^*$ where $l^* \times n^* \leq q$, our scheme is IND-CPA secure in the attack model 1.

Proof Suppose we have adversary A with non-negligible advantage ϵ against our scheme in the attack model 1. Moreover, suppose it chooses a challenge matrix M^* where both dimensions are at most q. We show how to build a simulator, B, that plays the decisional q-*parallel* BDHE problem.

Init. The simulator takes in a q-*parallel* BDHE challenge $\vec{y}, T$. The adversary gives the simulator B the challenge access structure (M^*, ρ^*), where M^* has n^* columns.

Setup. The simulator B generates the public parameter PK as follows. The simulator B chooses random $\alpha' \in Z_p$ and implicitly sets $\alpha = \alpha' + a^{q+1}$ by letting $e(P,P)^\alpha = e(aP, a^q P)e(P,P)^{\alpha'}$. It outputs public parameter $Q_1, ..., Q_U$ as follows.

1. For each x for $1 \leq x \leq U$ begin by choosing a random value z_x
2. Let X denote the set of indices i, such that $\rho^*(i) = x$.
3. The simulator B computes
$$Q_x = z_x P + \sum_{i \in X}\left\{\left(a^2 M^*_{i,1}/b_i\right)P + \left(a^2 M^*_{i,2}/b_i\right)P + \cdots + \left(a^{n^*} M^*_{i,n^*}/b_i\right)P\right\}$$

Note that if $X = \varnothing$ then we have $Q_x = g^{z_x}$. Also note that the parameters are distributed randomly due to g^{z_x}. The simulator B randomly chooses attribute keys $t_x \in Z_p$ for

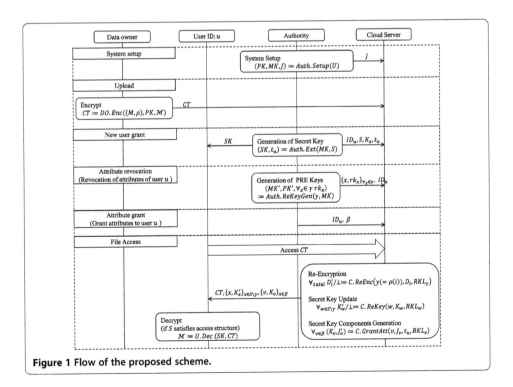

Figure 1 Flow of the proposed scheme.

$1 \leq x \leq U$ and computes public parameters $T_x = t_x P$. It gives the adversary A the public parameters $PK := (P, e(P, P)^\alpha, aP, Q_1, ..., Q_U, T_1, ..., T_U)$.

Phase1. The adversary A issues following queries:

Ext query : The adversary A submits a set of attributes S where S does not satisfy the access structure M^* to the challenger. The simulator first chooses a random $r \in Z_p$. Then it finds a vector $\vec{w} = (w_1, ..., w_{n^*}) \in Z_p^{n^*}$ such that $w_1 = -1$ and for all i where $\rho(i) \in S'$ we have that $\vec{w} \cdot M_i^* = 0$. The simulator B begins by implicitly defining t_{ID} as

$$r + w_1 a^q + w_2 a^{q-1} + \cdots + w_{n^*} a^{q-n^*+1}$$

It performs this by setting $L = rP + \sum_{i=2,...,n^*} w_i(a^{q+1-i}P) = t_{ID}P$. The simulator can compute K as

$$\alpha' P + arP + \sum_{i=2,...,n^*} w_i(a^{q+2-i}P)$$

The simulator B computes $K_x \ \forall_x \in S$ as follows.

Case 1. If there is no i such that $\rho^*(i) = x$, it computes $K_x = (1/t_x) \cdot z_x L$.

Case 2. If there is i such that $\rho^*(i) = x$.

1) Let X be the set of all i such that $\rho^*(i) = x$.

2) It computes K_x as

$$z_x L + \sum_{i \in X} \sum_{j=1,...,n^*} M_{i,j}^* [(a^j/b_i)rP + \sum_{\substack{k=1,...,n^* \\ k \neq j}} w_k \{(a^{q+1+j-k}/b^i)P\}]$$

3) It calculates $K_x = (1/t_x)K_x'$.

It gives the adversary A secret key $SK := (K, L, \forall x \in S \ K_x)$.

Add query : The adversary A submits a set of attributes S' where $S \cup S'$ does not satisfy the challenge access structure M^*. The simulator B computes $K_x \ \forall_x \in S'$ as follows.

Case1. If there is no i such that $\rho^*(i) = x$, it computes $K_x = (1/t_x) \cdot z_x L$.

Case2. If there is i such that $\rho^*(i) = x$.

1) Let X be the set of all i such that $\rho^*(i) = x$.

2) It computes K_x' as

$$z_x L + \sum_{i \in X} \sum_{j=1,...,n^*} M_{i,j}^* [(a^j/b_i)rP + \sum_{\substack{k=1,...,n^* \\ k \neq j}} w_k \{(a^{q+1+j-k}/b^i)P\}]$$

3) It calculates $K_x = (1/t_x)K_x'$.

It gives the adversary A the secret key component $\{K_x\}_{\forall x \in S'}$.

Challenge. The adversary A submits two equal length messages $\mathcal{M}_0$, $\mathcal{M}_1$. The simulator B flips a random coin $b \in \{0, 1\}$. It computes $C = \mathcal{M}_b T \cdot e(sP, \alpha' P)$, $C = sP$. It choose random $y_2', ..., y_{n^*}' \in Z_p$ and the share the secret using the vector

$\vec{v} = \left(s, sa + y'_2, sa^2 + y'_3, ..., sa^{n-1} + y'_{n^*}\right) \in Z_p^{n^*}$. In addition, it choose random values $r'_1, ..., r'_l \in Z_p$.

For $i = 1, ..., n^*$, we define R_i as the set of all $k \neq i$ such that $\rho^*(i) = \rho^*(k)$. The challenge ciphertext components are then generated as

$$D_i = -r'_i T_{\rho^*(i)} - s b_i T_{\rho^*(i)}$$

$$C_i = h^{r'_i}_{\rho^*(i)} + \left\{ \sum_{j=2,...,n^*} M^*_{i,j} y'_j (aP) \right\} - z_{\rho(i)}(b_i \cdot s)P + \left\{ \sum_{k \in R_i} \sum_{j=1,...,n^*} M^*_{k,j}\left(a^j \cdot s \cdot (b_i/b_k)P\right) \right\}$$

It gives the adversary A the challenge ciphertext $CT^* = \left(C, C', (C_1, D_1), ..., (C_{l'}, D_{l'})\right)$.

Phase2. Phase 1 is repeated.

Guess. The adversary A will eventually output a guess b'. of b. The simulator then outputs 0 to guess that $T = e(P, P)^{a^{q+1}s}$ if $b'. = b$; otherwise, it outputs 1 to indicate that it believes T is a random group element $R \in G_2$.

When T is a tuple the simulator B gives a perfect simulation so we have that

$$\Pr = \left[B\left(\vec{y}, T = e(P, P)^{a^{q+1}s}\right) = 0 \right] = \frac{1}{2} + \epsilon.$$

When T is a random group element the message $\mathcal{M}_b$ is completely hidden from the adversary and we have $\Pr = \left[B\left(\vec{y}, T = R\right) = 0 \right] = \frac{1}{2}$. Therefore, the simulator B can play the decisional *q-parallel* BDHE game with non-negligible advantage.

Security Proof in the Attack Model 2

Theorem 2 Suppose Waters's scheme [2] is IND-CPA secure, our scheme is also IND-CPA secure in the attack model 2.

Proof Suppose we have adversary A with non-negligible advantage ϵ against our scheme in the attack model 2. Moreover, suppose it chooses a challenge matrix M^* where both dimensions are at most q. We prove there is an simulator B which has advantage at least ϵ against Waters's scheme simulator (Given input, it responds according to algorithms of the Waters's scheme).

Init. The adversary A submits the challenge access structure (M^*, ρ^*) where M^* has n^* columns and version number ver^* to the simulator B. The simulator B submits the challenge access structure (M^*, ρ^*) to the Waters's scheme simulator.

Setup. The simulator B receives public parameters $PK' := (P, e(P, P)^\alpha, aP, Q_1, ..., Q_U)$ from the Waters's scheme simulator. It randomly chooses attribute keys $t_x \in Z_p$ for $1 \leq x \leq U$ and computes public parameters $T_x = t_x P$. It computes the key for granting an attribute $J := \{(1/t_1)Q_1, ..., (1/t_U)Q_U\}$. Then, the simulator B computes PRE keys and public parameters T_x for each version as follows. For x $(1 \leq x \leq U)$, for $1 \leq k \leq ver^* - 1$, the simulator B randomly chooses PRE keys $rk_{x^{(k)} \to x^{(k+1)}} \in Z_p$ and computes public parameters $T_{x^{(k+1)}} = rk_{x^{(k)} \leftrightarrow x^{(k+1)}} T_{x^{(k)}}$. $(k+1)$ and (k) denote the version number of PRE keys and public parameter. The simulator B gives the adversary A the public parameter $PK := (P, e(P, P)^\alpha, aP, Q_1, ..., Q_U, T_1, ..., T_U)$, the key for granting an attribute J and all PRE keys.

Phase1. The adversary A issues following queries:

K_x **query** : The adversary A submits a set of attributes S for version k, $1 \le k \le ver^* - 1$. we denote $V_{x^{(k)}} = \prod_{i=2}^{k} rk_{x^{(i-1)} \leftrightarrow x^{(i)}}$. The simulator B randomly chooses $t_{ID} \in Z_p$ and computes $\forall x \in S \ K_x = (t_{ID}/t_x \cdot V_{x^{(k)}})Q_x$. It gives the adversary A the secret key components $\{K_x\}_{\forall x \in S}$.

Challenge. The adversary A submits two equal length messages $\mathcal{M}_0$, $\mathcal{M}_1$, then the simulator B submits them to the Waters's simulator. The Waters's simulator flips a random coin $b \in \{0, 1\}$ and computes ciphertest $CT' := (C, C', (C_1, D_1), ..., (C_l, D_l)) \leftarrow Enc (PK, (M^*, \rho^*), \mathcal{M}_b)$. The simulator B receives the ciphertext CT', then it computes $CT := \left(C, C', \left(C_1, V_{\rho(1)^{(ver^*)}}D_1\right), ..., \left(C_l, V_{\rho(l)^{(ver^*)}}D_l\right)\right)$ from the ciphertext CT'. It gives the adversary A the cipertext CT.

Phase2. Phase 1 is repeated.

Guess. The adversary A outputs will eventually output a guess b' of b. The simulator B outputs b' as its guess.

The simulation above shows there is a simulator B that has advantage at least ϵ ageinst Waters's scheme simulator if there is an adversary A that has advantage ϵ against our scheme.

Result and discussion

In Table 1, we give two comparisons of the proposed scheme with the schemes of [3,4] that can revoke the only specified attributes. The first comparison is in terms of the size of the public key (PK), the secret key (SK), the ciphertext (CT), and the re-encryption key (RK). The second comparison is in terms of the computation amount of encryption (Enc), secret key generation (Ext), re-encryption (Re-enc), decryption (Dec), and secret key update (Re-key). As to the size of the public key, the scheme of [4] has the smallest one, followed by the proposed scheme. As for the size of the secret key,

Table 1 Key Size, Ciphertext Size and Computation Amount

	Yu etal's scheme [3]	Hur et al's scheme [4]	The proposed scheme
PK	$(3\lvert U \rvert + 1) \times \lvert G \rvert + \lvert G_T \rvert$	$2 \times \lvert G \rvert + \lvert G_T \rvert$	$(2\lvert U \rvert + 2) \times \lvert G \rvert + \lvert G_T \rvert$
SK	$(2\lvert U \rvert + 1) \times \lvert G \rvert$	$(2\lvert S \rvert + 1) \times \lvert G \rvert + \log \lvert N \rvert \times \lvert K \rvert$	$(\lvert S \rvert + 2) \times \lvert G \rvert$
CT	$(\lvert U \rvert + 1) + \lvert G \rvert + \lvert G_T \rvert$	$(2\lvert I \rvert + 1) \times \lvert G \rvert + \lvert G_T \rvert$	$(2\lvert I \rvert + 1) \times \lvert G \rvert + \lvert G_T \rvert$
RK	$r\lvert U \rvert \times \lvert Z_p \rvert$	$(2\lvert N \rvert - 1) \times \lvert K \rvert$	$r\lvert U \rvert \times \lvert X_p \rvert$
Enc	$(\lvert U \rvert + 2) \times exp$	$(2\lvert I \rvert + 2) \times exp$	$(2\lvert I \rvert + 2) \times exp$
Ext	$(2\lvert U \rvert + 1) \times exp$	$(2\lvert S \rvert + 2) \times exp$	$(\lvert S \rvert + 2) \times exp$
Re-enc	$\lvert R_{CT} \rvert \times exp$	$\lvert R_{CT} \rvert \times exp$	$\lvert R_{CT} \rvert \times exp$
Re-key	$\lvert R_{SK} \rvert \times exp$	$\lvert R_{SK} \rvert \times exp$	$\lvert R_{SK} \rvert \times exp$
Dec	$(\lvert U \rvert + 1) \times \hat{e}$ $+(\lvert U \rvert 1) \times exp$	$(2\lvert R \rvert + 1) \times \hat{e}$ $+(2\lvert R \rvert + 2) \times exp$	$(2\lvert R \rvert + 1) \times \hat{e}$ $+(2\lvert R \rvert + 2) \times exp$

Exp:ex ponentiation in G, $\hat{e}$: bilinear pairing,
$\lvert U \rvert$: the number of attributes defined in the system,
$\lvert S \rvert$: the number of attributes in user's key,
$\lvert R \rvert$ the number of user's attributes satisfying an acces structure,
r: the number of times the attribute revocation event occurs,
$\lvert R_{SK} \rvert$: the number of updated attributes (secret key),
$\lvert R_{CT} \rvert$: the numbet of updated attributes (ciphertext), $\lvert N \rvert$: the number of total user,
$\lvert I \rvert$: the number of attributes am acces structure, $\lvert K \rvert$: size of the common key.

Table 2 Comparison of Schemes

	Yu etal's scheme [3]	Hur et al's scheme [4]	Liang et al's scheme [5]	The proposed scheme
Suporting acces policy type	'AND'	'AND', 'OR'	Any LSSS	Any LSSS
Attibute level user revocation	Possible	Possible	Impossible	Possible
Grant attributes to users	The authority generates a new secret key	The authority generates a new secret key	The authority generates a new secret key	Cloud server adds attributes to user's secret key

the proposed scheme has the smallest one. Both the proposed scheme and the scheme of [4] have equally the smallest size ciphertexts. As to the size of the re-encryption key, if there are users more than the number of attributes, both the proposed scheme and the scheme of [3] have the equally smallest one.

As for the computation amount of encryption and decryption, the proposed scheme and the scheme of [4] have the equally smallest. As to the computation amount of secret key generation, the proposed scheme has the smallest. Finally, as to the computation amount of re-encryption and secret key update, all schemes have the same.

The differences, in terms of the requirements in Section I, between the proposed scheme and the schemes of [3-5] are summarized as shown in Table 2.

Conclusion

This paper proposed a ciphertext-policy attribute-based encryption scheme delegating attribute revocation processes to Cloud Server by proxy re-encryption. Cloud Server re-encrypts a ciphertext and updates a secret key by updating attribute key with PRE key for updating the attribute keys.

The proposed scheme meets three requirements as follows; First, the proposed scheme supports any LSSS access structure. Second, the authority can only revoke specified attribute by updating attribute key included in ciphertext corresponding to his attributes which are revoked. Finally, when granting attributes to a user, generation of a new secret key becomes unnecessary because Cloud Server generates secret key components corresponding to granting attributes.

The proposed scheme is secure against attack by unauthorized users and Cloud Server. Our future direction is to implement the proposed scheme and confirm its feasibility.

Competing interests
The authors declare that they have no competing interests.

Authors' contributions
TN designed the study and drafted the manuscript. MM and YS conceived of the study, participated in the design and drafting the article and revising it critically for intellectual content. They reviewed and approved the final, submitted version. All authors read and approved the manuscript.

Authors' Information
TN received B.E. degree from Nagoya Institute of Technology, Japan, in 2013. He is a graduate student of the institute. His current research interests include information security, cryptography. He received DICOMO2013 symposium Paper Awards and Presentation Awards in 2013. He is a member of IPSJ.
MM received B.E. and M.E. degrees from Ehime University, Japan, in 1993 and 1995 respectively. She received Ph.D degree in Engineering from the University of Tokushima, Japan in 2002. From 1995 to 1998 she was an assistant professor at the Department of Management and Information Science, Kagawa junior college, Japan. From 1998 to 2002 she was a research associate of the Department of Information Science and Intelligent Systems, the University of Tokushima, Japan. From 2003 to 2008 she was a lecturer of the same department. Since 2008, she has been an

associate professor at the Information and Multimedia Center, Gifu University, Japan. Her research interests are in coding theory, information security and cryptography. She is a member of IEEE and a senior member of IEICE.

YS received B.E. and M.E. degrees from Ehime University, Japan, and Ph.D degree from the University of Tokushima, Japan, in 1995, 1997, and 2000, respectively. From 2002 to 2006 he was a lecturer at the Department of Informatics, Kinki University, Japan. From 2006 to 2013 he was an associate professor at the Department of Computer Science and Engineering, Nagoya Institute of Technology, Japan. Since 2013, he has been an associate professor at the Department of Electrical and Electronic Engineering, Kobe University, Japan. His current research interests include information security, cryptography, computer network, and knowledge sharing and creation support. He received the SCIS 20th Anniversary Award and the SCIS Paper Award from ISEC group of IEICE in 2003 and 2006, respectively. He is a member of IEEE, ACM and a senior member of IEICE, IPSJ.

Author details

[1]Nagoya Institute of Technology, Nagoya, Japan. [2]Gifu University, Gifu, Japan. [3]Kobe University, Kobe, Japan.

References

1. Bethencourt J, Sahai A, Waters B (2007) Ciphertext-policy attribute-based encryption. In: Paper presented at the 2007 IEEE Symposium on Security and Privacy, Oakland., 20–23 May 2007
2. Waters B (2011) Ciphertext-policy attribute-based encryption: an expressive, efficient, and provably secure realization. In: Paper presented at the 14th International Conference on Practice and Theory in Public Key Cryptography, Taormina., 6–9 March 2011
3. Yu S, Wang C, Ren K, Lou W (2010) Attribute based data sharing with attribute revocation. In: Paper presented at the 5th ACM Symposium on Information. Computer and Communications Security, Beijing, 13 April 2010
4. Hur J, Nor D.K (2011) Attribute-based access control with efficient revocation in data outsourcing systems. doi:10.1109/TPDS.2010.203.
5. Liang X, Lu R, Lin X, Shen X (2011) Ciphertext policy attribute based encryption with efficient revocation. http://bbcr.uwaterloo.ca/~x27liang/papers/abe%20with%20revocation.pdf.
6. Beimei A (1996) Secure schemes for secret sharing and key distribution. Dissertation, Israel Institute of Technology.

Permissions

All chapters in this book were first published in HCIS, by Springer; hereby published with permission under the Creative Commons Attribution License or equivalent. Every chapter published in this book has been scrutinized by our experts. Their significance has been extensively debated. The topics covered herein carry significant findings which will fuel the growth of the discipline. They may even be implemented as practical applications or may be referred to as a beginning point for another development.

The contributors of this book come from diverse backgrounds, making this book a truly international effort. This book will bring forth new frontiers with its revolutionizing research information and detailed analysis of the nascent developments around the world.

We would like to thank all the contributing authors for lending their expertise to make the book truly unique. They have played a crucial role in the development of this book. Without their invaluable contributions this book wouldn't have been possible. They have made vital efforts to compile up to date information on the varied aspects of this subject to make this book a valuable addition to the collection of many professionals and students.

This book was conceptualized with the vision of imparting up-to-date information and advanced data in this field. To ensure the same, a matchless editorial board was set up. Every individual on the board went through rigorous rounds of assessment to prove their worth. After which they invested a large part of their time researching and compiling the most relevant data for our readers.

The editorial board has been involved in producing this book since its inception. They have spent rigorous hours researching and exploring the diverse topics which have resulted in the successful publishing of this book. They have passed on their knowledge of decades through this book. To expedite this challenging task, the publisher supported the team at every step. A small team of assistant editors was also appointed to further simplify the editing procedure and attain best results for the readers.

Apart from the editorial board, the designing team has also invested a significant amount of their time in understanding the subject and creating the most relevant covers. They scrutinized every image to scout for the most suitable representation of the subject and create an appropriate cover for the book.

The publishing team has been an ardent support to the editorial, designing and production team. Their endless efforts to recruit the best for this project, has resulted in the accomplishment of this book. They are a veteran in the field of academics and their pool of knowledge is as vast as their experience in printing. Their expertise and guidance has proved useful at every step. Their uncompromising quality standards have made this book an exceptional effort. Their encouragement from time to time has been an inspiration for everyone.

The publisher and the editorial board hope that this book will prove to be a valuable piece of knowledge for researchers, students, practitioners and scholars across the globe.

List of Contributors

Mohammad Malkawi
Jadara University, Irbid, Jordan
Cambium Networks, USA

Omayya Murad
Department of Computer Science, Jadara University, Irbid, Jordan

Shih-Ming Chang
Department of CSIE, Tamkang University, Taipei, Taiwan

Hon-Hang Chang
Department of CSIE, National Central University, Taoyuan, Taiwan

Shwu-Huey Yen
Department of CSIE, Tamkang University, Taipei, Taiwan

Timothy K Shih
Department of CSIE, National Central University, Taoyuan, Taiwan

Eman Elsayed
Department of Math and Computer science, Faculty of Science (girls), Al-Azhar University, Cairo, Egypt

Kamal Eldahshan
Department of Math and Computer science, Faculty of Science (girls), Al-Azhar University, Cairo, Egypt

Shaimaa Tawfeek
Department of Math and Computer science, Faculty of Science (girls), Al-Azhar University, Cairo, Egypt

Newton Howard
Massachusetts Institute of Technology, Cambridge, MA 02139, USA

Erik Cambria
Massachusetts Institute of Technology, Cambridge, MA 02139, USA

Rajinder Singh
Deenbandhu Chhotu Ram University of Science & Technology, Murthal, Haryana, India

Parvinder Singh
Department of Computer Science and Engineering, Deenbandhu Chhotu Ram University of Science & Technology, Murthal, Haryana, India

Manoj Duhan
Department of Electronics and Communications, Deenbandhu Chhotu Ram University of Science & Technology, Murthal, Haryana, India

Debotosh Bhattacharjee
Department of Computer Science and Engineering, Jadavpur University, Kolkata 700032, India

James McNaull
School of Computing and Mathematics, University of Ulster Jordanstown, Shore Road, Newtownabbey, Belfast

Juan Carlos Augusto
Department of Computer Science, Middlesex University, Hendon, London, UK

Maurice Mulvenna
School of Computing and Mathematics, University of Ulster Jordanstown, Shore Road, Newtownabbey, Belfast

Paul McCullagh
School of Computing and Mathematics, University of Ulster Jordanstown, Shore Road, Newtownabbey, Belfast

Prabhat Verma
Computer Science and Engineering Department, Harcourt Butler Technological Institute, Kanpur, 208002, India

Raghuraj Singh
Computer Science and Engineering Department, Harcourt Butler Technological Institute, Kanpur, 208002, India

Avinash Kumar Singh
Computer Science and Engineering Department, Harcourt Butler Technological Institute, Kanpur, 208002, India

I Diana Jeba Jingle
Department of Computer Science and Engineering, LITES, Thovalai, India

Elijah Blessing Rajsingh
KSCST, Karunya University, Coimbatore, India

Santosh Kumar Vipparthi
Department of Electrical Engineering, Indian Institute of Technology BHU, Varanasi, India

Shyam Krishna Nagar
Department of Electrical Engineering, Indian Institute of Technology BHU, Varanasi, India

Jaspher Willsie Kathrine Gnanaraj
Department of Information Technology, Karunya University, Coimbatore, Tamilnadu, India

Kirubakaran Ezra
SSTP Systems, Bharat Heavy Electricals Limited, Trichy, Tamilnadu, India

Elijah Blessing Rajsingh
School of Computer Science and Technology, Karunya University, Coimbatore, Tamilnadu, India

Hsiang-Yuan Hsueh
Computational Intelligence Technology Center, Industrial Technology Research Institute, Taiwan, R.O.C.

Chun-Nan Chen
Chunghwa Telecom Laboratories, Taiwan, R.O.C.

Kun-Fu Huang
Information & Communication Research Lab, Industrial Technology Research Institute, Taiwan, R.O.C.

Dong Hyun Jeong
Department of Computer Science and Information Technology, University of the District of Columbia, 4200 Connecticut Avenue NW, 20008 Washington, DC, USA

Soo-Yeon Ji
Department of Computer Science, Bowie State University, 14000 Jericho Park Rd., 20715 Bowie, MD, USA

Evan A Suma
Institute for Creative Technologies, University of Southern California, 12015 Waterfront Drive, 90094 Playa Vista, CA, USA

Byunggu Yu
Department of Computer Science and Information Technology, University of the District of Columbia, 4200 Connecticut Avenue NW, 20008 Washington, DC, USA

Remco Chang
Department of Computer Science, Tufts University, 419 Boston Ave, 02155 Medford, MA, USA

Masashi Katsumata
Department of Computer and Information Engineering, Nippon Institute of Technology, 4-1 Gakuendai, Miyashiro-machi, Minamisaitama-gun, Saitama, Japan

Takeru Naruse
Nagoya Institute of Technology, Nagoya, Japan

Masami Mohri
Gifu University, Gifu, Japan

Yoshiaki Shiraishi
Kobe University, Kobe, Japan

9 781682 852552